A WISE ADVENTURE II

A WISE ADVENTURE II

NEW ZEALAND AND ANTARCTICA AFTER 1960

MALCOLM TEMPLETON

VICTORIA UNIVERSITY PRESS
in association with
THE NEW ZEALAND INSTITUTE OF INTERNATIONAL AFFAIRS

VICTORIA UNIVERSITY PRESS
Victoria University of Wellington
PO Box 600 Wellington
http://www.vup.vuw.ac.nz

ISBN 9781776561681

First published 2017

The New Zealand Institute of International Affairs is an independent body which seeks to promote an understanding of international issues, particularly as they concern new Zealand. The Institute does not advocate any particular policy nor does it express opinions. The views expressed in this publication are, therefore, those of the author.

Printed by Ligare, Auckland

CONTENTS

	Foreword	7
Chapter VII	Conservation: The Protection of Fauna and Flora	11
Chapter VIII	Conservation: The Convention on Seals	31
Chapter IX	Conservation: Marine Living Resources	44
Chapter X	Mineral Resources: The Need for a Regime	74
Chapter XI	Mineral Resources: Negotiating a Convention	124
Chapter XII	Mineral Resources: Reaching Agreement	163
Chapter XIII	Mineral Resources: A Convention Under Fire	224
Chapter XIV	An Environmental Protection Protocol	269
Chapter V	A Balance Sheet	315
	Acronyms	322
	Notes and References	323
	Index	357

FOREWORD

Malcolm Templeton's *A Wise Adventure* was published in 2000. It is a rich and significant history of New Zealand's Antarctic policy from 1920 to 1960, chronicling the development of policy from a reluctant acceptance of responsibility for the Ross Dependency to the negotiation and adoption of the Antarctic Treaty in 1959. Since then, Antarctica has been governed through a unique system of international collaboration.

The central premise of the Antarctic Treaty system is to ensure that Antarctica is used for peaceful purposes only and that freedom of scientific investigation is maintained. Within that context, attention is then placed on environmental protection and the management of living resources in a sustainable way. It has also preserved a workable balance between those countries for whom sovereignty in Antarctica is an important national interest, and those who oppose such claims. As events are proving in other parts of the world, such a balancing act is indeed a remarkable diplomatic outcome.

As much as we might now take this status quo for granted, the path to achieving this was not straightforward. Nor can we assume an easy road ahead for the system and for the Antarctic environment itself, which plays such a key role in relation to the planet's ecosystems as we know them.

A Wise Adventure II sheds light on New Zealand's involvement in Antarctic policy since 1959, detailing the challenges the Antarctic Treaty system has faced and overcome since its inception, and focussing on the main legal instruments. This begins with the negotiations on the protection of fauna and flora, moving then to the history of the Convention on Seals and why New Zealand is not party to it. It explains the background to the Convention on the Conservation of Antarctic Marine Living Resources – today responsible for the management of the highly sought-after Patagonian and Antarctic toothfish and the still abundant krill that are at the heart of the Antarctic marine food-web. It documents the negotiations, which New Zealand led, to establish a regime to regulate mineral exploration. This regime was adopted but never brought into force. It also records the subsequent negotiations that resulted in the Madrid Protocol on Environment Protection.

The 60th anniversary of the establishment of New Zealand's station in the Ross Dependency, Scott Base, was marked on 20 January this year. Today, the base is a busy hub for Antarctic scientists, working on issues that impact us all. International collaboration is alive and well in Antarctica, and – while they are not perfect – permitting systems manage the impact of human activity on this pristine environment. In December we will see the entry into effect of the Ross Sea region Marine Protected Area. The Antarctic Treaty system, so carefully negotiated, is working. We need to ensure that it continues to do so. We must not be afraid to strengthen it where it needs strengthening, but most importantly we must continue to ensure it is upheld and implemented.

The views expressed in *A Wise Adventure II* are of course those of the author, and not the government.

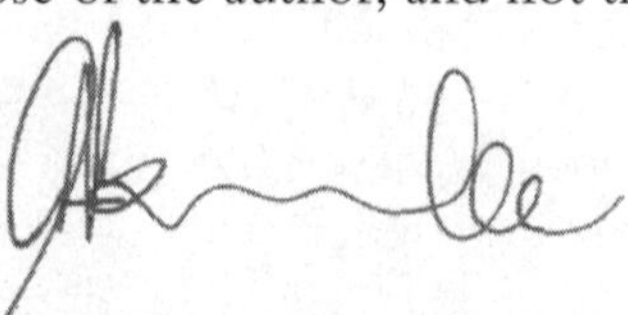

Hon Gerry Brownlee
Minister of Foreign Affairs

It should be noted that Malcolm Templeton undertook this second venture into the history of New Zealand's engagement in Antarctica some years ago. The Ministry of Foreign Affairs and Trade therefore contracted Alice Revell to update the text to take account of the most significant recent events. Alice's work is gratefully acknowledged.

VII

CONSERVATION: THE PROTECTION OF FAUNA AND FLORA

New Zealand ratified the Antarctic Treaty on 1 November 1960. The Treaty entered into force on 23 June 1961. A few days later, the Consultative Parties—that is, the club whose membership was defined in Article IX of the Treaty—met in Canberra. Meetings have continued to be held since 1961, at roughly two year intervals until 1994 and annually since then. The view of the New Zealand delegation to the Antarctic Conference that the machinery established by the treaty for subsequent meetings would not operate very productively or actively, has proved to be wrong.[1] The Treaty machinery has in fact gathered momentum as it continues, with a permanent secretariat established in Buenos Aires, Argentina, in 2004 (despite previous apprehensions of the devotees of national sovereignty about the implications of establishing a body with administrative or control functions, and the difficulty of achieving agreement on a permanent headquarters site). The delegation should not be blamed for lack of vision. It could not have foreseen the speed with which environmental issues have become the subject of international concern and action since the Treaty was negotiated. Sensitivity about actual and potential dangers to the environment, rather than the strategic concerns which were uppermost in New Zealand officials' minds in 1959, have undoubtedly been the driving force behind diplomatic efforts since that date to put flesh on the bones of the Treaty—and in doing so, to give to the international regime real powers which at the outset some of the original parties to the Treaty had sedulously sought to avoid.

This narrative will not attempt to cover New Zealand's contribution to every topic dealt with in the Antarctic Treaty Consultative Meetings (ATCMs) from 1961 onwards. Rather it will concentrate on the negotiation of the principal legal instruments devised by the Antarctic powers to give practical effect to Treaty objectives. All these have in fact had as their principal aims the protection of the environment and the conservation of wildlife.

The first agreement to be negotiated by the Consultative Parties dealt with the Conservation of Fauna and Flora (the order in normal English usage was reversed deliberately to emphasise the greater importance attached to the conservation of fauna: in practice, the indigenous species thought worthy of special protection were confined to mammals and birds; entomologists will no doubt regret that insects were left to fend for themselves). Those who believe that New Zealand has always been in the conservationist van may be disillusioned to learn that the initial reaction of New Zealand officials to proposals from conservationists on the protection of fauna in Antarctica was distinctly lackadaisical. Even before the Antarctic Conference met, a quango called the Fauna Protection Advisory Council had passed a resolution asking that the New Zealand delegation take up the question of the danger to New Zealand sea birds of oil pollution by ships in the Antarctica. The resolution drew the following minute in External Affairs:

> Dr Falla . . . says that the subject was not on the Council's agenda and the resolution was moved by a new member. [It] is apparently not to be taken too seriously, and Falla advises a polite evasive reply.[2]

Representations from the Forest and Bird Protection Society were dealt with similarly. However, as recorded earlier, a specific provision on the protection of living resources was in fact included in the Antarctic Treaty on the initiative of Chile, and in 1960 the question was taken up by the Special Committee on Antarctic Research of the International Council of Scientific Unions (SCAR).[3] Due note of this development was taken by the Ross Dependency Research Committee (RDRC).[4]

In the preparations for the first meeting of the Consultative Parties, both the United Kingdom and United States adopted a positive approach to the idea of a regulatory control system for the conservation of living resources on the continent.[5] The New Zealand Department of External Affairs, however, remained hesitant:

> In principle of course we favour the conservation of living resources in the area, and the government itself would doubtless be prepared to consider promulgating regulations . . . At present the leaders of New Zealand Antarctic Stations have an overall directive to conserve wildlife and more precise instructions govern the killing of seals for dog food.
>
> However, because of various doubts about the legal basis upon which the Ross Dependency has been administered we are not over-anxious to have states saddled in the near future with the responsibility for issuing such regulations. It would frankly suit us best not to have to pass regulatory measures . . . until we have put the administration of the Dependency upon a somewhat firmer footing than hitherto and this process may take some time.[6]

This was a rather timid attitude in contrast to the firmness with which New Zealand asserted criminal jurisdiction in the Dependency when the Antarctica Act was passed.

Specific proposals were put forward by SCAR in February 1961.[7] It is of interest that these would have permitted the 'exploitation of fauna for commercial gain, on terms which accord with sound conservation principles'. Despite this, the RDRC characterised the SCAR proposals as unrealistic and idealistic.[8] External Affairs agreed, noting that this view was shared by some other members of the consultative group which was preparing for the Canberra meeting.[9] The United States produced a draft recommendation for that meeting, which omitted the requirement for the parties to the Treaty to adopt national regulations. The recommendation adopted by the First ATCM was that governments should consult 'on the form in which it would be most suitable to establish in due course internationally agreed measures for the preservation and conservation of the living resources of the Antarctic', and as an interim step, issue general rules of conduct based on the SCAR recommendations.[10]

Even this would seem to be further than New Zealand wanted to go. When the United Kingdom representative raised with his Australian and New Zealand colleagues the idea of a draft convention for the conservation of wildlife, the New Zealand representative was instructed that New Zealand would prefer to have only a code of conduct:

> It would surely seem advisable to give the Treaty a reasonable breathing space before embarking on what might develop into a network of supplementary conventions. Without knowing what the British are worried about, we can see no real justification to press for a convention . . . We would not suggest that you put these views so bluntly to the United Kingdom.[11]

The British were not deterred by the evident lack of enthusiasm displayed by their Commonwealth colleagues, and produced a draft convention for consideration at the Second ATCM, held at Buenos Aires in 1962.[12] When they received the draft, the New Zealand lawyers produced a new argument:

> This Convention raises two difficulties. First is our own particular problem—since the 1923 Ross Dependency Order in Council is pretty shaky as a legal authority—of having to get legislation in New Zealand which would make the acts defined in the Convention, offences at our law, as required (apparently) by the draft. This is a domestic problem however, and should not stand in the way of our going along with a Wild Life Convention if other Contracting Parties to the Antarctic Treaty feel that one would be worthwhile and if our own wild life people agree.
>
> Secondly however, the draft Convention raises in concrete form the whole question of jurisdiction, so that it is really integral with the British proposal to raise jurisdiction as one of the topics for discussion. What the draft says is that each Contracting Party (and this would include even Contracting Parties which have no territorial claims in Antarctica) shall prohibit the killing, wounding,

etc. of Antarctic wildlife except as provided in the Convention. This presumably means that each Contracting Party shall exercise a criminal or similar jurisdiction over its nationals, in any part of Antarctica, in respect of the killing of and other acts against wildlife. It could also mean—though the draft is generally not clear on the point—that each Contracting Party would exercise similar jurisdiction over nationals of other Contracting Parties. The Convention is, however, obscure on this issue because it merely states that 'each Contracting Party shall prohibit the killing . . .', without clarification as to what persons shall be prohibited.

However, it looks in substance as though the intention is that wildlife offences throughout Antarctica shall be a matter for the national government of the offender i.e., the same jurisdictional principle as applies under the Antarctic Treaty in respect of observers and exchange scientists. Such a principle, no matter how logical, would be sure to run into difficulties with those states such as Chile and Argentina which may want to punish offences committed in their sectors even if committed by nationals of other Contracting Parties. Other countries such as the United States, however, would no doubt prefer the 'jurisdiction of the Government of which the offender is a national' since the United States in acknowledging no territorial claims would—even taking account of Article IV of the Antarctic Treaty—not want to submit its own nationals in Antarctica to the jurisdiction of a state claiming a slice of territory there and purporting to control all offences committed in that slice.

In short, therefore, the general question of jurisdiction over acts committed in Antarctica is directly raised by the draft Convention, and strictly speaking that question should be considered before the draft is discussed. It would, of course, be possible to argue that the Convention should be proceeded with in isolation and treated as a special case which does not prejudice or affect the question of jurisdiction in Antarctica in relation to other matters: but I doubt whether this will be possible since the Antarctic Treaty already provides. for the principle of governmental jurisdiction over nationals in regard to observers and scientists, and if this principle is also adopted in relation to persons who kill or wound wildlife, the precedents would be mounting up in favour of making this the general jurisdictional rule. One can foresee that at least some of the Antarctic Treaty powers will want to discuss jurisdiction before they commit themselves to this particular Convention.'[13]

These comments, while they raised a fair point about the desirability of some progress among the parties to the Treaty on the question of jurisdiction,[14] show a surprising degree of caution—lack of confidence, even—in regard to the assertion of New Zealand's national jurisdiction, which had been included in the Antarctica Act of 1960. The British, on the other hand, saw the conservation of living resources as one of the issues on which real progress could be made; they did not want to tie it to the general topic of jurisdiction, the solution to which was unlikely, in their opinion, to be found in the foreseeable future.[15]

In the event, the Second ATCM merely referred the British draft convention forward for further consultation, and did not pursue the question of jurisdiction.[16]

As preparatory meetings proceeded during 1963 for the Third ATCM to be held in Brussels in the following year, New Zealand officials remained unconvinced that the British draft convention was in an acceptable form:

> A treaty is a legal contractual document and should—indeed must—be capable of being put into effect with reasonable certainty as to what it means. Yet the present text is, in fact, obscure (and we are, frankly, not sure how we could 'sell' it to the Justice Department, who would certainly probe it, and the sort of laws which we might need to give effect to it, in some detail.)
>
> Politically one can sympathise with the desire to obscure or avoid issues of jurisdiction or of conflicting views as to sovereign claims. Questions of 'prohibitions' (which convey a notion of corresponding penalties) are, however, inherently ones bringing jurisdictional issues into the picture; hence the desire to avoid jurisdictional matters results in a rather doubtful document of a kind which should not really take a treaty form unless and until it is made more precise. (This consideration makes us wonder whether a convention should be tried for at all, and whether it might not be preferable to have a code, a declaration, or a statement of agreed principles, as some Contracting Parties have suggested.)[17]

Towards the end of 1963 the United States produced a new proposal which appeared to come closer to what New Zealand officials were advocating. The essential difference from the

British draft, as the United States Government explained in a note to the other Consultative Parties in January 1964, was that it took the form of 'agreed measures' rather than a convention. This term harked back to the language of the treaty, which in Article IX envisaged the recommendation by representatives of the Consultative Parties of measures regarding, *inter alia*, the preservation and conservation of living resources in Antarctica. The United States considered that the use of this form would be a recognition of the 'primacy of the Antarctica Treaty and of the authority and procedures it provides for dealing with measures to achieve its objectives'. A separate convention would set an undesirable precedent, creating pressure to have subsequent measures in the same form or risk having them considered less important.

The United States, however, believed that the instrument should create binding legal obligations, and that 'agreed measures' would do this. They would require affirmative action by the parties before entering into force. Each party would be free to determine how this affirmative action should be taken so as to be legally binding on its nationals. Some parties might consider it necessary to legislate, others might not. Similarly some parties might need to seek formal parliamentary approval of the agreed measures. The United States, for its part, considered that authority to approve agreed measures as an executive agreement had been conferred by its ratification of the Antarctica Treaty.[18]

The 'agreed measures' form, therefore, would permit the United States to ratify the instrument without the need to seek the advice and consent of the Senate. This was no doubt the nub of American concern: the ratification process in the case of the Treaty itself had not been entirely smooth. What the American authorities (and others) probably never envisaged was the length of time it might take for the Agreed Measures on Fauna and Flora to be approved by all the Consultative Parties involved in negotiating them, and thus to become fully effective.

The United States' proposal did not, of course, do anything to alleviate New Zealand's worries about the problem of jurisdiction which, officials recognised, would arise whether the agreement took the form of agreed measures or a convention. Surprisingly, however, New Zealand—which earlier had seemed happily prepared to settle for a code of conduct—now raised doubts about possible differences of interpretation in regard to the binding nature of agreed measures, given the wording of Article IX(4) of the Antarctic Treaty. It was also felt that if it were thought desirable to amend the agreement subsequently it would be more difficult to amend agreed measures in a manner that was equitable to Contracting Parties, other than Consultative Parties, which had accepted them. New Zealand, therefore, the United States was informed, was inclined to favour a separate convention as the appropriate form for the proposed agreement, although it would support the use of agreed measures if these two difficulties could be overcome! A detached observer might have felt that New Zealand was a little hard to please.[19]

However, there was reason for New Zealand's concern that not all parties to the Antarctica Treaty might share the American view of agreed measures as being equally as binding as a convention at international law. In particular, it seemed that Australia might not do so. In December the Australians had informed the New Zealand High Commission in Canberra that they were opposed to the registration of approved recommendations with the United Nations as international agreements in accordance with Article 102 of the Charter. They regarded approved recommendations as 'sufficiently binding', but it was not in their view the intention of governments that the recommendations after acceptance should create rights and obligations between parties which were subject to international law and thus justiciable, for example in the International Court.[20] It was also the initial view of New Zealand External Affairs lawyers that these recommendations need not be registered: this was based largely on their understanding of British practice, which did not call for the registration of agreements which were subsidiary to a principal treaty and did not materially add to, subtract from or alter it.[21]

The argument was undercut, however, by the British reaction to the Australian and New Zealand views. In the Foreign Office's opinion it was necessary to examine each recommendation to see whether it was 'intended to create rights and obligations, or to establish relationships, governed by international law'. They could not agree that all the recommendations of the Consultative Meetings were subsidiary agreements:

> To take an extreme example, we would not consider the Agreed Measures on Fauna and Flora to be subsidiary to Article IX(i)(f) of the Treaty; we feel that they do in fact add to the Treaty.

The British conclusion was that since it would very inconvenient to attempt to distinguish between registrable and non-registrable recommendations the best solution would be to register all the recommendations, without prejudice as to whether registration was required or not.[22]

At about the same time, however, the United States changed its position on registration in the opposite direction. The New Zealand Embassy in Washington was informed that the State Department

> was doing a backwards flip on this question, not because they felt the validity of their arguments could be called in question but because this was not a propitious time to press their case and because to win the agreement of the Treaty governments would require too much energy.[23]

New Zealand legal officials, reviewing their position in the light of the British opinion, agreed that as a matter of strict law it would probably be necessary to examine each separate recommendation to see if it needed to be registered. It was doubtful whether any of the recommendations of the first two ATCMs needed to be registered. They agreed, however, with the British view that the proposed measures on fauna and flora would need to be registered. It would be very difficult to argue that they were merely subsidiary to the Treaty and did not add anything to it. Whether or not the British suggestion that all recommendations should be registered was the best way of dealing with the problem; it could not continue to be shelved indefinitely. There was an obligation under Article 102 of the United Nations Charter to register international agreements as soon as possible. However, officials felt that it would be unwise to raise the issue before the measures had actually been agreed upon, since countries like Argentina and Chile were already unhappy at the idea of accepting an instrument imposing legal obligations upon them. This was no doubt the same line of reasoning that had led the State Department to decide that this was not the time to seek agreement to the registration of approved recommendations.[24]

The New Zealand delegation to the Third ATCM was therefore instructed that, while New Zealand had little doubt that the measures should be registered, there was no need for this to be stated explicitly in the text, and that it might be better therefore to agree to the deletion of the relevant paragraph in the existing draft, on the understanding that the question of registration would need to be taken up through the diplomatic channel immediately after the meeting.[25] New Zealand did not intervene in the discussion of this point at the meeting. The United States representative made it clear that in his delegation's view the Agreed Measures were a registrable agreement, and that registration should take place whether or not a provision to this effect was included in the text: however, he did not go so far as to commit his government to register the measures as a unilateral act in accordance with its Charter obligation. Argentina opposed the retention of the paragraph and it was deleted. The Argentine representative acknowledged privately to the New Zealand delegation that the Antarctic powers had individual obligations under Article 102 of the United Nations Charter. However, he favoured a discussion of the question of registration at the next ATCM, with a view to reaching agreement on which recommendation should be registered and which not.

In its report the New Zealand delegation urged an early exchange of views with the United States and United Kingdom authorities, both of whom, it said, appeared to favour the registration of virtually all recommendations adopted by ATCMs.[26]

Another concern of New Zealand officials was, as foreshadowed earlier, with the knotty problem of jurisdiction. The American draft of Agreed Measures had gone a good deal further than the British draft convention—which had been deliberately vague on jurisdiction—in requiring participating governments to prohibit various activities *within the Treaty area*. To do this they would have to pass legislation covering the whole of that area. If that were acceptable to those Treaty parties which were most sensitive about sovereignty, would it not be possible to remove the remaining vagueness concerning the nationality of the persons to whom the legislation would apply? New Zealand officials favoured the nationality rule for which Article VIII of the Antarctica Treaty provided a precedent—that the legislation adopted by each government should apply only to its own nationals.[27] When these views were conveyed to the working party in Brussels, however, it transpired that the Australian representative had already made this proposal and, when it was opposed by his Argentine colleagues, he had withdrawn it. The New Zealand representative reported that the British continued to favour clouding the issue, as the best way of getting the measures quickly into effect.[28]

However, Foreign Office lawyers were more sympathetic to New Zealand views, and told the High Commission in London that they had not closed their minds to the option favoured by New Zealand: if the circumstances looked favourable they might be ready to change their tack and see if they could introduce legislation for their nationals instead of, or perhaps as well as, for their territory.[29] After further consideration of the New Zealand arguments they conceded that it would be desirable for the Agreed Measures themselves to contain some generally acceptable jurisdictional rule, and for some such rule to appear more and more frequently under the Treaty. They doubted whether it would be possible in the context of the Agreed Measures to find any such rule, but—they added cheerfully—there was no harm in trying, and they suggested therefore that New Zealand should attempt to gain acceptance of some jurisdictional rule, without pushing things too far.

The British lawyers agreed with their New Zealand counterparts that Article VIII of the Antarctic Treaty contained the jurisdictional rule most likely to provide the basis for the solution of the general problem. They went on to offer an intriguing comment:

> If something very close to Article VIII can be included in the Agreed Measures, it is worth considering whether there would be a sufficient insurance of our territorial position. To accept such a rule would weaken the claims to sovereignty of all claimant states. But it would also point the way toward the internationalisation of Antarctica. We might under these circumstances be prepared to consider whether we should not accept the slight weakening of our claims to sovereignty in order to encourage a move towards internationalisation.
>
> There are obvious risks. We should have to be certain that the Argentines and the Chileans were only going to legislate for their nationals throughout the Treaty Area and not for the territories which they claim. Further, we should have to have an understanding with the other Treaty Powers that any Power would be free, if it considered it necessary, to legislate for its territory as well.[30]

New Zealand officials, after digesting this message, were doubtful whether it would be wise to raise the question of jurisdiction, especially if doing so seemed likely to prejudice the outcome of the meeting. On the issue itself, they considered it obvious that:

> if any government asserts a territorial jurisdiction based on claims, other claimant governments will follow suit (New Zealand alone among the claimant governments might refrain from doing so). It would not . . . be realistic to bank on a general renunciation of jurisdiction based on claims but there may be a rather better prospect of showing that the two kinds of jurisdiction are not mutually exclusive.
>
> There is in principle no reason at all why a claimant state should not assert a jurisdiction based on nationality instead of or in addition to a territorial jurisdiction based on claims. If all states concerned did assert a jurisdiction based on nationality that would be a step towards internationalisation even if jurisdiction based on claims should also persist.[31]

When they came to discuss the matter at the outset of the Brussels meeting however, the British and New Zealand delegations quickly agreed that to seek to introduce a jurisdiction rule into the Agreed Measures would antagonise Argentina and Chile and might jeopardise the chances of their adoption. The British delegation was much less flexible than its lawyers had appeared to be in London. They saw no possibility that Argentina and Chile would agree to refrain from legislating on a territorial basis, and were not even prepared to enquire. It seemed clear that their first objective was to avoid prejudicing the status of their own claim.[32]

The issue of jurisdiction was never raised in the meeting. The New Zealand and British delegations agreed that early consultations would be desirable with a view to harmonising legislation.[33] For whatever reason, this suggestion was not immediately pursued.

There was however a slightly odd final twist to this tangled, and no doubt boring, tale, which can conveniently be recorded here. Three years were to elapse before the United Kingdom enacted legislation to give effect to the Agreed Measures. By the time that legislation came to be drafted, British lawyers had done an about turn:

> In principle, the Agreed Measures impose the same obligations on all Participating Governments: in that case, the jurisdictional obligation cannot depend upon sovereignty since five participants do not claim it.
>
> We feel that to legislate [on the basis of nationality] would give effect to the intention behind the Agreed Measures and would not mark any weakening in our sovereignty over the British Antarctic territory (quite apart from the protection of Article IV of the Treaty). We continue to make laws in the territory from time to time and . . . the Bill when enacted might well be extended to it.

The writer of this letter, which was addressed to Australia as well as New Zealand, did acknowledge that in the case of New Zealand he was preaching to the converted.[34]

From the outset of the negotiations, therefore, New Zealand was aware that the draft measures had, and were likely to retain, features which were unsatisfactory from the legal point of view.

The delegation was instructed, however, that the value of having the measures agreed outweighed these considerations. There was a residual feeling in Wellington that in view of the Argentinian and Chilean opposition to a solution of the jurisdiction question it might well have been better to have been content with a non-binding declaration after all: but New Zealand was now saddled with something else and would have to make the best of it.[35]

As to the substance of the measures, perhaps the most significant defect in the draft was the fact that it would not protect fauna once they left the protection of the land and ice—shelves for the pack ice. Australia was particularly concerned about this aspect, and New Zealand scientists agreed that the value of the measures would be considerably reduced by the exclusion of the pack ice from their scope. All Antarctic animals spend at least part of their lives on or around the pack; some species, and in particular crabeater seals, live entirely on the pack. New Zealand supported the Australians on this issue in the preliminary meetings, but strong opposition was encountered. The Norwegians, whose delegation included influential commercial sealing representation, argued that the numbers of crabeater seals were such that conservation was unnecessary, and that sealing on the high seas and on the pack ice could be commercially profitable. Other delegations pointed out that extending the scope of the measures to the high seas on which the pack ice floated would take them beyond the limits established by Article VI of the Antarctic Treaty and thus render them *ultra vires*.

In the end, the meeting confined itself to a separate recommendation that the issue of pelagic sealing and the taking of fauna on pack ice be considered at the next ATCM, and that governments voluntarily regulate these activities in the meantime to ensure the survival of species and avoid disturbance of the natural ecological system. This result was not achieved without much hard bargaining, with the Norwegians resisting even the supplying of information on their possible pelagic sealing operations in Antarctic waters. The final compromise reflected Chilean keenness to have a substantial item on the agenda of the next meeting, to be held in Santiago.[36]

The substantive articles of the Agreed Measures were otherwise agreed relatively easily. The participating governments 'considered' Antarctica as a Special Conservation Area. The original proposal had been to 'declare' it an international wildlife reserve. The use of the expression 'international' encountered the usual objection from the more dedicated upholders of national sovereignty. Argentina objected also to the expression 'Reserve', with support from France, because—interestingly—it carried the connotation of a national park. Argentina further objected to the capitalisation, and as a consequence the capitals were dropped in the French and Spanish versions of the text.[37] An innocent reader might suppose that a special conservation area comprising a whole continent was difficult to differentiate from a world park, but of course the Agreed Measures do not touch on the question of non-living resources.

If the substantive prohibitions for the protection of fauna and flora were readily accepted, the same was not true of the machinery provisions—entry into force, amendments and accession—which were the subject of an interminable debate. For a start, Australia proposed the deletion of the accession article, and was supported by Argentina. Their argument was that the Agreed Measures should not be treated differently from other recommendations made by the Consultative Parties. The Soviet Union, on the other hand, favoured an open accession article. The United States, United Kingdom and New Zealand favoured the provision in the existing draft which would permit any country eligible to accede to the Antarctic Treaty to participate in the Agreed Measures: that is, a country might accept the Agreed Measures without becoming a party to the Treaty if it so wished.

At this point Australia effectively vetoed the three draft articles on amendment, accession and deposit, and for a time it appeared that no such articles would appear in the final text. The United States representative, however, succeeded in introducing revised articles on amendment and accession. It was provided that the Agreed Measures would become effective for the Consultative Parties to the Antarctic Treaty after *all* those parties had accepted them. *Thereafter*, other Contracting Parties to the Treaty might accept them by agreeing to apply and be bound by them. Non-parties to the Treaty are not permitted to accede.[38] It was no doubt assumed that the Agreed Measures would, under this provision, come into effect within a reasonably short period of time. It would certainly not have occurred to anyone at the Brussels meeting that they would not come fully into effect for eighteen years.[39]

The New Zealand delegation, which had participated quite actively in the detailed drafting of the Agreed Measures, viewed the result as generally satisfactory, although it did not meet New Zealand wishes in all respects, notably in restricting accession to governments which had already become parties to the Antarctic Treaty.[40] The insistence of some Consultative Parties on exclusivity was of course counterproductive, in that countries operating in Antarctica which were not permitted initially to accede to the measures later neglected to do so and were free to disregard them. (Only ten countries which qualified for consultative status after 1964 acceded to the measures before the ATCM decided in 2011 that the measures were 'no longer current' and further accessions were unnecessary.)[41]

New Zealand itself was in no hurry to take the necessary legal steps to give effect to the Agreed Measures. In September 1965, in response to an Australian enquiry, the Department of External Affairs believed that it would be necessary to pass legislation to implement the measures. Further, it was the New Zealand view that legislation should not be limited in scope to the New Zealand sector. That would leave a gap in respect of unclaimed areas, and furthermore would tend unnecessarily to bolster territorial claims.[42] (This last comment must surely have been added with a view to irritating the Australians.)

As already mentioned, the British produced their Bill to give effect to the Agreed Measures in 1966 and passed it in 1967. Meanwhile Chile, evidently concerned that the Measures as drafted in 1964 might have set the Antarctic powers on the slippery slope towards internationalisation, proposed amendments to them which were evidently designed to protect—if not to 'bolster' territorial claims and discourage the issuing of permits under the terms of the measures with validity extending beyond territorial boundaries.[43] At the Fourth ATCM in 1966, however, the British refused to consider any amendment because their Bill had already been introduced into Parliament.[44] New Zealand officials happily put off consideration of their legislation.[45] At the Fifth ATCM in 1968, agreement was reached on an addition to the text which satisfied the Chileans and seemed innocuous to everyone else. New Zealand officials then put off their legislation until 1970. The power to make regulations to give effect to the Agreed Measures was inserted in the Antarctica Act 1960 by the Antarctica Amendment Act 1970 (later repealed by the Antarctica [Environmental Protection] Act 1994).[46] The regulations could be applied to any New Zealand citizen or, in the Ross Dependency, to any person who is not a national of any Contracting Party to the Antarctic Treaty. The reasons for asserting a national rather than a territorial jurisdiction were explained to the Law Draftsman as follows: it was

> the most obvious way of giving effect to the broad intent of the Agreed Measures. They are said, in Article I, to apply to the whole of the Treaty area; and Article II requires each Participating Government to take appropriate action to carry out the Agreed Measures. In the light of Article I it is reasonable to interpret Article II as requiring appropriate action to be taken by each Participating Government *throughout the Treaty area.* This interpretation is supported by Article XI of the Agreed Measures which looks to nationality as the basis for the assertion of jurisdiction over ships. Secondly, the enactment of legislation applicable to New Zealand nationals anywhere in the Treaty area is consistent with the general spirit of the Antarctic Treaty and our traditional approach to it; because of the protection afforded by Article IV of the Treaty, legislation in this form would also not in any way weaken New Zealand's claim to sovereignty over the Ross Dependency. Thirdly, there is a significant difference between jurisdiction asserted for the purposes of or general criminal law and jurisdiction claimed to give effect to the Agreed Measures. If in the Antarctica Act 1960 we had not applied New Zealand Criminal law in general to all persons in the Ross Dependency this might have resulted in the enforcement in New Zealand territory of the criminal law of another country to which we took strong

> objection. The application by another country to its nationals in the Ross Dependency of the internationally agreed rules contained in the Agreed Measures is quite another matter and need not, in our view, be a cause for concern. Finally the application of our legislation to New Zealand nationals rather than to New Zealand territory will avoid the possibility of unnecessary skirmishing with the Americans over jurisdictional issues. It is most unlikely that the United States would accept a New Zealand claim to control the issue of permits under the Agreed Measures to Americans in the Ross Dependency. To make such a claim would lead us at once to unprofitable argument which, with luck (and the continued absence of crime from the Ross Dependency) we shall continue to avoid in relation to the criminal law jurisdiction we have claimed. If at any stage any serious doubt should arise as to the willingness or ability of the Americans to ensure the observance of the Agreed Measures by their nationals in the Ross Dependency, then we should probably have no choice but to face up to the consequences of applying our legislation to all persons in the Ross Dependency as well as to New Zealand nationals throughout the Treaty area. We don't expect this situation to arise and if it does, should prefer to deal with it by way of a subsequent amendment to our law.[47]

Another interesting feature of the New Zealand legislation which it shared with the corresponding British Act,[48] is that it empowered the extension of the regulations to the high seas within Antarctica. (It will be recalled that the Australian desire to have the Agreed Measures apply to the pack ice was frustrated by the argument that the harvesting of living resources was a legitimate high seas activity and that to attempt to control it through measures under Article IX of the Treaty would be *ultra vires*. It is also possible to argue, although this view does not appear to have been put forward at the Brussels meeting, that what Article VI of the Antarctic Treaty says is that 'nothing in the present treaty shall prejudice . . . the rights, or the exercise of the rights, of any State under international law with regard to the high seas within that area'. This formulation, the argument runs, does not preclude the adoption by the Consultative Parties of recommendations which would limit the exercise of their high seas rights.) In any case when regulations were issued under the amended Act in 1971[49] it was not thought necessary to extend them to the high seas. By that time, as will be explained in the next chapter, progress was being made towards dealing with the problem of pelagic sealing in the Treaty area by another method.

The New Zealand regulations having been promulgated in June 1971, New Zealand was at last able to formally approve the Agreed Measures.[50] The Agreed Measures were superseded by Annex II to the Protocol on Environmental Protection to the Antarctic Treaty when the protocol entered into force in 1998.

Following the Agreed Measures on Fauna and Flora, the Antarctic powers have proceeded to negotiate a series of international legal instruments designed to conserve marine life and protect the environment in Antarctica. In no case, however, has the experiment of formulating such instruments as 'agreed measures' under Article IX of the Antarctic Treaty been repeated. Substantively, the Agreed Measures on Fauna and Flora were a success and were incorporated into Annex II of the protocol. Under their terms, a number of species and areas have been given special protection and, so long as the moratorium on mineral exploitation continues to be respected, it can be said that Antarctica is the international wildlife reserve that was envisaged in the original draft of the Agreed Measures, or, *de facto*, a world park. Tourists have not yet become a significant problem.

As a legal instrument, 'agreed measures' have both advantages and drawbacks, as will have become apparent from this account of the Fauna and Flora exercise. Since in the negotiation of subsequent instruments it seems to have been the predominant view that the drawbacks outweigh the advantages, it may be useful to attempt a balance sheet.

It may be considered an advantage that the unanimity rule established by the Antarctic Treaty (Article IX 4) applies to agreed measures: this means that there is considerable pressure on the Consultative Parties which negotiated them to take the necessary steps to bring them into effect. A situation is unlikely to arise in which the instrument is in force but only partly effective because one or more of the Antarctic powers has failed to ratify it.

On the other hand agreed measures are less formal than a

treaty and ratification may be easier for some countries. This is notably so for the United States.

The unanimity rule, however, creates difficulty both in negotiation and in regard to entry into effect. In negotiation, extreme views (e.g., on sovereignty in the case of Antarctica) may carry disproportionate weight. Entry into effect may, as in the case of Fauna and Flora, be a long drawn out process. (Tills may matter less in practice if interim measures or a moratorium are in place.) Another drawback is the privileged position of the Consultative Parties. Even if they had agreed on a more liberal accession clause for Fauna and Flora, there is little incentive for countries other than the Consultative Parties to take the necessary action to enable them to accede. Finally, there is a lingering doubt whether agreed measures are equally as legally binding as a convention. Although this doubt is evidently not shared by a number of countries, including New Zealand, it is highlighted by the fact that neither the Depositary Power nor any Consultative Party has registered the Agreed Measures on Fauna and Flora with the United Nations, although there is an obligation to do so on each individual Party under Article 102 of the United Nations Charter. An Australian authority notes that there is no clear understanding among the Consultative Parties about the legal status of agreed recommendations. Some, such as the Agreed Measures for the Conservation of Fauna and Flora, are 'drafted in treaty form replete with mandatory language' and 'will almost certainly be regarded as legally binding'. But 'in the case of many others, one is not so sure.'[51] Eventually, the ATCM's decision in 1995 to divide recommendations into Measures (legally binding), Decisions (internal administrative matters) and Resolutions (hortatory) . . . clarified its intentions. [52]

One may speculate, however, that it was a desire to have international agreements in place quickly, and to place no obstacles in the way of their acceptance by governments with a direct involvement or interest in the activity to be regulated, that led the Antarctic powers to go for the treaty option in formulating regulatory regimes to control sealing and the exploitation of other marine resources in the Antarctic area and the Southern Ocean.

VIII

CONSERVATION: THE CONVENTION ON SEALS

Having decided at their third meeting to take up the question of pelagic sealing in Antarctica at their fourth meeting, the Antarctic powers turned their minds to the form which a regulatory instrument might appropriately take. A British working paper was circulated in March 1966, based in part on a SCAR recommendation of the previous year.[1]

There was no suggestion, fifty years ago, that sea mammals were not an appropriate object of commercial exploitation. The papers refer unselfconsciously to the 'harvesting' of 'crops'. The only concern was that 'this resource should not be needlessly depleted by over-exploitation'. Fur seals had been hunted almost to extinction in the eighteenth and nineteenth centuries. The scientists now warned that care was needed if the crabeater seal (the most numerous species in Antarctic waters) was to be exploited, because of lack of basic knowledge of the breeding biology of this species. The British paper did not take up this point, and suggested that an 'annual crop' of 650,000 crabeating seals could safely be taken. It did envisage that the killing of seals should be confined to those lying on the floating ice, 'in order to minimise loss through sinking'. New Zealand scientists thought that from an ecological point of view the paper was 'quite sound'.[2]

New Zealand officials believed the regulation of high seas sealing to be outside the ambit of Consultative Meetings under Article IX of the Antarctic Treaty. They noted that there was limitless scope for argument about the distinction between high seas on the one hand and territorial waters and land on the other in polar regions where ice flows and other formations made the delimitation uncertain. They were not prepared to commit themselves on whether conservation of seals in Antarctic waters could best be dealt with by a treaty or by non-binding 'standards'; but, in their view, where economic interests were affected a treaty would usually be the appropriate vehicle.[3] The British, however, followed up their first working paper with a draft of agreed measures, which would be applicable within the Antarctic Treaty area, including the high seas.[4]

At a preparatory meeting for the Fourth ATCM in 1966, there appeared to be considerable support for a treaty,[5] but by the time the meeting itself was held, the British had backed off the idea of proceeding immediately to the negotiation of a binding agreement, and proposed instead the adoption of 'interim guidelines' for the *voluntary* regulation of pelagic sealing in the Antarctic area. As the New Zealand delegation said in its report, there was no need for it to play any prominent role in the discussion, and it confined itself to general support for the British approach.[6]

At the Fifth ATCM, held in Paris in November 1968, the British delegation sought to move matters forward by circulating a draft Convention on Seals based on recommendations from SCAR. The draft received strong support from Norway, the country considered most likely to engage in commercial sealing in Antarctic waters.

The United States, however, sought—as it had at the Fourth ATCM—to slow things down. It was decided to defer the question until the next Consultative Meeting.[7]

At the Sixth Consultative Meeting, held in Tokyo in 1970, it was decided that the proposed Convention should be considered 'outside the framework of the Antarctic Treaty, since the conservation of seals in the sea does not fall within the scope of the latter and is of interest to countries which are not parties to the Antarctic Treaty';[8] but this did not prevent the Consultative Parties from meeting 'informally', outside the Consultative Meeting proper, to produce a revised draft. However, the host government was not keen to have a Convention concluded and signed in Tokyo, since its subject matter was unlikely to be welcomed by Japanese fishing interests.[9] It was envisaged, therefore, that a second meeting would be held at a later date to adopt the Convention, to which meeting a wider group of potential signatories would be invited. There was concern that Canada, as another country besides Norway which might wish to engage in commercial sealing in Antarctica, should become a party. Australia, in particular, felt that Canada should be given an opportunity to take part in the drafting of the Convention,[10] and at a preparatory meeting proposed that Canada and several other non-parties to the Antarctic Treaty be invited to the Tokyo meeting: but there was no support except for an invitation to Canada.[11] It turned out that Canada was not interested in Antarctic sealing and it declined the invitation to take part.[12]

Humanitarian questions about the killing of seals attracted remarkably little interest in New Zealand. One member of the public wrote to the Christchurch *Press* and to Ministers asking that the killing of seals under one year old and the use of clubs as killing weapons should be prohibited.[13] New Zealand officials noted, however, that there was no evidence of any widespread support in New Zealand for a review of killing methods, and that there was little sign of interest in the question on the part of other Treaty powers; nor, it was thought, was there any effective means of policing regulations of that kind. The New Zealand delegation to the Tokyo meeting was therefore instructed to let the matter rest. To raise the issue might have only encouraged those who would wish to reopen textual discussion of the draft and give them an excuse for further deferment.[14] There was no comment in the New Zealand brief on the proposed permissible catch, which, if large-scale commercial sealing had in fact been undertaken in Southern waters, could have resulted in an annual slaughter in six figures.

A draft Convention (without machinery clauses) was agreed in the meeting convened for this purpose 'outside the framework of the Consultative Meeting proper'[15] and a British invitation to hold a formal conference to conclude a Convention in London was accepted. It was convened in February 1972. The New Zealand delegation was composed of officials from the High Commission, the Prime Minister having declined to fund the attendance of the only New Zealand authority on seals, Professor G A Knox of Canterbury University.[16]

In the interval before the London Conference met, views were exchanged between several of the potential parties to the Convention. The Japanese were unenthusiastic. There was not enough scientific evidence, they claimed, to justify a restrictive regime of the kind envisaged. It was not that Japan was engaged in, or contemplated, a commercial sealing operation; it was evident that they were more concerned about the precedent that might be set in regard to other marine resources (e.g. Antarctic krill).[17] (Japan also had a problem about enforcement of penal provisions required to give effect to international agreements against Japanese nationals outside Japan; the Gaimusho found that it could not engage the cooperation of the other government departments and its United Nations Bureau later complained that 'it is enough to give one indigestion'.)[18] The United States, on the other hand, wanted to see teeth put into the Convention in the form of an independent scientific committee which would encourage research, assess data supplied by sealing expeditions, and recommend changes in the quotas set in an annex to the Convention.[19] The United Kingdom, taking a more cautious view, favoured a two-stage approach, bearing in mind that a sealing industry on floating ice in the Southern Ocean had not begun. Only when the permissible catch set in the annex appeared likely to be reached did they favour convening a conference to agree on more rigorous controls.[20]

The New Zealand delegation for its part was instructed that the existing draft provided 'the best possible basis' for a Convention, being based on the 'best available scientific information' and making adequate provision for review. The aim should be to conclude the Convention with the minimum of delay, and the evident desire of Japan, and to some extent of the United Kingdom, to amend the draft in ways which would water it down, should be resisted. So, however, should the United

States' proposal to create a scientific committee to monitor the operation of the Convention: 'sophisticated and costly control machinery' should not be established unless and until it was shown to be needed. New Zealand officials were sufficiently keen on the Convention to have full powers prepared in advance to enable the delegation to sign the instrument if it were agreed upon at the London Conference.[21] With retrospective wisdom one wonders, however, how deeply they had considered the 'scientific evidence', and whether they had taken into account the likely public reaction to a commercial sealing operation that even remotely approached the scale envisaged in the 'permissible catch' figures proposed for the annex.

Although the New Zealand delegation was under instructions that New Zealand's sole interest in the Convention was in conservation, since New Zealand had no interest in itself engaging in commercial sealing, its report shows greater sympathy with the attitude of the delegations representing actual or potential sealing interests—Chile, Norway and South Africa—than with the 'arch-conservationist' United States delegation, which unsuccessfully sought to insert control and inspection provisions into the Convention:

> Its hard-line, unwavering approach was undoubtedly attributable to the eighteen-man band of civil servants, congressmen and conservationists (e.g. representatives from the Friends of the Earth, the Sierra Club and the Sea Mammal Motivational Institute) who gave every impression of propelling the leader of their delegation . . . to take stands from which it was clear to all he would have to give way if any convention was to be finally agreed upon.

The New Zealand delegation reported that, despite this American 'obstructionist' approach, the Conference was held in a 'club like' atmosphere. Since only the members of the Antarctic Treaty consultative 'club' were invited to attend, this was not altogether suprising.[22]

It was also not surprising, therefore, that an attempt to extend the scope of the Convention beyond that of the Antarctic Treaty area met strong objection from the most determined of the claimant states—Argentina, Chile and on this occasion the United

Kingdom. Norway proposed that the area to be covered should be extended from 60° to 50° south latitude—but excluding the area in which the Falklands, South Georgia and the southern tips of Argentina and Chile are located. The proposal—which would have included the Auckland and Campbell Islands within the scope of the Convention—was justified by the experience of a Norwegian expedition which had taken nearly half of its catch on pack ice north of 60° south. This problem was met, to some extent, by a provision in the final text requiring the parties to the Convention to report to each other, and to SCAR, statistics on catches of Antarctic seals on floating ice north of 60°.

The scope of the Convention is defined in a curiously worded paragraph which reads:

> This convention applies to the seas south of 60° latitude, in respect of which the Contracting Parties affirm the provisions of Article IV of the Antarctic Treaty.

States not party to the Antarctic Treaty which might wish to adhere to the Convention are thus required to 'affirm' the provision of the Antarctic Treaty dealing with territorial claims; and, not surprisingly, none have done so. The exclusivity of the Convention was further reinforced by the accession clause, under which any state may accede provided that it is invited to do so by *all* the Contracting Parties. The refusal of the Western countries to accept the 'all states' formula, and of the Soviet Union to accept the 'members of the United Nations and its specialised agencies' formula, thus resulted in a formula considerably more restrictive than that in the Antarctic Treaty. Again not surprisingly, only five countries (Brazil, Canada, Germany, Italy and Poland) have been invited to accede to the Convention.[23]

On the initiative of the United States, a new provision was added to the Convention authorising the Contracting Parties at some future date to adopt 'an effective system of inspection'. A further American proposal to make provision for an international observer system was, however, not accepted. (The Whaling Convention of 1946 provides both for *national* inspectors and *international* observers). However, it was agreed, in an article dealing with consultation among the parties, that after commercial sealing had begun, a meeting might be held with a view to establishing (by a two-thirds majority including the concurring votes of all states signatory to the Convention present at the meeting) 'an effective system of control, including inspection'. Thus, yet again, the Consultative Parties to the Antarctic Treaty arrogated to themselves a right of individual veto.

The United States, with support from the United Kingdom, also proposed the establishment of a *new* scientific body, whose composition and functions would be laid down in the Convention, to police the fulfilment of the obligations undertaken by Contracting Parties. The Soviet Union and Chile were not in favour of a new committee, and proposed that SCAR should be designated as the independent scientific body to carry out the policing function. The New Zealand delegation, in accordance with its instructions, proposed that this responsibility should be given to the Food and Agriculture Organisation (FAO). The New Zealand brief favoured FAO over SCAR in the hope that this would encourage wider adherence to the Convention than just among the Antarctic Treaty powers; linking the Convention to SCAR could have an inhibiting effect. The Fish Stock Evaluation Branch of the Fisheries Resources and Exploration Division of FAO would be well suited to do the job. However, several of the Antarctic powers, including the Soviet Union and South Africa, were not members of FAO, and the proposal to assign the main task to SCAR (which might call on FAO for assistance) was eventually adopted. SCAR was not, however, empowered to call a meeting of the Contracting Parties on its own initiative (as the Americans had originally envisaged for an independent scientific body) but merely to warn them, through the depositary (the United Kingdom) when the permissible catch seemed likely to be exceeded.

In contrast to its efforts to strengthen the Convention, the United States proposed, and it was agreed, that parties to the Convention might—in contrast to the corresponding provision in the Antarctic Treaty—withdraw at relatively short notice. Thus an unwelcome precedent was set which was to be followed in subsequent Conventions forming part of the Antarctic treaty system. The only reason given by the United States was that a similar provision had been included in the Whaling Convention. The fact that the withdrawal provision in the Whaling Convention had in fact been frequently availed of might have been seen as a reason not to reproduce it in the Sealing Convention, but alas, New Zealand was in no position to say so, having itself withdrawn from the Whaling Convention in 1969.[24]

The Convention can be amended only by unanimous agreement of the Contracting Parties.[25] The Annex, which sets the permissible catch for certain species (and protects others either partially or absolutely) may be amended by a complicated process which has, as its bottom line, a requirement for approval by a two-thirds majority of Contracting Parties. A Contracting Party which objects, however, has considerable scope for delaying a decision.[26] In practice, the permissible catch figures have remained at 175,000 crabeater seals, 12,000 leopard seals, and 5000 Weddell seals, *per season*. (Ross seals, Southern elephant seals and fur seals may not be taken in the course of commercial sealing.)

The area covered by the Convention is divided into six zones, in each of which sealing may take place for five successive years, followed by a closed year, in rotation. There are three breeding reserves, one of which comprises a part of the south-western Ross Sea. It would thus be lawful, in terms of the Convention, to kill 175,000 crabeater seals in a single zone in each of five successive years. Although three species of seals are protected from commercial sealing, limited numbers may be killed 'to provide indispensable food for men or dogs', for scientific research or to furnish museum specimens.

The permissible catch is mandatory on the Contracting Parties, but there is no provision in the Convention for sharing it among them, should more than one sealing expedition be mounted simultaneously. At the Conference the United Kingdom sought to modify the mandatory character of this provision, given the difficulty of legislating to penalise violators in the absence of national quotas; but other delegations, including New Zealand, objected to weakening the draft, and the mandatory requirement stands, unenforceable though it may be in practice.[27] 'Commercial sealing', it may be added, is not defined in the Convention, so it may also be difficult in practice to determine whether a particular sealing expedition is commercial, or merely engaged in scientific research (or both). This is relevant to the question of whether a meeting of the Contracting Parties may or may not be summoned under the terms of the consultation article.[28]

New Zealand was one of seven countries that signed the Convention when it was opened for that purpose in June 1972, and the remainder of the participants followed suit within the year. It might be supposed from the instructions given to the delegation and the satisfaction expressed by the Minister of Foreign Affairs (Holyoake) on the occasion of New Zealand's signature,[29] that New Zealand would also have been among the first of the signatories to ratify the Convention. Not so.

The Convention entered into force after the deposit of the seventh ratification, on 11 March 1978.[30] By 1980, all the signatories had ratified except Australia and New Zealand. During the decade following its conclusion, the question of ratifying the Convention appears to have sunk to the bottom of successive pending trays in the Ministry of Foreign Affairs.

On 5 June 1975, World Environment Day, the Prime Minister (Rowling) issued a statement expressing concern about the depletion of whale stocks and foreshadowing the introduction of legislation to protect 'all sea mammals, not just whales' within New Zealand waters.[31] This was something of a political gesture, since New Zealanders had given up coastal whaling some ten years before, and New Zealand had not yet extended its maritime jurisdiction by declaring a 200-mile exclusive economic zone (EEZ). Nor did Rowling mention Antarctic waters.

In 1977 a correspondent who raised the issue of the protection of marine mammals in the Antarctic area was told by the Minister of External Affairs (Talboys) that the proposed Marine Mammals Protection Bill would apply in New Zealand's EEZ. Whether the Bill, when enacted, would apply in the Ross Dependency would depend, however, on whether New Zealand declared an EEZ there in terms of the Exclusive Economic Zone Act of 1977.[32] But, as explained in Chapter VI, there were inhibitions against New Zealand's declaring an EEZ for its Antarctic territory, of which the Government was aware when the Minister's letter was written.

The Marine Mammals Protection Act was duly passed in 1978.[33] It is not applicable in the waters of the Ross Dependency unless and until regulations are introduced for that purpose. As late as August 1978 diplomatic posts were informed that New Zealand intended to ratify the Convention on Seals shortly after the passing of the Act, but no action followed.[34] By 1977, the Antarctic Consultative Parties had decided to give urgency to the early conclusion of a 'definitive regime' for the conservation of Antarctic Marine Living Resources (although this was not to apply to species already regulated pursuant to existing international agreements, i.e., whales and seals) and were focussing also on the need for a parallel regime to deal with the question of mineral resources in Antarctica.[35] These developments were no doubt absorbing the full attention of the New Zealand officials responsible for Antarctic questions.

No doubt also the Convention on Seals, allowing as it does for large-scale commercial exploitation, was becoming progressively less attractive from the conservationist viewpoint that was now receiving growing publicity and support, in New Zealand and indeed worldwide. It seems likely that the Convention would have continued to be treated with benign neglect, in Australia as well as New Zealand, had it not been for an unexpected event.

In November 1986 the Soviet authorities notified the New Zealand Embassy in Moscow that it would shortly be conducting an experimental seal hunting expedition,[36] and the Soviet Embassy in Wellington advised the Ministry of Foreign Affairs that one of the vessels involved would be calling at Wellington for bunkering.[37] In response to an enquiry, the Soviets told the New Zealand Embassy that the principal purpose of the expedition was scientific research, and that the number of seals to be taken was very small. When asked for a figure, the Soviets said that 'several hundred' seals were likely to be taken. It was emphasised that the provisions of the Convention would be strictly observed.[38]

In mid-1987, following the return of the expedition, New Zealand again approached the Soviet authorities for information about its results. These were provided with some reluctance. The total catch had amounted, not to a few hundred, but to over four thousand seals, including 'a few' of the protected Ross and Weddell seals. As to the disposal of the seals, it transpired that rather than dump the carcasses overboard, the thrifty Russians had skinned them and minced up the meat and bones for subsequent sale as feed to mink farms. It was again stressed that the whole operation was well within the provisions of the Convention (which provides that special permits may be issued for taking limited numbers of protected species for the purpose of scientific research).[39]

This report raised some apprehensions that the Soviet Union might be about to begin sealing on a commercial scale. It was decided to inform the Soviet Union that if it were to mount further expeditions its sealing vessels would not be welcome in New Zealand ports.[40] When news of the expedition became public in August 1987, the Prime Minister announced that New Zealand had issued this warning, using language that might have suggested an intention to close New Zealand ports to all Soviet vessels en route to Antarctica. Commercial sealing, he said, 'need not and should not become the reality in the Antarctic'.[41] The Soviet authorities, in responding to the publicity, called the expedition 'a routine commercial catch and also the quest for scientific material'. The Prime Minister's demand that the Soviet Union should stop catching seals 'caused surprise'.[42]

The Soviet expedition led the New Zealand authorities to take another look at the question of ratifying the Convention. Officials were concerned, however, that to ratify the Convention, which permitted commercial sealing operations, would effectively disbar New Zealand from opposing seal hunting outright. It was felt that New Zealand's status in the Antarctic treaty system afforded it 'a sufficiently influential platform for the present on matters relating to sealing'. Moreover, the Antarctic Marine

Living Resources (AMLR) Convention with its ecosystem approach to conservation of Antarctic marine life had shown up the inadequacies of the Convention on Seals, which had been negotiated in 1972 at a time when conservation issues were less well appreciated.[43]

This was certainly true, and was accepted by the Minister: but it was perhaps overlooked that the AMLR Convention contained a provision acknowledging the existing rights of parties to the Convention on Seals, and so did not in fact give the seals any additional protection. Confronted with the same problem, Australia took a different approach and proceeded to ratify the Convention on Seals.[44]

In accordance with a provision in the Convention, a review conference was held in 1988. New Zealand sought and was granted permission to attend as an observer.[45] At the Conference it was clear, however, that the majority of the parties to the Convention (except Australia and the United Kingdom) were not prepared to consider any amendments, except for some minor changes to the Annex. The Federal Republic of Germany, a very recent party to the Convention, was especially resistant to change (apparently fearing, for obscure reasons, that the European Economic Community (EEC) might thereby be given an opportunity to seek membership). There was a general reluctance on the part of Consultative Parties to the Antarctic Treaty to 'tamper' with existing instruments, and a particular reluctance to establish a link with the AMLR Convention.[46]

The New Zealand observer explained to the Conference his country's attitude to the Convention on Seals. The conservation standards of the present day, he noted, are very different from those of 1972. The strong commitment that New Zealanders have to the protection of marine mammals made a Convention which allowed the taking of large numbers of seals much less easy to accept. New Zealand had not ruled out ratifying the Convention. But in judging whether to do so it would want to be satisfied that the Convention was capable of being brought into line with modern standards of conservation and take account of developments in the Antarctic treaty system. It would like to see much closer cooperation between the parties to the Convention and the institutions of the AMLR Convention.[47]

If the review meeting was anything to go by, that hope, and any prospect of substantial amendment to the Convention, was unlikely to be realised in the near future. The conservatism of some of the Consultative Parties to the Antarctic Treaty, and the continued interest of some countries, such as Norway, in possibilities of commercial sealing, were formidable barriers to reform of the Convention.

New Zealand was left in something of a dilemma. As a non-party to the Treaty, its voice was unlikely to carry much influence at future meetings convened under the provisions of the Convention. But Australia, holding similar views, did not achieve much success either. New Zealand, as a non-party, was not inhibited from taking a stronger line against commercial sealing than it would be able to do if it had acceded to the Convention. Other Consultative Parties to the Antarctic Treaty might have regarded such a course as 'opting out of the system', bearing in mind in particular that the AMLR Convention, to which New Zealand *is* a party and attaches great importance, defines 'conservation' as including 'rational use', and seeks to regulate rather than prohibit the 'harvesting' of marine living resources—including, presumably, mammals. There was also the question of what effective action New Zealand might take in the event that commercial sealing began in earnest. The closing of New Zealand ports to sealing vessels might have been seen as a little more than a gesture. To actually deter sealing in the New Zealand sector would require quite drastic steps, such as the declaring of an EEZ for the Ross Dependency—and policing it.

IX

CONSERVATION: MARINE LIVING RESOURCES

Even before the Convention on Seals came into force in March 1978, work had begun on an instrument of broader scope designed to protect all living species in Antarctic waters. The need for further measures was formally recognised by the Antarctic Treaty Consultative Parties at their Eighth Meeting in 1975.[1] The reasons for this recognition were several. On the one hand, environmental and conservation issues had come to the forefront of international attention as a result, in part, of the United Nations Conference on the Human Environment held in Stockholm in 1972 and the establishment of the United Nations Environment Programme. On the other hand, the question of sovereign rights over both living and non-living resources in coastal waters and on continental shelves had become a leading issue at the Law of the Sea Conference, which held its first substantive session at Caracas in 1974. Coastal state jurisdiction over the marine resources out to 200 nautical miles from the shoreline came to be widely asserted and accepted. Meanwhile there was growing concern about some of the living resources of the sea, notably whales, which seemed in danger of being hunted to extinction. Attention was beginning to be focussed on possible new food sources, and in the case of Antarctic waters, on a small crustacean, krill, which existed there in uncounted numbers, and appeared to offer the possibility of a huge supply of protein. Krill were (and are) an important part of the diet of baleen whales and crabeater seals,[2] but attention at the time was on their possible utilisation for human consumption.

In New Zealand, a small scale research project on the processing of krill was undertaken at Massey University in 1968. Work was concentrated on utilising the krill 'as a flavouring agent in sea foods to enhance the palatability of fish lacking a characteristic or attractive flavour'. The products that were developed were found 'well suited for home cooking and in industrial preparations of fish products'. It was also found that trout fed with krill grew twice as fast and twice as large as normal, and tasted better.[3] At an interdepartmental meeting in 1976, however, it was decided that there was 'no way in which New Zealand could benefit economically from the exploitation of the krill resources in the Antarctic region'. The reasons were not recorded.[4] At this time, the New Zealand authorities were more concerned with the immediate issue of how to protect the fisheries off New Zealand's coasts from excessive exploitation by distant water fishing nations. Thus, New Zealand's interest in the living resources of Antarctic waters appears to have been almost exclusively driven by concerns about conservation rather than possible exploitation by the New Zealand fishing industry.

At the Eighth Antarctic ATCM in 1975 Norway submitted a paper on the question of conservation measures,[5] and the United States a draft recommendation.[6] In its paper Norway noted that the Consultative Parties had recognised at their Fifth Meeting that the Southern Ocean was an integral part of the Antarctic environment. Exploitation of its living resources was thus a matter of common concern to the Contracting Parties to the Treaty, as had been recognised in Article IX 1(f). Scientific knowledge of the extent of these resources (e.g., of krill) was deficient, and SCAR should be asked to make an assessment. The United States took up this suggestion in its draft recommendation, which called for governments to make catch statistics available to SCAR as a basis for a 'coordinated international biological investigation of the Southern Ocean'. Predictably, this went too far for Argentina and Chile, and a less ambitious recommendation was co-sponsored by New Zealand and Australia. Governments would be asked to conduct detailed studies of the biology, distribution, biomass and population dynamics, and the ecology of Antarctic marine living resources, and SCAR to convene a meeting to discuss and report on this work. The New Zealand delegation was told that five expeditions were about to set out to study the krill resource in the Treaty area.[7]

Later in 1975 it was learnt that the Food and Agricultural Organisation was taking an active interest in the question. New Zealand officials, perhaps having overlooked the fact that it was New Zealand who had pressed hardest to have provision for 'cooperative working relations' with the specialised agencies of the United Nations included in the Antarctic Treaty (Article III 2),[8] took a somewhat negative 'claimant's' view of this intervention. An FAO paper referred to the need to control the exploitation of Antarctic resources 'so that their productivity should be maintained for the benefit of all mankind'. The Law of the Sea Conference was moving towards the establishment of an international regime which would treat areas outside national jurisdiction as 'the common heritage of mankind'. It seemed to New Zealand officials that there was a clear implication in the FAO paper that Antarctic fisheries should be subjected to the international regime foreseen in the Law of the Sea discussions.[9] Subsequently, they took a more relaxed view, and when a proposal emerged for a fisheries survey programme jointly sponsored by FAO and the United Nations Development Programme, it was decided to support it, provided that the Antarctic Treaty powers were consulted before it went ahead.[10]

The initiative of the United Nations agencies proved a useful spur to the Antarctic powers to reach some agreement among themselves in order to avoid being pre-empted. In May 1976 the Ministry of Foreign Affairs wrote to other government departments that:

> The need for some agreement regulating the exploration and exploitation of resources in the Antarctic is becoming increasingly urgent and if the Consultative Parties do not come up with a solution it will be difficult for them to justify resistance to demands to throw the whole question over to a wider international body. This would certainly put paid to the Treaty's already fragile status

> as an international (universal) agreement. Yet we must be aware that the very process of negotiations over the issue among the Consultative States themselves will put the Treaty under very considerable pressure as the divisions patched over by the Treaty, for instance, the question of sovereign claims in the Antarctic, are reopened under the additional pressure of vested interests.[11]

The Ministry noted that New Zealand had already promoted the concept of a scientific management regime for living resources, and would do so again at the Ninth ATCM. Both SCAR and SCOR (Scientific Committee for Ocean Research) recommended that arrangements should be made as soon as possible to ensure the conservation and rational utilisation of Antarctic fish resources, especially krill.[12] This provided the necessary impetus for a preparatory meeting, held in London in March 1977, to agree to send on to the Ninth ATCM the outline of a draft convention prepared by the United Kingdom. Again, as in the case of the seals, the Convention form was preferred to agreed measures.[13]

New Zealand officials, meanwhile, continued to worry about the interest displayed by FAO in the Southern Ocean and the motivation for that interest. Instead of waiting for the Antarctic powers to consider the proposed regime for living resources at their next ATCM, FAO officials decided to try to have a research programme adopted by its Committee on Fishing (COFI) in April. In instructing the New Zealand delegation to the COFI meeting, the departments in Wellington suggested that the FAO Fisheries Division might see in the programme 'the prospect of a new empire at a time in which the proliferation of 200 mile zones is rapidly doing them out of a job'. Even more worrying, New Zealand officials believed that the FAO proposals were

> the thin edge of a wedge which is being driven into the Antarctic Treaty framework by various countries and in various fora . . . Clearly one of the long term objectives is to internationalise Antarctica using 'common heritage of mankind' type agreements. Naturally this line of argument is particularly attractive to the developing countries. It is however essentially destructive of the Treaty itself.[14]

It should be noted that New Zealand officials were, at this time, more concerned with the issue of minerals exploitation than with Antarctic fisheries, which New Zealand was in no position to exploit or police. In March 1977 the Government approved a paper on future Antarctic policy which was almost solely concerned with mineral resources. The starting point for this paper was a belief that Antarctic minerals might be subject to 'limited commercial exploitation . . . in the reasonably near future'.[15] The need to put in place control measures under the umbrella of the Antarctic Treaty, and at the same time to safeguard New Zealand's own interests in whatever future exploitation might take place, was of paramount concern. Hence the slightly paranoid note in New Zealand's reaction to what might otherwise have been regarded as a harmless, and indeed commendable, extension of FAO's legitimate interest in the conservation of fish stocks in a southerly direction.

By the time the COFI meeting was held, however, consultation with Australia, the United Kingdom and the United States had revealed a consensus that FAO could not be frozen out of Southern Ocean fisheries questions.[16] The meeting itself agreed that FAO had a role to play, that there should be a close working relationship with the parties to the Antarctic Treaty, and that no new FAO machinery was required.[17]

In the preparations for the Ninth ATCM, it became evident that Australia, in contrast to New Zealand, was disposed to give priority to a regime for living resources over a minerals regime, having concluded that the latter was unrealisable in the short term.[18] In consequence the Australians were able to come up at the ATCM with a draft convention on living resources.[19] (This was largely the work of Eli Lauterpacht, the leading British international lawyer who was at that time Legal Advisor to the Australian Department of Foreign Affairs.)[20] The Australians had read well the developing mood among the Antarctic powers, which proved to be very much in support of priority for the living resources regime: the interest displayed by FAO, reports of a possible Sri Lankan initiative in the United Nations General Assembly, and 'a genuine recognition of a need for a regime to govern conservation and rational utilisation' together ensured that delegations were prepared to discuss the substance of a regime at this meeting.

The Australian draft did not, however, deal with utilisation. It envisaged a collective approach to conservation, with the establishment of a commission to adopt appropriate measures. While the draft included a provision to protect the rights of the claimant states, the Australians apparently took the pragmatic view that as no claimant state was currently fishing in Antarctic waters, there would be an obligation—under the rules envisaged in the draft Law of the Sea Convention—to allow foreign fishing fleets access to the entire allowable catch: thus the awkward question of sovereign rights over the resource might in practice be sidestepped. On this point, the New Zealand delegation reported, the position of Argentina and Chile had moved remarkably; they now spoke openly of the political necessity of subordinating these rights to a collective regime. They placed strong emphasis on the collective responsibilities of the Treaty powers, and on the importance of the Antarctic as 'a special conservation zone' (the Agreed Measures on Fauna and Flora, it will be remembered, considered it to be a Special Conservation Area).[21]

Under New Zealand chairmanship, a working group formulated a two-stage approach. The Australian and other drafts were not directly discussed, but interim guidelines were adopted calling for cooperation in scientific research and in the exchange of catch statistics, and for the exercise of great care in harvesting to avoid depletion of stocks and damage to the Antarctic marine ecosystem. A definitive regime should be concluded before the end of 1978. (This was optimistic.) It was agreed that the area to be covered by the regime should extend north of 60° south where necessary for effective conservation of Antarctic species. It was also agreed that the regime should not apply to species already regulated by existing international agreements, i.e., whales and seals. 'Conservation' was to include 'rational use', in the sense that harvesting would not be prohibited, but the regime would exclude catch allocation and other economic regulation of harvesting.[22]

Despite the recognition by claimant states that even a strictly conservationist regime required the renunciation of certain sovereign rights over living resources, the most concerned claimants—Australia, Argentina and Chile—argued as strongly as ever the need for a 'without prejudice' clause on sovereignty. There were 'constant and harassing interventions' by the Australian representative (Keith Brennan), and 'when he was not addressing the issue the Latins were'. There was no reluctance, the New Zealand delegation reported, 'to barter what would in any case have been somewhat illusory sovereign rights over resources on a 200 mile Antarctic EEZ for a secure right to share in the setting of allowable catches and access to catch and effort statistics and other data which could in the long run be of direct economic benefit.' (This comment is not easy to reconcile with the agreement recorded by the working group that the regime should exclude catch allocation and other economic regulation of harvesting: the Convention in its final form gives the Commission on the Conservation of Antarctic Marine Living Resources power to set catch *limits* by regions and sub-regions but not to fix national catch *allocations*.)[23] The objective at this meeting (according to the delegation) was not to draft a 'without prejudice' clause but to demonstrate to the non-claimants that the mere reformulation of Article IV of the Antarctic Treaty might not be enough. Finding an appropriate formula was not an easy task, and failing agreement on the wording finally adopted on New Zealand's initiative, the meeting might well have ended in disarray. According to the formula accepted by the Consultative Parties, the regime should ensure that

> the principles embodied in Article IV are safeguarded in application to the marine areas south of 60° south latitude.[24]

(A similar form of words, *mutatis mutandis*, was adopted in the Meeting's recommendation on mineral resources.)[25]

Although almost all of the Consultative Parties at their Ninth Meeting favoured establishing the 'definitive regime' for living resources in the form of a convention, Chile stood out in favour of agreed measures, in order to link the agreement more firmly to the Antarctic Treaty and the controlling hand of the Consultative Parties. A convention to which non-members of the Antarctic Treaty might accede could, in Chile's view, disturb the balance struck in the Treaty between claimants and non-claimants. At the London meeting Australia and New Zealand had worked hard, but unsuccessfully, to find a compromise acceptable to Chile. At the beginning of 1978 they made *demarches* in Santiago.[26] They pointed out that there were strong practical reasons for not confining the agreement to the Treaty partners. 'Outsiders' would not be bound by agreed measures. The Federal Republic of Germany, for example, not yet a party to the Treaty, was among the countries conducting exploratory expeditions.[27] The Chilean authorities were told that New Zealand, which had gone further than any other country towards applying 200-mile jurisdiction to its Antarctic Territory (a doubtful assertion) did not regard a regime of the kind contemplated in the Australian draft convention as undermining its claim. The powers which would be given to a Commission under the convention would be virtually impossible for a claimant state to enforce, given that krill were migratory, that knowledge about the stocks was minimal, and that enforcement would be extremely difficult. Whether or not these arguments were decisive, Chile agreed to drop its insistence on agreed measures.[28]

A Special Consultative Meeting (SCM) was held in Canberra in March 1978 to elaborate the draft 'definitive regime'. It was a measure of New Zealand's interest in the Antarctic fishing at the time that, apart from Foreign Affairs, none of the departments involved with Antarctica, or fishing, felt able to meet the relatively modest expenditure required to send a representative to Canberra.[29]

No less than eight draft conventions were submitted to the meeting. In a remarkable display of determination that the Consultative Parties should decide the shape of the regime, it was agreed to give the Chairman responsibility for producing a single negotiating text. In an intensive exercise the Chairman prepared a draft convention and two revisions within the space of a week.[30] Although the wording of the articles on sovereignty, the setting of conservation standards and on voting in the Commission remained to be agreed, considerable progress was made in the direction of a generally acceptable text. The compromise article on sovereignty, perhaps not surprisingly, leant somewhat towards the position of the claimants by introducing the concept of coastal state sovereignty:

> Nothing contained in this Convention shall be interpreted as a renunciation by any Contracting Party of any right of or claim to or basis of claim to coastal state jurisdiction in marine areas in which this Convention applies or as prejudicing the position of any Contracting Party as regards its recognition of any such right or claim or basis of claim.[31]

In mid-March the meeting adjourned until July, when it reconvened in Buenos Aires.[32]

In the interval a potential problem that had emerged at Canberra became more evident. At the Ninth ATCM it had been agreed that the proposed regime should 'extend north of 60° south latitude where that was necessary for the effective conservation of species of the Antarctic ecosystem, without prejudice to coastal state jurisdiction in that area.'[33] This begged the question of what precise geographical limits would need to be set in the convention to meet this criterion. The first Australian draft also begged the question. The New Zealand Embassy in Paris learnt in April that France was particularly concerned to retain control over the waters surrounding the French islands which were north of the Antarctic Treaty area but south of the Antarctic convergence (a suggested northern boundary for the convention).[34] There had been reports of huge catches by Soviet fishing vessels in the vicinity of Kerguelen; and in any case France was not disposed to concede rights which others were not prepared to concede elsewhere.[35]

This was not, however, the only obstacle that remained to be surmounted before a convention could be completed. Also in the interval between the meetings, the Soviet Union had (as recounted in Chapter VI) protested against the provision in the New Zealand Territorial Sea and Exclusive Economic Zone Act, permitting its application to the Ross Dependency. New Zealand had categorically rejected that protest. In turn the attitude of the Soviet Union—supported by Poland and Japan—to the reference in the draft Convention to coastal state jurisdiction had hardened considerably. The instructions for the New Zealand delegation to the meeting in Buenos Aires closely paralleled the position taken by New Zealand in rejecting the Soviet protest against New Zealand's assertion of a right to a territorial sea and an EEZ in its Antarctic territory.[36] Japan, the Soviet Union and Poland, the instructions said, were unhappy with the Canberra text because they contended that there could be no possibility of 'coastal state jurisdiction' in Antarctica. New Zealand found this attitude difficult to understand. They—the non-claimants—had accepted the reference to 'territorial' sovereignty in the Antarctic Treaty. How could the reference to 'coastal state jurisdiction' in this convention be more prejudicial? They asserted that in prohibiting the enlargement of territorial claims, the Treaty prohibited the establishment of jurisdiction over resources in the marine area. New Zealand considered this view legally unsound. In 1929 New Zealand had asserted jurisdiction throughout the Ross Sea over whaling activities. This jurisdiction had been actually implemented. Licences were issued to foreign vessels and licence fees collected. There were therefore in New Zealand's opinion strong grounds for saying that even if the Soviet argument were sustained that claims were proscribed, New Zealand at least (and probably Chile also) had implemented such claims well before the Treaty entered into force.[37]

The instructions also restated New Zealand's position on claims, as it had been formulated (or reformulated) by the Minister of Foreign Affairs (Talboys) in a speech a few months earlier. Pointing out that the legal merits of claims had been fixed in 1961, when the Treaty entered into force, Talboys had said:

> It is often asserted that the treaty extinguished the claims, or that they were frozen or rendered ineffective. Those who assert that have not read the treaty. The treaty specifically provides that the claims shall not be diminished. In practice the treaty places four limitations upon the claimant state in the exercise of its sovereignty in its claimed territory:

> (a) First, the obligation to refrain from establishing a military presence in its territory;
> (b) Secondly the obligation to refrain from testing nuclear weapons in its territory or dispose of nuclear waste there;
> (c) Thirdly the obligation to permit scientists of other parties free access to the territory (in other words it cannot require them to apply for visas);
> (d) Fourthly the obligation to refrain from exercising jurisdiction over inspectors and exchange scientists present in their territory.

It is therefore quite wrong to assert that the treaty has extinguished the claims. Apart from these four obligations—which constitute the practical framework within which scientific cooperation can take place—the sovereign claims continue as before.'[38]

This, it may safely be said, was the strongest assertion of New Zealand's sovereignty in the Ross Dependency since the Treaty had been negotiated. It was a very different approach from that of Walter Nash, who certainly hoped that claims would be regarded as frozen, or in abeyance, once the Treaty had entered into force. As Talboys went on to make clear in his speech, New Zealand's Antarctic policy was now very much resource driven and the resources in question were minerals, not fish. As the New Zealand delegation to the Buenos Aires meeting put it in its report:

> In everything they said and did . . . each delegation was conscious that a fisheries convention would need to be followed before long by a convention on the exploitation of minerals.[39]

Thus there were two aspects to the question of sovereignty in the minds of New Zealand and the other claimants: their desire to protect, in respect of their Antarctic territories, the off-shore rights in process of definition at the time in the Law of the Sea Conference; and equally a concern to ensure that their territorial claims should be fully maintained against the contingency of agreement on a minerals regime for the continent.

At the Canberra meeting the claimant states thought their position had been secured by a 'simple' provision to the effect that the provision of the convention which would give to a commission powers of conservation would not prejudice their sovereign rights as coastal states. This, the New Zealand delegation reported, could be interpreted 'bifocally', i.e., non-claimants would regard references to coastal state jurisdiction as applying solely to areas of undisputed national jurisdiction north of 60° south and claimants would regard such references as applying both north and south of that latitude.[40] At Canberra the 'bifocal' approach was acceptable to some non-claimants, including the United States, but at the Buenos Aires meeting the three distant water fishing states—Japan, Poland and the Soviet Union—resolutely opposed a text which, as the New Zealand delegation acknowledged, effectively reserved the right of the coastal states to implement and enforce 200-mile zones. Their adamantine attitude, now supported by the United States, effectively deprived the claimants of any advantage they might have thought they had gained. The text of the sovereignty article discussed (but not agreed) at Buenos Aires, while continuing to refer to coastal state jurisdiction in similar terms to the Canberra draft, contained an additional sentence which read:

> [In this connection] Contracting Parties confirm that no new claim or enlargement of an existing claim to territorial sovereignty in the Antarctic shall be asserted.[41]

As the delegation leader (Norrish) ruefully remarked in a personal letter:

> I am still on balance optimistic that a Convention can be successfully negotiated. The sovereignty issue, however, will have to be settled pretty much on the basis of what we came to call the Oelofsen text. . . This means of course that the attempt in Canberra to push through non-prejudicial language that was nevertheless very much in our favour has failed. Personally, however, I believe that the Oelofsen text is not too bad. It is a long step backwards and it is a pity that we should have to take a specific reaffirmation of the provision in the Antarctic Treaty forbidding the extension of existing claims. It seems to me, nevertheless, that the way in which that concept and the concept of coastal state jurisdiction appear side by side implies pretty clearly the two are different things. At least that is a respectable interpretation which is about the best we can hope to rely on.[42]

However, the participants in the Buenos Aires meeting were unable to agree on any text for this Article. Disagreement remained also on the question of voting. The United States was opposed to consensus decision-making. Other participants wished to retain a veto, for various reasons: South Africa, to guard against any expulsion move; Argentina and Chile, to protect their sovereignty; the Soviet Union and Poland, to protect their fishing interests. Japan favoured an objections procedure which would in effect give fishing nations a veto. The New Zealand delegation was instructed that this was quite unacceptable, as it would create an imbalance. New Zealand, although it had not openly advocated a consensus procedure at Canberra, in fact regarded it as the only politically acceptable procedure. (There is no mention in New Zealand's reporting of whether 'consensus' was interpreted as meaning 'unanimity', but this seems to have been the assumption.) At Buenos Aires, the United States came up with a formula combining two-thirds majority voting with an objections procedure on conservation measures which attempted to meet the concerns of both claimants and fishing nations. Despite its instructions, the New Zealand delegation's report implied that it supported the American proposal as 'just about the only possible solution to a knotty problem'. (It wasn't.) As with the sovereignty issue, the meeting was obliged to hold this issue over for the next round.

Also unresolved were the problems posed by French determination to retain sole jurisdiction over conservation and management of living resources in the 'economic area' of the Kerguelen and Crozet archipelagos, and by the demand of the EEC for the right to be a party to the convention on its own account.

The New Zealand delegation viewed with some foreboding the way things seemed to be heading. It seemed clear to them that the 1959 bargain on sovereignty would become more fragile as commercial activities in Antarctica developed:

> New Zealand's primary interest is in the prospect of the exploitation of valuable mineral deposits either on land . . . or more likely, offshore in the 200 mile zone. The debates so far . . . have made

> it perfectly clear that there is little prospect of non-claimant states . . . conceding that claimants have a right to special consideration in respect of minerals found off the Antarctic coast. The United States seems to concede that claimant states may reasonably *think* they have rights in the 200 mile zones but it . . . is not at all prepared to recognise or concede those rights . . . We have to accept, beyond the shadow of a doubt, that no one likely to be involved in exploitation in our area is going to concede us any legal entitlements.[43]

The delegation suggested, therefore, that New Zealand needed to show by its actions that it had confidence in its position in Antarctica and that it expected to gain advantage from the resources there because of its practical efforts as well as its legal and historical claims. Because of the particularly negative attitude that some delegations had shown to the 200-mile question, it seemed particularly important to do whatever was possible to extend New Zealand's research and similar activities off-shore. It was suggested New Zealand should also aim to take an active part in the work of the convention, once it had come into effect. It had emphasised the need for conservation and effective inspection, and had asserted the right and responsibility of the Consultative Parties to participate in the management of the marine living resources of the area. It would have to follow through if it was to be taken seriously as an Antarctic partner in 'activities of more importance to us' in the future. It would, for example, have to participate effectively in the work of the Scientific Committee for Ocean Research and the Commission, and from time to time make available a well-qualified inspector.

This exhortation, which does not appear to have had any discernible effect at the time, was no doubt prompted in part by the fact that the New Zealand delegation had once again included no scientists or fisheries experts; it was in fact comprised solely of diplomatic officials stationed overseas.[44]

Following the failure of the Buenos Aires meeting to settle a number of key issues, a further effort to resolve the remaining differences was undertaken in informal consultations in Washington only six weeks later. This time substantial progress was made. Among the unresolved issues left over from the earlier meetings was the question of whether the Commission should be empowered to allocate quotas when the total allowable catch of a species seemed likely to be reached, whether the claimant states should, in that situation, be entitled to a share, and whether as a *quid pro quo* they should agree not to apply 'national measures' in the Antarctic against other parties to the convention. Answering the questions in the affirmative (for tactical purposes) the claimants had, at the end of the meeting in Buenos Aires, put forward a working paper in the name of the United Kingdom delegation which embodied these points, but it had not been discussed.[45] It will be recalled that at the Ninth ATCM it had been agreed upon that the convention would *not* go so far as to deal with catch allocation. The New Zealand view on this point, as set out in the delegation's instructions for the Buenos Aires meeting, was that it was

> an essential element of this draft convention that the only rights pooled or ceded to the Commission are the conservation rights . . . The Commission will therefore have no powers of utilisation and management (i.e. it cannot set quotas or allocations or charge fees). Under our view of the legal position these powers will be reserved for the coastal state. Whether or not we exercise them and seek to have them recognised is a separate question and one which this convention will not resolve. Hence the need for Article XXI. In its absence the fishing countries could acquire 'traditional rights'. We can square the fact that they are fishing our waters with the fact that as there is no New Zealand fishing in the area, under international law we are obliged to let foreign countries have access to 100% of the surplus [total allowable catch].[46]

The New Zealand delegation at the Washington talks viewed the United Kingdom paper as 'introducing a very complex factor into an already difficult negotiation'. The non-claimants considered the proposal strongly prejudicial to their position on claims. Faced with likely deadlock, the meeting rather belatedly recalled that, in any case, consideration of economic questions such as catch allocation was outside the terms of reference laid down at the Ninth ATCM, and reverted to discussion of a regime which would be restricted to conservation. Taking up the draft article on claims, the meeting agreed that it should exactly parallel Article IV of the Antarctic Treaty. They were thus able to agree on language relating to coastal state jurisdiction within the convention area which survived into the final text.[47]

The New Zealand delegation submitted a working paper proposing the addition of a provision for a review conference at which the utilisation and economic aspects of harvesting could be onsidered.[48] There is no explanation in the delegation report for this initiative, which may have been taken for tactical reasons to mollify the other claimants for the abandonment of the proposals in the British paper. At any event, it appears to represent a step back from the uncompromising 'coastal state' position presented in the July instructions.

Agreement was reached surprisingly easily on voting procedure. When opposition emerged to the elaborate American proposal, it was quickly abandoned in favour of consensus for all decision-making, despite the fact that this had been unacceptable to the United States only a few weeks before. In addition, provision was made for an objection procedure, which in effect permitted a fishing state to reject any conservation measure adopted by the Commission, despite the fact that New Zealand had considered this 'quite unacceptable to the claimants'.[49] The delegation did not mention this considerable concession to the fishing nations in its report.

Although progress had been made, an apparently immovable roadblock remained in the form of a 'non-negotiable' determination on the part of France to redraw the northern boundary of the convention area in such a way as to exclude the Kerguelen and Crozet archipelagos.[50] The French delegation continued to insist on this position despite the fact that other Consultative Parties owning islands within the convention area—Australia, Norway, South Africa and the United Kingdom—were satisfied that the exercise of their sovereignty in the economic zones surrounding their islands would, for all practical purposes, be unimpaired: should the Commission seek to impose conservation measures in those zones at variance with the wishes of the sovereign state, the consensus rule could be invoked. The principal objections of other claimants were that, first, if the French position were maintained, all those countries possessing islands within the convention area would feel obliged to take a similar stand, and second—perhaps more important—the 'bifocal' interpretation of the sovereignty article would lose all credibility if France were not prepared to accept its validity in respect of its own possessions.[51] New Zealand made representations in Paris, but its arguments were not accepted. Among the French counterarguments, it was pointed out that the consensus procedure offered no real protection, since if there were no consensus fishing nations could do what they liked.[52] (This seems a fair point. The French might have added that even if there *were* a consensus acceptable to France, a fishing nation could still invoke the objections procedure.)

Yet another problem emerged as a serious obstacle after the conclusion of the Washington talks. At Washington, it had been assumed that the undecided question of EEC participation would have to be settled at the final conference in Canberra. However, the three Consultative Parties that were also members of the EEC insisted that the EEC would have to be invited to the conference as a full participant.[53] The rationale for this position was that members of the Community had transferred to it competence in respect of fishing by their nationals outside their metropolitan zones. Similar arguments were being advanced to secure the Community's right to full participation in the Law of the Sea Convention, which was no doubt regarded as much more important: the AMLR Convention would provide a precedent. In both forums, the Eastern European states were equally adamant in their opposition to giving the EEC a separate right to become a party to either convention, especially if that right were denied to the Council for Mutual Economic Assistance (COMECON). New Zealand pointed out that in the negotiation of a treaty to establish a South Pacific Fisheries Organisation, which was essentially similar in character, the Community members had not insisted on separate membership.[54] The rather lame response was that this had probably been 'overlooked'.

In reporting to Ministers on the results of the Washington meeting, New Zealand officials continued to lay emphasis on the implications of these negotiations for any subsequent attempt to negotiate a minerals treaty. The Soviet Union, they noted, had rejected the proposal in the British working paper that fish quotas should be allocated by the Commission to both fishing nations and claimant states:

> There was some justice in the Soviet argument. The British proposals, which raised economic issues, ran counter to the approach to the living resources issue which had been agreed at the London ATCM, i.e., that the Convention should be limited to conservation matters. It was clear that to open up the larger issue of a regime for sharing the economic benefits of Antarctic would, because of its inherent complexity and its precedent setting value for mineral resources, have delayed the living resources regime for years. Nevertheless we also gained the clear impression that the USSR had other motives. They have not yet reached the point where they are prepared to negotiate an economic settlement in Antarctica. Despite the success of the Washington consultations, the area for dispute between claimants and non-claimants remains. Moreover that area of dispute is coming into an increasingly sharper focus . . . It will be extremely difficult to negotiate a satisfactory economic settlement with respect to mineral resources. The success of the living resources convention will undoubtedly have created some political goodwill but little more. There are still no clear indications that the non-claimants are prepared to concede a share of the economic benefits of Antarctica to the claimant states. 'We believe from discussion with the United States Delegation . . . that the United States is perhaps the closest to accepting that some form of economic sharing may be necessary. Japan may also be moving in that direction in the field of fishing but probably not on minerals. The Soviet Union, however, is sticking rigidly to the view that all offshore areas are high seas.

New Zealand, the officials pointed out, would need to take a position on the application of the EEZ to the Ross Dependency after the living resources convention had been finally adopted. It had been a major objective of the claimant states to ensure that the convention did not limit their rights to apply an EEZ in their Antarctic territories. Equally it had been an objective of the non-claimants to ensure that the convention did not specifically legitimate such application. The convention was likely to strike a delicate balance between these positions and New Zealand and the other claimants in a similar position would need to weigh their next step most carefully.[55]

Faced with an impasse over EEC participation and the French islands, the Australians put off the diplomatic conference which it had intended to convene in January 1979, and instead organised informal discussions in which they aimed to settle both issues, in the case of the EEC by inviting the Commission to be represented at the Conference with observer status, and with the prospect of becoming party to the Convention.[56] These negotiations proved extremely difficult. The French demand for a more specific reservation of coastal state rights in respect of its island territories north of 60° south than was provided in the 'ambiguous' and delicately balanced claims article could only be satisfied, in New Zealand's view, at the expense of its own claim (and that of the other territorial claimants) to coastal state rights in Antarctic waters. An attempt was made to meet the French position in the form of an agreed statement, phrased in general terms, that in the case of territories within the convention area over which sovereignty was undisputed, the rights of the state exercising sovereignty would remain unimpaired; it might introduce its own conservation measures, which other states would be bound to observe: if the Commission sought to introduce conservation measures relating to the waters adjacent to the territories in question, the state exercising sovereignty could withhold its consent. This was not good enough for France: while all delegations agreed that this was a correct interpretation of the draft convention, the statement 'in and of itself did not overcome its objections to certain provisions of the . . . text'.[57]

A second piece of paper embodied the Australian approach to the question of EEC participation: observer status for the Community at the Conference, provision for accession to the convention by regional economic organisations to which members had transferred competence with respect to conservation of marine living resources, the EEC to be a member of the Commission, duplication of voting by the EEC and its members to be avoided.[58] This was not good enough for the EEC, which demanded to be treated exactly as if it were a sovereign state. The proposed limitations, even though the substantive right of full participation had been conceded, were described as 'an offence to the dignity of the Community'. While the package seemed likely to be acceptable to the Soviet Union, Argentina became apprehensive that it might allow COMECON the right to accede, which Argentina could not stomach.[59]

The outcome was an inevitable further delay. For New Zealand, an important concern was that progress on the question of a minerals regime was likely to be consequentially held up. But because New Zealand was having problems at the time in its relations with France over agricultural protectionism, New Zealand did not feel able to join with Australia and the United States in pressing France to soften its stand.[60]

Preparations were now beginning for the Tenth ATCM, to be held in Washington. In June 1979, yet another attempt was made under American chairmanship to solve the outstanding AMLR issues in conjunction with these preparatory meetings. The June talks again failed to produce solutions that satisfied France and the EEC. On the latter issue, however, several revised articles were produced by the United States, including the voting formula for the Commission which was eventually embodied in the final text of the convention. This provided that in a voting situation in which both a 'regional economic integration organisation' and any of its member states wished to participate, the number of votes to be cast by the organisation and its member states should not exceed the number of those member states which were members of the Commission.

France for its part reiterated its determination not to be drawn into a situation in which its conservation measures for its Antarctic island territories, including the total allowable catch in their EEZs, might be questioned in the AMLR Commission. It accepted that the draft Article IV established that its jurisdiction as a coastal state would in no way be prejudiced by anything in the convention. But it did not want the discretions which it applied in the exercise of that right to be subject to second guessing.[61] This was apparently regarded as a somewhat extreme attitude, but it did no more, in fact, than reflect the attitude adopted by the coastal states in the law of the negotiations. It would have been interesting to see what attitude New Zealand might have taken if any of its sub-antarctic islands had come within the area proposed for the convention. New Zealand, however, unlike other Antarctic claimants, did not have this problem.

Although agreement was not reached at this informal meeting, two documents were produced which were eventually to be amalgamated to produce the final 'compromise' on this issue. These documents, a revised 'Chairman's statement' and an alternative text produced by France, both differed from the Berne document in that they dealt specifically with Kerguelen and Crozet instead of simply attempting to state understandings applicable to all islands of undisputed sovereignty within the area of the convention. The Chairman's draft essentially restated the understandings enunciated in the Berne document as being specifically applicable to Kerguelen and Crozet with an additional paragraph stating that these understandings would also apply to other islands similarly situated. The change was therefore essentially one of presentation, for France's benefit. The French draft, however, made plain what it was that France wanted:

> If . . . the Commission should wish to undertake examination of the conservation needs of the general area in which the waters adjacent to Kerguelen and Crozet are to be found, it would be open to France either to agree that the waters in question should be included in the area of application of such measures taken to meet those needs or to indicate that they should be excluded. In the latter event, the Commission would give no consideration to conservation measures to apply in the waters in question unless and until France should indicate its agreement to see such measures discussed by the Commission.[62]

In September, the United States after informal contacts with 'several interested delegations' produced yet another text which appeared to go a long way towards meeting French demands. This text, which incorporated the substance of the French position as set out in the foregoing quotation, was further refined at meetings held contemporaneously with the Tenth ATCM, and agreed upon for reference to governments.[63]

The New Zealand representative found difficulty at this stage with the final paragraph of the proposed statement, which he reported on as follows:

> For our part we pressed for an amendment to the statement in order to alleviate the possibly prejudicial effects of the statement that the wording on Kerguelen and Crozet would also apply to waters adjacent to islands within the Convention over which state sovereignty is recognised by all contracting parties. We received little support from other claimant states, although all were prepared to concede the possibility of a prejudicial construction. In this regard it is of some significance that New Zealand is the only claimant state that does not have recognised territory north of sixty degrees within the convention area. Most of our claimant partners privately admitted the overriding importance to their governments of clearly avoiding any prejudicial effects for recognised territory, even if that meant forgoing similar protection for their Antarctic territories. We did not insist on the deletion of the paragraph but sought the inclusion of language that made it clear that the statement did not give rise to legal rights and obligations, that its sole purpose was to illustrate the application of the Convention to Kerguelen and Crozet and that its contents were to be read subject to the non-prejudice provision in Article IV of the Convention. The final text makes a very useful step in this direction.[64]

The additional language referred to consisted of a preface by the chairman of the informal consultations (Negroponte) noting that the statement was fully consistent with the draft convention, that 'it was prepared only to show the manner in which the convention would be applied to waters adjacent to the islands of Kerguelen and Crozet', and should be read in the context of international law. This exegesis is on its face not easy to reconcile with the terms of the statement itself, which appears to be equally applicable to all islands which are in a similar situation to Kerguelen and Crozet and whose sovereignty is not disputed.[65] Moreover, the remarks of the chairman of the informal consultations did not reappear when the statement was finally included in the Final Act of the Conference on the Conservation of Antarctic Marine Living Resources in the following year, so that their legal effect is uncertain.[66] What is clear is that the statement was more advantageous to France than to the other states owning islands within the convention area.

The draft convention now began to attract attention and criticism from non-governmental organisations concerned with the environment and conservation issues. In April 1980 the Antarctic and Southern Ocean Coalition (ASOC) wrote to the Prime Minister setting out a number of points on which the draft was considered to be deficient. In general, ASOC regarded it as oriented towards the harvesting rather than the protection and conservation of species. It seemed that it might not adequately protect species that depended on krill as their main food supply. Because it would take decisions by consensus rather than majority vote, it might not function effectively, there was no provision for adequate enforcement, and the draft did not 'establish a comprehensive conservation regime south of the Antarctic convergence so as to exclude lower conservation standards in recognised exclusive economic zones'.[67] (There is no record of any reply to this communication.) There was some disposition on the part of the United Kingdom and the United States to amend the article dealing with conservation principles to meet the first of ASOC's criticisms.[68] New Zealand officials reacted with some impatience to the prospect of further amendments when the draft appeared to have been virtually sewn up. They feared that the distant water fishing states, which had accepted the existing draft only with the greatest reluctance, would react negatively. Nevertheless, they recommended to the Government that New Zealand should speak in favour of any amendments that would strengthen the conservation standard and might stand some chance of success, even though the chance was fairly remote.[69]

The diplomatic conference was preceded by a special meeting of the Antarctic Consultative Parties to discuss procedure. The knotty issue of EEC participation inevitably reared its head. It was agreed that intergovernmental organisations could attend and speak at plenary meetings (but not working groups) and that non-governmental scientific organisations such as SCAR and the International Union for Conservation of Nature (IUCN) could attend but not speak; but environmental lobby groups were entirely excluded.[70]

New Zealand's main contribution at this Conference—apart from its participation in efforts to settle the EEC issue—was the promotion of an additional article requiring the Commission to cooperate with neighbouring coastal states such as New Zealand in respect of the conservation of fish species which migrate between the convention area and adjacent economic zones. (This appears as Article XI in the final text.) The *raison d'être* for this initiative was that

> First, the discussion . . . enabled us to emphasise our direct interest in the subject matter of the convention because of our physical proximity to the convention area. This helped to justify our fairly high profile at the Conference despite the fact that we are not a fishing state nor able to participate actively in the research effort represented by the biomass programme. Secondly, the environmental groups represented here appear to recognise that it does strengthen the text from an environmental standpoint and accordingly it can, if necessary, be pointed to as a counter to possible criticism that preoccupation with the EEC problem precluded any real efforts to improve the text.[71]

New Zealand did not, in fact, seek any radical change in the draft convention and emphasised its support for the recommendation of the Ninth ATCM that the regime should exclude catch allocation and other economic aspects of harvesting. This, the New Zealand representative said, 'would have raised issues involving the rights of coastal states with respect to those resources which may have protracted the negotiation'. It was not imperative to address the question at that stage: New Zealand had no doubt that it could and would be resolved 'at the appropriate time'.[72]

As for the European Community, its bottom line was an explicit understanding that it would, on accession, be automatically accepted as a member of the Commission; that it should be able to participate in budgetary decisions; and that it should not be precluded from subsequently offering amendments to the convention. These points were met. The Australian representative made a statement at the close of the Conference that his government, as depositary for the convention, would recognise the EEC's eligibility to become a member of the Commission when it had deposited an instrument of accession. The EEC's other stipulations were met by minor amendments to the draft.[73]

The Convention and Final Act were signed on 20 May 1980, and the Convention entered into force on 7 April 1982 after New Zealand had become the eighth signatory to ratify it.[74] The EEC acceded shortly afterwards. The Commission for the Conservation of Antarctic Marine Living Resources established by the Convention held its first meeting at its headquarters in Hobart, Tasmania, in May to June 1982, and has met annually since that year.

The Convention represents an extension and development of the Antarctic treaty system in a number of respects. Whereas it was thought in the case of the Convention on Seals that the conservation of seals in the sea did not fall within the scope of the Antarctic Treaty and the Convention was therefore concluded at a separate conference outside the framework of the Treaty, the preamble of the AMLR Convention recognises 'the prime responsibilities of the Antarctic Treaty Consultative Parties for the protection and preservation of the Antarctic environment, and in particular, their responsibilities under Article IX, paragraph 1(f) of the Antarctic Treaty in respect of the preservation and conservation of living resources in Antarctica'. It thus redefines and extends the responsibilities of the Treaty powers as they had been understood a decade earlier. (The Minerals Convention goes a step further in asserting its status explicitly as 'an integral part of the Antarctic Treaty system'.)[75]

The Convention area, moreover, is considerably more extensive than the Antarctic Treaty area, stretching northwards where necessary beyond 60° south to an approximation of the Antarctic Convergence.[76]

Thirdly, the Convention is designed to protect the entire

marine ecosystem in Antarctic waters, not only conserving the stocks of individual species but also taking into account the effect of the harvesting of particular species for human use on other species for which those particular species form an important food source.

Finally, the Convention for the first time established permanent machinery, in the form of a secretariat servicing a Commission and a Scientific Committee, the cost of which is, of course, shared by all members. Provision is also made for a system of observation and inspection. In theory, therefore, it should be possible for the Commission to adopt conservation measures based on adequate information about Antarctic marine resources and the effect on stocks of their exploitation, and to police those measures.

On the other hand, this Convention has been the object of a range of criticisms by Antarctic specialists and environmentalist organisations. The criticisms by ASOC have already been mentioned.

Like the previous Antarctic agreements, the Convention further entrenches and extends the privileged position of the Consultative Parties to the Antarctic Treaty. On ratifying the Convention, those states automatically became members of the Commission; there is no requirement, as there is for states subsequently acceding, that they be engaged in research or harvesting of marine living resources in Antarctic waters. The special obligations and responsibilities of Antarctic Consultative Parties are to be acknowledged by non-parties to the Antarctic Treaty (Article V of the Convention); these states are required to observe the Agreed Measures on Fauna and Flora and other measures recommended by the Consultative Parties for the protection of the Antarctic environment. While these somewhat draconian provisions may be held by the Consultative Parties to be justified in order to ensure that all parties to the Convention treat the Antarctic environment with the same degree of care as the parties to the Antarctic Treaty, they can scarcely be said to be an inducement to non-parties which might be disposed to start fishing in Antarctic waters to ratify the Convention. They could be regarded as highly discriminatory by developing countries seeking new food resources. (And Taiwan, already an important distant water fishing 'nation' in the Pacific, is of course, ineligible to accede to the Convention since it is not recognised as a state.)

Thus the lack of teeth in the Convention is of some concern. While the Commission may set total allowable catches for the whole area or for particular sub-regions, designate protected species, fix open and closed seasons, regulate methods of harvesting and so on, it has none of the powers of enforcement exercisable by a coastal state in its EEZ: and it cannot allocate the catch. Furthermore, there is some doubt whether the wording of the relevant Article gives unambiguous effect to the stated intention of preserving the ecosystem by ensuring that predators (other than human ones) continue to get their fair share of the various species. The doubt may be most easily explained by contrasting an unsuccessful British amendment with the text of Article II 3(a) as finally adopted. The United Kingdom proposed the addition of the underlined words in the first principle of conservation:

> Prevention of decrease in the abundance of any harvested population which is not subject to significant natural predation to levels below those which ensure its stable recruitment. For this purpose its size should not be allowed to fall below a level close to that which ensures the greatest net annual increment. For any other harvested population prevention of decrease in its abundance either as specified above or to a level below which the stable recruitment of species dependent on it cannot be ensured whichever is the higher level.[77]

Although the amendment was not adopted, several delegations recorded their view that this was in fact, the intention of the Article taken as a whole. In the event of a dispute, however, that interpretation of the article could well be contested.

The Convention is applicable to all 'living organisms' in the Convention area, but whereas finfish, molluscs, crustaceans and birds are specifically mentioned, marine mammals conspicuously are not (Article I 2). The rights of parties to the Convention on Seals and the International Whaling Convention are specifically preserved (Article VI). This means that seals and whales may be taken up to the limits set in those Conventions (very large numbers in the case of seals) irrespective of any effect that this might have on the Antarctic marine ecosystem. A commercial sealing industry has not been established since the Convention on Seals was concluded. Should this occur, however, there would be severe damage in the eyes of conservationists (and others) to the credibility not only of the Convention on Seals but of the AMLR Convention and the Antarctic Treaty system as a whole.

The Convention has been relatively effective in relation to the conservation of other species, notably finfish and krill. Although the annual krill harvest exceeded 400,000 tonnes several times during the 1980s, it has hovered around 100,000 to 200,000 over the past 30 years. Almost all of this catch was taken in the Atlantic Ocean sector. The Commission first set a total allowable catch for krill in 1991 of 1,500,000 tonnes per season for the Atlantic Ocean sector, with precautionary limits to be agreed upon if the total catch in any season exceeded 620,000 tonnes. This 'trigger level' remains in place and has yet to be exceeded. A catch limit for part of the Indian Ocean sector was first agreed upon in 1992, of 390,000 tonnes per season (increased to 2,645,000 tonnes by 2014/2015) and the remainder in 1996, of 775,000 tonnes per season (reduced to 440,000 tonnes by 2014/2015). However no krill fishing currently takes place outside the Atlantic Ocean sector.[78]

Over-fishing of one important finfish species, *notothenia rossi* (Antarctic cod) led to that fishery being effectively closed in 1984.[79] Stocks of another important species, *champsocephalus gunnari* (Antarctic icefish) were also over-fished in the South Georgia area and around Heard and McDonald Islands, with a peak catch of over 200,000 tonnes of icefish in 1983, resulting in the closure of the icefish fisheries in the early 1990s.[80] It would seem, however, that these measures were taken only after stocks had been drastically reduced, and after several years of meetings at which the Soviet Union (the main fishing state) took advantage of the consensus procedure to obstruct the adoption of conservation measures. Nowadays, icefish fisheries may only operate within two years of a survey that has assessed sufficient stock is available. The catch limit for icefish for the 2014/15 season is 2659 tonnes for the South Georgia area and 309 tonnes for Heard and McDonald Islands.[80a]

The two most commercially important finfish species in the Convention area today are *Dissostichus eleginoides* (Patagonian toothfish) and *Dissostichus mawsoni* (Antarctic toothfish). The Patagonian toothfish fishery began in 1977, with Japan, Poland and the Soviet Union catching 457 tonnes in the Atlantic Ocean. A catch limit for Patagonian toothfish was not established until 1990, however, when a 2500 tonne limit was set for the South Georgia area with catch limits later established for other Patagonian toothfish fisheries. The total catch limit for toothfish in the Atlantic sector is now 3008 tonnes and for the Indian Ocean sector it is 11,636 tonnes. New Zealand vessels were the first to fish for Antarctic toothfish, catching 128 tonnes in the Ross Sea in the 1996/97 season. The total catch limit for toothfish in the Ross Sea is now 3044 tonnes in the Eastern Ross Sea and the 619 tonnes in the Western Ross Sea (2014/15 season).[80b]

In the 1990s illegal, unreported and unregulated fishing (IUU fishing) for toothfish in the Convention Area was estimated to be more than six times the catch reported by authorised fishing vessels. A catch documentation scheme was adopted in 1999 to track toothfish through the entire supply chain and help reduce the problem of illegal, unreported and unregulated (IUU) fishing, and 'blacklists' of vessels involved in IUU fishing were established for contracting party vessels in 1998 and non-contracting party vessels 2002. IUU fishing in the Convention Area has since declined, but it remains a concern for the Commission as it could seriously undermine the Convention for the Conservation of Antarctic Living Marine Resources's (CCAMLR) objectives.[80c]

New Zealand also carries out regular surveillance under the CCAMLR system of inspection, with the aim of deterring IUU fishing. Although often supplemented by aerial patrols, in 2015 the surveillance efforts were led by the *HMNZS Wellington*, a modern off-shore patrol vessel. In January 2015 the Wellington encountered three vessels, the *Songhua*, the *Yongding* and the

Kunlun, that have been on CCAMLR's IUU Vessel List for many years, blatantly fishing for toothfish deep in the southern Indian Ocean close to the Antarctic continent. These vessels reported that they were flagged to Equatorial Guinea, which is not a Commission member.[81]

New Zealand has been active in the Commission since its early days, even in the 1980s and 1990s when New Zealand reports to the Commission indicated that New Zealand vessels were not engaged in commercial fishing in Antarctic waters, and that New Zealand had conducted no fishing research in the area.[82] New Zealand's interest, therefore, was in the conservation rather than the exploitation of the marine living resources in Antarctica. New Zealand in 1981 passed the Antarctic Marine Living Resources Act to enable it to carry out its obligations under the Convention,[83] which have become more onerous since New Zealand fishing vessels began operating in the area in 1996.

The Government, which had put off a decision on whether to formally declare an EEZ for the Ross Dependency until the Convention had been negotiated, did not revive the issue when it ratified the Convention. This was, in part, because such a step was thought unlikely to be helpful while negotiations were continuing for the establishment of an Antarctic minerals regime.[84] There are, course, other reasons of a practical kind why the declaration of an EEZ for the Ross Dependency would be of doubtful utility. In the first place, it would not be recognised by non-claimant nations, including those which fish in Antarctic waters. In a vast expanse of ocean at some distance from New Zealand, policing the activities of foreign fishing vessels which do not recognise New Zealand jurisdiction would be not only expensive but in all probability ineffective. Moreover, given that the Convention provides for the fixing of total allowable catches but not for their allocation, it would seem that effective enforcement of catch limits could only be accomplished in collaboration with other claimant states. The development of a more elaborate regime which would include catch allocation remains an unlikely prospect.

X

MINERAL RESOURCES: THE NEED FOR A REGIME

In July 1945, as the Second World War was coming to an end, the Secretary of the Department of Scientific and Industrial Research, Ernest Marsden, wrote to the Secretary of External Affairs in support of a proposal that the British 'Discovery Committee', which had been in recess during the war, should be revived. Marsden, a nuclear scientist who had worked in England with Rutherford, could always be counted on to provide the enthusiasm for Antarctic projects which might otherwise have been lacking in the New Zealand bureaucracy. After mentioning New Zealand's interest in meteorology, hydrology and plankton research, he wrote:

> Another matter which may be of considerable future importance is the exploitation of the mineral resources of Antarctica . . . It is therefore desirable that any geological expeditions which may be made to Antarctica should contain representatives of New Zealand. The last decade has brought about requirements in many minerals which were in short supply in the rest of the world. There is evidence that some of these minerals may be available on Antarctica and . . . with the advent of cheap aviation it is not improbable that at some time in the future they will be exploited. Much of this area is, as you know, under New Zealand jurisdiction.[1]

Marsden's views were put up to Peter Fraser, who sent them on to the New Zealand High Commissioner in London for transmission to the British authorities.[2] However, as was recorded in Chapter III, the New Zealand Government did not pursue the idea of a joint expedition and the opportunity for New Zealand scientists to engage in systematic activity in Antarctica did not arise until the International Geophysical Year in 1957.

In the interval, however, considerable interest in the potential mineral wealth in Antarctica was expressed in articles appearing in New Zealand newspapers,[3] and in May 1951 the Minister of External Affairs (Doidge) was moved to issue a press statement which, in essence, sought to explain away the unwillingness of the Government to undertake an active policy of its own on Antarctica. Other countries with greater resources than New Zealand, Doidge said, had not yet developed techniques for exploiting the mineral wealth of Antarctica. New Zealand had given up the idea of having its own expedition in 1949 because of the cost, but was keeping in close touch with the research being conducted in Britain and Australia; and it made annual grants to the Scott Polar Research Institute.[4]

In 1956, the Director of the New Zealand Geological Survey pointed out that South Victoria Land—the largest land area in the Ross Dependency—was a typical shield area in which large deposits of metallic ore were commonly found.[5]

As recorded in earlier chapters, New Zealand was not able to secure a specific reference to economic development in the Antarctic Treaty, although the wording eventually adopted for the consultation article left open the possibility of dealing with this issue through the consultation system at a later date. While Australia had been the prime mover in avoiding any reference to economic development in the Treaty, the Australian representative at the signature ceremony (Beale) referred to the continent as 'a great reservoir of raw materials capable some day of being exploited in the service of man'. The New Zealand representative (White) commented later that

> Australia has never been opposed to economic development in Antarctica. What they opposed was any treaty commitment in this matter. They are not giving up sovereignty and therefore regard themselves as being free under the Treaty to do what they please to promote economic development by Australians in the Australian sector. Thus, Beale may have meant that this was the sort of peaceful

> activity which could be proceeded with confidently now that any ideas of pooling of sovereignty had been pushed out of sight. As for exploiting the materials 'in the interests of man', this would naturally be intended to mean *homo Australis*.[6]

New Zealand officials, however, continued to take a different approach. According to guidance prepared for the first ATCM in 1961, New Zealand had been willing at the Antarctic Conference to consider the extension of cooperation in Antarctica to fields other than those to which the Treaty was limited, and believed in particular that it would be desirable to leave open the possibility of persuading other countries that it might be useful to consider in due course the regulated economic exploitation and development of Antarctic resources. While such economic activity could be in New Zealand's interests, it would not be possible to develop any resources found in the Ross Dependency without external assistance. The Treaty's silence on economic matters meant that a situation might arise where a national claim would be vigorously asserted in order to justify the unilateral exploitation of an economic asset. In the officials' view, however, it was naive to expect that unilateral exploitation would be feasible. Since the United States, for example, acknowledged no country's claim, it could hardly be expected to concede that a country would be entitled to exploit completely on its own account, and without regard to the views of other parties to the Treaty, a valuable raw material found in a sector claimed by that country. That would particularly be the case if American exploration and research had revealed the existence of that raw material. The United States had always been very much alive to the potential economic importance of Antarctica, and had conducted a survey of its resources. Although a prominent American scientist had declared that he 'would not give a nickel' for all the mineral resources in Antarctica, a report of the Senate Foreign Relations Committee acknowledged that important discoveries might still be made, and indicated probable United States support for the view that economic assets should be exploited by cooperative efforts rather than by the assertion of a national claim.[7] There was no disposition to take up the thorny question of economic exploitation at the early meetings of the Consultative Parties. In 1969, however, the New Zealand Government received an application for the granting of exclusive rights to 'explore, prospect and develop' the Ross Dependency for petroleum, coal and all minerals. The Prime Minister sent an interim reply saying that the application had raised new issues which were being examined by the government departments concerned. A substantive reply might be expected in the relatively near future. However, it was six months before a further reply was sent, in which the application was declined.[8] The same applicant and two others also sought licences from the Australian Government, which did not regard them as having sufficient substance to justify serious consideration.[9]

The effect of the application was, however, to stimulate the New Zealand authorities to canvass the possibility of raising the question of minerals exploration and exploitation for consideration at the Sixth ATCM in Tokyo in 1970, and they persisted despite adverse reactions from New Zealand's closest treaty partners.[10] Australia thought it would open a 'Pandora's box'.[11] The United States considered it premature.[12] British officials thought the question 'dynamite' and therefore requiring most careful handling, but were favourably disposed to a New Zealand initiative. They were, however, pessimistic about the likely reaction of Argentina, Chile and Australia, and distinctly dampening in their estimates of the likelihood of mineral exploitation becoming viable. It was likely to be quite a few years, one official remarked prophetically, before any agreement could be reached on the question 'of an internationally organised exploration of the Antarctic's mineral resources, and it would be necessary first to establish some permanent machinery under the Treaty.[13]

New Zealand was not deterred by the reaction: the fact that the question was 'dynamite' was no reason for burying our heads in the snow and hoping the problems would go away.[14] In a note circulated to participating governments, the New Zealand Government sought to separate mineral prospecting from exploitation as a first subject for consideration. The note raised the delicate question whether prospecting would be subject to Article III of the Treaty, requiring the free exchange of all scientific information.[15]

The enthusiasm of some New Zealand officials for opening up the subject was not shared by Lloyd White, now back in Wellington. From his experience as a New Zealander active during the negotiation of the Treaty, he was doubtful whether it would be any easier in 1970 than it had been in 1959 to reach agreement, within the context of the Treaty, for regulating the economic development of Antarctic mineral resources. The increasing interest in the possibility of such development would, if anything, serve to harden positions. There had been no indication, White said, of what the Government's current attitude would be, and there were not therefore, any positive suggestions for New Zealand to put forward on the main issue. The delegation's brief was, in fact, that 'although there may be good reasons, from New Zealand's point of view, for supporting internationalisation of Antarctica for purposes of developing its mineral resources—perhaps along the lines of current proposals for the internationalisation of the deep seabed—we cannot say at this point that New Zealand would necessarily be prepared now to abandon or modify its claim to the Ross Dependency as an area over which it asserts territorial sovereignty in the fullest sense.'[16]

White therefore advised the leader of the delegation (Hunter Wade) to take 'a fairly low key approach', adding

> I hope you can keep [the Department of Scientific and Industrial Research (DSIR) delegate] in line in the above sense. His enthusiasm is inclined to run away with him and I hope he will not be enabled to waffle at length on this aspect, at least during the formal sessions, in a way which will lead to the pointing up of issues which could prove embarrassing to us—especially with so many Americans squatting on our claimed sector.[17]

White's caution was reflected in the handling of the topic at the ATCM, where it was raised under 'any other business' rather than as a separate item, and discussed at an 'unofficial' session with no chairman, thus ensuring that no recommendation could emerge, had there been any danger of this. New Zealand kicked off the discussion, but Wade made it clear that his government had no proposals. New Zealand's initiative did however serve to break the (figurative) ice, and it was agreed that the possibility of an item on minerals could be discussed at the preparatory meetings for the Seventh ATCM.[18]

The next development on this issue was an initiative by a branch of the United Nations Secretariat to have the question of Antarctic natural resources discussed by the Committee on Natural Resources of the Economic and Social Council.[19] This attempt was headed off by Argentina, with support behind the scenes from other Antarctic powers, including New Zealand.[20] But it sent a warning signal that if the Antarctic powers did not address the issues themselves, they might find it opened up for discussion in a wider international forum and taking a turn that they could not control.

During 1972, the Antarctic powers continued their cautious discussion of the topic as they prepared for the Seventh ATCM, which was held in Wellington in November. Even the *title* of the proposed item provoked anxious debate. It was eventually agreed that it should be 'the *Effects* of Mineral Exploration'. The United States wanted to add the words 'and exploitation' but the United Kingdom thought this unwise. The immediate danger to the Treaty, in the British view, was the unilateral issue of a licence by, say, Chile: this could not be ignored by either Argentina or the United Kingdom and the ensuing row would inevitably result in serious damage to the Treaty. No doubt a serious applicant would be considering the possibility of future exploitation if exploration was successful, but so far most of the approaches by potential prospectors had been essentially speculative and there had been little serious intent to engage in exploration, let alone exploitation. It would be better to take two bites at the cherry, since there was a considerable risk that to attempt to deal with exploration and exploitation together would precipitate a Latin American veto. What the British wanted was an agreement that licences should not be issued by any Consultative Party without the consent of all the Consultative Parties, and secondly that there should not be two kinds of scientist working simultaneously in

Antarctica, one kind pledged to the free exchange of scientific information and the other to commercial secrecy. The process of consultation would probably prevent any exploitation in the foreseeable future—for 'say, fifteen years'. This, British officials thought, would be a good thing: it would defer exploitation until the resource was sufficiently valuable to justify the cost, and would guard the Treaty against the development most likely to disrupt it.[21]

Even the modest steps desired by the British were too much for the Consultative Parties to agree on at this session.[22] So was a French proposal for a ten to fifteen year moratorium.[23] Chile circulated a paper which opposed the initiation of economic activities in Antarctica on the grounds that this would 'destroy the delicate balance reached in Washington'.[24] Argentina proposed that discussion be put off until the next Consultative Meeting.[25] As so often is the case, the most modest proposal was what the representatives agreed to recommend. The most significant paragraph in the recommendation was one which recognised

> that mineral exploration is likely to raise problems of an environmental nature and that the Consultative Parties should assume responsibility for the protection of the environment and the wise use of resources.[26]

In reporting to the newly elected Prime Minister (Kirk) New Zealand officials claimed that the effect of the recommendation was to impose a prohibition for two years.[27] This was stretching the recommendation quite a bit: there was no suggestion of a moratorium in the text.

In January 1973 the United States research vessel *Glomar Challenger*, engaged in drilling in the continental shelf in the Ross Sea, unexpectedly found traces of hydrocarbon gases at shallow depth. The New Zealand authorities tried to avoid publicity for this accidental discovery, but that was of course a vain hope.[28] The discovery led New Zealand to take a keener interest in an initiative by the Nansen Foundation to hold an 'unofficial' conference of experts (geologists, lawyers, conservationists, and developmental economists) to consider the problems that might be involved in exploration for an exploitation of Antarctic minerals.

The Nansen Foundation Conference, which was attended by experts from all the Consultative Parties, took place in June 1973. New Zealand was represented by the Director of the Geological Survey (David Kear) and another DSIR scientist, R W Willett, attended as a representative of SCAR. New Zealand was the only country that did not send a legal expert. (Its Foreign Affairs lawyers were heavily involved with the International Court of Justice (ICJ) hearing of the case against French nuclear weapons testing in the South Pacific.) There was in fact some confusion as to whether the experts were representing their governments or not. The conference was poorly organised—'a shambles', according to a British official.[29] It is not surprising, therefore, that the Conference did not reach any startling new conclusions.

The less formal status of the meeting did, however, allow differences of approach among the Consultative Parties to emerge more clearly. The Conference sought to determine whether it was 'urgent' for the Consultative Parties to discuss and agree on a minerals policy. Speakers from three parties—Argentina, Chile and the Soviet Union—took the line that an agreement was not urgent, because they were opposed to any commercial exploration or exploitation of Antarctic minerals. (The term 'exploitation' appeared to have a particularly pejorative connotation.) The majority of participants, however, thought that the problem was urgent—not necessarily because they favoured early exploration or exploitation, but to ensure that any such activities were effectively controlled.

Dr Kear said in his statement (not based on any explicit instructions from Wellington) that:

> My realisation of 'urgency' arises from a scientific need that I see to continue investigations offshore, and also from the fact that I assess the chances of finding an economic mineral deposit to be greater offshore than on land, from the point of view of time taken until discovery. I do not think that I am alone in this assessment, as is shown by the reported enquiries of petroleum companies to various governments, and by the reported interest at ECOSOC. If others

> think this way, there will be real pressures for mineral exploration both within and without the Treaty area of influence, with the possibility of such undesirable developments as exploration under 'flags-of-convenience'. We cannot allow these pressures to build up to precipitate hasty decisions or undesirable situations. We need our decisions to be based on careful discussion.
>
> If the Treaty Nations decide that no exploitation of minerals should be permitted in Antarctica, it is urgent that they say so.
>
> If the Treaty Nations decide that exploration and/or exploitation is to be permitted in Antarctica, it is urgent that they say so and that they specify carefully the conditions under which this should take place.
>
> Because the process of reaching agreement within the Treaty organisation may well take 10 years, it is urgent that the above matters be discussed at the next Treaty meeting.[30]

The concept of treating Antarctica as a world park does not appear to have been debated as such at the Nansen meeting; in 1972, however, a World Conference on National Parks passed a resolution recommending that the Antarctic continent and the surrounding seas should be established as the first world park, under the auspices of the United Nations. This resolution was brought to the attention of the Prime Minister by a private citizen, to whom Kirk replied that it was particularly interesting and could well be a field in which New Zealand, as a party to the Antarctic Treaty, might take an initiative. Subsequently the International Union for Conservation of Nature (IUCN) wrote to say how splendid it would be if New Zealand would do just that.[31] Responding to an enquiry from the Director-General of Lands, the Ministry of Foreign Affairs, which up to that point had not been asked for its advice, poured lukewarm water on the idea. It pointed out that, as a result of the Agreed Measures on Fauna and Flora, Antarctica could already be considered 'in a sense' an international reserve or park. To go beyond that to the point of establishing Antarctica as a world park under United Nations auspices would 'involve some complex and rather sensitive legal and political issues which, at this point in time, it would appear to be extremely difficult, if not impossible, to resolve'. In a quite lengthy elaboration of this theme, the Ministry somehow managed to avoid mentioning the issue of mineral resources: to that extent, the reply was disingenuous.[32]

The interest of environmentalists in Antarctica would not, however, go away. In April 1973 it surfaced in the Governing Council of the United Nations Environment Programme (UNEP, of which New Zealand was not at that time a member). Agitated Consultative Parties who were members of the Council speedily drew the proposals of the UNEP Director-General (Maurice Strong, a Canadian) to New Zealand's attention. The New Zealand reaction was no less agitated. The UNEP Secretariat's proposal did not envisage a world park or the banning of Antarctic mining, but did stress the need for environmental protection and for the drawing up of rules for exploration and exploitation. The alarming aspect of the proposal, however, was that it spoke of achieving its environmental aim by amending the Antarctic Treaty.[33]

As New Zealand could not express its horror at this suggestion in the Governing Council itself, a message was shot off to Strong from the Prime Minister (Rowling) warning him that the course of action proposed 'could have serious consequences leading to the collapse of the Antarctic Treaty'. Rowling told Strong that New Zealand had raised the issue of exploration and exploitation of mineral resources with the other Consultative Parties and that they were making 'slow progress' towards agreement on a regime. If such an agreement could be reached Rowling was confident that agreement could also be reached on the consequent environmental measures. Any initiative outside the Treaty, however, could weaken it and reduce the chances of agreement. Exploitation activity might then begin outside the framework of the Treaty, with the possibility of damage to the environment of the area and its ecosystems through unregulated activities. Rowling urged therefore that the Governing Council confine itself to affirming its legitimate interest in conservation and environmental protection in Antarctica and pressing the Eighth ATCM to take the necessary measures in respect to the possible exploitation of natural resources in the region. Rowling concluded his message by offering a small carrot in the form of an invitation to Strong to visit New Zealand.[34]

Strong sent a soothing reply. Rowling's message, he said, would be 'extremely helpful' in dealing with the issue, and the UNEP Secretariat would have no problem in accepting a solution in line with New Zealand's position. In light of the difficulties raised for New Zealand and other Treaty countries by the specific proposal which the Secretariat had put forward, the proposal would not be pressed.[35]

Meanwhile, the New Zealand delegation to the preparatory meetings for the Eighth ATCM had been provided with a lengthy brief on the question of minerals exploration. New Zealand thinking on this topic was now much influenced by developments at the Law of the Sea Conference, which held a long but not particularly productive session in Caracas in 1974, and was due to hold a further session in Geneva in March 1975. One of New Zealand's objectives in the Law of the Sea (LOS) negotiations (shared with Australia and the United Kingdom, among others) was to protect its jurisdiction over the natural resources of its continental shelf. This was already one of the most contentious issues in the negotiations. The oil crisis was at its height. Continental shelves were seen as among the last areas where important new petroleum discoveries might be made. There were practical as well as legal difficulties in defining the boundary line between the continental shelf and the deep seabed. Because the deep seabed was now recognised as 'the common heritage of mankind', there was thus a direct conflict of interest between the broad shelf states and the developing countries, who saw the sharing of the mineral wealth of the seabed as one of the few potential benefits for the 'have-not' participants in the Conference. The states with shelves extending beyond the 200-mile limits of their EEZs were therefore seen as greedily seeking to extend their shelf jurisdiction to include the 'last grain of sand'. The negotiating position of these states was not helped by the fact that they were in a small minority in the Conference.

As it happened, most of the Antarctic claimant states were

also broad shelf states (although not necessarily in respect of their Antarctic territories). They thus had a common interest in how the maritime spaces of Antarctica were to be treated. There was a danger, from their point of view, of a move to deprive all Antarctic territory of an economic zone, to declare the adjacent seabed 'common heritage' right up to the shoreline, and even to extend the common heritage concept to the resources of the continent itself. It is not surprising therefore that the Antarctic powers, and especially the claimant states, were from an early stage agreed among themselves that Antarctic issues should be kept out of the LOS negotiations.

Even if this could be achieved (the brief paper noted) there would be formidable problems in applying the eventual LOS treaty to Antarctica. In some localities the Antarctic continental shelf extended north of the Antarctica Area as defined in the treaty, as would a 200-mile EEZ. Elsewhere, continental shelves and EEZs of territory outside the treaty area would extend into the area. The unclaimed sector of Antarctica posed another set of problems.

Mineral exploration, in the view of New Zealand officials, represented 'the greatest potential threat . . . to the survival of the Antarctic Treaty and all it stands for.' Ideally, the next ATCM should determine whether or not mineral exploration and exploitation should take place, and under what conditions. Such an expectation would, however, be 'naive in the extreme'. The most that could be hoped for could be a moratorium, but this would be no solution unless it were coupled with action on the issues of substance.

The brief paper emphasised that New Zealand's attitude on these issues was by no means clear:

> At no stage has the Labour Government enunciated a policy on Antarctica. One of the Ministry's tasks following the preparatory meeting will be to prepare a paper to Cabinet . . . recommending a New Zealand policy. Until that has been done it will not be possible to speak of a firm New Zealand view . . .

This did not inhibit departmental officials from expressing theirs:

> The question of whether or not mineral exploration and exploitation should be permitted is . . . not a real issue—we are of the opinion that it is inevitable. This should not be interpreted as signifying that we are necessarily in favour of exploration or exploitation or that we wish to encourage it. Indeed we have very real difficulty convincing ourselves that it is desirable. Certainly there is little hope of New Zealand being in a position to explore and exploit whatever mineral resources its own on and offshore territory may contain. Be that as it may, there appears to us to be little point in arguing blindly that it should not take place when we consider that once the outstanding technological difficulties have been solved and it becomes an economic proposition, it will. This could happen in a relatively short period of time.

The paper went on to consider how these developments could best be reconciled with the original objectives of the Antarctic Treaty. Officials thought some kind of international regime would be the best means of achieving these objectives:

> It would for example secure for New Zealand as a member of an international controlling authority a say in the manner and, extent of exploitation, i.e. a *recognised* influence which New Zealand might well not have if it tried to invoke a unilateral claim to exclusive jurisdiction over the resources of the Ross Dependency—bearing in mind that certain countries do not recognise the claims of others. An international arrangement would also more readily facilitate the sharing of facilities, equipment and expertise which could be of great benefit to New Zealand. It would overcome the problem likely to be involved with the issuing of licenses and their validity. An international regime involving close cooperation between the parties would be fully in keeping with the spirit of the Antarctic Treaty. It would also make it easier to give expression to the other main objectives of the Antarctic Treaty regarding the use of Antarctica for peaceful purposes, the prohibition of nuclear explosions and the protection of the Antarctic environment.

Officials considered that the international regime should be administered by the Antarctic powers rather than the United Nations, that any attempt to deprive Antarctic territory of the resource rights attached to other territories should be resisted, and that it was therefore of importance to persuade the Consultative

Parties to adopt a united front on the applicability in Antarctica of the new law of the sea.[36]

At two preparatory meetings, in October 1974 and February 1975, there was extensive discussion—in which New Zealand took an active part—of possible statements of general principles, or guidelines, designed to demonstrate the intention of the Consultative Parties to grapple with, and maintain control of, the minerals issue. But the discussions served only to demonstrate disagreement. The February discussion showed that there was no support for a public statement of principles. On the LOS issues, there was agreement only not to initiate discussion of Antarctica in the Conference and to consult if the topic were raised by someone else. The United States representative (Oxman) gave a virtuoso exhibition of his obstructionist skills on this occasion. He took the position that the United States would not discuss even the possibility of a minerals regime in the absence of a firm assurance from the claimant states that it would place no 'artificial' restriction on the extraction of resources, and that there would be non-discriminatory access for non-claimant states in all sectors. The United States was in the meantime totally opposed to any attempt to determine the entitlement of Antarctic territory to maritime spaces, since—Oxman argued—this would compromise its non-recognition of territorial claims. For similar reasons, he said, even a limited moratorium was out of the question. Oxman's obduracy incensed the Latin Americans, who took precisely the opposite stand—that sovereignty was the only basis on which they could agree to guidelines.[37]

The British position also regressed as United Kingdom Ministers became familiar with the issues, taking into account the implications for future oil supplies. In May, the New Zealand High Commission in London was told that the enthusiastic, almost idealistic, approach that the United Kingdom had pursued up to that time had been 'curtailed'. British Ministers were reluctant to endorse the negotiation of an international regime at that stage. The delegation to the Oslo meeting was given, in effect, a watching brief.[38]

By the time the Eighth ATCM opened in June 1975,

the attitude of New Zealand officials was one of diminished expectations. A lengthy submission was made to the Prime Minister which, with his approval, constituted the delegation's instructions. This submission laid great emphasis on the damage, both environmental and political, that would ensue from uncontrolled exploitation of mineral resources in Antarctica:

> The almost inevitable result of a scramble for Antarctic resources would be the collapse of the Treaty and the destruction of its main objectives—the maintenance of peace in the region, the promotion of cooperation among countries active there and the preservation of the unique environment. The only beneficiaries of a policy of 'open slather' would be those few Treaty powers including the United States, the Soviet Union and Japan, which have capital and technology to overcome the formidable obstacles to the development of Antarctic resources. New Zealand would gain little or anything. The ire of the Third World . . . would be justifiably aroused.

It may be remarked that, in a sense, this analysis was unfair to the Soviet Union which—because, as the submission later pointed out, its technology lagged behind that of the West—was opposed at that time to moves which would facilitate or legitimise mineral exploration in Antarctica.

The submission proceeded to set out 'two policy options; neither of them free from difficulty'. (There were in fact three, but the third—a total ban on resource exploitation—was subsumed in the first.)

The first option, the submission said, was an agreement to establish an international regime for the controlled exploration and exploitation of Antarctic resources. This would involve the establishment of an international authority which would be given the power to decide both where exploitation should take place and how the proceeds should be distributed—a policy of resources rights for the benefit of all. This would be consistent with what New Zealand had proposed in 1959. (There was, perhaps a *non sequitur* in the argument: it did not follow that the authority *must* be given control over distribution, or that such distribution should be 'for the benefit of all'.)

The paper went on to consider, as a subset of this option, the concept of a total ban. Very tight restrictions on exploitation would be needed, it said, to ensure the protection of the environment. The Second World Conference on National Parks had recommended that Antarctica be established as a world park, but since this would involve a total ban on exploitation, it was 'more than doubtful' whether this would ever be acceptable to all the Treaty powers:

> It ought, however, to be possible to reach agreement that very large areas of the continent, including those of special ecological significance, should be left untouched.

The submission noted that the idea of a resources regime was unpalatable both to the two Latin American claimants and to the United States. The attitude of Argentina and Chile on the question of sovereignty was 'little short of obsessive' and they were extremely wary of any 'internationalist' scheme that might cut across their claims. Whereas they insisted that any regime must give preferential rights to claimant states, the American position

> is an opposite and ugly one which is plainly closely related to and perhaps derived from, United States opposition to the notion of a new world economic order. The Americans will not contemplate any international regime for Antarctic resources unless the claimant States give them in advance a firm assurance that there will be a non-discriminatory system of access to resources for non-claimant States in all sectors of the continent. They want, in other words, a free-for-all with the lion's share going to those few countries with the necessary expertise and capital.

In the absence of any obvious means of reconciling the two extreme positions, the submission suggested, the other option New Zealand might pursue was the imposition of a *moratorium* on exploration and exploitation of Antarctic resources. A long-term moratorium would provide the *best possible means* of protecting the Antarctic environment and avert the threat of a break-up of the Antarctic Treaty.[39] The Soviet Union and the Latin Americans were strong supporters of a moratorium, and most of the other Treaty powers could probably accept it. But the opposition of the

United States to a long term moratorium had hardened, and it was felt that the most promising approach was to seek agreement on a short-term moratorium which would give a breathing space to allow the search for a more permanent solution to continue. This then was the course of action recommended to the Prime Minister, and specifically approved by him.[40]

When it came to the issuing of a press statement on the eve of the conference, however, a significant difference of emphasis was introduced into the presentation of New Zealand's position. The statement by the Prime Minister included a paragraph which read:

> The Government's long term objective will be to see Antarctic set aside as a world park, possibly under United Nations auspices. This has long been the position of Labour Governments in New Zealand. If the Treaty powers cannot agree to this there should at least be agreement that very large areas of the continent including those of special ecological significance should be left untouched. In the event that pressure for commercial exploration and exploitation is irresistible, New Zealand would insist that such exploitation should be rigidly controlled to minimise the damage to the region and to ensure that the profits of exploitation were shared fairly.[41]

In other respects the statement followed the language of the 'instructions' submission fairly closely: but this paragraph in stating as New Zealand's long-term objective the creation of a world park in Antarctica, possibly under 'United Nations auspices', diverged significantly from the principal emphasis and recommendations in the ministerial submission. While the idea of equitable sharing of the resources appears in both, equitable sharing by an international authority comprised of the Antarctic powers and equitable sharing under United Nations auspices could have distinctly different outcomes.

It might be imagined that the differences between the confidential instructions and the press statement represented a measure of disagreement among officials within the Ministry of Foreign Affairs. Since however both the substantive submission and the press statement were put to the Prime Minister under the signature of the Secretary, it is more plausible to suppose that it was thought politically expedient, in the light of environmental sensitivities at the time, to give the press statement a stronger conservationist colouration. The reference to the attitude of previous Labour administrations represented, and tended to perpetuate, a misunderstanding of Walter Nash's policy.

The New Zealand representative (Craw) was in fact instructed orally to express the Government's preference for a world park, and duly did so in the course of the Oslo meeting. If the phrase 'a lead balloon' was ever applicable, he says, it was on this occasion.[42] Clearly the attention of delegations was focussed not on the acceptability of otherwise of a world park, but on the acceptability or otherwise of a moratorium. The delegation reported that on this issue the conference came very close to breaking down.[43] In the end an uneasy compromise was worked out which resulted in a recommendation that Governments should study the question of mineral exploration and exploitation and consult 'with a view to convening a special preparatory meeting during 1976, the terms of reference of which will be determined precisely through diplomatic channels'.[44] At least the Consultative Parties were now agreed that they had to discuss the substantive issue of exploration and exploitation, not merely the effects of exploration. Secondly, as the delegation reported, there was 'perhaps the weakest possible formulation of an agreement that there should meanwhile be restraint in matters to do with minerals exploration and exploitation'. As the Australian representative (Keith Brennan) put it, what emerged was 'a little better than nothing'. One has to search for the agreement on restraint, which is tucked away in one of the preambular paragraphs in the recommendation, and in a paragraph of the final report. The latter document 'urged states and persons to refrain from actions of *commercial* exploration and exploitation' while the Consultative Parties sought 'timely agreed solutions to the problems raised by the possible presence of valuable mineral resources' in the Antarctic, thus begging the question of when exploration might assume a 'commercial' character.[45]

The delegation reported that the two major stumbling blocks were the Chileans and the Americans, Chile continuing to base itself on an unbreachable confidence in the principle of sovereignty, while the United States representatives very obviously looked over their shoulders at the minerals lobby in Washington. Despite 'some dickering on the part of the British, who are greedy for more than North Sea Oil', all the Treaty partners except the United States could have agreed to a firm restraint clause. 'The Americans however found it necessary to qualify and equivocate . . . in a way which lost them a great deal of support . . .

The New Zealand delegation found it difficult to be confident that the Antarctic Treaty would be strong enough to withstand a scramble for the exploitation of minerals. The constraints were the oil crisis and the rapid development of oil exploitation technology which seemed likely to lead oil companies almost indirectly to the conclusion that the Antarctic too must be explored for oil. 'Another view', the delegation said, was that Antarctica should be declared forever a form of international park; but even this laudable aim clearly raised questions of international administration and responsibility. A third view, strongly held in the Norwegian Foreign Office, was that the Antarctic Treaty approach should be abandoned, the problem handed to the United Nations, and such resources as could be mined without environmental damage exploited for the benefit of all mankind.

Given that the Ross Sea was a likely prospective oil-bearing area, the delegation suggested, the options for New Zealand seemed to be:

(a) An international park ('most unlikely to succeed');
(b) A joint exploitation—e.g., with the United States;
(c) An international regime of the Consultative Parties, with possibly some benefits for New Zealand; or
(d) A United Nations regime for the benefit of all mankind—'which could just conceivably be the worst of all?' (The delegation did not elaborate.)[46]

At the end of 1975 a new Government was elected in New Zealand. No attempt appears to have been made to develop a firm governmental position on the minerals issue (by preparing the Cabinet paper that had been envisaged as a follow-up to the Oslo meeting) in advance of the special meeting that was to be held in Paris in mid-1976. The new Minister of Foreign Affairs (Brian Talboys) was given an outline of the problem[47]—but only after he asked for it.[48] (The Ministry seems to have managed to avoid telling him about the meeting until after it had begun.) Officials had, however, been thinking hard about a New Zealand policy. Their concern was accentuated when, shortly after the Oslo meeting, Chris Pinto of Sri Lanka, a prominent player in the LOS negotiations, proposed taking the question of Antarctica to the United Nations with a view to bringing its resources under the control of an international regime. This may have been a tactical move, designed to strengthen the hand of the developing countries (the Group of 77) in demanding that the LOS Convention allocate to them a lion's share of the mineral wealth of the deep seabed. In any case, the move could not be taken lightly.

In April, Colin Keating, the Foreign Affairs lawyer who was to attend the Paris meeting, produced New Zealand's first attempt at the draft of a legal instrument to govern the exploration and exploitation of Antarctic mineral resources. The draft, entitled a declaration but effectively 'agreed measures', had the following features:

(a) The designation of prohibited zones;
(b) The establishment of a regulatory committee to designate such zones and to approve or disapprove proposals for the exploration or exploitation of Antarctic resources;
(c) Voting in the regulatory committee to be unanimous.

The Keating paper also envisaged a parallel United Nations Assembly resolution which would endorse the Consultative Parties' declaration and urge all states considering the initiation of commercial activities in Antarctica to submit proposals to the regulatory committee. That committee, it was suggested, might be enlarged to include the members of the Governing Council of UNEP.[49]

The initial response of the Ministry of Foreign Affairs to this initiative, and to reports of negotiations in New York among representatives of the Treaty powers about the agenda for the Paris meeting,[50] was extremely cautious. The time had not seemed propitious, it said in a telegram on 6 May, to seek Government endorsement of the policy line that had begun to evolve several years earlier. Nor was the Ministry optimistic that the international scene would permit an early solution to the awesome problems which had been revealed since New Zealand had started to nudge the Treaty powers to focus on the issues. There was a variety of departmental views on what New Zealand's future policy should be and it was hard to judge how the Government would respond if it were obliged to decide in the next few weeks on a particular policy line. The kind of long-term perspective that 'we' (the Ministry of Foreign Affairs) had tried to bring to bear on Antarctic questions might be no easier to argue domestically than in international bodies in the current climate. The Ministry had therefore 'reluctantly' concluded that not too much should be expected from the Paris meeting and that an outcome which simply continued the process of consultation would be preferable to another attempt at a quick solution which failed. This, it was acknowledged, was 'a step back from the imaginative and activist approach we have tended to adopt on Antarctic questions in the past'. The Ministry felt that it should now be accepted that the world park and moratorium approaches were good ideas that were not going to work. It was quite clear that 'the pressure is going on and that we and other Antarctic Treaty governments are going to have to face some difficult challenges in the next few years'. It would have been good if a regime for mineral and marine resources had been in place but 'frankly we do not think it is going to happen quickly enough'. What should be aimed at therefore was a framework for consultations 'in which we can reasonably defend our national interests'.[51]

Forty years later it is not so clear where the 'pressure', to the extent that it was internal pressure, was coming from. Ministry officials, it would seem, were making one of their periodic switches from internationalist idealism to nationalist *realpolitik*. If they were being pressed to do so it seems likely that the pressure was coming from other departments and not from Ministers, who had not yet been consulted.

The 6 May telegram was not the end of the story, however. The posts principally concerned—Washington, London and the Mission in New York—chirped cheerful assent to the demise of the world park and the moratorium, but to the suggestion that New Zealand back off from an active role on the minerals issue they voiced a chorus of polite disagreement.[52] As the High Commission in London put it:

> The alternative to rapid progress by the Treaty twelve is surely a takeover bid by the international community. This prospect is hardly likely to appeal to either government or public opinion in New Zealand and we should have thought that this gives good reason for a positive and active New Zealand role in trying to head off such an outcome.

In New York, a conversation with Zegers of Chile revealed the possibility of a significant loosening in Chilean and Argentinian policy:

> We can appreciate the reasons for the conclusion to which you are being reluctantly drawn, but it will be curious to say the least if . . . New Zealand should trail even behind the Latins in willingness to produce workable arrangements on Antarctic resources.

In response, Ministry officials swung the wheel over in a radical, if unacknowledged, shift of course. While adhering to the view that the 'worthy ideas' that the continent should be turned into a world park or made the subject of a long-term moratorium 'no longer constitute possible solutions', the instructions cabled to the Paris delegation at the end of June took as their starting point that:

> (the) main elements in the Treaty and the Treaty itself are now at risk and will be for so long as the problem of the exploitation of Antarctic resources remains unresolved. Unless the Treaty powers act quickly the prospect of an uncontrolled scramble for Antarctic resources of revived political rivalries, of damage to the Antarctic environment and of a breakdown of scientific cooperation, is a real one.

This was a very different assessment of the urgency of the problem from that expressed only six weeks earlier. Sooner, rather than later, the instructions went on, the Antarctic Treaty powers would have to come to terms with Third World pressure for the internationalisation of the continent. An agreed regime for resources would not be enough: the Antarctic powers would have to produce a solution which was saleable to the rest of the world. The instructions rejected the view that the claimant states could resist this pressure by simply sitting tight on what they regarded as their sovereign rights, as the broad shelf states—the margineers—were currently doing in the LOS negotiations in respect of their rights in their continental shelves. The analogy, it was argued, was a false one: the margineers were able to present a common front, whereas the Antarctic powers were deeply divided on the issue of sovereignty, and the claims were not recognised by those members of the club which would first have the technical capability and the capital to exploit Antarctic resources. The attitude of the United States, in particular, was uncertain. Presumably it would prefer an agreed regime within the club that would give it reasonable access to resources. But if that should fail, the United States could well consider it advantageous and consistent with its legal position to join with Third World countries in seeking the total internationalisation of Antarctica and its resources. The claimants would then be seen as the isolated defenders of the old economic order in Antarctica and could expect to salvage little of what they sought to protect. 'With Rochester, we should have the scandal of the whore and none of the joy.' (In retrospect it seems improbable that the United States would have compromised its consistently negative attitude to the 'common heritage' concept by adopting this approach to the question of Antarctic resources.) The attitude of the Latins and Australia, on the other hand, probably precluded internationalisation as a viable option from New Zealand's point of view. At this stage, anyway, New Zealand would need to seek a solution within the club. Such a solution would have to:

(a) satisfy the reasonable requirements of both claimant and non-claimant powers;
(b) protect those aspects of the privileged position of the Treaty powers which could be justified on grounds of prior interest, scientific activity and input of research and development funds;
(c) provide adequate protection for the Antarctic environment; and
(d) in order to head off a full-scale developing country takeover bid, recognise that the international community had some legitimate interest in Antarctica.

In this regard, the instructions suggested, the Keating paper deserved careful consideration. It placed a heavy and proper emphasis on environmental protection: it acknowledged the legitimacy of the exploitation of Antarctic resources, 'and must accordingly give the United States at least some comfort'; it followed the Treaty in side-stepping wholly intractable sovereignty issues; and through the provision for unanimity in a regulatory committee, it would give the claimant states a substantial degree of control over resource exploitation in the areas they claimed. A provision for some form of revenue sharing (also suggested by Keating) would increase the prospects of acceptance of a resources regime by the developing countries.[53]

The Keating proposal (not including the suggested United Nations resolution) was duly circulated at the Paris meeting on an informal basis (Ministers were informed that this was being done but that it would not commit the Government).[54] Although the New Zealand paper was well received as a focus for discussion, the meeting revealed no advance on the basic positions of the parties, with the Soviet Union and Japan arguing that discussion of the form of a regime was premature, while Argentina, Chile and Australia insisted that any acceptable solution must give preference to the claimants. The Australian representative initially described the New Zealand paper as 'essentially destructive of the Australian position', but later as 'an ingenious attempt to reconcile the irreconcilable'.[55]

The papers circulated to the meeting included an American report that 'the Antarctic continental shelf could contain potentially recoverable oil in the order of magnitude of tens of billions of barrels'. It was also possible, but less likely, that no potentially recoverable resources existed. Among the five most prospective areas, the Cenozoic portions of the Ross Sea basin were listed.[56] Another American report took a sanguine view of the ability of the oil industry to develop the necessary drilling and production technology for offshore operation in Antarctic conditions.[57]

The Soviet Union, by contrast, circulated a paper which stressed the danger to the environment and the 'ecological balance' in Antarctica which might result from offshore exploration for and production of petroleum. (Soviet concern for the ecological balance contrasts rather painfully with the subsequent behaviour of their fishing fleets). The Soviet Union proposed therefore that serious consideration should be given to the possibility of leaving the region intact for the next ten to fifteen years.[58]

The New Zealand paper which was annexed to the official report of the meeting contained an additional paragraph not found in the April document. This would have had participating governments recognise the importance of working towards arrangements which would ensure that any proceeds of mineral resource exploitation are shared on a just and equitable basis with the international community with due regard to:

> (a) the legal status of the continent and its continental shelf;
> (b) the efforts of the countries which have contributed to the exploration and development of the continent;
> (c) the needs of the developing countries.[59]

The specific mention of the continental shelf of course reflected the generally accepted view that any mineral resources likely to be recoverable in the foreseeable future would consist of offshore petroleum. As noted in Chapter VI the United States had taken the position in 1975 that the status of the Antarctic continental shelf was unclear.[60] At this meeting Australia and the United Kingdom argued that the scope of any minerals regime should be limited so as not to conflict with the principle that the resources of the deep seabed were the common heritage of mankind and therefore subject to appropriation only by the projected International Seabed Authority (ISA). New Zealand supported this concept, but argued that in view of the special environmental competence given to the Consultative Parties under the Treaty, any mechanism established by them for the purpose of imposing environmental controls on exploitation should also have some say in respect of environmental aspects of exploitation by the ISA. The United States suggested that it was possible to argue, in a juridical sense that in the absence of a sovereign on land there was no continental shelf. New Zealand countered by pointing out the impossibility of denying that in a geophysical sense there *was* an Antarctic continental shelf. The area controlled by the ISA was to be the deep seabed beyond the limits of national jurisdiction. New Zealand argued that any submarine areas which could not in a factual sense be classified as seabed must be excluded from the ISA's mandate, whether they were within or beyond the limits of national jurisdiction.[61]

The New Zealand delegation acknowledged that the outcome of the meeting, as expressed in the official report, was meagre.[62] Consensus was achieved only that

> (a) the Consultative Parties would continue to play an active and responsible role in dealing with the question of the mineral resources of Antarctica;
> (b) the Antarctic Treaty must be maintained in its entirety;
> (c) protection of the unique Antarctic environment and of its dependent ecosystems should be a basic consideration;
> (d) the Consultative Parties, in dealing with the question of mineral resources in Antarctica should not prejudice the interest of all mankind in Antarctica.[63]

The fourth paragraph was included only as the result of persistent efforts by New Zealand. (Argentina insisted that it use the word 'interest' and not 'interests'!).

The official report also noted, however, that 'several delegations spoke in favour of a moratorium and that one delegation had submitted a proposal to that effect.' Finally, it recorded the agreement of all delegations 'that regulations would sooner or later be needed and that protection of the environment was an absolute necessity', although they held differing views on how to achieve those aims. This was, as the New Zealand delegation noted, a step forward from the position taken at Oslo. The delegation also acknowledged that the Soviet proposal was an important contribution towards formalising the voluntary restraint measures agreed at the Oslo meeting. There was widespread support for its emphasis on ecological protection, but few delegations were prepared to consider it in detail, any more than they were to consider the New Zealand working paper. The New Zealand delegation saw problems in accepting that consideration of the legal and political issues should be deferred until the scientific issues had been resolved. It could not accept the Soviet contention that if a strict moratorium were established the developing countries would respect and understand the competence of the Antarctic powers. Throughout the meeting it emphasised that the 'twelve' must take account of the awakening interest of the international community in Antarctica arid move towards solutions of the resources question which would be saleable to the Third World: 'at Wellington or Oslo a moratorium would have been attractive but the situation has moved on since then'.[64]

While New Zealand officials' beliefs in the urgency of reaching agreement on a minerals regime was strengthened by the outcome of the Paris meeting, they had yet to convey this sense of urgency to their Ministers. Despite publicity about the possibility of oil being discovered in the Ross Dependency, the Minister of Science announced a cut in the funds allocated to New Zealand's Antarctic research programme.[65] Officials continued to neglect the task of briefing Ministers until, in October, they received a request from a Cabinet committee for information about the territorial sea and a possible EEZ in the Dependency. The Ministry of Foreign Affairs, in addition to answering the question, undertook to produce a Cabinet paper on New Zealand's future Antarctic policy.[66] A draft was prepared and circulated for comment to other departments.[67] The comments received ranged from advocacy of a world park,[68] or of treating Antarctic mineral resources as a 'nest-egg',[69] to a

Treasury view that New Zealand should 'take a firmer line and seek a greater share of any resources discovered'.[70] There was what one official described an 'incredible wrangle' with Treasury on this issue,[71] in the course of which Treasury complained to the Minister of Finance (Muldoon) that Treasury had not been adequately consulted, that the issues ought to be referred to the Cabinet Economic Committee, that it might be unwise for New Zealand as a 'weak' claimant to be taking any initiatives on the minerals issue, and that in any event it would be preferable for discussions with the Australian and United States governments to be conducted at the ministerial or prime ministerial level rather than by the officials attending Antarctic Treaty meetings. Perhaps as a result of these disagreements, the paper did not reach Cabinet until March 1977, although it did so substantially in the form that the Ministry of Foreign Affairs had drafted it before receipt of Treasury's complaint.[72] The Cabinet agreed that New Zealand's policy should be based on the following principles:

> (a) preservation of the Antarctic Treaty;
> (b) negotiation among the twelve Treaty powers of a regime, designed to control and limit resource exploitation, which
>> (i) protected the Antarctic environment to the maximum practicable;
>> (ii) secured and safeguarded the advantage which should accrue to New Zealand in view of its prior interest, scientific activity, input of research and development and in particular its sovereign claim;
>> (iii) bore in mind the ultimate need for acceptance by the international community, both within and outside of the Antarctic Treaty;
>
> (d) the undertaking of any additional actions necessary, in the light of developments, to preserve and remote New Zealand's special position in the Ross Dependency.[73]

In giving its approval, Cabinet directed officials to consider the areas in which New Zealand activities in the Ross Dependency could be developed, authorised them to consult with other claimant states on the question of the application of EEZ legislation in the Antarctic, and in effect gave the Minister of

Foreign Affairs, acting in consultation with other Ministers concerned, a free hand to develop initiatives in future Antarctic Treaty meetings based on these principles.

This paper was later interpreted as proposing that officials should in due course consider the possibility of becoming actively engaged in petroleum exploration in the Ross Sea.[74] It in fact spoke only of the desirability of expanding New Zealand activities in the Dependency, especially into the offshore area with, for instance, a scientific research programme on the mineral and energy resources there. The question whether such a programme should be purely scientific (and subject to the disclosure requirements of the Antarctic Treaty) or should in effect amount to commercial exploration, was not discussed.

The newly defined policy should in any case have been nationalistic enough even for Treasury. How realistic it was, given the relative positions of New Zealand and the United States on the ground in the Dependency, was another matter. The Ministry of Foreign Affairs had won the bureaucratic battle for the time being, but not necessarily the war, and so long as the oil crisis lasted it was obliged to continue looking over its shoulder at those power centres within the Government that were inclined to adopt a more gung-ho approach to the issue of New Zealand's sovereignty in the Dependency and to its international relationships. Inevitably the Ministry itself tended to adopt a more nationalistic approach.

Attention now focussed on the preparations for the Ninth ATCM, to be held in London in September 1977. New Zealand was strongly represented at a preparatory meeting in March—although only by Foreign Affairs officials. The meeting provided an opportunity for the New Zealand representatives, aimed with the Government's new (but flexible) policy, to engage in extensive discussion of the minerals issue behind the scenes. The delegation reported with some optimism that in these talks the attitudes of both claimants and non-claimants showed a significant advance on the positions they had taken in Paris the previous year.[75]

Encouraged, New Zealand took the opportunity of the Australia, New Zealand, United States Security Treaty (ANZUS)

Council meeting held in July to have an exchange of views with Australia and the United States at ministerial level. In a preliminary message to New Zealand's posts in Canberra and Washington, the Ministry explained its reasons for doing so:

> We have come reluctantly to the view that it is unrealistic to think New Zealand (or any other claimant) will ever achieve sole rights to the resources of any one part of the Antarctic Continent. Neither the non-claimant Treaty nations nor the rest of the world is ever likely to agree to such exclusivity. However, we continue to believe extant territorial claims do give claimants a special position from which some advantage should accrue. If any agreement is to be achieved on the exploitation issue within the Treaty framework, therefore, the obvious requirement is for an accommodation between claimants and non-claimants which on the one hand preserves the most important aspects of sovereignty (i.e. jurisdiction) while on the other it satisfies the reasonable requirements of non-claimants (i.e. access). The informal paper which we tabled at the Paris special preparatory meeting was a first step in this direction. We would like to know whether either Australia or the United States accepts this view, or sees other possible solutions.

The New Zealand Government's position, it was suggested, was somewhere between that of Australia and the United States, and not too radical for at least parts of it to find acceptance in both camps. The main point was to convince them both of the need for quick action.[76]

Ministry officials regarded the discussion at ANZUS as 'extremely useful', although it is difficult to see from their report of the views expressed by Peacock and Christopher any substantive shift in the Australian and American positions.[77]

It was also clear that Australia considered that priority should be given to completing a convention on marine living resources. Nothing daunted, the Ministry made a further attempt in August to nudge Australia into a greater sense of urgency on the minerals issue. This took the form of a personal letter from Talboys to Peacock, which stressed the basic similarity of Australia's and New Zealand's interests in the continent. There was agreement, Talboys wrote, about the need for an agreed regime for living resources, but the area where most work needed to be done was on mineral and energy resources. A moratorium on its own was unlikely to be more than a palliative: there was need for agreement on the principles which would govern an eventual exploitation regime. Australia and New Zealand both approached the problem as claimant states: Peacock had stressed in the ANZUS meeting that Australian public opinion identified closely with Australia's sovereign claim, whereas in New Zealand Talboys believed that there was acceptance of the need for the claimants to make some compromise in the face of international reality. New Zealand could not accept a policy which effectively destroyed New Zealand's sovereign claim, but on the contrary, wanted to negotiate a regime which safeguarded the advantages which should accrue to New Zealand in view of its prior interest and activity in Antarctica. 'What we are interested in is not a sterile legal claim but a share in the real stuff of sovereignty.' Oil, presumably.

Talboys added that recent discussions with the Treaty powers had led New Zealand to the conclusion that the question of exploration required separate treatment from exploitation. It seemed, he said, that few if any of the Treaty partners would be happy with a situation in which they were precluded from undertaking exploration activities, particularly in their own claimed sector.[78]

This is a puzzling comment. There is no record of discussions of this point between New Zealand and other Treaty partners. Did other New Zealand government departments want to keep a free hand? There is no direct evidence. Treasury and Energy Resources officials continued however to complain about lack of consultation by their Foreign Affairs counterparts, following the unusual course of grizzling to the New Zealand High Commission during a visit to Canberra. Given New Zealand's possibly long-lasting economic plight, they said, New Zealand might very much want the (putative) oil in the Ross Sea for itself if it could get at it. There was, in their perception, a sharp divergence of opinion on this issue between 'resource' departments and Foreign Affairs. But it was now possible for

Foreign Affairs to respond that New Zealand policy had been determined by Cabinet.[79]

Peacock's reply to Talboys did not significantly advance matters. Politely acknowledging the similarity of Australia's and New Zealand's interests in Antarctica, he equally politely disagreed about the best means of advancing them. Australia clearly wanted to give priority to the protection of marine living resources, and was about to produce a draft convention. But in regard to minerals, Australia had been confirmed in its belief that full studies of the environmental implications of their exploitation were necessary before any exploitation took place. Australia was therefore anxious to see in place a more effective moratorium pending the results of these studies. The moratorium was essential if there was to be any hope of convincing the Third World that the Antarctic Treaty partners were not at the point of beginning exploitation without any regard for the concerns of others. Without it they would not believe that exploitation was at least a decade away, and the pressures from them would accelerate and intensify. Subject to this first step, Australia was prepared to 'explore the possibility' of developing a resource regime within the Treaty framework.

Australia, Peacock said, sympathised with New Zealand's objectives in putting forward its informal proposal at the Paris meeting. It felt, however, that the approach of turning together environmental, legal and political issues would transfer to the proposed regulatory committee all the problems which the Consultative Parties had found it so difficult to solve. Australia would 'of course' be interested in any New Zealand ideas, but their preference would be 'to grapple with the details of each of the issues to be faced in advance of the receipt of any exploitation proposals'. Peacock also expressed reservations about the suggestion that exploration and exploitation should be dealt with separately. Some commercial exploration activity, such as drilling, could have a serious environmental impact; moreover, if a significant resource was found, companies that had spent money on exploration might be less willing to observe a moratorium.[80]

The somewhat condescending tone of these remarks, one

is tempted to observe, was nicely attuned to the Australian Minister's personality as well as to the views of his officials. It is important to remember, however, that there were more weighty issues at stake than exercises in political one-upmanship. Despite the polite protestations of identity of interest, there was (and is) at least one fundamental difference in the positions of New Zealand and Australia on the minerals issue. If they exist, the most readily exploitable and valuable resources in Antarctica are, in all probability, likely to be discovered in the New Zealand, British, Argentinian or Chilean sectors. It is much less likely that large quantities of petroleum will be found off the coast of the Australian territory. In addition, it is likely that Australia, the most dedicated of the 'margineers' in the LOS negotiations, felt a keener concern than New Zealand to avoid antagonising the 'have-not' nations while negotiations were continuing on the delicate issue of coastal state jurisdiction over the continental shelf out to the margin's edge.

As recounted in Chapter IX, the Antarctic powers gave priority at the Ninth ATCM to making progress towards a convention on living resources.

The New Zealand authorities did not therefore have much expectation of progress on the question of minerals. The Ministry of Foreign Affairs told the Ministry of Energy Resources and the Treasury in advance that progress on the legal and political aspects was likely to be very limited, not only because of the disposition among Treaty partners to deal with living resources first, but because some of them were likely to insist that there be no discussion of these aspects until scientific examination enabled the potential environmental impact of exploitation to be better understood. It was not necessary, therefore, for the Government to reach an agreed position on the energy resources of the Ross Dependency. The New Zealand delegation would be working to have the question of exploitation dealt with urgently, and would argue the need for a resources regime to satisfy the reasonable requirements of both claimant and non-claimant states.[81]

Treasury and Energy Resources were not happy with this formulation, which did not square with their interpretation of the policy that Cabinet had laid down earlier in the year. The delegation was therefore warned, after the meeting had started, of the need to ensure that the line it took was not at variance in any way with the Cabinet directive, and in particular the provision that 'the advantage which should accrue to New Zealand' from any minerals exploitation in Antarctica should be secured and safeguarded. Clearly for Treasury and Energy Resources the need to satisfy the reasonable requirements of non-claimant states was not something to be pursued at New Zealand's expense.[82]

The delegation must have felt some uncertainty, not to say unease, as to where precisely New Zealand stood. When and if the crunch came, would the Government insist that it had exclusive sovereign rights over a major oil find in the Dependency's continental shelf? Not surprisingly, the delegation was at pains to confirm that no substantive progress on minerals was likely at the Ninth ATCM and to recommend that 'further interdepartmental consideration . . . be delayed until the various positions have been clarified . . . The delegation also considered that an indefinite moratorium would not serve New Zealand. In contrast, Australia wanted a strict, legally binding moratorium, and even the United States was prepared to acquiesce, 'at the end of the day'. The delegation proposed therefore to work actively to secure the limitation of the moratorium 'both in time and content'; this would not be easy, as New Zealand would be in a minority of one.[83]

The delegation received fresh instructions which broadly followed its advice. Acceptance by all the Antarctic powers of the need for restraint while practical answers were being sought was an essential part of the overall exercise: but the danger in agreeing to a moratorium at an early stage in the meeting was that it would encourage some Treaty members to think that nothing more need be done at this meeting, or in the near future. The delegation was therefore instructed to encourage discussion of the wider issues and only at the end of the day, as an interim measure, should it agree to a qualified moratorium which did not restrict scientific research and which would be reviewed at the next Consultative Meeting, preferably in 1978.[84]

The New Zealand delegation was not able to dissuade Australia from tabling a proposal for a moratorium which would remain in force for an initial period of at least five years. It did however find support from the United States, Japan, France, Norway and the United Kingdom, who were unhappy with this proposal, and took initiative in the production of a draft which recommended Treaty parties urge their nationals and other states to refrain from mineral exploration and exploitation, in particular drilling activity, thus making timely progress towards achieving an internationally agreed approach to mineral resource activities in Antarctica.[85] This formulation was followed fairly closely in the recommendation eventually adopted,[86] and to the extent that it was something less than a strict and binding moratorium, New Zealand must accept a considerable share of the responsibility: but its good intention was, of course, that it should be replaced by a comprehensive regulatory regime as soon as possible.

The New Zealand delegation was highly satisfied with the outcome of the meeting, given the lower priority assigned to the minerals item. It was agreed that it should be placed on the agenda for the Tenth ATCM, and that the United States would convene a special preparatory meeting on the legal and political aspects in 1978. The four principles adopted at the Paris meeting were endorsed, and a further principle accepted:

> . . . the provisions of Article IV of the Antarctic Treaty shall not be affected by the regime. It should ensure that the principles embodied in Article IV . . . are safeguarded in application to the area covered by the Antarctic Treaty.

The delegation regarded this as an important new principle. It reported that the drafting, for which New Zealand was largely responsible, owed its origin to the principle in the March Cabinet paper concerning New Zealand sovereignty. (This observation was no doubt meant for the benefit of Treasury and the Energy Ministry). There was now perhaps for the first time, the delegation added,

> an appreciation that a regime for mineral exploitation will require a deal with the claimant states, whereby the balance in Article IV

> of the Treaty is struck again but in a way which will ensure that certain practical attributes of sovereignty in respect of resources accrue to the claimant states.

'Certain practical attributes of sovereignty' is a nice phrase.

The delegation stressed (also for the edification of the resource departments) that:

> the political weight both within the Treaty forum and outside it (in the media, the United Nations and the Law of the Sea Conference) is strongly against any form of commercial exploration before a regime is set in place. The group of experts made the point strongly that a great deal more environmental work should be done—either in national scientific programmes or at the international level. Prior to any decision on New Zealand involvement in any commercial exploration programme it would be essential that we should make a significant contribution to the recommended scientific studies. It would be equally important that a major commitment be made to securing the negotiation of a regime . . .[87]

In November 1977, a meeting of officials from interested departments reviewed New Zealand's position. It was agreed that while New Zealand needed to remain closely involved with the negotiations for a convention on living resources, the minerals question was far more difficult and should therefore be concentrated upon. It was also agreed that New Zealand should actively assert its interests, as defined in the Cabinet paper. The possibility of New Zealand's participating directly in the exploration and exploitation of potential petroleum deposits was clearly in the minds of Treasury and the Minister of Energy Resources.[88]

In May 1978, the Officials' Economic Committee submitted recommendations to the Cabinet Economic Committee designed to give practical effect to Cabinet's presumed wish to 'actively assert New Zealand's interests'. The paper pointed out the inadequacy of New Zealand's activity in the Dependency up to that point. It was, for example, entirely dependent on the United States for ship transport and for air support on the Continent. If New Zealand were to engage in investigation of offshore petroleum resources, whether scientific or commercial, the first requirement was a suitable ship. Additional air support, in the form of helicopters, was also needed. Officials recommended new legislation to establish a legal framework for the administration of the territory.[89] Despite the impressive line-up of departmental support for these proposals, Ministers evidently took fright at their potential cost and the Cabinet Economic Committee took no action upon them.[90]

Officials continued to urge an expanded Antarctic programme on their reluctant masters. In August, a memorandum addressed to the Minister of Foreign Affairs suggested that the negative attitude of the non-claimant states to the rights of claimant states, as demonstrated at the meeting on living resources in July, could well be carried over to subsequent negotiations about minerals. New Zealand's ability to secure its share of resources would depend more on what it actually did in the area than on its legal and historical claims. This underlined the need, the memorandum urged, to extend New Zealand's research and other activities to the offshore area.[91] Ministers were unmoved.

By mid-1979, as the Antarctic powers met to prepare for the Tenth ATCM (scheduled for September in Washington) officials had somewhat shifted their ground in the face of the evident unwillingness of the Government to assume the risks, financial and other, involved in a national programme of offshore exploration in the Dependency. In light of New Zealand's current energy situation, officials were still interested in establishing with some precision the petroleum potential of the Ross Sea continental shelf. One way to do this, they thought, was in a joint venture with another treaty partner. The obvious partner was, of course, the United States. In 1975, New Zealand had been in the position of urging a moratorium pending the conclusion of a minerals regime, while the United States had been opposed. Now, it became necessary to approach the United States to ascertain whether it was prepared to agree to a relaxation of the moratorium and whether it was interested in a joint exploration venture. The Minister of Foreign Affairs agreed that bilateral consultations with the Americans should be undertaken during the preparatory meeting in Washington.[92]

In addition, the New Zealand delegation to the preparatory meeting was authorised to circulate a working paper outlining the possible framework of an international regime. In this paper, it was suggested that a regime which was linked to the Antarctic Treaty and maintained the provisions of that Treaty intact might include the following substantive provisions:

(a) commitment that the environment should be protected;
(b) agreement that certain extremely sensitive areas (e.g. breeding grounds) should be specially protected from exploitation;
(c) establishment of a regulatory body to approve and monitor exploitation activity from an environmental viewpoint;
(d) establishment of an agreed set of anti-pollution guidelines;
(e) provision governing the relationship between the regime and the International Seabed Authority to be established by the Law of the Sea Conference;
(f) provision for possible revenue or resource sharing arrangements with the international community; and
(g) provisions on dispute settlement.

Most important (the paper argued) was the balance to be struck between a solution based solely on sovereignty and one based solely on unrestricted access, with no economic return for the claimant state. Unlike the proposed convention on living resources, a mineral resources regime must deal with the question of the utilisation of the resources. These, moreover, were non-renewable. Thus, the claimant state could not contemplate a simple environmental protection regime which would permit the exploitation of non-renewable resources in the absence of an overall settlement.

The paper suggested alternative approaches to this issue:

(a) Mineral Resources Convention could provide for access to defined areas considered potentially exploitable, pursuant to an authorisation by a Committee or Commission composed of each of the Consultative Parties. This regulatory body would be responsible for monitoring environmental safeguards and for imposing environmental protection measures. The Convention might provide in terms similar to Article IV of Living Resources Convention that Article IV of the Antarctic Treaty is unaffected and that the mineral resources regime and exploration and exploitation activities do not prejudice the position of either claimants or non-claimants. It might then provide in simple terms for a payment of a percentage of revenue and/or resource to the state or states in whose claimed territory or continental shelf the exploitation was to take place.

(b) Alternatively, a Mineral Resources Convention, in addition to the provisions on Regulatory Machinery and Article IV of the Antarctic Treaty, might adopt a less direct approach to the question of shared benefits. It could proceed on the basis of a bilateral (or side) arrangement between the claimant state in whose sector exploitation was proposed and the exploiting entity. An intending prospector would have to make satisfactory private arrangements with the relevant claimant state regarding revenues and a share in the resource or his proposal would not receive support from the claimant state at the international level. The system would be predicated on the consensus decision-making process upon which the Treaty meetings operate and which is also provided for in the Antarctic Living Resources Convention. Such a system would carefully avoid including in the text any wording which might be thought tantamount to the recognition of the claims.[93]

This paper, it will be seen, elaborated the proposals first put forward by New Zealand in 1976. It may be compared with the final text of the Convention. In the bilateral talks between New Zealand and the United States, it transpired that the United States was not disposed to seek any modification of the moratorium, for the continuance of which there was in fact overwhelming support among the other treaty partners. New Zealand was somewhat out of step. On the question of investigating the offshore resource, the United States also made it clear that it had no intention of conducting or permitting any geophysical programmes that would obtain 'proprietary' (i.e., commercially secret) information: any such programme, in their view, would prejudice the negotiation of a minerals regime. Thus, it was not possible for the New Zealand delegation to get very far with the idea of a joint venture.[94]

In September, therefore, Cabinet approved the recommendation of officials that New Zealand should accept the continuance of the moratorium until the Eleventh ATCM. At the same time the delegation to the Tenth ATCM was to urge the need for 'an accommodation between the claimant states and the non-claimant states based on a reasonable portion for the claimant state of the royalties/taxes/resource that it would derive if the resource were exploited on recognised territory'. It was, finally, to 'make known New Zealand's interest in ascertaining the petroleum potential of the Ross Sea continental shelf', and to make it clear that New Zealand's agreement to the continuance of the moratorium would depend on substantial progress towards the conclusion of an international regime. Cabinet directed that the New Zealand Antarctic Research Programme should be maintained at least at the existing level, but that it should be reviewed in order to concentrate as far as possible on resource-related research, including research into the possible environmental impact of resource development.[95]

The press statement issued by the Minister of Foreign Affairs on the occasion of the ATCM in September was somewhat less stridently nationalistic than the Cabinet paper. It indicated, for example, as the Cabinet paper had not, that New Zealand would be prepared to consider some form of revenue sharing with the international community at large;[96] and this point was included in the opening speech of the New Zealand representative at the ATCM, together with an assertion of New Zealand's expectation of 'an appropriate economic return' for itself.[97]

Although the Tenth ATCM had as its first priority the draft Convention on Living Resources, some progress was made on the minerals issue, which continued to be New Zealand's main preoccupation. Australia, the delegation reported, continued to be cautious, but it was now clear that other claimants—New Zealand, Argentina, Chile and the United Kingdom—had already reached the point where they were seriously prepared to negotiate a compromise. There was general agreement on the need for a solution to the sovereignty question and for an acceleration of the negotiating process. It was also recognised, the delegation reported, that 'the interests of the international community, including a future seabed authority, would have to be recognised and that this would probably involve benefit sharing.

The need to accelerate the negotiations was reflected in the recommendation adopted by the Consultative Parties, which called for a further meeting on mineral resources before the next ATCM, preferably in the first half of 1980. The Soviet Union, however, continued to attempt to apply the brakes. Although it no longer sought to confine a regime to environmental aspects, it argued that the 1977 moratorium was of indefinite duration and that the system of voluntary restraint needed no renewal.

New Zealand, keen to push ahead with the negotiations, took the opposite view: the delegation asserted that New Zealand would not consider itself bound by the moratorium unless it could interpret the recommendation as having been renewed. The Chairman, it reported, produced 'an ingenious form of words that leaves open both interpretations'. There was no doubt, according to the delegation, that New Zealand could opt out of the moratorium if it was dissatisfied with the rate of progress towards a regime.[98]

The delegation noted that the United States was now much more constrained by environmentalist pressure than in the past, and seemed unlikely to encourage or sanction the commencement of commercial exploration in advance of the conclusion of a regime. This left New Zealand as perhaps the leading proponent of urgency in the negotiation of a regime, and it was therefore not surprising that New Zealand was pressed by a number of delegations to act as host for the meeting that had been recommended. Although the suggestion met with ministerial favour[99] the general disposition to deal first with living resources, and the difficulty faced by the New Zealand authorities in finding the necessary manpower and finance to run a meeting in 1980, led to a delay in taking this initiative, and it was eventually agreed that a preparatory meeting should be held in Washington to discuss the procedure to be followed in future negotiations on a minerals regime.[100]

Before this meeting took place, however, New Zealand came under renewed pressure to take the lead in moving matters forward. In August, Fernando Zegers of Chile approached members of the New Zealand delegation at the Law of the Sea

Conference to express his concern that the moment the southern hemisphere claimants had most feared was fast approaching, when Third World countries might be in a position to raise the question of an international regime for Antarctic resources in the General Assembly of the United Nations, without upsetting the LOS negotiations on deep seabed mining. The claimants, he believed, could count on one or, at most, two Assembly sessions before this issue was inscribed. Therefore, a meeting should be held as soon as possible to prepare the first draft of a treaty. This meeting should be held in a southern claimant country, and preferably an English-speaking one, to facilitate its drafting. Since Australia had handled the negotiations on living resources, the finger now clearly pointed at New Zealand. (It seems probable that Chile did not want the leadership role to fall to Argentina, which might have seemed the obvious candidate, for other than linguistic reasons.) Financial and administrative considerations, Zegers was told, would preclude New Zealand from convening a meeting before the ATCM, which was to take place in Buenos Aires in June 1981. There was, however, a reasonable chance that the Government would be prepared to act as host to a meeting in the latter part of 1982. It was not, at this stage, in any way committed. The LOS delegation summed up:

> This would be an ambitious undertaking for New Zealand, requiring a diversion of scarce manpower. The stakes however are high. The topic is going to become one of intense political and public interest in New Zealand whether or not we attempt a leading role. The advantage for New Zealand of having direction of the drafting exercise needs no elaboration.[101]

In a letter to the Head of the Legal Division (Mansfield) in the Ministry of Foreign Affairs, Keating wrote from Washington in October to underline the importance of strong representation if New Zealand was to play an influential role in the minerals negotiations:

> I believe that the Law of the Sea Conference has demonstrated, so clearly that there can be no dispute about it, that a country's ability really to move a negotiation of this sort depends on the people

> more than any other single factor; I am confident that if we can put into the mineral resources negotiations a capable delegation leader who will stay with the issue for more than one meeting (and hopefully through to its conclusion) we will be able to achieve a very great deal. The question is who . . . Clearly Chris [Beeby] would be an ideal candidate . . .

Beeby, who had recently returned from his Ambassadorship in Iran to a position as Assistant Secretary in the Ministry, was in fact sent to the preparatory meeting in Washington that December.

Keating also reported a talk with Tucker Scully, the State Department official who was to handle the minerals negotiations for the United States until their conclusion. They reviewed in very general terms the possible ways ahead which had appeared during the discussions at the Tenth ATCM. They noted that there had been two approaches. Some participants had clearly been attracted by the idea of a 'common enterprise' which might have sole rights to extract resources and which would pay dividends in pre-agreed proportions to the Consultative Parties and any other beneficiaries that might be agreed upon. Others favoured the more traditional concept of private and government entities extracting resources on a free enterprise system. It seemed important, in terms of progressing the negotiations rather than addressing any one country's national interests, that whatever framework was established should not conclusively rule out either of these two alternatives. (One wonders whether Scully might not have had a mental reservation on this point.)

Keating and Scully proceeded to discuss the stages in which minerals activities would be conducted, moving from scientific research which would be shared, to research that would produce proprietary information (i.e., prospecting), then to drilling (exploration) and finally to production. Scully took the line that it would be much easier if the regime could be drafted in such a way that it would be possible to move from non-commercial research to prospecting 'without requiring a specific decision by any institution established under the regime' (which was to be a consistent American theme throughout the negotiations). While environmental considerations would be the prime factor in the operation of the regime, there was not any serious evidence, in Scully's view, that any of the activities envisaged at the second stage would be environmentally harmful. It was at the third stage that a prior environmental test would be required.

Keating gained a distinct impression that:

> Scully's own thinking on the possible solutions to this question is moving increasingly in the direction of the proposal which New Zealand floated in Paris in 1976 and which has been implicit in some of the papers prepared in recent years. In particular Scully seemed highly attracted by the 'minimalist' approach which avoided going into the kind of detail that has been necessary in the Law of the Sea Conference negotiations on Committee One. He said that if a regime is ever to come about, the Consultative Parties will probably need to take quite a lot of the detail on trust.[102]

The encouragement for New Zealand to take a lead continued at the meeting in Washington in December. The New Zealand delegation described developments there as 'a major breakthrough'. Both the Americans and the Russians indicated that they wanted a regime, and that they accepted the need for 'a meaningful accommodation' with the claimants—although there was little clarification of what such an accommodation might involve. There was increased support for the idea that it would also be necessary to have an accommodation between the Consultative Parties and the international community, including some form of economic benefit-sharing. There was a 'shared perception' that the next ATCM should adopt a recommendation which would set in train a formal negotiating procedure. The New Zealand delegation circulated an informal draft of such a recommendation. The Chilean representative (Zegers) summed up the situation:

> The superpowers have very strong interests in maintaining the Antarctic Treaty. Their only alternative to an Antarctic Treaty solution is a common heritage solution. Provided the economic concessions to claimants are approximately of the same order as would otherwise be forfeited to the common heritage then political interests will continue to motivate them to seek an Antarctic Treaty solution.[103]

Argentina continued to hanker after holding the 'last meeting' on a minerals regime in that country, no doubt with a view to having the headquarters of a regulatory body located there. A number of countries, however, privately expressed the hope that some of the negotiations might be held in New Zealand. They did so again at a preparatory meeting for the Eleventh ATCM in February 1981.[104]

In late May of that year, a draft Cabinet paper was submitted to the Minister of Foreign Affairs seeking approval to offer New Zealand as a venue for the first negotiating session. The arguments for doing so, according to the draft, were these. Now that the Law of the Sea Conference was very close to a conclusion, the need for action on a minerals regime had become increasingly urgent; there was every likelihood that the idea of an international regime for Antarctica would be raised in the United Nations General Assembly at an early date. It had become clear, as it had not been earlier, that all the Antarctic powers, including the Soviet Union, were now ready to engage in a serious effort to negotiate a minerals regime. The stakes for New Zealand were high. There were strong indications that the continental shelf of Antarctica might contain valuable resources of hydrocarbons, the technology to exploit which, even in the extreme conditions of Antarctica, was either in existence or near at hand. At issue, therefore, would be two matters of direct concern to New Zealand: the benefits New Zealand might receive from mineral exploitation, and the possible environmental dangers of exploitation for countries like New Zealand whose waters bordered those of Antarctica. For tactical reasons (the paper contended) it was highly important that at least the first and final negotiating sessions should be held in a southern hemisphere claimant state. For various reasons (some more convincing than others) it was argued that this should be New Zealand rather than any of the other three. The principal reason, clearly, was self-interest. New Zealand would be in a position 'directly to influence the course of the negotiations and to ensure that as far as possible our interests are accommodated. Conversely, to fail to make the necessary financial and administrative effort involved in holding the meeting would send a very clear signal that New Zealand did not attach great importance to the negotiations, to the potential economic benefits of exploitation or the environmental risks.[105]

This paper was not, however, submitted to Cabinet: Treasury refused to agree to the expenditure in the 1981–82 financial year, since no provision had been made for it in the Estimates.[106]

Instead it was proposed to the Minister of Foreign Affairs, who agreed, that the New Zealand delegation to the Eleventh ATCM should be authorised to extend to the participants an invitation to attend the first of a series of special meetings on mineral resources in this country. If the invitation were accepted, the proposal would be included in the Ministry's new policy proposals for 1982–83, and in case it was not approved, the cost would be met from savings from the Ministry's allocation for that year.[107]

This somewhat topsy-turvy procedure, viewed in retrospect, may have had consequences that were less than fortunate, though unforeseeable. While it may have short-circuited possible disagreement at the time about the strength of the arguments for a high New Zealand profile, the decision to go ahead did not have the backing that a Cabinet decision, based on thorough debate in a Cabinet Committee, would have provided. There was an election in late 1981. Cabinet portfolios were reshuffled. The Minister of Foreign Affairs (Talboys) retired and a less experienced, more sceptical Cabinet member (Cooper) succeeded him. No one could or did foresee that six years of arduous negotiation lay ahead. In any event, the new Minister in January 1982 accepted the 'new policy' proposal, which had the general support of the other departments concerned. He did not have much choice, since the invitation had in fact been accepted by the Consultative Parties the previous June.[108]

The ATCM, after arduous negotiation, had adopted a lengthy recommendation that set the scene for the forthcoming negotiations.[109] For once, it was not the Latins who were taking the extreme claimant position, but the British, whose Government was passing through a nationalistic phase in its Antarctic—and energy resources—policy-making.[110] At the opposite extreme was the position of the Soviet Union, which had begun from a position of unwillingness to make any concession to the claimants.[111] Disagreement focussed on two issues—whether there was to be an 'accommodation' of the respective interests of the claimants and non-claimants, and the formulation of the description of the area to which the regime would apply.

On both issues, language was incorporated in the resolution which was technically ambiguous, but the general intention of which seems clear enough. On the first issue, the Soviet Union baulked at the word 'accommodation' but eventually accepted a formulation which read:

> Any agreement . . . should be acceptable and be without prejudice to those states which have previously asserted rights of or claims to territorial sovereignty in Antarctica as well as to those states which neither recognised such rights of or claims to territorial sovereignty in Antarctica nor, under the provisions of the Antarctic Treaty, assert such rights or claims.[112]

Whether the word 'acceptable' did (or, as the Soviet Union chose to interpret it, did not) apply to the remainder of the sentence does not now seem to matter. It is of interest, however, that this formulation did not refer to states which had a 'basis of claim' and which have been accorded a special status in the Minerals Convention as finally adopted.

On the second issue, the recommendation stated that the regime should

> apply to all mineral resource activities taking place on the Antarctic Continent and its adjacent offshore areas but without encroachment on the deep sea-bed. The precise limits of the area of application would be determined in the elaboration of the regime.[113]

The Soviet Union was not prepared to have the offshore area defined in terms of the definitions in the Law of the Sea Convention. The Latins reluctantly accepted this language on the understanding that 'encroachment' meant *illegal* intrusion, and did not therefore affect the rights of the coastal state on the deep seabed within the EEZs provided for in the Law of the Sea Convention.[114] This *was* a point of substance. The recommendation could equally well be read as depriving claimant states of minerals in the seabed beyond the edge of the continental margin, but within 200 miles of the coastline; and in the end it became necessary to include an interpretative sentence in the Final Act of the Fourth Special Consultative Meeting (SCM) to ensure that the term 'continental shelf' as it appears in the definition of the area of application of the Minerals Convention is interpreted as meaning the continental shelf as defined in the 1982 Convention on the Law of the Sea, and not in its 1958 predecessor.[115]

The stage was now set for detailed negotiations to begin under New Zealand chairmanship in 1982. This will be a convenient point at which to end an excessively long chapter with some reflections about New Zealand's stance on the minerals issue up to the commencement of the negotiations.

There were several consistent threads in New Zealand's attitude to the minerals issue throughout this period. From the time that the negotiation of an Antarctic Treaty was undertaken, New Zealand regarded the absence of an international agreement to regulate mineral exploration and exploitation in Antarctica as a gap that needed to be filled. Credit is due to New Zealand for continuing to press for action on this touchy issue in the face of indifference, reluctance and at times outright opposition on the part of the other Consultative Parties to the Antarctic Treaty. First and foremost, it attached importance to the protection of the fragile Antarctic environment. This principle appeared prominently in every proposal that New Zealand put forward from 1970 onwards. At the same time, there was recognition that discovery of valuable mineral resources in Antarctica would almost certainly lead to competitive efforts to exploit . . . them. It would not be difficult to see how unregulated activity in the area could lead to a breakdown of the carefully constructed Treaty system, as well as creating environmental hazards.

When the Antarctic Treaty was being negotiated, New Zealand's policy was to encourage both scientific investigation and economic exploration of Antarctic resources 'for the benefit of all'. Walter Nash would have supported the concept of the 'common heritage of mankind' had it been international currency at the time. This was a very different idea from that of a world park, in which all exploitation of non-living resources would be forbidden.

The idea of making the continent a world park, or an international nature reserve, was inherent in the Agreed Measures on Fauna and Flora, but a number of countries, such as France, rejected the use of those actual terms. As already recounted, New Zealand had to fight virtually alone to have the question of non-living resources included in the agenda of later ATCMs. Only in the face of a possible takeover of the issue by the developing countries in the United Nations did the other Antarctic powers accept the need to agree on a regulatory regime within the Antarctic system.

During the seventies, Labour and National Governments in New Zealand, while continuing to work for an international regime, took different approaches to the question of what that regime should be designed to accomplish. The Labour Government favoured a world park, and failing that supported a moratorium on mineral exploitation. But it must be said that it did not pursue the idea of a world park with any vigour. Nor was that at any time a central tenet of Labour policy. There is no record that the issue was ever submitted for consideration by a Labour Cabinet.

By the time that a National Government came to office in 1975, it had become widely accepted that any mineral resources in Antarctica that might become exploitable in the foreseeable future were most likely to consist of petroleum deposits in the continental shelves, one of the largest of which was in the Ross Sea. The Middle East oil crisis was seriously affecting the supply to New Zealand of petroleum products and its ability to pay for them. Inevitably, departments other than Foreign Affairs and Scientific and Industrial Research developed a new interest in Antarctica, and demanded a voice in the formulation of policy. Some officials, with a valour born of ignorance, advocated the assertion by New Zealand of exclusive rights over minerals within the area of its claim. The Ministry of Foreign Affairs had little choice but to develop a policy line that now had two objectives—to protect New Zealand's potential economic as well as environmental interests in Antarctica. In the atmosphere engendered by the oil crises of the seventies, it was far from unwilling to work for an international regime designed to achieve both aims. Its numerically limited legal resources, hitherto heavily engaged in seeking to protect New Zealand's maritime interests, were now focussed on this new task. The Government of the day was fully briefed. Notoriously tight-fisted though it was when it came to spending money on international conferences—especially those attended by officials—the Government nevertheless accepted a leadership role without apparent demur. Neither it nor anyone else had any idea of the complexity of the task that lay before it.

XI

MINERAL RESOURCES: NEGOTIATING A CONVENTION

It may be asked why, after twelve years of intermittent discussion of the need for a minerals regime for Antarctica, it should have taken a further six years to complete the negotiation of a text on which all the Consultative Parties (fourteen in number in 1982, twenty in 1988) seemed ready to agree. Only a little reflection, on the other hand, might lead the historian to wonder how agreement could ever have been achieved at all, given the diversity of interests among the participating governments—a diversity in their approaches to Antarctic issues in general, and to the question of mineral resources in particular. Agreement on any substantive matter among the Consultative Parties requires not merely consensus, but unanimity. Readers who have struggled through the accounts in previous chapters of the negotiation of the earlier agreements forming part of the Antarctic Treaty system will appreciate how difficult it had proved to agree on anything, even on matters of a relatively uncontentious character. Now the Antarctic powers had to face up to the question of who—if anyone—was to have access to potential sources of enormous—if undiscovered—wealth: included among these, and in everyone's mind, was a resource of prime strategic importance, as well as economic value.

In 1959, when the Antarctic Treaty was being negotiated, the claimant states were in the majority. In 1982, the Consultative

Parties were evenly divided between claimants and non-claimants. By 1988, the claimants constituted only one-third of the total, and the proportion of non-claimants could only increase. Not surprisingly, therefore, some claimants were extremely defensive in their initial approach to an issue affecting their sovereign rights in such a concrete way. But the division between claimants and non-claimants was only one of the divergences among the Consultative Parties. The situation was more complex. It was assumed that while mineral resources might be expected to be found throughout Antarctica in comparable variety and quantity to mineral deposits in other continents previously joined with Antarctica in the supercontinent known as Gondwanaland, the only significant resource that could offer the prospect of early exploitation—if it existed in quantity, and if its extraction proved technologically and economically feasible—was petroleum. The most likely location of any significant deposits of this resource was in the continental shelves. The only large continental shelves in Antarctica containing thick sedimentary rock likely to contain hydrocarbons are in the sectors claimed by New Zealand and by Britain, Argentina and Chile (in the latter case, the subject of dispute). Thus it did not follow that only non-claimant states were concerned to ensure non-discriminatory access (by members of the Antarctic club) to mineral resources in Antarctica; countries like France, which lacked indigenous petroleum resources, had a keen interest in access to any exploitable resource that might be found. Non-claimant countries such as the United States, Japan and the Federal Republic of Germany, which had or could obtain access to the most advanced technology, were insistent that they should be able to explore for and exploit resources on an equal footing with the claimants. It was the position of all the claimants, however, that they should have preferential rights. The Soviet Union, for its part, not having the latest technology at its disposal, began by attempting to delay as long as possible the commencement of serious work on a regime; and when that work did begin, its initial bid was for *compulsory* joint ventures, which would ensure that the Soviet Union was able to secure a share of the resource or the profits, irrespective of whether it could contribute its share of the expertise. Australia, which also initially sought delay (advocating instead a stronger and more long lasting moratorium) may have done so for a different reason. One of the last issues to be settled by the LOS Conference, the definition of the continental shelf, was also for Australia one of the most important, for Australia has important offshore petroleum resources in its very large continental shelf. It seems unlikely that Australia wanted controversy to be aroused in international forums about Antarctic mineral resources until the boundary of the continental margin had been fixed by the LOS Conference.

When and if the archives of the principal participants are eventually opened, some of these speculations about their motives may need to be revised. What was undoubtedly true, however, was that there was a range of conflicting interests among the negotiating parties, and that these were exacerbated by uncertainty about the existence and exploitability of an important strategic resource, and in the early 1980s by a deterioration in political relations among several of the principal players. East–West tensions heightened after a Republican administration assumed office in the United States in 1980, and in 1982 war broke out in the Falkland Islands between two Antarctic claimant states, Britain and Argentina. That the mineral negotiations were able in these circumstances to continue without interruption is a matter for retrospective astonishment: all the more so since New Zealand, the provider of impartial chairmanship in the negotiations, was giving Britain all support in the Falklands war short of directly taking part in the hostilities.[1]

There was one danger, however, already mentioned in the previous chapter, which caused the Consultative Parties to suspend the differences and draw up their wagons in a defensive laager. This was the threat that the question of a regime for Antarctic mineral resources might be placed on the agenda of the United Nations General Assembly with a view to promoting a 'common heritage' solution on the analogy of the LOS provisions relating to the deep seabed. Thus there was no disposition at the first session of the SCM on Mineral Resources, held in Wellington in June 1982, to retreat from the judgment reached at the Eleventh Consultative Meeting a year earlier,[2] that the task of producing a minerals regime was urgent. There had been suspicion that the Soviet Union might be tempted to curry favour with the developing countries (the so-called Group of 77) by lending its support to the common heritage option. That proved not to be the case.

The Chairman (Chris Beeby) reported to the participants after the meeting[3] that in addition to the desire for urgency, there was broad agreement that the regime should not constitute a comprehensive mining and environmental code resolving all the issues that might arise, but should be 'dynamic' in character: it would, however, need to provide a clear picture of the decision-making process and of the standards on which decisions would be based.[4]

There was a wide measure of agreement on the need for a decision-making Commission, an Advisory Committee on scientific and technical questions, a Secretariat and perhaps an Arbitral Tribunal. (All these institutions were provided for in the text of the Convention.) The Chairman made only oblique reference to another category of bodies, the Regulatory Committees (which had been envisaged in earlier New Zealand working papers), saying that there might be advantage in having one or more institutions, perhaps regional in scope, that did not comprise all the Consultative Parties. There was consensus, he reported, that the regime should effectively protect the environment; and set standards as a basis for decision-making on environmental issues.

Turning to 'areas of greater difficulty' (i.e., disagreement), the Chairman noted a widely held view that the regime should be flexible on the question of who should be entitled to mine: private companies, consortia, governments or public sector organisations, or any combination of these entities, might be eligible. Beeby noted that the restrictive alternative to this (as mentioned earlier, the Soviet Union had advocated compulsory joint venture arrangements, under which the applicant for a licence would be *obliged* to accept partners seeking that status) was not easy to reconcile with the more broadly held view that both governments and private sector interests should be free to decide themselves on the shape that mining organisations should take.

Beeby noted differences of view on how the area to be covered by the regime should be defined. The nature of the problem has been mentioned in Chapter X.

The Chairman trod carefully round the issue of the interests of the wider international community, which the Eleventh Consultative Meeting had agreed should not be prejudiced.[5] There was a widely supported view, he said, that a regime based on exclusionary principles or which implied that only the Consultative Parties had an interest in Antarctic minerals, would be unacceptable to the international community. The regime should be, 'in some measured way', an open system. Some delegations thought that a distinction should be made between the right to mine and the right to participate in the institutions of the regime. Others felt that since many countries would not have the technology or resources to mine in Antarctica, it would be necessary to consider whether adhering states which engaged in mining should not also have the right to participate in decision-making institutions. It had also been suggested that provision should be made in the regime for sharing with the international community, and in particular with developing countries, a portion of any revenues derived from Antarctic mining. Some delegations, however, regarded this suggestion as 'premature'. In fact some of the Consultative Parties with extensive continental shelves in their metropolitan territories, and notably Australia, had been adamantly opposed to the concept of revenue sharing in the LOS negotiations. The inclusion of a modest revenue sharing clause in the relevant chapter of the LOS Convention[6] had been reluctantly accepted by them at a very late stage only as part of the compromise that ensured the retention of coastal state jurisdiction beyond 200 miles, out to the edge of the continental margin. The most important issue remaining to be resolved, Beeby went on, was the requirement for an 'internal accommodation' between conflicting positions on the issue of sovereignty. Only a beginning had been made in the search for such an accommodation, and the gap was wide. Only by forbearance in pressing opposing views on sovereignty to their logical conclusion could failure in the minerals negotiations, and consequential damage to the Antarctic Treaty system, be avoided. At this stage, the main stumbling block was the question of where power to regulate mineral resource activities should reside. The non-claimants took the view that regulation would have to be undertaken by the parties to the regime acting collectively through its institutions: to the extent that enforcement would remain wholly or partly in the hands of individual states, the states in question would be those of the operating entity. In other words, the claimant states would have no special role or powers. Claimant states naturally took the opposite view: the individual states exercising the major regulatory and management role, they asserted, would be those claiming sovereignty.

One avenue worth exploring, Beeby suggested, was a solution to the problem of where the regulatory power should be located, based on selective *membership* of the proposed institutions and on the voting formulas for decision-making, which need not be the same in all cases.

Modest though these suggestions may seem in retrospect, the Chairman was already moving on to delicate ground. His report represented his personal views, and was put forward as such. The New Zealand Government's position was that of a claimant, and the Cabinet paper which reviewed New Zealand policy in preparation for the meeting had reiterated that, in addition to ensuring maximum protection for the environment, the regime should

> (a) secure and safeguard the benefits which New Zealand can reasonably expect in view of our claim to sovereignty over the Ross Dependency, our proximity to Antarctica, our operational expertise in Antarctica and our contribution to scientific research on the continent, and
> (b) take account of the need to secure the toleration of the regime by the international community at large, and
> (c) involve minimum costs which should ultimately be recovered from mineral activities.

The paper continued to be based on the premise that 'the continental shelf in the Ross Sea area appears highly prospective and is likely to be the focus of early interest in exploitation'. It argued that the negotiation of a regime within the Treaty system in which New Zealand could exercise a major voice offered the best hopes of a result which protected New Zealand's interests. Other options such as unilateral exploitation (which New Zealand could not in any case sustain by itself) or a broader international regime would have serious disadvantages. The second option would reduce New Zealand's say in Antarctic affairs, would not recognise New Zealand's claim to preferential benefits in the Dependency, and would offer few guarantees of protection to the Antarctic environment.[7]

While the Minister of Foreign Affairs signed the memorandum to Cabinet, which had interdepartmental endorsement, it was to become apparent later on that he was highly sceptical of these basic premises and, therefore, implicitly, of the desirability of New Zealand's high profile in the negotiations. This was not however apparent to the officials at the time. They felt some satisfaction with the progress that was made at the meeting. The United States had shown readiness to accept the need for an accommodation between claimants and non-claimants. The Soviet Union had shown that it was ready to begin serious negotiations. The flexibility shown by the United States had been matched by three of the claimants, Britain, Argentina and Chile. The only real exception to this trend had been Australia, which submitted an extreme hard-line paper and was roundly and bluntly criticised by the non-claimant states. New Zealand, in view of its chairmanship, refrained from submitting a paper on the hard issues. Instead, it offered suggestions during the discussion of possible areas of compromise. It also circulated two papers and cosponsored a proposal designed to stimulate and guide future work on the environmental system to be incorporated in the regime. The delegation felt justified, therefore, in recommending that New Zealand continue to take a leading role and offer to hold a further meeting of the negotiating powers in New Zealand.[8] The Minister did not demur.

During the June meeting and the months that followed, New Zealand officials[9] were at work on a draft convention that was designed, among other things, to offer a solution to the need for an 'internal accommodation between the aspirations of the claimants and non-claimants'. Beeby himself visited a number of capitals of the Consultative Parties and tried out some of the ideas in the first draft. He was generally encouraged by the reaction to the idea of a regulatory body or bodies of limited membership, at which he had hinted in his personal report. The Soviet Union, however, took the position that it could not accept any regime that excluded it from important decisions. The Latin Americans took a similar stand, at least in respect of the territories they claimed.[10]

At the next meeting held in January 1983, there was a general disposition on the part of the participants to modify the positions they had taken the previous June in order to achieve progress. They found it difficult, however, to conceive of a scheme which preserved their legal positions on sovereignty and accommodated their various interests in the negotiation.[11] The fact that they were stumped for a formula provided the opportunity, for which Beeby and the New Zealand delegation had no doubt been waiting, to produce a partial draft convention as an annex to the Chairman's personal report on the outcome of the meeting. This was to achieve a certain fame, perhaps more extensive than its authors envisaged, under the document reference MR/17.[12]

The draft, as the Ministry of Foreign Affairs instructed its posts to explain to their host governments, was drawn up in such a way as to put an appropriate emphasis on the preservation of the environment. This emphasis was both inherently important and important in terms of its perception by the wider international community. There would be an initial determination by the proposed Commission (of which the Consultative Parties would be the foundation members) on whether the opening of an area for minerals exploration was acceptable on environmental grounds. This decision would be taken by consensus, i.e., any of the Antarctic powers could veto it. (This provision has been carried through into the final text of the Convention.)

The question of the 'internal accommodation' was dealt with by providing for Regulatory Committees of not more than eight members. These would include:

(a) in respect of an application relating to an area in claimed territory, the claimant state;
(b) the two countries which had asserted a 'basis of claim' prior to the entry into force of the Antarctic Treaty; and
(c) including (a) and (b), an equal number of claimant and non-claimant states.

Voting on the adoption of a management scheme would be by simple majority including the state sponsoring the application and the claimant state affected. (Although the size of the committees, their composition and the voting procedure were all changed or elaborated in subsequent negotiations, the basic features just described survived into the final text of the Convention). As the Ministry told its posts (but not the other participating governments):

> The basic approach adopted in Beeby's scheme is to construct the regime in such a way that there is no overt distribution of powers which might be seen as prejudicing the legal position of either side but to set up the institutions in such a way as to force a deal between the claimant state (if there is one in the relevant area) and the state whose company wished to engage in mineral resource activity. At the heart of the scheme is the idea that the critical decisions will be taken in a limited membership body whose membership is carefully balanced between claimant and non-claimant states and which cannot arrive at its critical decisions without the agreement both of the state in whose claimed area a potential activity is planned and of the state whose company wishes to engage in that activity.[13]

A further feature of the membership of the regulatory bodies, it will be noted, and one which survived into the final text of the Convention, was that the two superpowers were to be members in every case. This was not very palatable to other non-claimants with great power pretensions, but as the principal architect of the draft has pointed out:

> We had to bear in mind that the Soviet Union in the first and second sessions had shown itself to be suspicious of the whole

> process of negotiation and very negative towards the creation of anybody in which it might not be represented. The Soviet Union spoke consistently of all decisions being taken by a Commission on the basis of consensus, i.e. a Soviet veto on everything to ensure that it never missed out on participation in decisions or benefits. Part of the Soviet perception undoubtedly was that it was miles behind countries like the United States, Japan and the FRG in terms of technology for the extraction of oil in both Arctic and Antarctic areas.
>
> It was against this background that we took the decision that if the Soviet Union was to be brought along in the negotiating process that we hoped would be initiated by MR/17, it would have to be in every Regulatory Committee. The United States was also given the benefit of automatic membership of every Regulatory Committee (although in fact it had no anxieties of the kind displayed by the Soviet Union since it was pretty confident that it would be a member of the Regulatory Committee in most cases as a sponsoring state).
>
> Having taken the decision to put the superpowers in every Regulatory Committee the question then was how to name them. We decided that they should not be named directly because we predicted (rightly as it turned out) that countries like Japan and the FRG would have serious reservations of the same kind that they have in relation to permanent membership of the Security Council, about giving the superpowers a guaranteed part in the important decision-making in the Regulatory Committees. We judged that they might be a bit less offended if a different basis were found for their inclusion and the basis we hit upon was to describe them as the two states which, prior to the entry into force of the Antarctic Treaty, had asserted a basis of claim in Antarctica.[14]

Even this formula caused some unhappiness to Japan and the Federal Republic of Germany, and also to Argentina and Chile, which were reluctant to accept a text which might be taken as implying that the Americans and Russians had a basis of claim to the whole of Antarctica. It was to undergo several revisions,[15] but the substance remained.

It was agreed that the next meeting should be held in a non-claimant country, the Federal Republic of Germany. New

Zealand officials were, however, determined to keep control of the negotiating process. Their hand was strengthened by the generally favourable reception given to the Chairman's initiative, not only by most of the claimants but also by the United States and the Soviet Union. Some delicate manoeuvring was required to save Teutonic face—the Germans not unnaturally were reluctant to see their role reduced to the provision of tea and sandwiches[16]—while at the same time retaining the chairmanship of the key negotiating group on the contents of the regime in Beeby's hands. Before the meeting could take place, however, there were a number of developments, not all of them auspicious.

The fact that the majority of the participants were prepared to accept MR/17 as the basis for further negotiations did not mean that the balance it attempted to strike was equally acceptable. The Germans, who were perhaps the least enthusiastic of the participants, were prepared to regard the draft only as 'a point of departure'. They and other non-claimants were disposed to criticise it as excessively weighted in favour of the interests of the claimants. Colour was lent to their suspicions, perhaps, by the fact that the reaction of the claimants, including Argentina and Chile, was much warmer.

New Zealand officials saw the principal key to progress in the attitude of the two most important non-claimants, the Soviet Union and the United States. The fact that the Soviet Union professed to perceive in the Beeby text 'elements which might be suited to push the negotiations forward on the right track' was highly encouraging. The reaction of the United States was seen as even more crucial. The Reagan administration had just rejected the LOS Convention on largely ideological grounds—i.e., that it sought to impose international controls on the exploitation of the mineral resources in the deep seabed. The parallel with what the authors of the minerals regime were aiming to achieve was uncomfortably close. However, a system operated by a relatively small group of Antarctic powers was infinitely preferable to a system operated on 'common heritage' principles by a Third World-dominated control body. The American negotiators thus had a four-way battle on their hands: to restrain the more extreme elements in their own government, who favoured a full frontal free enterprise approach to the exploitation of natural resources in Antarctica (or anywhere); simultaneously to satisfy the growing environmental movement in the United States; to deflect the threat of an initiative by the developing countries to hijack the whole question of the administration of Antarctica into a United Nations forum; and at the same time to ensure that any minerals regime that might be negotiated by the Antarctic Treaty Consultative Parties would give the American mining industry a fair crack of the whip if and when exploitation of Antarctic mineral resources became technologically and economically feasible. The chief American negotiator (Tucker Scully) handled this complicated agenda with considerable finesse.

The New Zealand officials therefore took Scully's criticisms of MR/17 very seriously, and in the interval between the second and third sessions of the SCM, Beeby and Keating engaged in anxious correspondence about how these could or needed to be met.[17]

Scully's first objection was to the provision that decisions by the Commission as to whether an area should be opened up for mining should be taken by consensus and thus subject to (Soviet) veto. New Zealand officials thought that in the end the Americans would accept this—it was a *sine qua non* for the Russians and probably for the Latins—but only if they were satisfied on other major issues. Secondly, Scully pointed out that the voting procedure proposed for Regulatory Committees, although ostensibly balanced, would in fact be weighted in claimants' favour in a situation where the state sponsoring an application was itself the state claiming the territory in question or another claimant. It would be possible, Scully suggested, for a claimant state to set terms and conditions for its own sector, let its own companies in and veto all applications from other sponsoring states.[18] Even if this difficulty could be overcome, there was really still no equivalence between the position of the claimant and that of the sponsoring state. Each might have a veto, but a veto was an instrument for blocking something, not for moving it forward, as the sponsoring state would wish. Thus the Americans were really opposed to the veto in the Regulatory Committees as well as in the Commission.

Beeby's comment was that at this point they had come up against 'one of the main boundaries in the negotiations'. One of the realities was that for reasons of domestic politics, the claimants would have to be able to point to the fact that they could, by one means or another, block the carrying out of any activity in their claimed sector. It might of course, be possible to hedge the blocking power around in such a way that it was very difficult to exercise it—just as it was very difficult within the Antarctic Treaty system for any one Consultative Party to stand forever against the general tide of opinion.

The 'reality' of the need to cope with domestic political concerns was shortly to be brought home to the New Zealand delegation in an unexpected and disagreeable way. More immediately, however, the Antarctic Consultative Parties were confronted with a growing interest in Antarctica on the part of a large group of countries that hitherto had had no involvement in the development of the Antarctic Treaty system. The developing countries, many of them only recently emancipated from colonial rule, had through the seventies been seeking to increase their influence in world affairs through such groupings as the Non-aligned Movement, and to obtain a greater share of the world's wealth and resources through such concepts as the New International Economic Order. The thought that they were entitled to a share of the supposed wealth locked up in Antarctica was a direct extension of the concept of the common heritage of mankind, as applied to the deep seabed in the recently concluded LOS Convention. Inspired by a kind of neo-imperialist activism, some of the more ambitious leaders of the Non-aligned Movement and its economic counterpart, the Group of 77, now looked around for fresh worlds to conquer.

India's interest in Antarctica, it will be remembered from an earlier chapter, dated back to when the Antarctic Treaty was being negotiated. Nehru had been dissuaded from raising the question of internationalisation in the United Nations by Walter Nash, who spoke—perfectly sincerely—of a regime in which access to Antarctica's economic resources would be open to all countries without discrimination.

Indian interest in Antarctica appears to have revived contemporaneously with the decision of the Antarctic powers to begin serious negotiations to draw up a minerals convention. India may have been decided to adopt a two-pronged approach: first to initiate activities in Antarctica which might qualify India to adhere to the Treaty and seek consultative status, and at the same time to promote discussion of the future of the continent in wider international forums, such as the United Nations and the Non-aligned Movement. An Indian scientific expedition visited Antarctica in the summer of 1981–82. It was not immediately clear whether India had in mind acceding to the Treaty, as a number of other countries—the Federal Republic of Germany, Brazil, Italy and China, for example—had recently done or were contemplating. In 1982 there was an apparent revival of interest in Antarctica in various United Nations forums. A draft resolution calling in effect for a United Nations takeover of Antarctic policy-making was put about by non-governmental organisations during a special UNEP meeting in May. There were rumours that a study of legal aspects of the New International Economic Order, to be presented to the United Nations General Assembly, would include a section on Antarctica. Then in August the New Zealand Mission to the United Nations was approached by its Malaysian counterpart in search of information about the Treaty and the June 1982 meeting on minerals.[19] It transpired that the Malaysian Prime Minister (Mahathir) had hit on Antarctica as the centrepiece for his general debate speech at the forthcoming session of the Assembly. There were dark suspicions, since Malaysia had not hitherto displayed the slightest interest in Antarctic affairs, that he had been put up to his initiative by the Prime Minister of India (Mrs Gandhi). If so, this represented the second prong of India's policy.[20] New Zealand was not surprised that the issue should be raised in a United Nations forum, but was concerned that it was Malaysia, a 'moderate' developing country with which New Zealand had had close and friendly relations antedating even its independence, which was taking this initiative. (On the other hand Malaysia, under Mahathir, was keen to burnish its non-aligned credentials and loosen its 'colonial' ties with Britain, Australia and New Zealand.)

New Zealand took a very strong line with Malaysia in an endeavour to head off this move. In discussions with Malaysian representatives, it was stressed that New Zealand regarded the Ross Dependency as an integral part of its territory. To bring the subject up in the United Nations

> would amount to a direct challenge to New Zealand's territorial sovereignty and New Zealand, like any other country, could be expected to respond vigorously to any attack on its sovereignty.[21]

Tough stuff. Mahathir was not to be deterred, however, by the representations from the Antarctic powers. In his General Debate speech he said bluntly that:

> . . . it is now time that the United Nations focused its attention on these [uninhabited] areas, the largest of which is the continent of Antarctica. A number of countries have in the past sent expeditions there which have not limited themselves to mere scientific exploration but have gone on to claim huge wedges of Antarctica for their countries. Those countries are not depriving any natives of their lands, and they are therefore not required to decolonise. But the fact remains that those uninhabited lands do not legally belong to the discoverers, just as the colonial territories do not belong to the colonial Powers. Like the seas and the sea-bed, those uninhabited lands belong to the international community. The countries now claiming them must give them up so that either the United Nations can administer those lands or the present occupants can act as trustees for the nations of the world. At present the exploitation of the resources of Antarctica is too costly and the technology is not yet available, but no doubt the day will come when Antarctica can provide the world with food and other resources for its development. It is only right that such exploitation should benefit the poor nations as much as the rich.
>
> Now that we have reached agreement on the law of the sea the United Nations must convene a meeting in order to define the problem of uninhabited lands, whether claimed or unclaimed, and to determine the rights of all nations to those lands. We are aware of the Antarctic Treaty, concluded by a few nations, which

> provides for their cooperation for scientific research and prohibits non-peaceful activities. While there is some merit in this Treaty, it is nevertheless an agreement between a select group of countries and does not reflect the true feelings of the Members of the United Nations or their just claims. A new international agreement is required so that historical episodes are not made into facts to substantiate claims.[22]

Clearly,. Mahathir now regarded Malaysia's relations with the non-aligned movement as more important than its relations with the former colonial power and the other Commonwealth countries that had helped it to cope with the threat of communist insurgency. A senior Malaysian official confirmed to the New Zealand High Commissioner in Kuala Lumpur that the Malaysian initiative had had its genesis in a letter Mahathir had received from Mrs Gandhi in which she referred to India's interest in Antarctica and advocated the internationalisation of the continent. The official thought that Mrs Gandhi would not be very happy with the Malaysian statement because it did not go far enough towards the Indian position.[23] (One wonders how the Malaysians may have felt about the fact that India was simultaneously seeking to qualify as one of the 'select group of countries', to use Mahathir's phrase, which exercised a dominant role in the management of Antarctic affairs. New Zealand, Australia and other Treaty partners encouraged India to pursue this alternative.)[24]

There followed a lengthy diplomatic exchange among the Consultative Parties about the response they should make to the Malaysian challenge. This only served, however, to show once again how difficult it was for the Antarctic powers to agree about anything. One proposal was that a rebuttal should be made in the Assembly on behalf of all fourteen Consultative Parties, and it was also proposed that the task should be assigned to New Zealand. However, the Soviet Union and Poland refused to associate themselves with a joint statement.[25] It was then proposed that New Zealand should make a statement on its own behalf, with the other Consultative Parties refraining from making statements of their own which might reveal disunity within the group! At this point, however, the proposal ran onto the rocks in Wellington. The New Zealand Prime Minister was about to attend a regional Commonwealth Heads of Government Meeting in Suva, at which he was to have a bilateral meeting with Mahathir. The Minister of Foreign Affairs approved the proposal for a unilateral New Zealand statement, but it was then vetoed by the Prime Minister,[26] who evidently felt that it was not an issue worth quarrelling with Mahathir about. The subject did not, apparently, come up in their conversation, although the Prime Minister was briefed to raise it.[27] The Australian Prime Minister likewise was not disposed to take the matter up in his bilateral discussion with Mahathir.

As it turned out, Mahathir's reference to Antarctica was something of a damp squib at the Assembly. Other speakers did not mention it, and the Malaysians did not make a move to have the topic discussed at this session. The New Zealand Prime Minister's reaction, however, was a pointer to a certain lack of commitment on the part of Ministers to the policy that had, with their agreement, been so actively pursued by officials. When the Minister of Foreign Affairs expressed scepticism about the practicability of exploiting any petroleum resources that might be discovered in the Ross Sea, enquiries were made about the relevance of Canada's experience in the Arctic. A Canadian engineer in the department concerned advised that:

> while the production of oil in the Ross Sea area would be undoubtedly difficult, current and likely future developments in the relevant technology would make the exercise a practical one provided, of course, there was an adequate economic return. He guessed that a discovery of approximately two billion barrels would be required to justify the investment needed for exploitation.[28]

(Canada had not at that time proceeded beyond the exploration phase in the Arctic.) The scepticism of New Zealand Ministers remained, however,[29] and was accentuated by their sensitivity to the views of an increasingly vocal environmentalist movement.

Although Malaysia did not seek a debate on Antarctica in the United Nations in 1982, its determination to broaden international discussion of the future of the continent did not diminish, and in 1983 it scored a significant success by having the Non-aligned Movement (NAM) pronounce on the subject. At the NAM Conference held in New Delhi in march, the only Antarctic Consultative Party represented was Argentina—whose first preoccupation, inevitably, was the Falklands. However, Argentina, with help from Australia behind the scenes, managed to produce a watered-down version of the resolution which Malaysia had sought to have the Conference adopt. In the final version:

> the Heads of State or Government noted that the continent of Antarctica has considerable environmental, climatic, scientific and potential economic significance to the world. They expressed their conviction that, in the interests of all mankind, Antarctica should continue forever to be used exclusively for peaceful purposes, should not become the scene or object of international discord and should be accessible to all nations. They agreed that the exploration of the area and the exploitation of its resources should be carried out for the benefit of all mankind and in a manner consistent with the protection of the environment of Antarctica. The Heads of State or Government while noting the relevant provisions of the Antarctic Treaty related to international cooperation in the area and in view of increasing international interest in Antarctica, considered that the United Nations in its 38th session of the General Assembly should undertake a comprehensive study taking into account all relevant factors including the Antarctic Treaty with the object of widening international cooperation in the area.[30]

For the Antarctic Treaty powers, the good news in this outcome was the positive reference to the Treaty and the absence of a specific reference to Antarctica as the common heritage of mankind. The bad news was the fact that Malaysia, which had intended to raise the question again in the Assembly anyway, could now do so on the basis of a non-aligned position that would assure it a healthy majority for the inscription of an item.

The Malaysian paper circulated to the non-aligned was headed 'Antarctica as a Common Heritage of Mankind', and proposed that the United Nations General Assembly should at its 1983 session order a study to be made for further consideration in 1984. An international regime might follow the precedent of the LOS Convention in creating international machinery for the exploration of Antarctica's resources: 'perhaps in the not too distant future the international community will witness the establishment of a second "Enterprise" which would be another symbol of its ability to suppress narrow national interests for the betterment of mankind'. The emphasis, it will be noted, was on exploitation of resources rather than on environmental protection.[31]

There followed a further lengthy exchange of views among the Consultative Parties on how to handle the Malaysian initiative at the next Assembly session, and in particular on whether the inscription of an item on Antarctica should be opposed. At a preparatory meeting for the Twelfth Consultative meeting (held in April 1983 in Canberra) it was agreed that the Consultative Parties faced a new and serious situation and should seek to coordinate their strategy and actions to deal with it. As usual, they found this easier to say than to do. The New Zealand delegation prepared an informal paper which appeared to represent a consensus of opinion. The main points were that, given a satisfactory Assembly resolution, a United Nations study on Antarctica could be accepted; a satisfactory resolution would include 'adequate reference' to the Antarctic Treaty, contain some recital of its benefits and require that the study take account of its essential provisions; a resolution which stated or clearly implied that Antarctica and its resources were the common heritage of mankind would be unacceptable, as would a resolution which sought to call a halt to the minerals negotiations until the United Nations study had been completed.[32]

Although the paper did not explicitly discuss the pros and cons of a move to reject the inscription of the Malaysian item, there was in it a basic assumption that confrontation was to be avoided and that inscription should not be resisted. This was soon, however, to become a point of contention rather than consensus.

When the focus of discussion on tactics shifted to New York, the 'consensus' embodied in the Canberra paper soon began to unravel. The United States Mission to the United Nations, a much more highly politicised group than the American Antarctic experts, appeared not at all averse to having a confrontation with the non-aligned group over the question of inscribing the item. What stuck in their craw was the belief—not an unreasonable one—that however a Malaysian item might be worded, debate would be bound to focus on extending the concept of common heritage to Antarctica. To the Reagan administration, collectivism in any form was anathema, and the LOS provisions relating to the seabed had provoked it into an ideological frenzy. The reaction of the American United Nations team was, therefore, predictable. More surprising was the fact that by May the Soviet Union had decided to adopt a similar hard-line position. An exchange of views between the two superpowers served to stiffen their determination.

As the New Zealand Embassy in Washington remarked: It is almost as if they are delighted to find a political issue on which they both agree and can cooperate.[33]

New Zealand officials were disconcerted. A confrontational approach would preclude an attempt to negotiate an acceptable resolution before the Assembly began and the Malaysian initiative became set in concrete. New Zealand officials saw no possibility that a blocking move on inscription would succeed. After all, it was very hard to produce convincing reasons why the United Nations should not have a discussion of Antarctica.[34] Moreover, New Zealand attached great importance to its relations with ASEAN. The annual ministerial dialogue with the members of that organisation was about to take place. ASEAN solidarity would undoubtedly swing the other members behind the Malaysian initiative, whatever their private reservations.

The reaction of one New Zealand official was to point out that the Malaysian initiative impacted most severely on the interests of the claimants. In bilateral discussion with the Malaysians, he suggested, they should be left in no doubt that, while New Zealand had long supported some form of sharing of the benefits of resource exploitation with the developing countries, their attack on the claims cut most intensely against the interests of their friends (Australia and New Zealand) and the two developing claimant countries (Argentina and Chile).

For these geographically contiguous countries the question of sovereignty in the Antarctica was an important as the Arctic was to Canada, in terms of security, resources and national integrity. If the Malaysians did not ease up on the anti-claimant pedal, the real winners would be the superpowers.[35]

When the opportunity came, however, for the question of Antarctica to be raised bilaterally between New Zealand and Malaysia on the ministerial level, Cooper took a softer line, avoiding the sovereignty issue. His 'one to one' meeting with Tan Sri Ghazali during the annual dialogue with ASEAN Ministers in June was largely taken up with discussion about Antarctica, but it was not productive. The New Zealand officials present reported that there had scarcely been a meeting of minds. What came through 'rather starkly' was that Malaysia had no real interest in Antarctica as such, nor, if Ghazali himself were anything to go by, in becoming more knowledgeable about the area. Ghazali (a man not prone to excessive modesty, or to prefer listening to talking) displayed some quite basic misconceptions about the Treaty itself, about the way the Treaty partners worked, and about the status of claims. Cooper's line was to urge that Malaysia's interest in Antarctica take the form of acceding to the Treaty and sending scientists to Antarctica, but Ghazali showed no interest and criticised the Treaty as 'archaic'.[36]

The Australian Minister (Hayden) did not raise the question with Ghazali at all. The other ASEANs did not show interest in Malaysia's initiative, but it was equally clear that ASEAN solidarity would oblige them to support it.[37] This then was the unsatisfactory situation—from the Antarctic Treaty partners' point of view—at the outset of the Bonn session of the SCM on Minerals in July 1983.

The Malaysian initiative was by no means the only problem faced by the New Zealand negotiating team in the run-up to the Bonn meeting. In mid-June, a leaked copy of MR/17 was published in Britain by Roger Wilson, a New Zealander associated with both Greenpeace and Antarctic and Southern Ocean Coalition (ASOC).[38] New Zealand Ministers, who had not been consulted on the subject since January (and may not have read the report in any case), were probably startled to find that the subject had become controversial and that a New Zealand public servant appeared to be the main focus of the controversy. When the leaked document was released by ASOC in New Zealand, it was accompanied by an attack on its contents which struck a radical new note in opposition to the prospect of commercial minerals activity in Antarctica. Speaking for ASOC, Catherine Wallace said that the draft

> showed an alarming disregard for protection of the Antarctic environment from the impacts of mining and oil exploration.
>
> The negotiations—which were held in secret—were leading to unacceptable threats to Antarctica and to the Treaty itself . . . The contents of the draft made it plain that arrangements would be adopted for reasons of political expediency which would sacrifice environmental protection . . . the best minerals regime in the world won't mend the damage from an inevitable oil well blowout—environmentally disastrous anywhere—but a catastrophe in Antarctica.
>
> . . . The valuable treaty qualities of scientific freedom and cooperation could be lost as the nations which had hitherto been 'guardians' of Antarctica set up a system to commercially exploit the minerals and oil of the continent, once nations became dependent on Antarctic resources or even jealous to retain their share of future supplies, peace in the area would be threatened, and so would the Antarctic environment.[39]

Since the 'best minerals regime in the world' would be inadequate from the environmentalists' point of view, it was thus clear that they would be satisfied with nothing less than a complete ban on minerals exploration and exploitation in Antarctica—something quite different from the objective set by the Non-aligned Movement in March. The Antarctic powers and the environmental groups were now, it would seem, on a collision course.

Further publicity was given to the paper at a conference on Antarctica held by the New Zealand Institute of International Affairs, where the offending document was again excoriated in an environmental publication circulated to participants, under the heading 'Beeby's slick solution'.[40]

Ministers showed themselves to be sensitive to the publicity. A Cabinet paper was prepared to explain the draft Convention to them and seek their approval for the continuance of New Zealand's role, but unfortunately when it came up for consideration in a Cabinet Committee the officials most knowledgeable in the subject matter had already departed for Bonn.[41] The paper had a rocky passage, and in consequence the delegation received a distinctly intimidatory message reporting the ministerial reactions.

Ministers, the delegation was told, had displayed a quite unexpected disposition to go back to first principles and ask whether the course on which New Zealand had embarked was the right one. They questioned whether the draft regime did not take matters far beyond any situation that was likely to arise in the foreseeable future. In view of the world energy situation and the reluctance of oil companies to engage in marginal ventures, they asked whether New Zealand should not be taking advantage of the hiatus in commercial interest to consider other options for Antarctica rather than playing a leading role in the negotiation of a minerals regime. Should not New Zealand be using its influence in the direction of a complete prohibition of minerals exploitation, or of extending the moratorium? Would that be a credible approach for New Zealand, and one that would gain wider acceptance? Would a convention drawn up by the Antarctic Treaty powers deter undesirable activities by other countries, or would a United Nations treaty offer greater certainty? It was evident that ministerial knowledge of the basic principles of the Antarctic Treaty system was scanty indeed. They were concerned that although Beeby's paper was drafted in his personal capacity as Chairman, it would be regarded as a New Zealand paper reflecting the Government's position—without the Government having any very clear idea what was in it. If anything, Ministers appeared to have a preference for a moratorium, and the delegation in Bonn was asked to assess the reaction of other delegations to a two-pronged approach in which the establishment of a regime would be accompanied by an extension of the moratorium 'pending the establishment of fully acceptable standards and mechanisms to protect the environment'.[42]

The response of the delegation to this unwelcome, and no doubt unexpected, communication was to stress that:

> the purpose of these negotiations is not the Promotion of Antarctic minerals development . . . it is the establishment of a mechanism for ensuring that, if and when mineral development in Antarctica becomes an economically realistic possibility, well informed decisions are taken about the environmental acceptability of particular proposed activities in particular areas.

There was a widespread view, the delegation said, that every member of the regime must be able to exercise a veto on environmental grounds against the opening of any part of Antarctica for minerals development. Thus every party to the Convention, including New Zealand, would effectively be able to put an indefinite moratorium into effect. The delegation pointed out the superior effectiveness of a binding treaty in comparison to a loose and shaky 'best endeavours' moratorium which, it considered, would last only as long as progress was being made in the negotiations. As to a permanent prohibition, this would not be regarded by the other Antarctic powers as a serious position:

> It has been apparent throughout these negotiations so far that our treaty partners have concluded that it is most unlikely that any minerals will be commercially extracted from Antarctica this century. It is equally apparent, however, that they are not prepared to enter into a commitment that they will never in any circumstances at any time in the future seek to extract minerals from Antarctica.

Any move to transfer the issue to the United Nations, the delegation went on, would bring New Zealand into serious conflict with its Treaty partners. From an environmental viewpoint, such a move would in any case be self-defeating since the third world majority in the United Nations was a great deal more interested in the development of resources (as the common heritage of mankind) than in environmental protection. The delegation suggested that if Ministers wished to give even greater weight to this latter consideration its instructions might be modified to the effect that it should make every effort to ensure

> (a) that the regime specify that no mineral resources activities take place unless and until:
>
> (i) it is possible to make the judgment, on the basis of adequate information, that their impact on the environment will be limited and in conformity with rigorous standards spelt out in the regime;
>
> (ii) technology and procedures are available to ensure safe operations in compliance with those standards;
>
> (iii) adequate arrangements are made for monitoring such activities.
>
> (d) that the regime specify, in addition, that the opening of any part of Antarctica to mineral exploration or development, in terms of the principles specified above, would require a consensus decision commanding the support of all parties to the regime;
>
> (e) that the regime further specify that areas of Antarctica of special sensitivity be placed off-limits;
>
> If these objectives were not being met, the delegation should seek further instructions.[43]

This formulation proved so appealing to the Cabinet Committee that after very little further discussion it adopted it *verbatim*, and in addition agreed that New Zealand should offer to host the final session of the SCM.[44] Cooper, however, who was absent from Wellington for the second meeting of the Cabinet Committee, remained a sceptic. Attending a meeting of the ANZUS Council in Washington, he questioned whether it was realistic for the Treaty countries to think they would be able to defend a minerals agreement which gave them a preferential position in the face of pressure in the United Nations year after year. The prospects of early exploitation, he said, had receded. It might be necessary to rethink whether it was possible to defend the existing system. Before the next session of the SCM it might be necessary for the Consultative Parties to address themselves to the problem of making the regime viable in the United Nations in the long term.

These heretical views did not strike a chord with the Australian and American representatives. The Foreign Minister of the recently elected Labor Government in Australia (Hayden) said that neither the common heritage principle nor the idea of turning Antarctica into a world park was acceptable to his country, which was opposed to any United Nations involvement. The American Deputy Secretary of State (Dam) was equally blunt. The United States did not want United Nations involvement either. The principal interest of the United States in the minerals negotiations was to ensure future access to resources. The common heritage principle, as the LOS negotiations had shown, would result in restriction of access to minerals by the United States. Even if exploitation was a long way off, the next generation would be grateful for the efforts which were made now to protect American interests.[45]

All in all, it must have been with some relief that the New Zealand delegation was able to report at the end of the Bonn meeting that the negotiations remained on track. It is a measure of the difficulties it faced from all sides (and from behind) that it described the acceptance of MR/17 as the basis of negotiation and its reissue as a Conference document as 'a major breakthrough'. Some delegations had been seriously unhappy with MR/17 and the Germans, for example, would have liked formally to table an alternative text. It was 'progress', therefore, that none of the papers circulated by the Americans, the Russians or the Germans had actually been tabled. The American paper had in fact kept closely to the Beeby text and was presented as an evolution of it.[46]

Progress was made on definition of basic terms and on the question of environmental protection, on which Cabinet had focussed: the delegation considered that there was every prospect that its concerns could be met. But the problems arising from the conflicting interests of the major participants remained. The main continuing division was between claimants and non-claimants. The delegation felt that the position of the claimants (about which Keating had expressed particular concern beforehand) had been maintained.

A second major problem arose from the differing objectives of the Soviet Union and the United States. The Soviet Union wanted a minerals regime which would help preserve the Antarctic Treaty but which would also deny the West access to a potential source of scarce resources. They would therefore like the regime to give them a clear and unqualified veto over any minerals development activity. It should also recognise that the Soviet Union as well as the United States had interests throughout Antarctica and that parity should therefore be maintained in decision-making within the institutions to be established. The United States was probably prepared to accept parity but was

> certainly not prepared to allow the Soviet Union to use the regime in such a way as to deny the West generally, and the United States in particular access to potential resources. Specifically they could never accept a regime which gave the USSR a veto over a US-sponsored mineral resource activity which met all the requirements of the regime regarding environmental protection.

At the same time, the delegation went on, this problem had to be balanced against the concern of the claimant states that the regime must be so structured that no mineral resource development could take place without their acquiescence and without taking account of their essential interests. Many if not all states wished to be able to block the opening of any part of Antarctica for mineral resource activities if they believed that such activities would be environmentally unacceptable.

The alert reader will have noted a measure of contradiction between what the delegation was telling the Government at the beginning of the meeting and what it was saying at the end. Initially it argued for the view, reflected in Beeby's paper, that every country, including New Zealand, should have the right of veto on environmental grounds against the opening of any part of Antarctica for development. Now it was saying that the *claimants* were insistent on this right but that the United States was not prepared to have the Soviet Union exercise a veto to deny the United States access. But the Soviet Union might well say that it was as well qualified as any other country to judge the extent of environmental risk.

A third problem which was apparent at the Bonn session was the reluctance of the Germans and Japanese to accept that the importance of the presence of the United States and the Soviet Union in Antarctica as well as their global standing justified their being represented on all the institutions of the regime, including those of limited membership. The delegation considered that 'in time the Germans and Japanese will have to come to accept these political realities'.

Because the negotiations now seemed unlikely to be completed in 1984, the delegation did not make the offer to host the 'final' session. (It did however advise some key delegations—those of Australia, the United Kingdom and the United States—of New Zealand's interest in providing a site for the regime headquarters.) It was agreed that the working group that had been reviewing MR/17 under Beeby's chairmanship should reconvene in Washington in January 1984 for an 'informal session' on the same basis. A side effect of this was that Cabinet's wish, conveyed to the delegation at the beginning of the Bonn session, to have the Beeby paper 'de-individualised',[47] was effectively frustrated.

The Minister of Foreign Affairs put out a statement laying emphasis on the progress made in identifying the relevant environmental principles—a matter on which, he said, the delegation had been given 'strict instructions'.[48] (In fact, it was the British view that a lot more progress could have been made on the environmental aspects if it had not been for Soviet obstructionism: the Soviet Union did not want to have environmental safeguards in place before its other concerns were met.)[49]

In August, India acceded to the Antarctic Treaty: Since it appeared to be qualified as a Consultative Party, it was now also a player in the minerals negotiations. Brazil quickly followed suit.

The Malaysians, ignoring all pleas from the Antarctic powers to drop or even delay the submission of their item for inclusion in the agenda of the 38th session of the General Assembly,[50] produced a draft resolution replete with references to the desirability of making Antarctic resources available for the benefit of mankind as a whole, which completely ignored the Antarctic Treaty.[51] The Consultative Parties, facing the usual problem of agreeing on a course of action, managed eventually to present a united front against this threat. They circulated a document which praised the achievements of the Antarctic Treaty system and rejected the implied need for its replacement, which

> would undermine this system of international law and order in Antarctica with very serious consequences for international peace and cooperation. It is unrealistic to think that, in the present state of world affairs, a new or better legal regime for Antarctica could be agreed upon. The undermining of the Treaty could open the way to an arms race in the region and might lead to new territorial claims. It would not serve the interest of any country, or group of countries, if Antarctica became an area of international conflict and discord.[52]

The Consultative Parties, instead of forcing a vote (which they would have lost), decided not to participate in the decision to inscribe the item, but negotiated a 'gentleman's agreement' with Malaysia that in return for their not opposing inscription every effort would be made to ensure that a resolution could be adopted by consensus.[53] (Had there been a vote, New Zealand would in fact have abstained, unless the whole group of Consultative Parties had been united in their determination to cast a negative vote. Australia and the United Kingdom would also probably have abstained, while the United States and the Soviet Union would have voted against.)[54] The resolution that eventually emerged did not mention the proposition that the resources of Antarctica should be made available for the benefit of all mankind. It requested the Secretary-General

> to prepare a comprehensive, factual and objective study on all aspects of Antarctica, taking fully into account the Antarctic Treaty system and other relevant factors.[55]

The resolution was adopted by consensus. The Antarctic powers, recognising that they were on a slippery slope, were by and large agreed that the best course to follow was one of full cooperation with the United Nations Secretariat in the preparation of the study.[56]

In October, officials reported to the Cabinet Economic Committee on the outcome of the Bonn meeting.[57] Attention focussed on the proposition that New Zealand might provide the headquarters site for a regulatory authority to administer the minerals regime. Ministers were cautious, and asked for information about the obligations that this would entail for New Zealand, including the cost. Nevertheless, they agreed that New Zealand should continue to explore the possibility.[58] In the course of this discussion they appear to have been successfully diverted from further consideration of the desirability or otherwise of the negotiations being conducted by a New Zealand official. Ministers would sooner discuss a topic of a concrete nature (or at any rate, bricks and mortar) than one raising abstract legal problems, any day. The Minister of Foreign Affairs now wrote to his Australian opposite asking for Australian support.[59] The main purpose of this move was to head off Tasmanian ambitions to have the minerals headquarters in Hobart as well as those of CCAMLR. The Australians were, however, in a political bind. The Federal Government had already been approached by the Tasmanian Premier seeking support for a bid to have the minerals headquarters based in their capital. Hayden acknowledged the merits of the New Zealand case, but declined to give any commitment.[60] Subsequently the Australian Minister of Science told Beeby that the way Australia's decision went depended on whether rationality or atavistic tribalism won out. If the decision were taken in an election context, the latter seemed more likely.[61]

The next round of minerals negotiations was held in Washington in January 1984. Although this round was 'informal' in character, it required the participation on the New Zealand side, in addition to Beeby, of both the Head of the Legal Division in the Ministry of Foreign Affairs and his predecessor.[62] They had a formidable task. Although Beeby's continuing chairmanship of the working group was now accepted and although they had, in effect, stolen a march on the other parties by producing MR/17 at the beginning of 1973, the leading players were now honing their own drafting skills with a view to pushing the negotiating barrow in the directions they wanted it to go. These directions were, in some cases, opposite. The United States had produced operator-friendly articles at Bonn. The British in December quite openly told New Zealand that they were producing alternative articles of their own that were designed to produce a more claimant-friendly text.[63] They wished, for example, to have stricter controls on prospecting, and in regard to exploration, greater powers for the Regulatory Committees. In their view the membership of each Committee should be limited to three: the sponsoring state, the claimant state and a third appointed by the Commission. Effectively therefore, the British took the same view as the Federal Republic of Germany and Japan, that the United States and the Soviet Union should not automatically be members of all Regulatory Committees, as proposed in MR/17. The management scheme to be adopted in each Committee should, in their scheme, be drafted by the claimant state, negotiated with the operator and approved by the Committee with the concurrence of the claimant state. It should not go to the Commission for approval. The New Zealand Commissioner for the Environment was 'critical' of the British proposals, 'too much of a fast tracking process', which by restricting the roles of the Commission and the Advisory Committee, would 'encourage' minerals activities and fail to provide for adequate environmental controls.[64]

It was the aim of the New Zealand team to have the Washington meeting concentrate on the rules for prospecting, the procedure for opening up an area to exploration, the composition of the Regulatory Committees, the procedures for dispute settlement, participation in the Commission and the 'external accommodation'—that is, how the concerns and demands of countries outside the Antarctic Treaty system might be met or propitiated.[65]

In the delegation's report at the end of the meeting there may be detected a certain sense of relief that the negotiations had not been pushed off the rails by the Malaysian initiative in the United Nations or by the entry into the Antarctic club of two large and influential developing countries. All the principal protagonists, according to the report, were 'now' ready to make a serious and good faith effort to negotiate an effective and credible minerals regime. The delegation had, of course, said much the same thing after earlier sessions. The amount of work remaining to be done was reflected in a decision to schedule two more meetings in 1984 and 1985, to be held in Tokyo and Brazil. The delegation thought (optimistically as it turned out) that it might then be possible for New Zealand to offer to host the final meeting.[66]

Progress was, nevertheless, made. There was a profusion of proposals at this meeting. Beeby was able to respond to an invitation from the participants by circulating, in March, a revision of MR/17 which filled in many gaps in the earlier text so as to comprise a much more comprehensive and detailed draft convention.[67]

The revised draft now contained a preamble (which the final version closely resembled). It contained important definitions of 'exploration', 'development', 'prospecting' and 'mineral resources'. These made it clear that prospecting stopped short of dredging, excavation or drilling beyond a limited depth (eventually fixed at 25 metres). Exploration would include drilling but stop short of pilot projects or commercial production. Development would comprise subsequent activities aimed at exploitation. Mineral resources meant all non-living natural non-renewable resources (thus excluding, for example, ice).

The article setting out environmental criteria, in its revised form, was strengthened to make it clear that: *no* minerals resource activities should take place until an impact assessment had been completed and a reasonable judgment, based on adequate information, had been made that the activities would not cause a significant degradation of the Antarctic environment from which effective recovery was not possible within a reasonable period of time; they would not affect global or regional climatic patterns; and would not disturb the environment and associated ecosystems beyond the Antarctic area. (Substantially similar provisions, in more detailed form, appear in the final text of the convention.)

The new text included much more detailed articles on

prospecting, making it clear that this did not require prior authorisation by the institutions of the regime. It also laid down rules for the guidance of the Commission in dealing with applications and identifying areas in which exploration would be permitted. It provided that there should be only one Regulatory Committee for each area that had been the subject of an application to explore and exploit, rather than one for each individual block opened up for exploration and exploitation within that area. The implication of this was that the Regulatory Committee for an area would need to be established, and to divide the area into blocks, before applications to explore and exploit any or all of the blocks in that area would be entertained. This in turn involved a change in the composition of the Regulatory Committees. Since a Regulatory Committee would be established in respect of an area before applications could be received to explore and exploit a particular block within that area, the membership of the Committee would initially include the state requesting the designation of the area. Once an application had been made, it would be replaced by the state sponsoring an application for as long as that application was under consideration in the Committee. Instead of the sponsoring state nominating up to two members of the Committee, the Chairman of the Commission in consultation with the Chairman of the Advisory Committee would appoint a sufficient number of parties to maintain equal numbers of non-claimants with the claimant membership of the Committee. (One can only hope that this simplification of an extremely complicated provision is clear: the main point is that the intended balance between claimant and non-claimant members was maintained, eliminating the possibility, about which the United States had complained, that in certain circumstances the claimants might outnumber the non-claimants.)[68]

Among other changes, the United States and the Soviet Union were now described as the two states which *had maintained the largest presence* in Antarctica at the time the Antarctic Treaty entered into force. This was intended to meet the Argentinian and Chilean objections mentioned earlier. However, the Americans and Soviets would much have preferred the original language, while Japan and Germany would have preferred a formula which would allow each of them at least the theoretical possibility of becoming one of the two members at some future date. (In subsequent revisions, an attempt was made to combine the two formulae but the version which eventually appeared in the Convention went back to the 'basis of claim' criterion and, although slightly ambiguous, would, in Beeby's opinion, be interpreted by an arbitral tribunal as applying only to the Soviet Union and the United States.)[69]

New Zealand had been almost alone in pushing the idea that one means of getting the international community to accept a Convention would be to follow the precedent set in the Law of the Sea Convention by making some provision for revenue sharing with developing countries. Only Norway gave explicit support to this idea, and MR/17 had provided rather obliquely that the Commission should 'consider the establishment of measures to ensure participation of the international community in benefits derived from the regime'. The revision provided even more obliquely that it should 'elaborate by consensus the principle of non-discrimination with a view to ensuring full and fair opportunity, without discrimination, for participation in Antarctic mineral resource activities'. Even this attenuated provision was too much for the developed countries; and the developing Consultative Parties proved to be more interested in getting special preferences for themselves into the Convention rather than provisions for the benefit of developing countries at large. So, in subsequent revisions, this provision was dropped altogether, never to reappear.[70]

In presenting the revision of MR/17, Beeby as Chairman of the working group noted that further work was required on the questions of responsibility and liability of sponsoring states and of operators for damage done to persons, property, and the environment in the course of exploration or mining. He also stressed the importance of establishing a regime which would be credible to the international community as a whole and stand the test of time. This raised the question of whether states seeking to become party to the regime should first be required to adhere to the Antarctic Treaty, whether there should be a forum in the regime in which all acceding states might participate, and whether there should be a fund to encourage and promote scientific research in Antarctica by developing countries. The provisions for dispute settlement and the final clauses covering *inter alia* eligibility for membership remained blank in the revised text. There was, therefore, much difficult work still to be done.

After extensive interdepartmental discussion, a lengthy paper was submitted to the Cabinet Economic Committee in May 1984 seeking guidance for the New Zealand delegation to the forthcoming session of the SCM, which was to be held in Tokyo later that month.

The submission is of special interest as representing the last occasion on which the Government was consulted about Antarctic policy before the 1984 elections. It is evident that officials were determined that Ministers should have no grounds for suggesting, as they had in 1983, that they had not been kept sufficiently informed about the way the negotiations were heading and the implications for New Zealand.

The paper began by recalling that the Government had in 1977 'reversed' the policy of its predecessors, on the grounds that a total moratorium was unrealistic. (This may have been news to some Ministers.) It again laid stress on the elements of the 1977 policy, subsequently reaffirmed by Cabinet on several occasions and most recently in 1983, that had underlined the importance of environmental safeguards. It outlined the general trends which had emerged from the negotiations so far, with particular attention to progress on environmental protection. The 'trends' were summarised as follows:

> (a) the inclusion of a detailed list of environmental criteria against which future decisions on mining applications would be judged;
> (b) a distinction between 'prospecting', which would not require advance approval—because it would be limited to an 'environmentally relatively benign range of activities'—and 'exploration', which would cover activities, short of exploitation, which would include activities, such as drilling, likely to have significant environmental impacts. But even prospecting would be

subject to strict environmental rules and if necessary to collective review;
(c) to move from 'prospecting' to 'exploration' would require a decision by the Commission which would be taken by consensus. In other words, New Zealand would have a veto which could be exercised on political, environmental or economic grounds and would not be limited to the Ross Dependency;
(d) if an area were opened for exploration in the Ross Dependency, New Zealand would be able to choose half the members of the Regulatory Committee;
(e) the detailed legal, political and economic accommodation between New Zealand, as the claimant state, and the state sponsoring exploration the Dependency would be negotiated in the form of a 'management scheme' which would be legally binding and would cover taxes, royalties, inspection procedures, employment practices, liability bonding, insurance and the full range of technical matter;
(f) environmental protection would be assured both by detailed principles binding on operators and on institutions in the region, and by a requirement for a detailed environmental assessment to be provided by the operator before any decisions were taken;
(g) the regime would provide for the Commission to consider that if mining ever became feasible, a system of revenue sharing for developing countries. (The paper noted that the United States, the Soviet Union, the United Kingdom and Australia had expressed reservations about making any provision for participation by developing countries in decision-making and in the sharing of benefits. Officials were optimistic that they would eventually come round to the New Zealand point of view rather than risk a United Nations takeover bid.)

It would seem that some concern had been expressed by Treasury, if not also by Ministers, at the possible cost to New Zealand of establishing a regime. The paper sought to reassure Ministers that the regime would be eventually self-financing. It was acknowledged that much more information would be required before an application to open an area for exploration could be properly considered. This might require some additional scientific and financial resources to be provided. However, the paper went on:

> Delegations are conscious of the need to avoid establishing an elaborate or top-heavy administrative machinery. Given the unattractiveness, in the present economic climate, of mineral exploration in the Antarctic it seems that at the outset and perhaps for a good number of years assessed costs would be either non-existent or negligible. However, in the mid term if an interest is shown in prospecting, there would be greater cost implications. Prospectors could be made to cover some of these costs and financial decisions would be taken by consensus which would ensure that New Zealand has a veto to keep the system under control. Financial implications are at present unquantifiable but should additional expenditure by New Zealand on Antarctica be required at some future time this would be handled in the normal way as new policy.[71]

The Cabinet Committee noted that New Zealand would have a veto on expenditure proposals. It agreed that New Zealand should support a British proposal that, once the system was actually operating, there should be an environmental review involving independent scientific advice and procedures for ensuring that scientific advice could not easily be overridden; a proposal by Britain and the United States for interested international and non-governmental organisations to have access to information and input into decisions on environmental matters; the idea that the Commission should establish both protected and restricted areas of special environmental sensitivity; and proposals to give all states that joined the regime some part in decision-making. It agreed (for the first time) to the inclusion of an 'acceptable' NGO representative in future New Zealand delegations to minerals meetings.[72]

The Australian (Labor) Government accepted the revised MR/17 as 'a good basis on which to proceed'. It too laid emphasis on environmental concerns and instructed its delegation to seek to strengthen the relevant provisions in particular at the prospecting stage. It sought the right to tax earnings from exploitation conducted in the Australian Antarctic Territory and contemplated with reluctance the concept of an external accommodation that involved tangible benefits for the developing countries. It agreed with an American view that it would be bad tactics to offer concessions at that stage, since that might only lead to further demands later on. It would not be prepared to encourage proposals for 'major resource transfers'.[73]

The environmental publication ECO again obtained a leaked copy of the revised MR/17 and offered a commentary on its provisions during the Tokyo session. At this point it did not insist on a permanent ban on mining, but appeared ready to accept a long-term moratorium or a 'protection regime'. However, if mining and drilling were ultimately going to be allowed, a minerals regime should provide 'the most rigorous and effective protection for the Antarctic which can be devised'.[74] A press statement by the Chairman at the end of the meeting responded to these concerns. Beeby said that the negotiations were not based on the knowledge that there were great riches to be harvested in Antarctica. There was no certainty that minerals would ever be found there in commercially exploitable quantities. Development, if it ever took place, would be many years away; but against the possibility that it might one day become feasible, it was important to agree in advance on a regime that would ensure such activities proceeded in a regulated and disciplined manner. A basic consideration would be the preservation of the unique Antarctic environment and a commitment not to prejudice the interests of all mankind in Antarctica. It was agreed that at the next session, observers from Non-Consultative Parties to the Antarctic Treaty would be admitted.[75]

Reporting on the meeting, the New Zealand delegation acknowledged that on this occasion there had not been a breakthrough. For the first time there had been detailed discussion on such issues as liability, responsibility, jurisdiction and dispute settlement, to which potential miners—the Germans, British and Americans—attached importance. Now that all the cards had been dealt, the delegations said, the stage had been set for a serious negotiation. Heads of delegation, at the end of the session, recognised that the time had come to cut a deal. This would require tough bargaining on the unresolved issues.

Perhaps foremost of these was the problem—in Soviet eyes—of East–West, or Soviet–US, parity. The Soviet representative was himself uncertain how this could be achieved. He wanted parity not only in the institutions of the regime, which the revised MR/17 gave his country, but some kind of parity in terms of opportunity to mine. The New Zealand delegation believed that there was a Soviet economic interest that had to be accommodated. 'Obviously,' it said, 'they would be happy with what they have got under the Law of the Sea—a guaranteed mine site—although they seem to accept that given the lack of knowledge of Antarctic resources it is not feasible to go that route in this negotiation.'

Another problem was created by an Australian proposal that would have prohibited prospecting until two-thirds of the Commission could agree on rules to govern it. Previously there had been an apparent consensus that prospecting—defined in such a way as to be benign in environmental terms—could proceed without prior authorisation. Since the United States attached 'enormous significance' to that proposition, the Australian proposal was effectively a backward step in the slow march towards agreement.[76]

Although the delegation did not say so, the date for the 'final' session seemed to be receding. A further revision of the draft regime was not issued. Three more meetings were to be held, and nearly two years to pass, before that step could be taken.

XII

MINERAL RESOURCES: REACHING AGREEMENT

In July 1984, the New Zealand officials advising on Antarctic policy were confronted unexpectedly with the accession to office of a new Government. David Lange, the new Prime Minister and Minister of Foreign Affairs, had not been in Parliament during the previous Labour administration, and thus had no first-hand knowledge of the policy decisions on Antarctic matters taken by that Government—although when he entered Parliament in 1975 he showed a lawyer's interest in the validity of New Zealand's claim.[1] The first task of officials, therefore, was to ascertain whether the new Government was prepared to back the policy endorsed by the previous Government and continue New Zealand's active role in the minerals negotiations. Because of more pressing issues facing the incoming Government, this process took a number of months.

Before the election, the Labour Party had included in its manifesto a section on Antarctica which read:

> Labour supports the preservation of the Antarctic as an international resource, free from conflict, military activity, nuclear contamination and other environmental damage, and recognises the value of the Antarctic Treaty system and its achievement in protecting the environment and demilitarised status of Antarctica.
>
> Labour will continue to concentrate its efforts on the preservation of the fragile Antarctic environment and on the maintenance of Antarctica as an internal zone of peace, cooperation and scientific endeavour.

Labour will therefore:

(a) encourage other states to accede to the treaty;
(b) support open international consultation and debate on any proposed minerals regime for Antarctica;
(c) support the continuation of New Zealand's scientific endeavours in the Antarctic region and facilitate joint scientific ventures with other states;
(d) ensure that no minerals exploration occurs in the Ross Dependency unless New Zealand is fully satisfied the most stringent safeguards will be met, and that it will in no way endanger the Antarctic environment;
(e) encourage other states to take a similarly responsible attitude in the rest of Antarctica;
(f) participate fully and actively in the treaty system to these ends.[2]

Like all good election planks, this one combined a ringing declaration of principles with careful avoidance of commitment on the nitty gritty issues of controversy. It did not call for a world park or a permanent ban on mining in the Antarctic. By implication it accepted the possibility that there could be a minerals regime with sufficiently stringent safeguards for the environment that would permit minerals exploration to be conducted in the Ross Dependency. In short, it did not appear to require a radical shift in New Zealand policy on Antarctic issues.

This was confirmed in the Government's first response to an approach from Greenpeace urging a 'more enlightened' policy on the new Labour administration. Greenpeace was told that it was not correct that there were fundamental differences of policy between the major political parties:

> [The] Antarctic is very important to New Zealand and I think it is close to a bipartisan consensus on what is a realistic and appropriate policy for New Zealand.[3]

This letter was signed by Geoffrey Palmer on Lange's behalf.

The Government also lost little time in declining to change the policy of the previous Government in regard to the inclusion of NGO representatives in New Zealand delegations to Antarctic conferences, which was to require the organisations to bear the cost of such representation themselves.[4] And to Richard

Northey, an enthusiast on the left wing of the parliamentary party, the Acting Minister of Foreign Affairs wrote that the Prime Minister had decided that it was not necessary to focus immediately on Antarctic policy issues.[5] These reactions were no doubt a considerable disappointment to environmental activists who had been looking for a more sympathetic response from the incoming Government to their point of view.

One new Minister with his own special angle on Antarctica was Mike Moore, who urged an enhancement of New Zealand's Antarctic activities in his capacity as Minister of Tourism and also as a Christchurch MP. The Prime Minister's response, based on a departmental draft, was that New Zealand could best increase New Zealand's involvement in Antarctica by pursuing its scientific effort and taking steps to lessen New Zealand's dependence on the Americans for transport, and by continuing New Zealand's role in international negotiations on Antarctica. However, Lange added, New Zealand's case for having the site of the headquarters of the minerals regime in New Zealand would be prejudiced by talking about it in public at that stage.[6] Moore was none too happy with this response, which he judged to be 'the conventional departmental line'. In his view:

> there is an opportunity to do more at Harewood and make Christchurch the capital of the Antarctic. Why shouldn't we have half a dozen countries based in Christchurch using the best airport and the best harbour facilities? Indeed the Americans spend $10 million a year on Canterbury. More countries spending that kind of money would be of assistance to the city.[7]

Perhaps miffed at the implication that he was stooging for his newly acquired officials, Lange wrote 'seen' on this letter. Not to be put off, Moore wrote again demanding a reply.[8] The Ministry put together a brief for Lange pointing out the obvious fact that Antarctic bases could most easily be serviced from the continent closest to Antarctica. There were therefore 18 bases in the Antarctic Peninsula, immediately to the south of Argentina and Chile. Only the United States and New Zealand had bases to the south of New Zealand. Other Antarctic powers were unlikely to be induced to shift their operations from the Antarctic Peninsula, where it was easier and cheaper to operate and which was in most cases closer to their home ports. Even if they were so induced, they would be looking for technical advice and back-up from New Zealand, which the New Zealand Antarctic Research Programme was too poorly equipped and financed to be able to provide. The first requirement, therefore, would be more money, and quick results could not be expected. However, the brief continued:

> The picture would, of course, change dramatically if a substantial minerals find was made in the area. The Ross Sea is one of the most prospective areas for a substantial petroleum discovery. The necessary logistic support infrastructures for an exploration and production project could have a large economic spin-off for New Zealand. However, you have stated publicly that it is not the Government's policy to encourage mineral exploitation in Antarctica. Such exploration may come about in due course, although it will be tightly regulated and controlled once the current negotiations on a minerals regime are concluded. We would assume, however, that you would regard it as inconsistent with Government policy (and indeed it would be inconsistent with the undertakings made by the Antarctic Treaty Consultative Parties to restrain such activity while the negotiations are under way) for New Zealand agencies, eg Petrocorp or the domestic petroleum industry to be encouraged to pursue this option.[9]

Lange minuted this paper, 'Good'. Moore's reaction is not recorded.

Unwilling to accept that the Government seemed ready to stay with the *status quo* in Antarctic policy-making, the environmental groups loosely coordinated under the ASOC umbrella mounted a concerted public campaign seeking a shift in New Zealand's minerals policy, and also more vigorous action by New Zealand to discourage France from building an airstrip in Adélie Land. The campaign included some 2000 pieces of mail addressed to the Prime Minister. Goodwill began to run thin on both sides. Letters from the Convenor of the New Zealand Organising Committee of ASOC (Cath Wallace) acquired an increasingly peremptory tone.[10] On the other side, it was noted that ten per cent of the replies to the mail received by the Prime Minister was returned by the Post Office as undeliverable. An inference was drawn from this.[11] The Prime Minister sent a fairly stiff reply to Ms Wallace's demands.[12] He accepted a recommendation that, while dialogue with the non-governmental organisations should be maintained, receipt of repetitious correspondence should simply be acknowledged. He minuted, 'Cath Wallace is a bubble off plumb'.[13]

Consultations among the participants in the minerals negotiations continued after the Tokyo meeting in the hope of facilitating progress at the next session, due to be held in Rio de Janeiro in February 1985. In September, an 'informal' meeting was held on Australian initiative, with participation by the United States, the Federal Republic of Germany and the United Kingdom, as well as Australia and New Zealand, purportedly to attempt to 'nail down' the issue of the balance to be struck between the rights of claimants and non-claimants. The meeting, however, discussed a range of outstanding issues, without appearing significantly to narrow differences.[14]

The United Nations General Assembly, meanwhile, adopted a resolution which thanked the Secretary-General for his study on Antarctica and reinscribed the item for its 1985 session.[15] In December, a policy paper was presented for consideration by the Cabinet Committee on External Relations and Security. This paper sought to align New Zealand policy with the general principles enunciated in the Labour Party's election manifesto and in doing so reduced to the point of near (but not complete) invisibility the earlier emphasis on the need to preserve a direct interest in any future exploitation of minerals in the sector of Antarctica claimed by New Zealand. But while downplaying New Zealand's interest in exploitation, it played up the kind of economic benefits that had been envisaged by Moore:

> A New Zealand presence in Antarctica is essential. The Ross Dependency is under New Zealand sovereignty. Antarctica is our nearest neighbour and we have a major commitment to its protection and preservation. New Zealand's ability to play a leading role in international discussion of the content has been

> underpinned by the excellent scientific record which has been built up by the members of the New Zealand Antarctic Research programme. Our credibility in advancing a tough environmental protection policy is dependent upon first hand practical experience and effort in Antarctica.
>
> There is also an economic interest. While the Government's policy is not to give narrow economic considerations primacy, it is a fact that our proximity to Antarctica has led some other countries to use New Zealand as a jumping off point for Antarctic expeditions. If resources are ever exploited in the region that process can be expected to continue and increase. In this event there would also be spin-off benefits to the New Zealand domestic energy sector. Spin-off benefits to New Zealand from other countries routing scientific expeditions through our ports are more likely but such countries will only want to use New Zealand as a partner if we can offer practical on the ground expertise as well as a staging point.

The paper went on to point out, however, that these benefits could only be ensured by a greater scientific and logistic effort on the part of New Zealand (the proposal for the acquisition of a suitable ship surfaced for the umpteenth time) and a greater willingness to provide the necessary resources for an adequate input into international negotiations. The Cabinet Committee was asked to approve a twelve point brief for the continuing minerals talks. The first seven points dealt with the protection of the environment. The eighth called for increased participation by international organisations, including non-governmental organisations, in the negotiating process. The ninth said that New Zealand 'should receive an appropriate economic return for any exploitation in the Ross Dependency'. The tenth acknowledged that any agreement must be acceptable to the international community, and mentioned revenue sharing for developing countries as a possible option. The eleventh and twelfth proposed that New Zealand should seek to have the headquarters site and should offer to convene the final meeting.[16]

In accepting this paper, Cabinet effectively agreed to the continuance of the Antarctic policy that had been followed, not necessarily with any great enthusiasm on the part of individual

Ministers, by the previous Government. It did so on the premise, stated in the paper, that it was

> clear beyond any doubt that the Antarctic Treaty countries, even those for whom environmental protection is the major consideration, are not prepared to foreclose the possibility of extracting minerals from Antarctica if, at some time in the future, it is proved that a resource exists and that it can be extracted without serious environmental risks.

The Special Consultative Session held in Rio de Janeiro in February 1985 was the first which Non-Consultative Parties attended as observers. The New Zealand delegation reported that they had played a moderate and constructive role and appeared satisfied with the opportunities. There was no doubt an educative process to be undertaken, however, and the addition of fifteen observers to sixteen Consultative Parties in a two-tiered conference arrangement could not but add to the complexity of the organisational arrangements and of the negotiations themselves.

The principal outcome of the meeting was a 'very informal' paper dealing in summary form with the key issues in the negotiations—the composition and functions of the institutions in the regime, the rules for decision-making and the right to participate in mineral resource activities. This paper, the product of informal consultations by the Chairman with the principal protagonists, was given to heads of delegations at the end of the meeting. It came to be known as the 'Rio package'.[17]

This paper was in fact the culmination of a series of informal consultations conducted by Beeby with progressively larger groups of representatives before and during the Rio meeting. Some of these consultations took place behind the scenes during a workshop that was held in an American camp on the Beardmore Glacier in Antarctica in January 1985. According to Beeby:

> A lot of the 'Rio package' work consisted of ideas of mine on which I invited comment from Scully and Rybakov, first in Christchurch before we moved to the Beardmore Glacier and then at the seminar itself (in an ice cave!), then on the plane home and

> then at a meeting in Wellington the day after we got home from the ice. This produced a text which had most of the elements in what became the 'Rio package'. The process was then taken forward in Rio in a series of further discussions involving Rybakov and Scully. Those discussions were then broadened out to include Zegers (Chile)—the package had to be sold to the claimants and he was perhaps the most reasonable of them—and later to a larger group including, as I recall, the US, UK, USSR, Chile, Argentina, Brazil, Norway and the FRG. The package had a mixed reception in this larger group, and it was with some trepidation that I put it to all the Consultative Parties' meeting in the final hour of the Rio meeting. I told them to take it home and think about it and I only just escaped having the thing torn up in front of me. By the time we next met it had become pretty clear that the package was accepted, for want of any other, as the way forward to a final solution.[18]

A principal purpose of the paper was to produce a solution of the East–West problem as it had presented itself in Tokyo. The Soviet Union's position was that if the regime seemed likely to ensure in practice that any mining that took place in Antarctica would be carried out exclusively by Western private enterprise, the Soviet Union would simply block any progress towards its completion. The new idea embodied in the package was that no application for mining rights would be considered unless the opportunity had been offered for other parties that indicated an interest to participate up to a defined level. This would encourage joint ventures. There would be no compulsion, but priority would be given to the application with the widest degree of international participation. This idea would be attractive not only to the Soviet Union, but also to industrialising developing countries such as Brazil and India. There would also be provision for developing country representation in the Regulatory Committees.

Another element designed to give the regime wider appeal was a proposed new mechanism to allow *all* parties a voice in the fundamental first decision to open a particular area for mineral resource activities. This would take the form of a special meeting of parties to consider all applications to open up an area for exploration. Voting in these meetings would be by a simple majority, with the concurring votes *all* the Consultative Parties. Thus New Zealand would retain its veto, on which such importance was placed by the Government.

Commenting on the question of participation by the Non-Consultative Parties in the negotiations, Beeby says that, by this time:

> it had become clear to me and most others that the NCPs had to be given a reasonably full opportunity to participate in the consultations. If they felt totally excluded, this would not have prevented the Consultative Parties from adopting a Convention because the decision-making power was theirs alone. But exclusion of the NCPs would undoubtedly have made it harder to sell the Convention to the rest of the world and it could have a corrosive effect on the business of maintaining solidarity in New York against the Malaysian initiative there. From the Rio meeting onwards the NCPs participated in the main formal working groups established on the basis of procedural equality with the Consultative Parties. This is not to say that anyone, including me, took as much notice of the views they expressed in such working groups as was taken of the views of the Consultative Parties. But they were heard. When it came, as it did progressively more often, to dealing with the really hard issues which had to be negotiated in small groups, I adopted a variety of techniques for dealing with the NCPs. If I excluded them from a small group I would give an account of what that group had been talking about to a selected group of NCPs, and in particular to the more sensible and influential among them. Sometimes I would negotiate key issues in a very small group of Consultative Parties and then have the same discussion again with some more of the Consultative Parties and some of the NCPs. Sometimes, as a variation, I put one or two NCPs in the first group and quite a lot of them in the second group. By way of another variation and in relation to issues of particular importance to the NCPs I would call in a group composed of about half NCPs and half Consultative Parties.[19]

While the paper proposed to retain the possibility of a veto by any Consultative Party on opening up an area for exploration, it acknowledged by implication that the unqualified veto which the revised MR/17 gave to claimants, through the voting mechanism in the Regulatory Committees, in respect of all decisions on mining applications within their claimed sectors, would not in the end be achievable. Their concern to control what happened in their territory would have to be met in some other way. The paper therefore altered the membership of Regulatory Committees yet again, so that they would comprise the two superpowers, together with four non-claimants and four claimants, including the claimant state to whose territory the application applied. As Beeby explains:

> It was obvious to me that the claimants' veto at the Regulatory Committee stage would never get past some of the non-claimants. The Rio package replaced this veto with a chambered voting mechanism which still gave the relevant claimant a very high degree of protection.[20]

This mechanism would provide for a qualified majority, including a majority of both the claimants and non-claimants. Thus:

> In a chamber of four, three of the other claimants would have to desert the relevant claimant before he lost his ability to block deals he did not like. To put it another way, if the claimants in any Regulatory Committee maintained a reasonable degree of solidarity, nothing could get through that they did not like.[21]

A further element in the Rio Package was intended to satisfy the view of several countries, in particular the Soviet Union, who were worried that they might be out-voted in the Regulatory Committee, or not represented on it. The paper provided the opportunity for any member of a Regulatory Committee to request a review of a management scheme, and for the Commission by a qualified majority to send the scheme back for reconsideration.[22]

The delicacy of the balance offered by this package—in form, the barest of outlines, offering formidable problems of drafting—was illustrated by the reflections offered by the American representative to New Zealand officials in Washington after the meeting. He thought it might eventually offer the basis for a favourable United States inter-agency consensus, but only when it became clearer that the alternatives were 'even more horrible'. It was 'a mutually unsatisfactory balance' close to (if not in excess of) the limits of what would ever be negotiable within any reasonable time-frame. He was cautious about the degree to which the Soviet Union was willing to accept the concept of decisions by qualified majority (rather than consensus) but the very fact that the Soviet representative had been prepared to see it aired informally suggested that at least there was some Soviet awareness that the time-frame was not open-ended, and that such options merited consideration if they brought the end closer in view.[23]

If the American reaction was one of less than unbounded enthusiasm, that of the hard-line claimants was to complain about almost all its principal elements. The British representative acknowledged that the meeting had been positive and that the log-jam was beginning to ease. However, 'the sort of ideas being floated by the Soviet Union and the United States were pretty awful for the claimants and would cause the United Kingdom a lot of problems . . . They were sorting out something to suit themselves.' There were worrying signs of a weakening in claimant solidarity. The French had virtually deserted the ship, seeing their primary interest as a potential operator rather than as a claimant. The British were nervous also about 'one or two others'.[24] There may have been some unspoken criticism in all this of the role of the Chairman, and by extension New Zealand, in pandering too much to the demands of the superpowers.

Further complaints emerged from a meeting of claimants held in Brussels in April. It seemed that their purpose was primarily tactical, to signal to the superpowers' that further negotiations on the basis of the Rio package would not be acceptable unless additional elements of vital concern to the claimants were included. The Russians and Americans both reacted vigorously, rejecting the view that they had been the only participants in the Rio negotiations; the United States further rejected any suggestion that it should compensate the claimants elsewhere in the overall package for the damage done to their interests in the process of getting the Russians back into the negotiations.[25]

The British then proposed a more formal claimants' meeting to consider the Rio package, which it described as 'the US/ Soviet ideas recorded in the paper prepared by Mr Beeby'—thus distancing themselves from the paper despite the fact that the British representative had participated in the consultations that had produced it. They did not 'exclude the possibility that the paper may contain the seeds of an acceptable way forward'. However, they felt that if a new institution (the Special Meeting of Consultative Parties) was found to be necessary, its powers should be reduced: the provision for simple majority voting could enable the regime to be hijacked by acceding states who, despite Consultative Party unity, could use their majority to prevent areas ever being identified. The British were also unenthusiastic about the idea of wider international participation in minerals activities, and disliked the linkage between that concept and the problem of competing applications. Their strongest criticism was reserved for the new proposals on the composition of Regulatory Committees, which they regarded as too broadly based, providing for 'unnecessary' permanent membership for the Soviet Union and the United States, and unacceptably weighted against the claimants.[26] In saying this they seemingly ignored the fact that the package provided for qualified voting in the Regulatory Committees, including majorities of both claimants and non-claimants—in other words, a veto for either group. However, their concern was based on the fact that MR/17 had provided for decisions by Regulatory Committees on the approval of management schemes (in effect, on whether an exploration/exploitation project could proceed) to be taken by a simple majority including *all* the claimant members. Thus each claimant member would have an individual veto, whereas under the Rio package proposal all the claimants would have to vote together (three out of four) to be sure of blocking an acceptable management scheme—and that, although likely, could not be guaranteed. From the point of view of a non-claimant with aspirations to sponsor a mining venture, of course, it could be said that MR/17 and its revision were unfairly weighted against the non-claimant interests.

An Australian paper analysing the Rio package supported and elaborated on the British objections to it.[27] Australian officials commented that the consultation process from which it had emerged 'had not worked very well' (perhaps because they were excluded from it?).[28] In bilateral talks with New Zealand officials, the Australians noted the fact, remarkable in their view, that the Australian Labor Government had adopted the Antarctic policy of the previous Government as a matter of national interest.[29] That was, of course, a policy based firmly on the concept of Australian sovereignty over Australia's Antarctic Territory. At a claimants' meeting held in Canberra at the end of August an Australian official (from the Treasury) proposed that there should be a single Regulatory Committee for the whole regime on which all claimants should be represented, with rotating membership for non-claimants.[30]

The Australian view of sovereignty was reflected in an Australian paper on revenue sharing. In this context revenue sharing meant provisions to ensure for claimants a special share of revenue from minerals exploitation, not—as in earlier New Zealand policy papers—the sharing of benefits with developing countries. Australia wanted claimants' rights in this regard to be specifically recognised in the regime.[31] The United Kingdom, on the other hand, considered that any extra benefits for a claimant state should be negotiated in the course of preparing the management scheme for an area within its territory.[32] New Zealand officials leant to the British view, telling the Australians in a letter from Keating that:

> We do not want the regime to provide artificial incentives or windfall profits to exploit Antarctic mineral resources. We feel therefore that tie real cost of production ought to be similar to that in other parts of the world where taxes are imposed on mining. Otherwise exploitation in Antarctica might be more rewarding to tile operator-than elsewhere.
>
> As to the allocation of revenue, as you know we have taken the view that a middle course needs to be steered between the claimants getting rights written into the regime, which is quite obviously unacceptable to the non-claimants . . . and the claimants getting

> no special rights in this respect in the regime. This middle course we see as being the 'institutional arrangement' which would have the effect of enabling the claimants to reach an accommodation on these financial aspects. The management scheme is just such a vehicle if the relevant claimant is given a major role in respect of its negotiation and can through it impose certain financial obligations on the operator. This will be possible by maintaining in the draft a distinction between the management scheme addressing in this regard both institutional costs as well as payments in the nature of taxes and royalties.
>
> I am not clear what the practical advantage would be of insisting that the regime state that this claimant advantage is based on its 'sovereignty' or on its 'management role'. While claimant rights clearly flow from our sovereignty, it may well be appropriate at the time a particular management scheme is being negotiated to call it whatever we wish so as to reach an acceptable deal with an operator whose sponsoring state may outrightly refuse to recognise an exercise of our sovereignty.[33]

The Australians were not at all convinced by this line of argument and by the following year it appeared that the British had veered round to the Australian point of view, joining with them in proposing the inclusion of an additional article in the regime to give claimant states a 'special' revenue share.

It may be noted in passing that while the officials involved in the negotiations were arguing about the financial benefits to be gained from minerals exploitation, ministerial opinion in New Zealand appeared to be veering in the direction of a regime which would have as its main objective the blocking of such activities in Antarctica. Commenting on a remark by the Associate Minister of Foreign Affairs (O'Flynn) at a Labour Party Conference that one of the prices of keeping the Antarctic Treaty intact was to allow some minerals exploration there, the Prime Minister said that that proposition

> begs the question of what constitutes a minerals regime. A minerals regime, you see, can consist of banning minerals exploitation.

Any regime which allowed any kind of exploitation, he added,

> would run straight into conflict with a great mass of world ecological opinion.[34]

The Minister for the Environment (Russell Marshall) told James Barnes, an American environmentalist, that New Zealand was attracted to the concept of a (separate) Antarctic Environmental Protection Agency 'of some type'.[35] This was done without interdepartmental consultation.

The session of the SCM held in Paris from 23 September to 4 October 1985 provided the first opportunity to judge the reaction of the Consultative Parties as a group to the acceptability of the 'package' approach to the solution of key issues. While the idea of a package was not rejected, it became evident that the Consultative Parties—ever conservative and jealous of their pre-eminent role in the development and control of the Antarctic system—were not prepared to go as far as the authors of the Rio package in sharing that role with the Non-Consultative Parties. In particular, they rejected the idea of giving a special meeting of all parties the responsibility for identifying and opening the areas in which resources activities might take place (even though each of the Consultative Parties would have a veto on its decisions). There was a strongly held view that the Consultative Parties should have the right to determine that an area should be opened, as well as that it should not. They were not prepared to have their collective will overruled by the Non-Consultative Parties in a way which did not meet the criterion for decision-making in the Antarctic Treaty. It seemed, therefore, that if the special meeting were to remain in the package it would do so on the basis that the views it might express would not be binding.

The composition of, and voting procedure in, the Regulatory Committees remained a major difficulty. The New Zealand delegation continued to believe that a solution which did not include a claimant veto on activity in the claimed area was a possibility, although agreement on an alternative means of satisfying claimant concerns in this regard would be a critical element in that solution.

Progress, the delegation reported, was made in other areas.

It seemed likely that agreement could be reached on the definition of prospecting. This would permit drilling (the most sensitive aspect) up to a depth of twenty-five metres only. This compromise was to survive into the final text.

A number of legal issues were explored in detail. On the question of liability for damage, it was 'reasonably common ground' that for pollution damage, an operator would be strictly liable and no proof of fault would be required. This was to prove optimistic. It was not possible to agree that liability should be unlimited, and the extent of any limits, the delegation foresaw, might need to be left open for consideration by the institutions to be established under the regime.

Another legal question was the procedure for disputes settlement. Because of 'the traditional Soviet position on compulsory dispute settlement' (i.e., non-acceptance) it was not possible to reach agreement. The delegation hoped, however, that in the end the Soviet Union would accept a compulsory third-party procedure, as they had at the Law of the Sea Conference.[36]

The delegation felt that agreement of a regime was within reach, requiring perhaps three more meetings. (This was a little optimistic too.) The next meeting was set for Hobart in April 1986. Before then, however, Beeby decided to try to speed things up by holding an informal meeting of key heads of delegation in New Zealand. These were the representatives of Argentina, Australia, Brazil, Chile, France, the United Kingdom and the United States. The meeting was convened in some secrecy (although word of it leaked to a New Zealand newspaper)[37] in a remote resort accessible only by boat. The participants in this meeting, which came to be known as the Whangaroa meeting, produced drafts and redrafts of a number of articles. These texts covered the SCM (now with an advisory role), the connected questions of wider participation in minerals activities through joint ventures and the method of resolving competing applications. A new paragraph in the article enumerating the functions of the commission would implicitly permit it to set up a fund that might be drawn on by developing countries. A new article assumed that parties to the regime would be required to have acceded to the Antarctic Treaty. On the topic of 'stages of activity' (prospecting, exploration and development or exploitation) discussion was confined to prospecting, with Australia and the United States unable to reach complete agreement. It was acknowledged by the participants that if the timetable for completing the negotiations—the next meeting at Hobart plus two more—was to be met, a further revision of MR/17 would need to be issued after the Hobart meeting.[38]

The participants, however, did not include the Soviet Union[39] and at the Hobart meeting the Soviet representative refused to agree to the production of another revision of the Chairman's text for consideration at the next session. This may have been, as the New Zealand delegation thought, because the Soviet Union wished to retain as many bargaining chips as possible to the very end of the negotiations; but it may also have been that the Soviet Union was determined to have a voice in any further intersessional consultations among an inner group before a new text was permitted to emerge. Thus, although there was a 'new sense of urgency' at Hobart, the actual progress achieved in terms of firm agreements was disappointing. On the one hand the United States took, if anything, a harder line in opposition to the demands of the claimants. Its fundamental objective was to ensure that the regime was workable, that there was sufficient certainty about the rules to enable operators to make sensible decisions and that projects were not subject to unpredictable blockages. The claimants on the other hand were insistent that to achieve their aim of a major say over mineral activities in their respective territories there must be 'decision points' in the progression of those activities at which they would have a real chance to protect what they regarded as their interests—whether economic or environmental. While the claimants felt the need for more effective intersessional coordination within their own group, the achievement of this objective was made more difficult by the attitude of France, which on many issues tended to adopt the position of a potential sponsor of mining activities rather than that of a claimant. (This no doubt reflected the relatively small size of the French territory and the unlikelihood of exploitable mineral resources being found there.) The claimants' position was not made easier by the unrealistic expectations among some of them, including Australia and the United Kingdom, of the economic returns that might be exacted by them from mining operations on their claimed territories. The issues of the functions and decision-making rules of the Regulatory Committees, and the unspecified 'additional elements' envisaged in the Rio package, therefore remained of central importance to the claimants and in the delegation's view would require further work to permit the preparation of a text to take a further step forward. The next meeting was fixed for October 1986 in Tokyo, with the possibility of a further session in Montevideo before the final meeting which the delegation expected to be held in Wellington.[40] Meanwhile, the Chairman organised a further round of informal consultations among a limited group, this time including a Russian.

During 1986 a growing belief that, despite the failure of a revised text to emerge at Hobart, the end of the negotiating process was not far off led to increasing internal tensions in a number of the participating states, not excluding New Zealand. The Director-General of the Department of Scientific Research wrote to his Foreign Affairs counterpart complaining that his department had been left out of the negotiations for the previous two years.[41] (It was pointed out to him that in the past his staff had flagged away the opportunity, pleading lack of personnel and travel funds.)[42] The opposition of environmental groups grew in intensity: whereas initially their aim had seemed to be to secure watertight environmental safeguards in a minerals regime, it was now clearly to derail the negotiations and substitute a total and permanent ban on minerals development in Antarctica. The representative of the non-governmental organisations in the New Zealand delegation at Hobart, Alistair Graham, who had also attended previous sessions as a member of the New Zealand delegation, in each case on condition of confidentiality, produced a report (paid for by the Commission for the Environment) which Beeby described to the Commissioner (Ken Piddington) as defective in judgment and in its language abusive and verging on defamatory.[43] This contrasted with Graham's relatively cooperative behaviour at earlier sessions. Beeby raised the question with Piddington, and subsequently with Ministers, as to whether Graham could be regarded as a fit member of future delegations. It was eventually decided, but only after a discussion involving three Ministers, that he should be included in the delegation to the Tokyo meeting, with what amounted to a formal warning to abide by the conditions under which he was appointed.[44]

Media reports were along the lines of one on television that New Zealand diplomats were masterminding an agreement that would clear the way for the exploitation of oil and gas reserves in Antarctica.[45] In Parliament, Helen Clark asked whether the report was accurate. The Deputy Minister of Foreign Affairs (O'Flynn) replied:

> The statement was a complete distortion of the nature of the negotiations that were undertaken. The facts of the position are exactly the opposite.

The second sentence was perhaps an unfortunate embellishment, since it permitted an Opposition MP (Muldoon) to ask whether this meant that someone else was masterminding the agreement, or alternatively that there was to be no exploitation whatever. The Minister, skirting round both alternatives, said that New Zealand's aim was to put in place institutions and machinery to control mining activity, and to lay down effective environmental protection measures.[46] On behalf of ASOC, after being given a summary of the New Zealand brief for the Tokyo meeting, Cath Wallace wrote to the Prime Minister complaining that ASOC had not been consulted in its preparation; that it contained no mention of a New Zealand move to a fifty year moratorium, nor any hint that Beeby had been persuaded to 'slacken the rush to conclude the regime'. The Prime Minister's reply was terse: he resented the implication that the Government was rushing recklessly to conclude a regime. Wallace, he said, knew very well the reasons why the Government did not think a moratorium was a feasible or realistic alternative, and he did not intend to repeat them. As to consultation, given the pressures people were working under, her demands were unreasonable.[47]

That there were internal tensions in other participating countries became evident when Beeby summoned the 'select' group to Whangaroa for the second time. On this occasion those invited were representatives of Argentina, Brazil, Chile, the Federal Republic of Germany, India, Norway, the Soviet Union, the United Kingdom and the United States. (Australia and France, which had attended the first Whangaroa meeting, were separately advised of the outcome.) Only one person was invited from each country, but on this occasion some of the invitees sought permission to bring another delegation member with them. The German representative wanted to bring a representative from the Economics Ministry.[48] The American representative had a worse problem, since even within the State Department there was rivalry between the legal and economic bureaux, each claiming a better case to accompany him; so his proposed 'delegation' numbered three.[49]

The United Kingdom for its part had substantive worries about the trend of the negotiations. British Ministers were evidently taking a hard line (or British officials were so representing them for tactical reasons). British officials said they understood why the developing countries and the Soviet Union wanted to be able to participate in mining operations but 'the idea that they had the right to do so even if mining companies did not want them was anathema to the British Government'. This view, they went on, was shared by France, the Federal Republic of Germany, Italy and Japan but not, seemingly, by the United States. The British position had hardened since Hobart in the face of the emerging trend. They were worried also that when the claimants had sought preferential treatment in regard to benefits, the United States and other non-claimants had met their demand with a flat negative. It was 'inconceivable' that British Ministers would agree to a regime which treated developing countries more favourably than claimants.[50]

The most significant outcome from the Whangaroa meeting in September was an indication from the Soviet representative that his country would no longer stand in the way, as it had at Hobart, of a further revision of MR/17. Beeby therefore lost no time in whipping out the second revision, in time to be circulated at a claimants' meeting held in Santiago in September 1986.[51] (It is perhaps indicative of the relative importance attached by New Zealand to the claimants' meetings that by contrast to other claimants, it was represented at this meeting by a junior member of the Embassy staff in Santiago: New Zealand's concerns were sufficiently removed from those of the hard-line claimants that its representative could be given a 'watching brief'.)[52] In the new revision, Beeby had another go, on the basis of the discussions at Whangaroa, at producing articles on the composition of the Regulatory Committees and their voting procedure that would meet all the competing demands. Not surprisingly, this resulted in a further increasing the size of the Committees. Among the changes, the United States and the Soviet Union were described as the two states which had had 'the largest presence' in the Antarctica at the time the Antarctic Treaty entered into force. The claimant state asserting sovereignty in the relevant area was now to have the support of four other claimant states, and the Chairman of the Commission was to choose four non-claimants to serve on the committee. In regard to both claimant and non-claimant members, care was to be taken to include some states which had made a substantial contribution of relevant scientific and environmental information, and some developing states. (If the area in question was not the subject of a territorial claim, all eight states were to be selected by the Chairman of the Commission.) It will be seen that the basic membership of a Regulatory Committee would informally be eleven, of whom six would be non-claimant states. However, if the state sponsoring an application for an exploration permit was not one of the eleven, it would be added to the membership of the Committee for the purpose of dealing with its application and setting up a management scheme. Thus the Committee was likely to have a majority of non-claimants. However, in voting to designate a member to present a draft management scheme, and in approving that scheme, the simple minority must include both the state claiming the area in question and the sponsoring state: in other words, a two-way veto.

This proposal was not good enough for the Federal Republic of Germany, which thought that under these criteria it would find it difficult to secure membership, and complained that there was still an imbalance between claimant (seven) and non-claimant (eleven) Consultative Parties. But the question of securing a decisive voice (at least in the negative sense) in relation to the management of activities in areas over which they had sovereignty was a *sine qua non* for the willingness of the claimants to accept a minerals regime.[53]

The Chairman, in his introduction to the revised text, suggested that it might be necessary to make provision for preparatory work on a management scheme to be done initially in a relatively small sub-committee of the Regulatory Committee. This proposal could be justified on technical grounds but, perhaps more importantly, was desired by the claimants as one of the 'additional elements' foreshadowed in the Rio package. Equally, it was opposed by the Americans and Germans and did not appear in the revised or subsequent text.

The articles relating to participation in minerals activities were revised to meet Soviet and developing country desires that technologically advanced nations be encouraged to include them in minerals activities—a notion to which, as already mentioned, the United Kingdom for one had strong objections. The Special Meeting was another device to give Non-Consultative Parties a role in the regime, but as this concept emerged in the draft, their role would stop short of a decision-making function.

This revision did, however, contain a provision for dealing with competing applications to explore and develop the same block in a given area which at least gave a sympathetic nod in the direction of developing country interests. It directed the Regulatory Committee in question to determine a method for resolving competing applications which should give 'priority for the application with the broadest participation among interested parties which were Antarctic Treaty Consultative Parties, and other interested parties, in particular, developing countries in either category'. This provision survived into the final text of the Convention, modified only by a requirement that the competing applicants should first seek to resolve the competition among themselves.

The aspiration of some claimants, in particular Australia, for a special share of revenues from mining activities in their territories was not mentioned by the Chairman in his introduction to the revised text. The 'watching brief' for the New Zealand representative at the claimants' meeting in Santiago acknowledged that this was an important proposal, which New Zealand supported, but told him that for tactical reasons it would prefer 'general but firm' wording rather than an explicit reference to the special share. At the claimants' meeting, most participants, rather than seeking a reference to a specific percentage share, also favoured the inclusion of a more general reference, or peg, to be used in negotiating the claimant's revenue share after the 'convention' had come into force.[54] (Revision two of MR/17 was the first of the Chairman's drafts to carry the heading 'Antarctic Mineral Resources Convention: Draft Articles'.)

The New Zealand delegation to the second Tokyo session of the SCM, which opened on 27 October 1986, included representatives of the DSIR, Energy and Environment, as well as an NGO representative.[55] It was equipped with a brief on environmental issues which had been prepared jointly with the Commission on the Environment. By seeking to flesh out the relevant provisions of the draft Convention, it was hoped to satisfy the insistence of both the Ministers and the non-governmental organisations concerned with environmental matters that the Convention must include adequate protective measures. After discussing the contents of the brief with Cath Wallace and other ASOC representatives, officials expressed optimism that she had been 'surprised by the degree of coincidence between her views and much of the material contained in the brief'. However, as already mentioned, the aims of ASOC now extended well beyond the inclusion of adequate environmental provisions in a minerals convention.

The proposals in the brief included a strengthening of the

role of the Advisory Committee, including the publication of its reports. The delegation was directed to seek to insert in the Convention more detailed provisions for monitoring and inspection. There should be a requirement for sponsoring states to report regularly to the Advisory Committee, the Regulatory Committee and the Commission. The monitoring process should 'include repetitive measurements of key environmental parameters or phenomena to test for and document any environmental change'. Management schemes should be publicised. The function of monitoring should be not only to detect and deter non-compliance but also to facilitate a review of exploration and development whenever the relevant institutions considered this to be justified by the information they were receiving. In addition to the inspection system provided for in the Antarctic Treaty (which should be preserved) there should be a separate and comprehensive inspection system for the minerals regime. Liability for damage should be unlimited.[56]

At the end of the Tokyo meeting, the delegation was cautious in its report of this area of the negotiations. Progress has been made in terms of New Zealand's objectives; but New Zealand was out in rolling on environmental issues. The Australian delegation placed much greater weight on the economic aspects and was not prepared to spend much of its negotiating capital in support of New Zealand's environmental stand; and most of the other Consultative Parties felt similarly constrained, for a variety of reasons. While things were moving generally in the direction indicated in the delegation's brief there was important work still to be accomplished in regard to the environmental input into decision-making at various key points:

(a) examination of the initial exploration application;
(b) examination of a management scheme for exploration, with a clear right to decline an environmentally unsound scheme; and
(c) similarly, at the development stage.

New Zealand's proposals had been articulated, but the delegation saw a need for effective lobbying at the next meeting if they were to succeed. On the technical aspects of exploration and mining the New Zealand voice had been virtually alone against the operator-oriented expertise in the British, German, American and French delegations.[57] In his separate report, the New Zealand representative from the Commission for the Environment (Harry Keys) commented on the fact that texts agreed by representatives in the Environmental Impact Assessment group consistently failed to secure endorsement from their delegations: 'when New Zealand spoke . . . in the main contact group the other delegations, particularly Australia, failed to support us'.[58]

On legal issues, progress had been made towards a text on liability for damage that would meet New Zealand's desire for it to be unlimited: but important subsidiary issues remained. There were good prospects for eventual agreement on a compulsory procedure for the settlement of disputes.

On the 'key issues' of the Special Meeting—participation in mining ventures and membership of the Regulatory Committee—progress was limited. On the first issue, it was clear that a decision-making role for the Special Meeting was not acceptable to the Consultative Parties, and the German Democratic Republic suggested as a compromise that it be given the power to make recommendations, rather than simply offer advice. (Even this was in the end to be too much for the Consultative Parties.) A feature of the discussion on the other two issues was the forceful approach of both the developing countries and the Soviet Union in defence of the provision in MR/17 Rev 2 on participation. The New Zealand delegation saw this as a tactical reaction to the hardened position of the United Kingdom, supported by Japan. The concerned caucusing of the developing countries was a new feature which, the delegation observed, was not going to make it any easier to agree on the final package.

The delegation's report revealed some nervousness—not only on New Zealand's part—that the appetite for unravelling existing accommodations would only grow the longer the negotiations dragged on. There was some disposition to set a cut-off date for concluding them, but in the end the decision to hold the final session in New Zealand was made subject to confirmation at the next meeting, to be held in Uruguay in May 1987. Meanwhile, there would be a third Whangaroa meeting in March to work on technical, environmental and legal issues, with a view to a further revision of the Chairman's text.

These two meetings were preceded, as was customary, by a meeting of claimants which convened in Canberra on 17 March, with a wide-ranging agenda that included an Australian–British proposal to include in the Convention provision for a special share of revenue for claimant states.[59] While there is no record of the line taken on this proposal by the New Zealand delegation at the claimants' meeting, its tenor may be deduced from a file note written by Beeby shortly before.

In his note Beeby recorded the strong criticism of their proposal that he had registered with the British and Australian representatives during the Tokyo meeting. There was no dispute, he had told them, with the proposition that the claimants should aim to get as much as possible in the way of revenue from Antarctic mineral activities, paralleling what they could expect to get in areas of undisputed sovereignty outside Antarctica. It was equally obvious that there must be nothing in the regime calling in question the right of claimants to get revenues from activities in their claimed areas. The Beeby drafts, however, left the issue of the share of the revenue for each relevant claimant to be negotiated in the preparation and approval of a management scheme: they neither asserted nor called into question special claimant rights in relation to other issues to be negotiated in the management scheme. Australia and the United Kingdom, in the proposal they were now putting forward for a separate article on claimants' rights to a special share of net revenue, were reverting to an approach which had got nowhere in Wellington in 1982, and in 1983 and had been overtaken by MR/17. Their proposal had even less prospect of succeeding in 1987. This was not simply because there was no claimant unity on the proposal—although New Zealand and some others had grave doubts about the wisdom of presenting a text which showed on its face that the claimants had abandoned an important aspect of their claim to sovereignty. Apart from that all the non-claimants would be quite unwilling, as they had been all along, to give overt recognition to substantive rights for claimants, as distinct from conceding them certain procedural advantages which they could exploit at the time of the negotiation of the management scheme. Undoubtedly pressing the proposal would lead *developing* non-claimants to counter it with proposals spelling out special rights to net revenues for *them*. The more Australia and the United Kingdom pushed it the worse the counter-proposals would get.

Beeby noted that the British seemed to take the point but the Australians were relatively unmoved. Far from conceding that he was right, they talked about an elaboration of the proposal which would provide a certain percentage of net revenue for all members of the Commission, a certain percentage for members of the Regulatory Committee and a certain, very large percentage for the relevant claimant. This suggested to Beeby that they were even further into cloud-cuckoo-land than he had thought.[60]

That Beeby's fears had not been groundless was shown by a paper circulated by Australia to the participants in the claimants' meeting. This was by any criterion a remarkable document. It argued that the proposal for an article reserving a special share of net revenue for claimants (which proposal, according to the paper, had the support of all claimants subject to 'some reservations on the part of New Zealand and Norway') did not in fact go far enough. Claimants had been unable to agree whether the article should be worded in general language, for example, 'a special and substantial share', as a peg to be used in negotiations *after* claimants had joined the Convention, or alternatively, the inclusion in the Convention of a specific percentage to be negotiated before claimants decided to join. Australia regarded the first alternative as unsatisfactory. For example, a 3 per cent share would be 'special' and might well be 'substantial' in absolute terms but 'would, of course, fall well short of claimant ambitions'. Elsewhere in the paper a share of 5 per cent was similarly disparaged. Australia and the United Kingdom had put forward in Tokyo the proposition that all revenue accruing to the Commission and surplus to the requirements for financing the operation of the Convention should go to the claimants. This would recognise their sovereignty claims, the 'considerable derogation from that sovereignty inherent for practical purposes in the existence of the Convention', and their special management responsibilities. To the argument that reference to a specific percentage share of revenue would increase the opposition of non-claimants to any reference to a special share, the paper suggested that claimants ask themselves not whether non-claimants could accept such a proposition but whether claimants could accept anything less. The negotiations, it asserted, had seen an erosion of the claimant position on decision-making and management, and the share of revenue would be the only special economic benefit the claimants would receive in return for the derogation of their sovereignty and the imposition on them of special responsibilities. Claimants were *entitled* to a precise and unambiguous answer from non-claimants on this issue before they decided whether or not to accept the Convention.[61]

At the third Whangaroa meeting, held from 21 to 27 March, the participants from the previous meeting were joined by representatives of Australia, China, France, Japan and Uruguay. It was proposed to concentrate this time on 'non-key issues', including the area of application of the Convention, the question of who might participate in mineral resource activities (in effect, the definitions of the terms 'sponsoring state' and 'operator') and the final clauses. The description of these as 'non-key' issues did not of course mean that they were non-controversial. Beeby noted in his letter of invitation, with which he included drafts of the final clauses, that in preparing them he had proceeded on certain assumptions: that the Consultative Parties alone would participate in the decision to adopt a convention, that the Convention would be open for signature to all the participants in the SCM, and that there would be 'some role' for the Non-Consultative Parties in the article dealing with the entry into force of the Convention. Beeby remarked, prophetically, that there were many possible variations on that article in particular.[62]

The Whangaroa meeting did not produce a more widely acceptable article on the area of application of the Convention. On the other hand, Beeby was able to insert in the definitions article MR/17 Rev 3 (which he circulated within a few days of the conclusion of the meeting)[63] definitions of the terms 'sponsoring state' and 'operator', which were close to those finally adopted. For the first time, an article on liability for damage was included in the new revision, although it was to undergo much subsequent elaboration. For the first time also, two articles on dispute settlement were included in the draft Convention. One of these provided for reference of disputes to either the International Court or to an arbitral tribunal to be set up under the Convention. The crucial question of whether such reference should be compulsory or by consent of all parties was not resolved. The other article provided for a special procedure for summary settlement of disputes concerning a breach or threat of a breach of the provisions of the Convention dealing with the protection of the environment.

The draft final clauses on signature and entry into force, prepared by Beeby for discussion at Whangaroa, appeared unchanged in the third revision. Characteristically, however, the participants did not accept his suggestion that the Non-Consultative Parties should have 'some role' in bringing the Convention into force; in the third revision, entry into force was to be effected by the ratifications of a number, yet to be fixed, of Consultative Parties alone. It was decided that reservations should not be permitted. Beeby's original draft on amendments was altered to provide that no amendment should be considered until a period of years (later fixed at ten) after entry of the Convention into force. The provisions regarding withdrawal remained substantially as Beeby had proposed them pre-Whangaroa. (They had been based on an earlier report prepared under the chairmanship of a German delegate, Rüdiger Wolfrum.)

The Montevideo session moved the negotiations forward to the point where it was possible publicly to announce that a final meeting to conclude a Convention would be held in Wellington in the first half of 1988.[64] One key issue—the composition of the Regulatory Committee—was virtually settled. Attempts by the four developing non-claimant countries and by the Federal Republic of Germany and Japan to improve their chances of securing membership by increasing the size of the Committee were firmly resisted by the claimants and others. The size of the Committee was to remain at ten so members—four claimants and six non-claimants, including the United States and the Soviet Union—and although the method of selection was to be modified subsequently, no further change was made to the Committees' composition in later revisions. On the question of the need for a technical sub-committee of Regulatory Committees to draw up management schemes—a provision desired by the claimants but opposed by industrialised countries—the delegation reported, more optimistically than later proved justified, that Beeby had found the middle ground in the form of a draft article. It provided that a sub-committee was to be established unless the Regulatory Committee provided otherwise, and that its role would be to assist the Regulatory Committee in carrying out its functions, and that the Regulatory Committee should take full account of the sub-committee's work. This draft did not, however, find a place in the next revision. On the question of the powers of the next Special Meeting, the Consultative Parties were prepared to make only a minor concession to the Non-Consultative Parties. Beeby indicated at the final plenary that he was, in effect, unhappy with this outcome and that he felt more could be done to meet the wish of the Non-Consultative Parties and that this body should have an effective role.[65]

Beeby reported to his Minister that New Zealand had

> played a prominent role in advocating improvements to the text from an environmental/conservation perspective. The Montevideo meeting was probably the last effective opportunity to turn around some of the provisions which the environmentalists have opposed. By and large our initiative seems to have been successful. Certainly the NGOs have expressed privately their pleasure at what has been achieved. It remains to be seen whether this will be reflected in any meaningful way in their public statements.[66]

'Good,' minuted Lange. The hope for public demonstrations of pleasure by the New Zealand environmental lobbyists was not, however, to be realised.

To understand Beeby's comment about the New Zealand

initiative, it is necessary to go back to the second revision of MR/17 and in particular to the articles setting out the functions of the Advisory Committee and its role in the examination of applications. Those drafts in effect transformed the Advisory Committee into a decision-making body. The article dealing with the examination of applications by the Regulatory Committee provided that:

> In the event that the Advisory Committee advises that the application, if approved, would involve an unacceptable risk to the environment, the Regulatory Committee shall either:
>
> (a) reject the application, or
> (b) refer the application to the Commission which may by [ ] authorise the Regulatory Committee to proceed with the application subject to such conditions as it sees fit.'

At the Tokyo meeting, this provision was redrafted in a way that went too far in the other direction and threatened to leave the Advisory Committee as no more than a provider of information that may or may not be heeded by the Regulatory Committee. At Montevideo, the New Zealand delegation 'made its strongest pitch' to get the balance readjusted so as to ensure that the Advisory Committee's advice was given due weight in the Regulatory Committee's deliberations. In particular, it argued that the relevant article should:

> (a) enable the Advisory Committee to request more information;
> (b) state that the Advisory Committee's report would be publicly available; and
> (c) ensure that if the Advisory Committee advised that an application could have adverse consequences for the environment, the Regulatory Committee must either decline the application or at least defer a decision for a set period.[67]

A redraft was duly produced at Montevideo which provided that:

> . . . taking full account of the advice of the Advisory Committee, the Regulatory Committee shall make the judgements called for in Article 4 [the Article setting out the environmental criteria for allowing mineral resource activities]. In the event that such

> judgements are affirmative it shall proceed with the preparation of a Management Scheme . . . otherwise it shall decline the application.[68]

The delegation felt that this text took account of the concerns it had expressed. An environmentalist critic might, however, have considered that this language, which was not in any case agreed, went part-way only towards restoring the role of the Advisory Committee as set out in MR/17 Rev 2, and—despite the requirement to take 'full account' of the advice of the Advisory Committee—left it to the Regulatory Committee in the last resort to take the decision on acceptance or rejection of a mining application. That this was in fact the official New Zealand view was subsequently clarified in a commentary sent to the Deputy Prime Minister (Palmer) by the Foreign Minister (Marshall) on a letter from a correspondent concerned about the environmental provisions in the draft Convention, who had advocated giving the Advisory Committee a decision-making role. Marshall commented that:

> All Treaty Parties including New Zealand accept that the Advisory Committee must stick to its advisory role. The reason is simple enough. If the Committee were to have a decision-making role, its decisions would eventually become politicised. It would in effect lost its objectivity. We want to be sure that the Committee is free to give the best scientific and technical advice possible in order to provide an appropriate basis for responsible decisions to be made by the Regulatory Committee. Moreover, the New Zealand delegation has been working very hard to ensure that negative advice from the Advisory Committee cannot lightly be put aside by the Regulatory Committee.[69]

The redraft already quoted was produced in consultation among the New Zealand, Australian, British and American delegations. But although the actual drafting was done by a British representative (Heap) the New Zealand delegation was concerned that the United Kingdom was most reluctant to accord much of a role to the Advisory Committee.[70] (This did not prevent Heap from producing a series of revisions at a later meeting, and a still further strengthened draft of this Article survived substantially into the final text of the Convention [Article 26], which in paragraph 4 sets out an environmental impact procedure.)[71]

Much work was done at this session on legal issues, including the difficult question of liability for environmental damage. The main areas of disagreement were: whether there could be limits or defences to strict liability; whether the liability should extend to the sponsoring state and to the members of the regime as a whole if the operator's resources were insufficient to cover the damage; and whether the liability should cover all phases of minerals activities, or should exclude the prospecting phase. New Zealand and other claimants argued for broad coverage, and the United States, Japan and the Federal Republic of Germany, potential sponsoring states, sought to restrict it. The most difficult issue was the question of residual liability in the event of catastrophic damage to the environment. The potential sponsors resisted the position of Argentina and Chile that sponsors should have a direct responsibility to make good damage that operators could not meet, and proposed instead that in that event recourse should be had to a special fund set up by the Commission. On this issue there was a split among the claimants, with Australia and New Zealand supporting the concept that members of the Commission should accept the ultimate liability (this concept had been embodied in the third revision of MR/17) and the Latin American claimants opposing it. This issue was left over for resolution in the next round of discussions, but in the end had to be left out of the Convention for later settlement in a separate protocol.

On the question of dispute settlement, the main point of contention concerned the question whether an operator, or a sponsoring state on behalf of an operator, could take the institutions of the regime to arbitration. In particular, the Germans and Japanese wanted the right to take a Regulatory Committee before an arbitration panel in the event of its misapplying the principles of the regime. No agreement could be reached, and in fact the compulsory dispute settlement provisions in the Convention apply to parties only. The creation of a procedure to permit proceedings against a Regulatory

Committee was left as a task for the Commission.

While most of the text of the final clauses in MR/17 Rev 3 was accepted, no agreement was reached on the number of parties required to bring the Convention into force. Some wanted a straightforward high majority, some a qualified majority including all the claimants and perhaps the superpowers, and some a majority that included all the Consultative Parties.

Despite the progress made, the Chairman in his final statement at Montevideo acknowledged that there was much work to be done, listing no less than fifteen topics on which finality had yet to be reached. Nevertheless he secured agreement that after a further revision of the text and the establishment of a drafting committee, a final two-part meeting should be held in New Zealand to finalise the text and formally adopt it. On the question of the rules for its adoption, he made the following statement:

> It would need to be clearly understood . . . that the rules of procedure would be those applicable to all Consultative Meetings, whether regular or special, on the understanding that the rule [23] relating to the adoption of recommendations and requiring the approval of representatives of all the Consultative Parties present would apply to the adoption of the Convention on Antarctic Minerals.
>
> I understand from my consultations that some Non-Consultative Parties would prefer a different arrangement. By way of reassurance to those delegations, I should point out that the rules of procedure which underlie all Antarctic Treaty meetings have, in my experience, been very rarely appealed to or formally applied. There is also a distinction to be made between the legal rule relating to the adoption of a convention and the political imperative that is undoubtedly relevant to that act. I believe it is widely understood and accepted on all sides that the major purpose of our negotiations on Antarctic Minerals is to support and strengthen the Antarctic Treaty in the Antarctic Treaty system. That was spelt out clearly in Recommendation XI. It is also acknowledged in the Preamble to our text and stated very firmly indeed in Article 2 of the text. If we are to achieve that highly desirable goal of supporting and strengthening the Antarctic Treaty it is important that we produce a convention that is acceptable to all the parties to the Antarctic

> Treaty. I have no doubt that that judgment is accepted by all delegations here and it will certainly continue to guide me as chairman. The final point I would make on this matter is that I envisage that as we move to the stage of adoption of a convention arrangements should be made to allow all delegations, on the basis of equality, to have an ample opportunity to make their views known about the final package and to consider the need for any adjustments in the Convention before it is formally adopted. I would hope that these arrangements, which would seem to require a pause before the final adoption of the Convention, would be regarded as satisfactory to all.[72]

In New Zealand the prospect that the negotiations might soon be successfully concluded was received by ASOC not with satisfaction but with alarm. Papers were prepared for a combined meeting of the Environment and Foreign Affairs Committees of the Government caucus, which charged the New Zealand diplomats engaged in the negotiations with secrecy, haste and an unworthy desire to conclude an inadequate convention in order to establish the headquarters of the regime in New Zealand.[73] The Prime Minister annotated the papers with such comments as 'nonsense', 'ridiculous' and 'libellous'. He wrote to Helen Clark, who had chaired the meeting:

> I have had the benefit of a quick look at the papers and am annoyed at the extent to which they are off beam. Just one example. As you know there is no legislation relating to Antarctic minerals in the pipeline. That would come way down the track, well after the completion of the convention, when ratification was being considered. There is also a lot of exaggerated nonsense about secret meetings and imminent major policy decisions here in New Zealand. The fact is that Ministers established the major outline of New Zealand policy some time ago. We receive regular reports on progress and I am satisfied that things are progressing well in accordance with the guidelines we set. The hype from ASOC is unnecessary and its tone is unhelpful.[74]

Clark replied that Lange's irritation with Wallace and ASOC was largely shared by the Committee. The background document supplied by ASOC contained statements about Beeby which were probably defamatory, and other suggestions in the paper were quite off track. She had learnt from Simon Upton, the National Party spokesperson for the environment, that Wallace, having gained the impression that the members of the caucus committee were a little less than impressed with her presentation, had gone to him to urge that he become involved in the matter.[75]

Wallace had meanwhile written to Lange complaining that ASOC was 'disconcerted and disappointed' 'that Beeby had refused it a briefing on the negotiations prior to the Montevideo meeting in May. (ASOC had in fact had meetings with Lange and with officials on the question of consultation.) She indignantly rejected the suggestion by one official that, in arguing for further amendments to the draft Convention to strengthen its environmental provisions while at the same time calling for its replacement by a total prohibition on mining, ASOC's position was 'intellectually bankrupt'. ASOC's position, she said, was 'analogous to a passenger asking the driver of a dangerously speeding juggernaut to drive less dangerously while also pointing out that they are anyway headed in the wrong direction'.[76] Lange responded that:

> this Government is by far the most sympathetic you are going to find, not only here but anywhere in the world towards environmental protection issues in the context of the minerals negotiations. Furthermore I am satisfied that this is true of New Zealand officials. I do not accept that there is a cleft between the Ministry and myself on this matter.[77]

Before producing another draft for consideration at a full session of the SCM, Beeby followed what had become his customary practice of holding a preliminary consultation with a group of Consultative Party representatives. On this occasion all the Consultative Parties except Belgium, India and South Africa sent representatives to a meeting in Auckland in November 1987. The meeting lasted twelve days and some participants felt it necessary to send three or even four representatives. Things were heating up. Despite the range of issues discussed, Beeby was able to put out a new text, revision four of MR/17, within nine days of the end of the meeting.[78]

One issue that remained to be settled was the area to which the Convention should apply. The area covered by the Antarctic Treaty included a large expanse of high seas, south of 60°S. A part of the sea floor beneath the high seas within the Antarctic Treaty area is now defined by the LOS Treaty as the common heritage of mankind, subject to the provisions of the latter treaty that regulate seabed mining. The problem was therefore to draw a clear line between the land areas and continental shelves of the Antarctic continent and the common heritage area usually described (but not in the LOS Treaty) as the deep seabed. An additional complication in Antarctica was the presence of ice-shelves. An appropriate article therefore had to include its own definition of the deep-sea bed, which must however not conflict with the extremely complicated provisions in the LOS Treaty for drawing a boundary line between the continental shelf areas subject to national jurisdiction and the common heritage area. The draft article negotiated in Auckland, and reproduced in MR/17 Rev 4, made a gallant but clumsy effort to solve the problem. In doing so it treated the outer edge of ice-shelves as coastline for measurement purposes.[79]

There was further extensive discussion on the subject of liability for environmental damage. A definition of such damage was prepared for inclusion in the next revision. The principal article on liability was redrafted to impose strict liability on operators, except in the case of an unforeseeable act of God, armed conflict, or gross negligence by a third party. An additional paragraph was drafted by the Chairman providing for the later elaboration of rules and procedures regarding review of these three defences for the assessment of liability, and for the establishment of a fund to meet a situation where the full amount of damages could not be recovered from an operator. This fund could be financed by operators but underwritten, in the last resort, by members of the Commission. Provision might also be made for a limitation of liability in the case of loss or impairment of an established use of the Antarctic environment or its associated ecosystems, or loss of or damage to life or property: but in the case of damage to the Antarctic environment itself there would be no such limitation.[80] Beeby noted that there was as yet no agreement on the terms of this paragraph or indeed whether some of the issues it covered should be addressed at all. When these texts appeared in MR/17 Rev 4, Beeby noted that there was also no agreement as to whether the proposed elaboration should be in the form of measures adopted by the Commission or of a separate protocol, but that there was a trend in favour of the latter.

Beeby introduced successive drafts of the Article dealing with the procedure for the settlement of disputes between parties. Amendments by the Federal Republic of Germany and Japan designed to extend the settlement procedure to disputes between a party and the Commission or a Regulatory Committee, and between an operator and a Regulatory Committee, did not find their way into the fourth revision of MR/17.[81] The Statute of the Arbitral Tribunal, which would deal with disputes in terms of the Convention, did, however, appear for the first time as an annex to this text.

Beeby also introduced a new article providing for inspection of mineral resource activities by inspectors appointed individually by members of the Commission and also by the institutions established under the Convention. These inspection rights would be in addition to the existing inspection machinery in the Antarctic Treaty. Earlier drafts of MR/17 had provided that inspectors appointed in terms of the Antarctic Treaty should have access to mineral resource operations, and the Beeby draft retained this provision, so that mining sites and activities would effectively be subject to inspection from three sources. The new proposal was not sufficiently acceptable at the Auckland meeting to be included in the fourth revision.[82]

The Auckland meeting discussed what might best be described as the German problem, which had surfaced at earlier meetings. This amounted to an unwillingness, purportedly for constitutional reasons, to accept that a state would be obliged to give effect to decisions of the institutions of the Convention taken by majority vote when the state concerned had either opposed the decision or was not a member of the organ in question (i.e., a Regulatory

Committee.) Since no other participant saw this as a problem, the Federal Republic representative was told, in effect, that as this was a difficulty only for his country, it was up to the Federal Republic to find its own solution.[83]

Australia continued at this meeting to maintain its argument in favour of allocating to claimants the major share of surplus revenues, to be fixed as a specified percentage in the Convention. It also argued for the inclusion of an anti-subsidy article designed to prevent parties sponsoring mining activities from offering subsidies or incentives that might give an unfair competitive advantage to a party or an operator compared with other producers of the same mineral.[84] Neither proposal found its way into the fourth revision, nor did the Chairman feel it necessary to advert to them in his introductory speech.

The meeting discussed the wish of the prospective miners to have a small technical sub-committee of the Regulatory Committee to do the work of preparing a management scheme for the mining operation in question. The previous version of MR/17 had provided that the Regulatory Committee 'might' designate more than one member to present a draft management scheme. Claimants were generally opposed to a formalised technical sub-committee which might effectively make decisions adverse to their interests. The provision in the third revision of MR/17 was not changed in the fourth.[85]

At about the same time, the United Nations General Assembly resumed what had now become its annual debate on Antarctica. Its African members were particularly peeved that South Africa, which by now had been ejected from attendance at almost all United Nations and related conferences, was still taking a full part in meetings of the Consultative Parties. In 1985 and 1986 the Assembly had called for the 'racist apartheid regime of South Africa' to be excluded from meetings of the Consultative Parties, with a fine disregard for South Africa's legal rights under the Antarctic Treaty.[86] In 1987 the Assembly repeated this demand, and in addition urged Consultative Parties to invite the United Nations Secretary-General or his representative to all their meetings including the minerals negotiations. It also demanded that they impose a moratorium on the minerals negotiations 'until such time as all members of the international community can participate fully in such negotiations'.

Along with most of the other Consultative Parties, New Zealand did not participate in the vote on these unacceptable resolutions.[87] It took this position for the sake of maintaining a unified front on the part of the Consultative Parties, although non-participation went against New Zealand's general policy on voting in the United Nations. There were 44 'non-participants' on the substantive resolution, reflecting, as the New Zealand delegation reported, the 'strong and welcome sense of unity among the Antarctic Treaty parties', and also 'the sterile nature of a non-consensus approach to which so many, including major United Nations members of differing groups, are opposed'.[88] New Zealand had in fact no difficulty with the suggestion (which originated with the Australian Permanent Representative in New York) that the United Nations Secretary-General might be invited to attend meetings of the Antarctic Treaty Consultative Parties, but a number of the Consultative Parties (including Australia) were not in favour of it.[89] On second thoughts, moreover, New Zealand officials were concerned that the Secretary-General might not be treated with the degree of dignity and respect to which he was entitled: the treatment of observers at the Fourteenth Meeting of Consultative Parties—caused by the negative attitude of Argentina—had amounted to outright discourtesy.[90] The resolution eventually adopted in any case contained an unacceptable call for a moratorium on the negotiation of a minerals regime 'until such time as all members of the international community can participate fully in such negotiations'.

The session of the SCM held in Wellington in January 1988 made further attempts, and in some cases progress, towards settling the remaining troublesome issues.

The meeting had another go at defining the area to be covered by the Convention, an issue which seemed to present the legal draftsmen with dreadful difficulties. The solution adopted on this occasion, which duly appeared in revision five of MR/17, involved separating the component parts of the definition into three parts: a definition of 'deep sea-bed' in the definitions article; an article defining the area of application as covering the continent of Antarctica and all Antarctic islands south of 60° south, and the seabed and subsoil of adjacent offshore areas; and a second article excluding the deep seabed from the area. If this was not complicated enough, the definition provided for 'deep sea-bed' was, to say the least, obscure:

> 'Deep sea-bed' means with regard to the area south of 60° south latitude the sea-bed area seaward of the margin adjacent to the relevant land area or more than 200 nautical miles from its coast, including the ice front of ice shelves, if that distance is further from the coast or icefront.

As the Chairman remarked in his introduction to MR/17 Rev 5, the wording of these provisions required further refinement.[91]

The article concerning liability for damage was extensively redrafted, building on the provisions tentatively agreed upon at the Auckland consultations. The text in revision five was strengthened to provide that an operator should be responsible not merely to pay for damage to the environment, but should be required to take 'necessary and timely response action, including prevention, containment and clean up and removal measures', and also remedial action if its activities cause or threaten to cause environmental damage. The paragraph concerning provisions to be subsequently elaborated, which Beeby had tentatively included in revision four, was redrafted and retained. It was now accepted that a separate protocol would be required for this purpose, and that no application for an exploration or development permit could be made until the protocol was in force. The New Zealand delegation noted in its report of the meeting that environmental groups which had criticised the liability article had not grasped the fact that the possible limits and defences to an operator's liability would not affect its responsibility to restore damage to the environment, which was unqualified.[92]

It was also agreed that an article on inspection along the

lines drafted by Beeby during the Auckland consultations should be included in the Convention. At this session the United States dropped their insistence that inspections to ensure compliance with the minerals regime should be conducted by the Commission or subject to its control. Virtually all other participants accepted that the best deterrent to would-be violators was the possibility of an unannounced unilateral inspection by any member of the Commission. The article provided for inspection both by representatives of the Commission or a Regulatory Committee, and by individual Commission members. To satisfy the Americans, it also provided that inspections must not impose an undue burden on minerals activities.

On the question of dispute settlement, the remaining issue was largely one between the Federal Republic of Germany and the great majority of the other participants. The Federal Republic continued to push for a provision which would enable an operator to take a Regulatory Committee to dispute settlement on the grounds that it had acted contrary to the Convention in the negotiation of a management scheme. The Federal Republic failed to understand, according to the New Zealand delegation, that such a provision would negate the basic compromise between claimant and non-claimant positions embodied in the concept of the Regulatory Committee. The claimant position—that they must control minerals activities in their claimed areas—was reflected in the fact that they would have a major voice in Regulatory Committee decisions, particularly in the adaptation of management schemes. If an operator were able to challenge a Regulatory Committee decision in this area, it would make explicit in a way unacceptable to the claimants the notion that the Committee itself as an institution, rather than the claimants represented on it, controlled minerals activities in the claimed areas.

An alternative explanation for German stubbornness on this question might be that they understood very well the nature of the compromise embodied in the provisions relating to the Regulatory Committee, and were determined to shift the balance—which, as the New Zealand delegation's comments showed, tended to favour the claimant position—in the direction of the non-claimant and the operators they might sponsor. However, the Federal Republic seems to have become rather isolated on this issue, although it had received a measure of support from Japan (at Auckland), the Soviet Union and the German Democratic Republic. Other non-claimants such as the United States were said to be unhappy with the Federal Republic's proposal. They did not, the New Zealand delegation reported, accept that decisions of the institutions of the regime, which after all were states acting in a legislative capacity, might be challenged through dispute settlement procedures. This was particularly so with respect to the adoption of a management scheme which was, in essence, a politico-legal accommodation worked out among the states represented on the Regulatory Committee (or preferably, the delegation might have added, a small sub-committee of the Regulatory Committee). Dispute settlement procedures would in effect give to a single arbitrator the power to review and overturn such an accommodation. (The proposal does nevertheless seem more objectionable from the claimants' point of view, since it would provide a possible means of circumventing the claimants' blocking power in Regulatory Committees.)

Attempting to meet the Federal Republic part-way, the Chairman proposed a revised draft of the article in the Convention providing for review of management schemes by the Commission. This proposed that the Commission and, as appropriate, Regulatory Committees should establish procedures for the determination by the Arbitral Tribunal of disputes in which it was alleged that in adopting or rejecting a management scheme a violation of the Convention or an abuse of power had occurred.[93] This, the New Zealand delegation reported, was the maximum limit to which the claimant countries were prepared to go but the Federal Republic insisted on holding out for more. There was no chance that it would get what it wanted, and if there were to be a satisfactory outcome, it would need to be more flexible than it had been so far.

There was further discussion of the idea that provision be

made for the real work of preparing management schemes to be delegated by Regulatory Committees to much smaller groups. Claimants were disturbed, said the New Zealand delegation, at the extent to which the size of Regulatory Committees had grown in response to pressure from the developing countries and others to be represented. (In fact, the size of the Committees, normally ten members, had not been increased for some time.) The (putative) growth in membership would inevitably reduce the ability of the claimant countries to have a decisive say in deliberations on activities in their claimed sectors. From the environmental perspective, said the delegation, this meant that countries such as New Zealand would have less ability to ensure that the environmental principles of the regime were observed in any management scheme. At Wellington, the report went on, the claimant countries secured acceptance of the principle that while the Regulatory Committee as a whole must approve a management scheme, a smaller group of countries comprising the interested claimant and the sponsoring state had the responsibility of preparing the draft. The relevant article, it should be added, does not set up a formal sub-committee (as had earlier been envisaged) but in rather fuzzy language provides that the Regulatory Committee, in preparing a management scheme, 'shall have recourse' to the claimant state, the sponsoring state and, if required, an additional state.

Among the unresolved issues, finally, were the King Charles's Heads of the Australian delegation, of which there were two—revenue sharing and protection against subsidisation. The wish of Australia, with support from the United Kingdom, for a provision determining a special share of surplus revenues for claimants, has already been described. The New Zealand reaction to this proposal, a mixture of pragmatism and principle, was that on the one hand it would not be possible to get the non-claimants to agree to an explicit recognition of claimant rights in the text, and on the other that anything less than a right to 100 per cent of the surplus from activities in the Ross Dependency would amount to an unacceptable derogation of New Zealand's sovereignty. Another concern was that the Australian approach would encourage the stimulation of minerals activities by claimants in the hope of financial reward. New Zealand had always argued that the Convention must provide no incentives to carry out mining in Antarctica. The Australians showed little disposition at this meeting to moderate their approach.

The second Australian concern was the possibility that the Australian mining industry might face unfair competition from subsidised activities in Antarctica. Australian efforts to get an anti-subsidy provision written into the text had been opposed by the United States, who was not prepared to rule out the possibility of subsidised production in Antarctica, in the event that sources of or access to other supplies, particularly of strategic minerals, were to dry up. At Wellington the Australians held a seminar to explain their approach, but it was evident that they had not done enough to meet concerns about how their statement of principle would operate in practice.

During this meeting, a group of representatives chaired by Andersen of Norway undertook an article-by-article reading of the text. In the course of this exercise the New Zealand representatives introduced a number of verbal amendments designed to strengthen the environmental provisions: for example, references to 'wilderness values' in the articles dealing with environmental principles; amendments to the definitions of prospecting, exploration and development to ensure that logistic support was covered in the Convention; and a requirement in the chapter on prospecting requiring the removal of installations and site rehabilitation after the completion of a prospecting operation. A French proposal relating to the articles on observers would have excluded non-governmental organisations completely from attendance at meetings of the institutions of the regime. This initiative, which had been endorsed at the highest levels of the French Government, was thought to reflect their pre-occupation with and distaste for Greenpeace. There was much opposition to and little support for the French proposal. Even the Soviet representative, in what struck the New Zealand delegation at that time as a remarkable display of glasnost, said that Soviet public opinion would not understand it if NGOs were excluded from observing the work of the institutions.

At the end of the meeting, however, the main New Zealand concern was with the attitude of the Federal Republic of Germany. At the final plenary, it was agreed to maintain a May target date for the conclusion of the negotiations. This agreement was only forged after a lengthy meeting at which the Federal Republic, with some support from the Soviet Union and the German Democratic Republic, had argued that the possibility of carrying on beyond May should also be considered. This was strenuously opposed by the Americans, British, French, Chileans and Argentinians. A number of difficult issues remained to be resolved, however. The Federal Republic was acutely conscious that all Consultative Parties would have to agree to the adoption of the final text and it had given the occasional signal that it might be prepared to withhold its consent if its demands were not met. The New Zealand delegation did not, at this stage, register any particular concern about the attitude of Australia.

The worry about the Germans, however, was such that Beeby made a special visit to Bonn in March in an attempt to loosen up the rigidity of their position. He tried to demonstrate, he said afterwards, that it was simply not possible to reach a solution which any delegation would regard as fully satisfactory, and that each Consultative Party would have to ask itself whether it was better to have a treaty that was in some respects unsatisfactory, or no treaty at all. The German representative who had led the Federal Republic's delegation at the January session 'once again demonstrated the full range of his inability to understand or accept either proposition'. To New Zealand's relief, however, it was learnt that the Federal Republic's delegation to the May session would be led by a more senior diplomat, and that under his leadership the Federal Republic would join in a serious effort to reach successful conclusion at that session.[94]

The continuing Australian unhappiness with aspects of the draft Convention was highlighted in a letter circulated by the Australian Foreign Minister (Hayden) to the Foreign Ministers of the other Consultative Parties.[95] This was, it seems, the only occasion in which a participating government intervened directly in the negotiations at a political level with a view to influencing the positions of the other participating governments. In view of this and of Australia's later attitude to the Convention, the contents of the letter are of particular interest. It began by stressing Australia's important national interests in Antarctica, including security interests: in addition, Australia was 'one of the few countries in the world in which Antarctica is a matter of considerable domestic interest'. Australia was therefore a strong supporter of the Antarctic Treaty system and its evolutionary development, 'including the need to put into place a Convention to regulate any minerals resource activity'. Australia believed that the time had come to conclude the Convention:

> There have been intensive negotiations since 1982 which, in our view, have now fully canvassed all the major issues at stake and the early conclusion of these negotiations is now necessary in the interests of the standing of the Antarctic treaty system which continues to be under external challenge. Much progress has been made under the able chairmanship of Chris Beeby of New Zealand and the outstanding issues are well understood. What is required now is a serious commitment to negotiate a formal text in the context of the political and legal realities of Antarctica and the central position of the Antarctic Treaty. Any other approach will raise doubts in many countries about the seriousness of our common commitment to the Antarctic treaty system. We would hope therefore that all Consultative Parties are now at one in their commitment to work towards conclusion of a balanced convention in Wellington.

The letter then went on to explain Australia's remaining concerns about the draft. First, Australia regarded the protection of the environment as of high priority, and therefore sought further strengthening of the relevant provisions, including in particular those relating to liability for damage. The definition of damage needed refinement, especially with regard to the basic question of liability standards. The defences to liability, 'if there must be defences', were too broad, especially the defence of 'a violent act by a third party'. Nor was the treatment of residual liability adequate: it was important that participants be seen to shoulder responsibility for activities they authorised and regulated. The New Zealand Government did not take issue with Hayden: as Marshall said in his reply, there was widespread public support in New Zealand for environmental protection, and this was New Zealand's highest priority also.[96]

Hayden went on, however, to restate the financial demands which had so far failed to gain support (except in some degree from the United Kingdom). These included a provision recognising special economic benefits for claimant states, and a specific provision for a substantial share of net revenue deriving from mineral resource activity in Antarctica. Such provisions were 'essential to the striking of the appropriate balance between the interests of claimant and non-claimant states which lies at the root of the Antarctic Treaty system'. Furthermore, the role of the claimants in managing any minerals activity in Antarctica would place considerable burdens on them, and these should be taken care of in the financial provisions:

> Given that it deals with access to non-renewable resources, the Convention will inevitably contain elements which would not normally be seen as consistent with traditional notions of the exercise of territorial sovereignty. This reality has throughout been reluctantly recognised by the claimant states: but they need to have appropriate recognition from others for the apparent derogation from their sovereignty inherent for practical purposes in the existence of the Convention.

Another basic matter, according to Hayden, was:

> the need to ensure that any minerals development in Antarctica occurs only on the basis of market need and in accordance with sound commercial principles. The distortions resulting 'from non-commercial practices such as subsidisation are widely recognised as requiring elimination from a broad range of international economic activity. With this in mind and also recognising the need to ensure that the interests of existing minerals producers are not adversely affected by subsidised Antarctic minerals development, we believe it is necessary to include disciplines against subsidisation in an international agreement covering a potential new source of mineral production. Not to do so in the Antarctic Minerals

> Convention will raise problems for its external acceptability, given that a wide range of lion-parties to the Antarctic Treaty who produce minerals might see their interests as prejudiced. It could also raise questions as to the seriousness of Antarctic Treaty parties' commitment to environmental protection, as failure to include an effective anti-subsidy provision would indicate a shift in the direction of artificially encouraging mining. I would therefore urge all participants to recognise the need for an effective anti-subsidy provision in the Convention at Wellington.

Marshall acknowledged that the Australian and New Zealand delegations had differed on the question of a specifically identified economic benefit for claimant states. Both started from the same position that as claimant states Australia and New Zealand wanted a treaty that would enable them to receive an appropriate economic return from any future mining activity. The difference of approach related to means. One major concern was that once figures were being traded, the developing countries, the Soviet side and everyone else would want a slice of the action. That route led inexorably to equal shares and a convention under which everyone had a vested interest in granting approvals to mine. Such an outcome would result in the rejection of the convention by even moderate environmentalists and to an extremely hostile atmosphere at the United Nations. But even if that were not the case, New Zealand had always regarded a provision specifically identifying a rate of return for claimants as not negotiable. The claims were not recognised (by the non-claimants) and that degree of specificity would carry with it just too much prejudice to the other side's legal position: and to the extent that the provision was less than 100 per cent there was an equal prejudice to the claimants' position. Marshall was hopeful that the Australian position was tactical, and that they had appropriate fall-back positions, since there was only token support among the claimants for a hard line, and a general view that claimant economic interests could be secured by other means. This was, however, to underestimate Australian persistence.

In April, a paper was submitted to New Zealand Ministers which analysed the draft Convention in terms of the objectives which the Labour Cabinet had approved in December 1984, shortly after its accession to office.[97] The paper claimed that these objectives had been very substantially met in the draft, but outlined a number of additional points which the delegation believed should be pursued at the final session.

On the question of environmental safeguards, all exploration and development activities would be prohibited until positive decisions to permit them had been taken by the institutions set up under the Convention. While prospecting could proceed without prior authorisation, it was defined narrowly so as to exclude all activities that were not environmental benign. A prospector would require to be sponsored by a state party to the Convention and would be obliged to observe the strict environmental criteria set out in the Convention. Its performance would be guaranteed by the sponsoring state. No activities could be undertaken until information was available to permit the institutions of the Convention to assess whether its environmental standards had been met. Prospective operators would therefore have to disclose all relevant information if they were to get permission to go ahead. No activities could take place unless it had been judged that there would be no serious harm to the environment, that there were technology and procedures in place to provide for safe operations, and that there was a capacity to monitor environmental effects and respond to accidents. At each major decision point, a comprehensive environmental evaluation would be prepared. This would be assessed by the Advisory Committee, comprised of experts. Permission to go ahead with exploration and development would be granted in a detailed management scheme which would set out conditions consistent with the standards set by the Convention.

Minerals activities would be monitored by the Regulatory Committee which had negotiated the management scheme with the operator. The Advisory Committee would have an input into the monitoring process. There would be a comprehensive system of inspection, as already described. The threat of random unannounced inspection, backed by the threat of suspension or cancellation of the management scheme, should constitute a sufficient deterrent against malfeasance by operators.

One of the objectives set out in the 1984 Cabinet paper was that any decision to open up an area for exploration and development must be taken by consensus. This, the 1988 paper noted, had been agreed. The objectives of having areas of special sensitivity placed off-limits would also be met.

On the question of ensuring that the environmental review process was based on independent scientific advice that could not easily be overridden, the 1988 report was somewhat less unequivocal. It noted that the Advisory Committee, the environmental watchdog, was 'not formally' a decision-making body. This meant that it should be protected in some degree from the political considerations that might intrude into the deliberations of the Commission and the Regulatory Committees. But its advice must be taken into account by those bodies, and must be publicly available before major decisions were taken, and thus could not easily be ignored. If it was nevertheless arbitrarily ignored, there was the ultimate sanction of legal review in the form of arbitration. Perhaps not entirely convinced themselves, the authors of the paper added that the New Zealand delegation would be trying during the May session to have spelt out with greater clarity some of the roles that the Advisory Committee must play at key decision-making points.

Cabinet in 1984 had agreed that international organisations, both governmental and non-governmental, should have access to information before decisions were taken, and an opportunity for input into them. The draft Convention now provided for observers from international organisations to attend meetings of the Commission and the Advisory Committee and for NGO observers to attend the latter. Officials were reasonably confident that at the May meeting it would be agreed that NGOs could attend Commission meetings as well and that both international organisations and NGOs could attend some meetings of Regulatory Committees. (In the event, it was agreed that observers from both intergovernmental and non-governmental organisations could attend Commission and Advisory Committee meetings, and Special Consultative Meetings, at the discretion of the Commission. But no provision was made for attendance at Regulatory Committee meetings.)

It was an objective in the 1984 paper that New Zealand should receive an appropriate economic return from any exploitation in the Ross Dependency. In 1988 officials said that in their view it was not possible to secure an explicit recognition in the text of a claimant state's right to revenue from activities undertaken in its sector, because such recognition would compromise the fundamental legal position of the non-claimant states. The best way to secure such a benefit was in the negotiation of the management scheme. The New Zealand delegation had grave doubts, therefore, about the Australian proposal for a special share for claimants, especially when they had tried to sell it by offering the prospect that in return for recognition of claimants' rights, all countries might get a share in the benefits. This would be undesirable from the environmental viewpoint, in that it created an incentive for the approval of mineral activities. Officials hoped, optimistically, that Australia would be prepared to modify its position at the forthcoming meetings.

The 1984 paper contended that the agreement must be acceptable to the international community at large, and noted that one of several options under consideration was a system of revenue sharing for developing countries. It was not possible for officials to argue that this objective had been met. Surprisingly, they failed to mention to Ministers the continuing debates in the United Nations General Assembly on this issue. On the other hand, they were able to point to the growth in membership of the Antarctic Treaty during the six years the minerals negotiations had been under way, and in particular the accession to Consultative Party status of Brazil, China and India. It was therefore more difficult for 'outsiders' to argue that the Consultative Parties were an exclusive club trying to carve up the resources of Antarctica to the detriment of the wider international community. Nevertheless, officials believed that it was important the Convention should be defensible to, and demonstrably an instrument that took into account the interests of, that community. It was clear, however, that the United States,

United Kingdom and the Soviet Union were not prepared to contemplate the idea of revenue sharing for developing countries outside the Convention: they were prepared to offer some accommodation to enable a special share of revenue to be made available to developing countries that were party to the regime. Realistically, officials believed, nothing more could be achieved.

That, it must be admitted, was not much: especially as revision five of the draft Convention (and the final text) confined the allocation of funds for developing countries to those wishing to engage in scientific research in Antarctica. Undoubtedly among all the objectives set out in the 1984 paper, this was the one towards which the least progress had been made.

The final objective that Cabinet had accepted in 1984 was to have it agreed that the headquarters of any organisation established by the Convention should be located in New Zealand. While the draft Convention did not yet say so, officials considered that it was well understood by participants in the negotiations that the Secretariat and the Commission would be established in New Zealand, although this might be many years in the future. As had been discussed with Ministers, the most appropriate place for this headquarters would be Christchurch, New Zealand's gateway to Antarctica.

Officials told Ministers that there were a number of other points remaining to be settled, the most important of which was the question whether the requirement that operators should be liable for damage to the environment should extend without limit to its restoration and rehabilitation. Although it was mentioned that other environmental provisions could be strengthened by drafting changes, this paper did not mention other contentious issues that remained unsettled. These included the area to which the Convention would apply; the number of ratifications required to bring the Convention into force; the composition of the Regulatory Committees (the developing countries in particular were still dissatisfied with the representation); the voting procedure for decision-making in the Commission and the Regulatory Committees; the function of the Special Committee of Parties; the question whether budgetary contributions should be 'equal' or 'equitable'; the Australian proposal for an anti-subsidies article; and so on.

When the final session of the SCM convened in Wellington on 2 May 1988, the Chairman in fact had a list of eleven major issues, nineteen 'middling' issues, and thirteen minor issues which remained to be settled.[98] In this narrative I shall touch on only a few of the more difficult problems that were resolved in five weeks of intensive negotiations. The Chairman alone issued some 75 drafts (not counting revisions) and other documents relating to the text. For example, he produced six successive drafts on the question of *liability*. Article 7 of the Convention left 'further rules and procedures' to be negotiated subsequently in a separate protocol, including such knotty questions as the provision of moneys, for example through an operator-financed fund, to ensure that compensation for damage would in practice be available.

After many redrafts a definition of the area of application of the treaty was achieved which (with the assistance of an explanatory sentence in the Final Act) was consistent with the relevant provisions of the Law of the Sea Treaty.[99] The Article setting out the requirements for the entry of the Convention into force was radically revised during the course of the meeting. MR/17 Rev 5 had provided merely that it should enter into force after ratification by an unspecified number of the Consultative Parties who had participated in the final session of the Fourth Special Meeting. The text which was ultimately adopted (Article 62) set that number at sixteen, with the proviso that:

> that number includes all the States necessary in or to establish all of the institutions of the Convention in respect of every area of Antarctica, including the five developing countries and eleven developed countries.

The effect of this proviso was to ensure that the Convention would not enter into force until ratified by all the claimants, together with the United States and the Soviet Union, since the membership of the Regulatory Committees established in respect of each area was to include both the claimant state in respect of each area together with the two states that asserted a 'basis of claim'. In case this was not clear, the Final Act stated with respect to Article 62 that:

> the meeting agreed that all of the institutions of the Convention could not be established in respect of every area of Antarctica unless all the states referred in Article IV (1) (a) and (b) Antarctic Treaty and at least our states referred to in paragraph 1(c) of that Article were Parties to the Convention and that these included at least three development countries.

The process by which this text was arrived at is unclear. A draft was introduced by the Chairman to a small group (Australia, Argentina, Brazil, Chile, France, Japan, Norway, New Zealand, the Soviet Union, the United Kingdom and the United States) on Sunday 29 May. The notes taken of the meeting, which ran from 10 am to 11.30 pm, were sketchy, 'the note-taking being subject to frequent interruption'. At the end of the meeting, a revised draft was circulated, which corresponded to the final text except in one respect. At a further meeting on 31 May the required number of ratifications was reduced, on the motion of the United States, from seventeen to sixteen, and the number of developed countries within that number from twelve to eleven.[100]

After the marathon session of Chairman's consultations on 29 May, only a handful of particularly difficult problems remained. These were:

> (a) decision-making in the Regulatory Committees and the Commission;
> (b) the extent to which Regulatory Committees would be subject to either judicial or political review;
> (c) the Australian anti-subsidies proposal; and
> (d) the proposal by Australia and the United Kingdom for a special share of any revenue for the claimants.[101]

It is of interest that only the first two of these issues had been included in Beeby's initial list of major outstanding problems. These issues were of course interconnected, and this was recognised by the Chairman in the package which he submitted by way of compromise. It was on the fourth revision of this document, CH/60, that the crunch negotiation took place in a resumed session of the Chairman's consultations, which began at 8.15 pm on 30 May and continued until 5.30 am on the 31st.[102]

In MR/17 Rev 5 it had been provided that a Regulatory Committee should adopt the management scheme for the area in question by a simple majority which must include the state or states which laid claim to the area together with the state sponsoring the application to mine. The Chairman's paper provided that decisions on the adoption of management schemes and the issue of development permits should be taken by a two-thirds 'chambered' majority. The claimants in the Chairman's group were unhappy that this qualified majority was to apply only to decisions on those two matters, while the developing countries wanted these decisions to be taken by a three-quarters majority, which would enable the developing countries to muster a blocking vote.

The agreement eventually reached and embodied in Article 32 was typically complex. It provided that the two decisions in question should be adopted by a two-thirds majority, which must include a simple majority of both the claimant and non-claimant members of the Committee: this meant three out of four claimants and four out of six non-claimants (which six in all cases included the United States and the Soviet Union). Unlike MR/17 Rev 5 this formula did not give an outright veto to the state claiming the area affected, but since that state needed only the support of one of the other three claimant states on the Committee to reject a management scheme or a development permit, its position was pretty well safeguarded.

An additional paragraph in the Article, proposed at the last minute by the United States, provided for a slightly less restrictive qualified majority in deciding on the guidelines for exploration and development in each area. This compromise helped to make the proposal more acceptable to the claimants.

The foregoing, it should be stressed, is a simplified description of Article 32: but it covers the contentious points. This was not the last to be heard of Article 32, however.

There were several other elements in the package. The

Germans were insistent on having a provision that would permit decisions to decline a management scheme, to refuse to issue a development permit or to suspend or cancel a management scheme to be referred to the Arbitral Tribunal to determine whether the decision in question was in violation of the Convention. This provision, Article 59 in the final text, was now accepted by the claimants.

The United States had been concerned that a provision requiring states to provide for recourse in their national courts for adjudicating liability claims against operators (Article 8, paragraph 19) might permit more than one judgment to be issued in respect of the same claim. This difficulty was overcome by the inclusion of a paragraph in the Final Act recording the meeting's agreement that if a liability claim had been referred for adjudication in the courts of one party, it should not be subject to additional adjudication.

There were still the Australian and British proposals to be dealt with. On the anti-subsidies draft, the Australians had a very hard time making any headway. Eventually the British representative (Watts) responded to an Australian appeal for some movement by the United Kingdom and the United States by producing a weak formula that was eventually incorporated into the Final Act. This merely recognised that unfair economic practices, including subsidies, could adversely affect the interests of parties, and indicated that 'such effects should be addressed in the context of the relevant multilateral agreements'. This was a far cry from the original Australian proposal which required parties to refrain from offering subsidies or other substantial incentives to potential operators and provided for consultation and arbitration in the event that a party had failed to comply with this requirement.

The New Zealand delegation felt that 'the British and the United States dug Brook [the Australian lawyer] a hole and he jumped into it' while Tormey (the Australian Treasury representative) 'stayed in the wings'.

On the special share for claimants, Australia and the United Kingdom were again obliged to accept a much weaker formulation than they had originally put forward in Tokyo in 1986. The

Convention eventually provided only (in Article 35 [7]) that the Commission, in disposing of the revenues available to it, should ensure that the members of the Regulatory Committees 'hav[e] the most direct interest in the matter in relation to the areas in question are respected in any disposition of that surplus'.[103]

It may well be deduced, with the benefit of hindsight, that the Australian delegation, and in particular the Treasury member, went away dissatisfied with the degree to which their position on two issues to which they attached great importance had been met—isolated though they were on the one, and in a minority of two on the other. That dissatisfaction was to have consequences that could not be foreseen. At 5.30 am on 31 May, however, the New Zealand delegation 'retreated exhausted . . . believing that subject to some tidying up of some issues, the deal had been done'. That tidying up was largely completed the following day.

This, however, was not the end. The Chairman's consultative group had not included the Indian representative, Quasim. When he discovered that the proposal of the four developing countries (Brazil, China, India and Uruguay) suggesting there should be three-quarters majority voting in the Regulatory Committees had not been accepted, and was told that there was no possibility of consensus on that basis, he prompted the Chinese representative to raise the issue in plenary. When no agreement could be reached in that forum, it was decided in a smaller meeting to have resort once again to the expedient of a mollifying paragraph in the Final Act. This states the desirability that the two-thirds majority referred to in Article 32 should include one developing country. The Indian representative was still unhappy, and it became necessary for the Chairman, through the New Zealand High Commission in New Delhi, to make a direct approach to the Indian Government. At 3 am on 2 June, the High Commissioner called to say that India would probably go along with the consensus.[104]

On the final day, one more hurdle was raised, this time by the Americans. A State Department lawyer was now insisting that there must be an amendment to the text, or an unchallenged statement by the Chairman, that sovereign immunity would need to be available to a defence of a claim brought under Article 8 (10)—the provision which, it will be recalled, had already presented the United States with difficulties. Eventually the Chairman persuaded all the delegations to allow him to make a statement which would not be recorded and which no one would challenge. The Argentinian representative was unhappy and was persuaded only with great reluctance to refrain from referring home for instructions. The agreement not to record the Chairman's statement did not prevent the United States authorities from incorporating its substance in a statement accompanying the American signature of the Convention.[105]

A word might be added about the Final Act which, as will have been seen, had become a rather unusual document. In normal circumstances a Final Act records in a factual way the proceedings which have resulted in the conclusion of a Convention. In this case the meeting included most of the factual record in a Final Report, and the Final Act largely noted certain tasks that remained to be completed and recorded a series of understandings about the interpretation of the substantive text. (By comparison, the Third Law of the Sea Conference *annexed* four resolutions and a 'Statement of Understanding' to its Final Act.) A Final Act is not a legally binding instrument—full powers are not required for its signature—but it constitutes an authoritative source of interpretation of the Treaty to which any tribunal considering its meaning would give great, and in most cases decisive, weight.[106]

There was justifiable euphoria that the long and arduous negotiations had come to a successful conclusion. From most of the leading delegations there came warm, and indeed effusive, congratulations to the Chairman on the skill with which he had conducted them. The French representative, for example, remarked that:

> The texts we have just adopted represent a happy balance between concern for protection of the environment and the wish to allow, if it ever becomes necessary and possible, a reasonable exploration and exploitation of Antarctic mineral resources. [The Treaty is] a triumph of legal ingenuity for conciliating divergent positions on fundamental points . . .

> On this day of celebration let me tell you, Mr Chairman, that had, it not been for your dynamism, your understanding of the situation, your diplomatic sense and your courteous authority, perhaps there would not, or not yet, be any Convention . . .[107]

In a public statement on 2 June Beeby described the adoption of the Convention as an historic occasion which would go down as the most important political development in the regulation of Antarctica since the conclusion of the Antarctic Treaty itself. It was not, he added, an invitation to start mining in Antarctica: in fact it was quite the reverse. In environmental terms this was its most significant achievement. The Convention prohibited exploration for and extraction of mineral resources in Antarctica. That prohibition would stand unless the institutions established in the Convention gave specific approval, in accordance with a rigorous process which involved an initial consensus decision and stringent environmental protection criteria and safeguards.[108]

Despite the rejoicing among the negotiators, however, there were three small dark clouds on the horizon. In the first place, although Australia had joined in the consensus for the adoption of the Convention, there was an ominous absence from the congratulatory speeches of any statement by the Australian representative. This, it would emerge, was not simply a matter of trans-Tasman ungraciousness.

Significantly, also, if not unexpectedly, the adoption of the Convention was greeted by the environmental lobby with unalloyed dismay. Cath Wallace, its harshest critic, expressed the hope that some of the claimants at least would refuse to ratify the Convention, and thus prevent it from coming into force. They had been 'pressured and bludgeoned' to agree, making compromises on environmental protection, on revenue sharing with miners on the territory they claimed (a touching expression of concern on Wallace's part) and on the liability issue. It was possible that when their representatives got home, the governments of the countries that had had to make the biggest compromises—Argentina, Australia and Chile—would not be very happy with those compromises. Greenpeace planned a worldwide campaign to block ratification. The choice, said

Wallace, was a world park or world shame.[109]

By contrast, Guy Salmon (Director of the Maruia Society), wrote a letter of congratulations to Beeby in which he said he suspected that history would view the agreement in a more favourable light that some contemporary opinion.[110]

Finally, on the initiative of Malaysia, nineteen countries issued a statement in New York which described the adoption of the Convention by the Antarctic Treaty Consultative Parties as 'a matter of utmost regret and deep concern'. This had been done in 'complete disregard' of the Assembly's resolution of the previous year, which had reaffirmed the need for any minerals regime to look fully into account the interests of the international community, and called for a moratorium to be imposed on the negotiations until all members of the international community could participate fully in them.[111]

Despite these somewhat ominous developments, there was no reason at this stage to suppose that the treaty-making process would not proceed smoothly to signature of the Convention and its ratification in due course by the governments which had participated in the negotiations. The events of the next few months were unexpected, and will require a further chapter to describe.

XIII

MINERAL RESOURCES: A CONVENTION UNDER FIRE

In the second half of 1988 New Zealand officials were working hard to produce a definitive text of the Minerals Convention (CRAMRA) and to organise a signature ceremony in November. Conservationist organisations such as Greenpeace continued to lobby against signature and ratification of the Convention. This was to be expected. There was solid support for the Convention at this stage from both the New Zealand Government and the Opposition. Warren Cooper, a former Foreign Minister (and a master of the epistolary art), told Greenpeace's Antarctic Campaign Coordinator that representations to him on the subject were 'as numerical as the moa', that Chris Beeby had done an excellent job and that the final draft would satisfy a huge majority of his constituents.[1]

In August, however, there came the first rumblings of discontent with the Convention from one of the negotiating parties. This was Australia. In the talks held regularly between legal officials of the Australian and New Zealand Foreign Ministries, the Australians said that the New Zealanders 'should not hold their breath' about an early Australian signature. The Australian Treasury and the Department of Primary Industries and Energy were very dissatisfied with the results of the negotiations, specifically in respect of revenue-sharing and (lack of) an anti-subsidies provision.[2] This was in marked contrast to the statement issued by two Australian Ministers on 2 June, which had welcomed the Convention as strengthening the Antarctic

Treaty system as a whole.[3]

On 18 October, New Zealand posts were instructed to issue invitations to a signing ceremony on 25 November.[4] The reaction of a number of Western European countries, starting with Britain, was to indicate that they thought it unlikely that their interdepartmental examination of the Convention would be completed in time for them to sign on that date.[5] These countries did not include France, which as late as 9 November informed the New Zealand Embassy in Paris that their Ambassador in Wellington would almost certainly sign the Convention.[6] The New Zealand Government pressed the British authorities hard to sign on the due date, emphasising the desirability of concerted action by the Consultative Parties and especially the claimant states, to counter criticism of the Convention by Malaysia and others at the United Nations. Although the Deputy Prime Minister raised the matter directly with the Foreign Secretary, the British declined to be hurried.[7]

The Australian press now carried a report that the Treasurer (Paul Keating) had written to other senior Ministers urging against signature of the Convention. In what was apparently an authentic summary of Keating's letter, he was reported to have asserted that signature would 'concede our economic claims over Antarctica for virtually nothing'. He was said to believe that Australia's interests had been poorly represented in Wellington, and that Australia was in a strong position to change the Convention. Specifically, he was critical of the provision for claimants to share in mineral wealth that might be discovered on their territories. Australia, he said, 'must be prepared if necessary to stand alone' on the issue of the revenue share for claimants. Secondly, he regarded as 'completely unsatisfactory' an alleged loophole which could allow the superpowers to subsidise unprofitable mining operations for strategic purposes. Thirdly, he cited environmental concerns, noting that the Convention would limit the liability of a mining operator for environmental damage.[8] (It will be recalled that the liability Article in the Convention was to be elaborated in a separate protocol.)[9]

Keating's letter was a very far cry from a call for a ban on mining in Antarctica. Rather it was a demand for a convention much more favourable to claimants' interests, with provisions for sharing of revenue with claimant states and for an anti-subsidies article that had proved to be clearly unacceptable to the other participants in the lengthy negotiations leading up to the adoption of the Convention. Even the environmental issue was approached purely from a financial point of view. Clearly the letter embodied the reaction of a disappointed Treasury representative in the Australian negotiating team. Its effect, however, was to reopen the whole question of whether mining in Antarctica under any regime would be in Australia's interests.

Right up to the date of the signature ceremony, it seemed more likely than not that the signatures would include France. However, France did not sign, and on the day before the signature ceremony there was a significant development. In an interview in a French newspaper, France's leading environmentalist and ocean explorer, Jacques Cousteau, declared that the 'most urgent task' was to 'fight against a project which truly makes me blow my top [*sortir de mes gonds*]'. This was the Convention, according to Cousteau signed three months (sic) earlier in Wellington 'for the exploitation of the coal of Antarctica'.[10]

The New Zealand Embassy in Paris was told that the Quai d'Orsay had tried 'desperately' to 'sort out the departmental hitch which had arisen at the last moment'. The French Ambassador in Wellington had actually been provided with full powers to sign. But the Environment Secretary (Lalonde) had withheld his approval, saying that he wanted to have a thorough look at the Convention. Apparently his department had attended none of the interdepartmental meetings to discuss the Convention and had taken an interest only at the last moment.[11]

Although New Zealand officials tried to put the best face on the situation, there was disappointment that only nine countries—Brazil, Finland, New Zealand, Norway, South Africa, Sweden, the Soviet Union and Uruguay—signed the Convention on 26 November.[12] (Chile, United Kingdom and United States announced their intention to sign in the near future, which they did.)

There were indications that even in New Zealand there were those in Government who were prepared and indeed keen to take a stronger line against Antarctic mining, especially in the Ross Dependency. The Chairman of the Labour Caucus committee on foreign affairs and security (Richard Northey) wrote to the Minister of Foreign Affairs advocating that when New Zealand legislated to give effect to the Convention, it should go beyond ratification to provide additional controls over mining. There probably should be, he said, bars on New Zealand citizens taking part in mining; bars on the use of New Zealand ports and airports being used to facilitate mining; and, if possible, an undertaking not to mine in the Ross Dependency.[13] Foreign Affairs officials noted that these proposals were very close to the kind of provisions that the Department of Conservation had been thinking about: DOC officials had already briefed the Caucus Committee.[14] Ministers, however, continued to express to correspondents their confidence that the Convention had sufficiently strong safeguards over the Antarctic environment:

> The Convention does not open up Antarctica for mining . . . It prohibits all significant minerals activities in Antarctica unless all the Consultative Parties to the Antarctic Treaty agree otherwise. That is a powerful prohibition and a much more effective barrier to mining in Antarctica than was the case prior to the Convention when there were no agreed rules to control minerals activities there.

The Convention, Geoffrey Palmer concluded, was 'the best deal attainable in an imperfect world'.[15]

It was evident by now that Cousteau's attitude would be the key to the French decision on signature, which would inevitably influence the decisions of other members of the European Community. Cousteau had followed up his first interview with an emotional denunciation of the Convention in *Calypso Log*:

> Citizens of the entire world, be on the alert! The Wellington Agreement is nothing more than a hold-up on a planetary scale. It involves the smashing open of the safe that contains the most fantastic treasure: the last water reserve that cannot be controlled if it is set free! The hostages: seals, birds, penguins, whales . . . threatened is the whole of humankind whose conscience in managing the future

of our planet risks being sacrificed to the cult of a meaningless golden calf.[16]

The debate, it seemed, was being shifted beyond the reach of rational discussion. Cousteau appeared unaware that the 'safe' containing the fantastic treasure had never, in fact, been locked. It was decided that Beeby should attempt to brief Cousteau on the merits of the Convention. A téte-a-téte meeting was arranged. Beeby sought to convince Cousteau that the choice was not between a total ban and the Convention but between the Convention and no rules at all.[17] Cousteau was not convinced. Beeby found him both ill-informed and 'more than a bit arrogant as well'; Beeby did not make much progress in their discussion.[18] In the light of subsequent events, Cousteau would no doubt claim that he was right. In any event, he gave a further interview, the day after his meeting with Beeby, in which he denounced the exploitation of Antarctica as immoral, and called for it to be declared a world park under United Nations protection. (It is of passing interest that he declined at the same time to join in environmentalist criticism of a proposed airstrip in the French sector. He was, like Walter Nash, neither for nor against that project; he had been told that it was necessary and the penguins would not often be disturbed.)[19] Beeby found the Minister of the Environment (Lalonde) equally ill-informed about the content of the Convention, and adamantly opposed to it.

In an opinion poll about this time, Cousteau was voted France's most influential person. President Mitterrand came tenth. Not surprisingly, the efforts of the Quai d'Orsay to 'push matters along' on the Convention proved ineffectual.[20]

By 22 March, when the United Kingdom signed the Convention, there were fifteen signatories, including all the claimant states except Australia and France.[21] On 20 April, the French Prime Minister (Rocard) in a muddled reply to a television interviewer, said that France would not ratify the Convention as it stood. Cousteau was right to say that industrial development in Antarctica should be prohibited and only research allowed. The present situation, however, was worse than it would be under the Convention. Things could not be left as they were. The negotiations must be reopened, and Rocard hoped that the Convention would be greatly improved. But he recognised that France could not expect to have things all its own way.[22] *Le Monde* followed with a well-informed account of the content of the Convention, noting that New Zealand, by far the most environmentally conscious of the Consultative Parties, had taken in 1972 the initiative of the mineral resources Convention, not, obviously, to promote geological exploration, but to endow Antarctica with the essential framework to prevent any attack on the environment. The Convention, therefore, raised barriers against the day—unforeseeable at present—when mining might be technically and economically feasible.[23] For once, an influential organ of French opinion had got it right, but this was not enough.

The month of May 1989 saw developments which were, in the end, to seal the fate of the Convention. Although five of the seven claimant states continued to support it, of the remaining two Australia publicly committed itself in the course of the month not to sign it. While the French position remained as in its Prime Minister's equivocal statement, Australia took the lead in seeking to convert the other parties to the Antarctic Treaty to its point of view. The provisions for the entry into force of the Convention meant, in any case, that Australia had a power of veto. New Zealand worked desperately to stem the tide.

A preparatory meeting for the Fifteenth Meeting of the Consultative Parties was held in Paris during May. There was a strong emphasis on environmental issues. Chile proposed, as a new item, 'measures for the protection of the Antarctic environment', which was received with enthusiasm.[24] Australia went a long step further, however, in circulating a paper which envisaged a comprehensive conservation convention that might over time subsume existing instruments already part of the treaty system.[25] There was concern among other parties, the New Zealand delegation reported, at the apparent premise that there were serious flaws in the existing system. Argentina and Chile openly warned the Australian delegation against going down a path that was bound to lead to confrontation.[26]

There is little doubt that the Australian paper was a first move towards superseding the Minerals Convention. Senior New Zealand Ministers now sought directly to persuade their opposite numbers in Australia and France that their negative attitudes to the Convention were misconceived. It was evident that the Australian Cabinet was split on the issue. The Foreign Minister, Gareth Evans, spoke in strong support of the Convention in the Australian Senate on 3 May;[27] and while he and the Minister for the Environment maintained that stand, there seemed a good possibility that they would prevail in Cabinet. However, the Prime Minister (Hawke) saw advantage in joining Keating in advocating a ban on all mining. The *Sydney Morning Herald* (which had supported the Convention) said that Hawke's economics advisor, Craig Emerson, was a 'closet greenie' who was 'passionate about stopping [sic] mining in the Antarctic'. Hawke was also concerned not to be 'out-greened by the apparently born-again greenie, Opposition Leader John Howard', who was now 'very much on the environment tram'.[28] Whatever Hawke's motivation (and a decision by the Federal Opposition to oppose signature may also have been a factor),[29] it now seemed that the balance in the Australian Cabinet had swung against signature.

The New Zealand Prime Minister nevertheless wrote to Hawke, recalling that when New Zealand had 'tried to sell' the concept of a world park in 1975, no treaty partner had been prepared to enter into a commitment not to engage in mining in Antarctica at some future date. What they were prepared to do was to negotiate an agreement to regulate mining on the basis of strict environmental standards. The choice, Lange wrote, was not between a world park and a more limited convention, but between a convention and nothing at all. New Zealand's judgment was that a return to the idea of a world park would be even more unacceptable than in 1975.

It was neither politically not legally possible, Lange told Hawke, to renegotiate the Convention. But no minerals development could ever be considered until the parties had concluded a protocol on liability whose main purpose would be the enhancement of the protection of the Antarctic environment. The reality was that, under the Convention, operations in Antarctica were prohibited and would be most unlikely ever to be permitted. A number of countries which, like Australia and New Zealand, faced vociferous opposition to the Convention, had identified certain steps which might help to placate that opposition, including a decision at the Fifteenth ATCM to go ahead with the liability negotiations, stressing the need to give further precision to the environmental safeguards in the Convention, and a further decision to take a comprehensive look at the protection of the environment.[30]

There was an unfortunate delay of a few days between the initial drafting of this message and its despatch. It is unlikely, however, that it would have affected the course of decision-making in Australia. The weakness of the New Zealand argument, of course, was that the more it stressed the improbability of mining ever being permitted under the Convention, the more pertinent became the question why in that case the Convention, with all its elaborate machinery, was preferable to a simple outright ban on all mining. The strength of the New Zealand argument lay in the opposition to an outright ban on the part of powerful countries which were determined to retain their option to mine at some time in the future. There was an unresolved contradiction between the two lines of argument.

In any event, the Lange letter was not cleared for transmission until 22 May.[31] On the same day a joint statement by the Australian Ministers of Foreign Affairs and the Environment announced that Australia would not sign the Minerals Convention, but would pursue the urgent negotiation of a comprehensive environmental protection convention within the framework of the Antarctic treaty system. Australia's commitment, the Ministers said, was to the proposition that no mining at all should take place in and around the Antarctic continent. Australia would work in international forums and in bilateral discussions for a consensus on that position. Specifically, Australia would explore the prospects for an 'Antarctic Wilderness Park'. In the meantime, it would seek to strengthen the moratorium which at present was to remain in place until the 'timely' entry into force of the Minerals Convention.[32]

Hawke's reply to Lange—three weeks later—conceded nothing to New Zealand's arguments. Australia, he said, had decided to go down a different track. The time was ripe to explore some of the ideas that New Zealand had previously advanced:

> While acknowledging the undoubted achievements of the Minerals Convention I believe its underlying assumptions, particularly the assumption that mining can co-exist with adequate environmental protection, now deserve reconsideration by governments.

Hawke rejected the suggestion that Australia's concerns could be met by developing the Convention protocol on liability, and instead suggested that New Zealand cooperate closely with Australia at the Fifteenth ATCM in October to advance the Australian initiative. It was Hawke's firm intention, he said, to keep in close touch with New Zealand, as it would be of great value for the two countries to speak with one voice.[33]

This was an admirable thought. New Zealand Ministers and officials may have considered it a trifle belated. What was evident was Australia's determination to wipe the work of the Fourth SCM (and with it New Zealand's leading role) and start again with a clean slate, Australia holding the pencil.

The Australian initiative came as a considerable surprise to many of the Consultative Parties, and two in particular—the United States and the United Kingdom—did not trouble to conceal their anger. A senior American negotiator, Tucker Scully, spoke to Richard Woolcott, about to take up his position as Australian Secretary of Foreign Affairs. Woolcott, Scully reported afterwards, was 'openly horrified', attributed Australia's motivation to purely domestic considerations, and suggested that its position was not irrevocable.

Scully commented that the interdepartmental splits in Canberra had been a significant factor behind the Australian decision. The domestic political opponents of the Convention had taken advantage of these splits, in which those who opposed the Convention within the Government did so for reasons that had nothing to do with environmental concerns. In Scully's view France, Australia and, to a lesser extent, the Federal Republic of Germany, were the three countries which had paid least attention to their own environmental lobbies throughout the negotiations. Their negotiators were now receiving their comeuppance, as the environmentalists had managed to mount a successful counter-attack. While the Australians had pushed for some environmental elements in the Convention, their dissatisfaction at the end had nothing to do with the environment.

The Australians' argument, said Scully, was intellectually bankrupt, fallacious and internally inconsistent. They said they supported the treaty system but they were trying to reject one of its major achievements. They wanted a mechanism by which to judge whether prospective mining was environmentally sound, but they had prejudged the issue by saying that all mining was bad. They were declaring publicly that Australia was not interested in mining, but privately they were not ruling it out.

The Australians, Scully added, were now claiming that they had already raised their proposal (for an outright ban on mining) at the preparatory Consultative Parties meeting in Paris. In fact they had merely tabled 'an ill-prepared and badly written' paper after discussion on the environmental item had been completed. There was no reference in it to a wilderness park or to a ban on mining. Whereas they had claimed that it had drawn interest from the South American countries, it was clear that Chile supported the Convention, and the only country to express a view on the Australian paper—Argentina—had savagely attacked it.

Scully told Woolcott that the lack of prior consultation on Australia's part was especially troubling. The failure of the Convention to enter into force, should this transpire, would undermine the status of Antarctica as a zone of peace. In that event, if the demand for mineral resources were there and if it looked viable, countries would go down to Antarctica. The pressure from American mining companies would be irresistible. The moratorium provisions would also lapse; the United States for one would be under pressure to undertake prospecting in Antarctica.

Woolcott had said that if the Australian initiative did not get anywhere the position would have to be reassessed after the Australian elections. Scully felt that once the elections had taken place the heat would go out of the issue and by October, provided the Australians had received a clear enough message, they might be prepared to reconsider.[34]

The United Kingdom authorities also hoped that the Australians would not close the door against the possibility of eventually acceding to the Convention. They themselves had already put legislation before Parliament which would enable the United Kingdom to ratify the Convention before the end of the year. The effect of the legislation would be to prohibit any British national or company from undertaking any mineral resource activity in Antarctica, except prospecting, until the liability protocol had been concluded and effect given to it in United Kingdom law. In urging other countries to sign or ratify the Convention, the British noted that Australia had *not* said it would not accede to or ratify, only that it would not sign. The United Kingdom would meanwhile give a sympathetic hearing to the Australian case for a comprehensive approach to the protection of the environment, would seek to make progress at the October ATCM on such issues as waste disposal and marine pollution, and stood ready to embark on the negotiation of a liability protocol which would strengthen the environmental protection already afforded by the Convention. In the light of these possible courses of action, the United Kingdom did not believe that it was in the interests of the Consultative Parties, or of the Antarctic treaty system (as the only available mechanism for managing the interests of states in Antarctica) or in the long-term interests of the wider international community, to decide to exclude the possibility of Antarctic mining. Such a decision would, in the British view, be the subject of international challenge by those who saw Antarctica as part of the common heritage of mankind.

The British authorities, addressing themselves specifically to the Australians, said that it was of the utmost importance to the United Kingdom that none of the Treaty partners should read the Australian decision as final and irrevocable. If anyone took the view that the need for restraint with respect to mineral activities was at an end, British security interests in Antarctica could be endangered. Australian officials responded that at their level the possibility of signing the Convention at some future date was not excluded, but their Ministers did not entertain the possibility. They had refused to add the words 'at this stage' to their statement about Australia's not signing the Convention.[35]

New Zealand, meanwhile, had not given up hope of persuading the French not to follow Australia in publicly refusing to sign. The Deputy Prime Minister, Geoffrey Palmer, met the French Prime Minister, Michel Rocard, in Noumea and the Minister of Conservation, Philip Woollaston, talked with the French Secretary of State for the Environment, Brice Lalonde, at a UNEP meeting in Nairobi. Palmer followed this up with a letter to Rocard in which he reiterated a suggestion discussed in Nairobi that a declaration should be issued immediately before the October ATCM. This, by signifying a common intent to take further measures to protect the Antarctic environment, could 'pave the way' for all countries to sign the Convention.

There was a notable difference of emphasis in the representations being made by Britain and the United States and those by New Zealand. It had, of course, always been the objective of the industrialised Consultative Parties to keep the door open for mining-under safeguards—but New Zealand Ministers were now laying more and more stress on the Convention as an obstacle to the commencement of mining operations. It was 'most unlikely' that they 'would ever be permitted', Palmer told Rocard, as Lange had told Hawke—and with the same lack of effect.[36]

The Opposition in New Zealand now adopted the same position as its Australian counterpart. Why, the Leader of the Opposition (Bolger) asked in Parliament on 30 May, would the Minister not support the total ban on mining in Antarctica? 'The document that has been negotiated among the Treaty partners,' Palmer replied, 'allows any of those parties to ban any mining in Antarctica, as the Leader of the Opposition should know.' This was somewhat of a simplification.[37]

At the same time the Government Caucus Committees on Foreign Affairs and the Environment, while continuing to contemplate the ratification of CRAMRA and legislative provision for its 'stringent' application by New Zealand, made it clear that they regarded it as a second best to the world park proposal that New Zealand had favoured in 1975, and that 'our goal remains the total protection which is offered by the Antarctic park'.[38]

The Foreign Minister, Russell Marshall, sent a conciliatory letter to his Australian counterpart, Gareth Evans. 'Many of us here,' he said, 'in our hearts would very much have liked from way back to take the line Australia is now taking.' They had, however, crossed that bridge much earlier in their term of office and they had seen nothing recently to convince them that their decision to stay with the negotiation of the Convention had been wrong. New Zealand accepted that Australia was now in a situation where it had to have a decent crack at airing its initiative. New Zealand would work constructively with Australia towards putting in place expanded environmental, measures for Antarctica. However, Marshall added, it would be very difficult to do this if Australia was simultaneously seeking to persuade others to reject the Minerals Convention.[39] A few days later, the New Zealand press reported that the Government was 'softening' its criticism of the Australian proposal, and was considering legislation to forbid New Zealand companies to mine in Antarctica. New Zealand, according to Marshall, still intended to push for the acceptance of the Minerals Convention at the October ATCM.[40]

In mid-June, Palmer, as Minister of the Environment, held a meeting with the other Ministers concerned (Foreign Affairs, Conservation, and Science and Technology) to review New Zealand's strategy in the light of developments. The meeting concluded that New Zealand should support:

(a) the ratification of CRAMRA;
(b) an explicit moratorium on mining in the meantime;
(c) a collective commitment to work vigorously for a world park as soon as possible.

Policy was to be coordinated by a group of four officials—Beeby, Hugh Logan of DSIR, Roger Blakeley from the Environment Ministry and David McDowell from the Department of Conservation. These officials were invited to produce a Cabinet paper 'fleshing out' the proposals and a strategy for implementing them.[41]

This was a key document. Assuming that a world park meant no mining, it implied that New Zealand's ultimate objective would be to supersede CRAMRA. It also had important implications for the bureaucracy. Up to this point New Zealand's Antarctic policy had been seen primarily in terms of its relations with its Antarctic Treaty partners, and had been conducted primarily by the Foreign Ministry (known at this time as MERT) with input from other interested departments. While DSIR was responsible for New Zealand's science programme in Antarctica, it would be fair to say that the input from other departments into the development of the Antarctic treaty system had been small. Now the two departments responsible for environmental issues were demanding an equal say, and had the advantage that the Minister for the Environment was also Deputy Prime Minister. In turn, the non-governmental organisations concerned with the protection of the environment could expect to have a greater influence on the formulation of New Zealand policy.

A wrangle ensued among the departments over the preparation and content of the Cabinet paper. Foreign Affairs officials circulated for comment a draft which they intended for submission to Cabinet by their Minister.[42] The Secretary for the Environment took exception to the fact that it had not been prepared as an Officials Committee paper and claimed that it did not focus on a strategy for the future. Working with remarkable speed he and the Director-General of Conservation produced an alternative draft within twenty-four hours of receiving the Foreign Ministry draft.[43] (It seems likely that they had concerted their positions well in advance.) The tone of the two drafts was very different but the basic recommendations remained the same. It was also accepted that the paper should be submitted to Cabinet by the Minister of Foreign Affairs. As finally agreed, it proposed that Cabinet:

(a) agree in principle that New Zealand should promote an initiative for an integrated and binding environmental protection regime for Antarctica;
(b) approve the introduction of legislation to give effect to CRAMRA and its accompanying moratorium as a matter of urgency;
(c) agree, subject to the passage of the legislation, that New Zealand should ratify CRAMRA;
(d) agree that the environmental initiative should be put forward at the October ATCM and that the New Zealand delegation should actively promote a special ATCM 1990 to advance that initiative;
(e) direct officials to produce a paper developing the initiative by 15 September 1989.[44]

What Cabinet decided was very different. The Cabinet Policy Committee recommended that there should be no decision on legislation to give effect to CRAMRA or on ratification until after the October ATCM. New Zealand should press for the proposed environmental protection regime both at the ATCM and bilaterally. A statement of the Government's policy should be promulgated in a White Paper, a draft of which was to be submitted for consideration by Cabinet on 31 July, in 12 days' time. Cabinet, in accepting the Committee's recommendation, decided also that the Government's position on CRAMRA was that New Zealand would rather there were no mining of Antarctica whatsoever, but the Convention was the preferred method of regulating mining (if it did occur).[45]

A few days earlier, at the South Pacific Forum meeting in Tarawa, the Prime Minister had received from the Australian Prime Minister, neatly tied with green-and-gold ribbon, Australian proposals for an Antarctic Environment Protection Convention. These obviously also envisaged an integrated approach to the development of an environmental regime, but differing from New Zealand ideas in that they featured a new, over-arching Convention. They also specifically rejected CRAMRA and proposed the exploration of the concept of an Antarctic wilderness park.[46]

In mid-July the Leader of the Opposition again challenged the Government in Parliament on its attitude to the Australian proposal. In defending its environmental credentials, the Government took several steps away from its support of CRAMRA, and also from historical accuracy. In answer to a series of questions from Bolger and Government members, Palmer said that in 1975 the Labour Government had had a proposal for a world park, but that the succeeding National Government 'had reversed that policy'. He agreed with Labour questioners that 'as early as 1956 Walter Nash proposed a similar protection' and that when it assumed office in 1984 the fourth Labour Government 'had to instruct its negotiators to put environmental protection at the top of the agenda rather than at the bottom'. There was a mythical element in all these assertions. More significantly, Palmer said that the Government would still like a world park or a wilderness park in Antarctica, and that the question was how to get to that position. He did not say that the best way was through CRAMRA.[47]

A draft White Paper was produced after a week of what Foreign Affairs officials told their Ministers had been 'lengthy and difficult negotiations'. Competing drafts had been prepared of the final section of the paper by the Ministry of External Relations and Trade (MERT) on the one hand and the Departments of Environment and Conservation on the other. Both drafts proceeded from the premise that the Government needed to be able to say that a total ban on mining was its preferred objective. There was a clear implication in the Environment/Conservation draft that the White Paper constituted a rejection of the Minerals Convention, and that New Zealand's position was now virtually identical with Australia's. It contained no defence of the Convention and suggested that its replacement would be part of the agenda for the Paris ATCM. This would have three serious negative consequences, the Ministry argued: a public repudiation of the stand taken by the Prime Minister, the Deputy Prime Minister and the Foreign Minister in defence of the Convention following its rejection by Australia; the loss of New Zealand's credibility with its Treaty partners and thus its ability to promote any new initiative; and a 'terminal impact' on the Convention, with no rules on mining and no protection for the environment. The validity of some of these arguments was accepted by the other officials and the text was modified. But the result was a long way from what MERT officials had proposed and from what they considered desirable as a statement of Government policy. MERT noted that at the Cabinet Policy meeting of 19 July, Palmer had stated that the Government remained committed to CRAMRA and that this should be the basis of ongoing diplomatic discussions. The MERT Ministers were asked to secure written confirmation of this position when Cabinet considered the White Paper.[48]

It was the hope of MERT officials that the draft of the White Paper would not be further amended to weaken that position. Their hope was not to be fulfilled. The paper as issued contained a paragraph not found in the draft agreed upon by officials, which read:

> Whether or not any mineral extraction should take place in Antarctica remains to be decided. The Convention offers a means of making that decision—the only means which has attracted the necessary consensus. Ultimately, changing world opinion may lead the Treaty nations to reach a consensus that Antarctica should be accorded permanent protection from extraction industries *in toto*. Such a consensus, if reached, would be in accord with New Zealand's policy goals.

This paragraph, drafted by the Minister of Conservation (Woollaston),[49] was a pretty clear indication that New Zealand was prepared to abandon CRAMRA if a consensus on a total mining ban could be reached.

A White Paper is a political document in which a Government is entitled to present its policy to best advantage. In this instance, historical accuracy requires some comment on its account of past events.

The Paper begins with the assertion that New Zealand had been 'in the forefront of Antarctic policy-making for more than thirty years', and that a succession of Labour Governments under Prime Ministers Peter Fraser, Walter Nash, Bill Rowling and David Lange had 'steered New Zealand into a position of acknowledged leadership in Antarctic affairs'. The implication is that this leadership was exercised *only* when Labour was in office. There were Labour governments, however, in only 11 of the 32 years between 1957 and 1989. It is difficult to point to any great interest in or active policy towards Antarctica on the part of the first Labour Government between 1935 and 1946. After the Second World War it was prepared to contemplate an international regime for Antarctica under United Nations auspices, but it remained reluctant to spend money on establishing a New Zealand presence there. When Walter Nash became Prime Minister in the second Labour Government, he did indeed take a great interest in Antarctica, but his aim was an international regime along the lines of what has since been proposed by Malaysia; there is no indication that he would have been opposed to the exploitation, under international controls, of its natural resources. In 1975 Rowling issued a press statement advocating a world park; but Labour did not pursue it. When Labour again returned to office in 1984, as I have recorded, it did not change New Zealand policy in the direction of a world park, but continued the existing policy of working for agreement on a Minerals Convention. The need for a minerals regime was first raised by New Zealand in 1970, raised again in 1972, and a decision to take the lead in negotiations for a Convention was made in 1976. New Zealand was an active participant in the negotiation of other legal instruments forming part of the Antarctic Treaty system, including the Agreed Measures on Fauna and Flora (1964) and the Convention on the Conservation of Antarctic Marine Living Resources (CCAMLR) (1977–80), while National governments were in office. New Zealand, as a claimant state and then as a Consultative Party to the Antarctic Treaty, was *continuously* active in Antarctic affairs from 1955, when New Zealand decided to participate in the International Geophysical Year and to establish a permanent Antarctic base, irrespective of which political party was in power.

The Paper says that New Zealand 'formally' proposed the establishment of a world park at the Oslo ATCM in 1975. I have been unable to trace any such formal proposal, although the New Zealand delegation appears to have informally (and unsuccessfully) canvassed the idea with other delegations in the course of the meeting. In 1984, the newly elected Government seemed content to allow the ongoing negotiations to continue, even telling Greenpeace that there was 'close to a bipartisan consensus' on a realistic New Zealand policy.[50] This policy, of course, laid strong emphasis on the importance of protecting the environment. The record does not bear out the assertion that there was a marked reordering of priorities after the change of government.

The Ross Dependency Research Committee subsequently pointed out a couple of factual errors in the Paper. Inexplicably, the Paper described Antarctica as New Zealand's nearest neighbour—closer even than Australia. The Paper described Antarctica as the world's first nuclear-free zone. The RDRC considered it, instead, a nuclear weapons-free zone, but the Committee did not get it right either. The Antarctic Treaty (Articles I and V) forbids both nuclear weapons tests and so-called 'peaceful' nuclear explosions within the Treaty area. It does not forbid the construction of nuclear power plants on the continent (see Chapter VI).[51]

The Paper outlined the way in which an environmental protection regime, in New Zealand's view, might quickly and effectively be established. This was by way of a range of conventions or other agreements to cover such matters as tourism, enforceable environmental impact procedures, waste disposal, scientific drilling, marine pollution, expansion of the network of protected areas, uses of Antarctic ice, monitoring and compliance, and better baseline data on the environment. The alternative approach of seeking to negotiate one total all-embracing Convention, the Paper said, would be likely to take many years.[52]

Thus the Paper sought to regain the initiative which had been so brutally pre-empted by Australia. But it was attempting to cover too many bases. By expressing a preference for a no-mining regime as the 'ultimate' objective, while giving lip service to CRAMRA as the only means of attaining that objective which had attracted the necessary consensus, the Government effectively abdicated New Zealand's role as the leading defender of the Convention. The question now became whether a new consensus could be forged on a 'no-mining' agreement; and that would depend on how strongly the Consultative Parties which wished to preserve the right to mine were prepared to resist environmentalist pressure for a world park.

Cabinet, in approving the text of the White Paper, endorsed the paragraph drafted by Woollaston. The Minister of Foreign Affairs was not happy. He had told his officials, in writing, that at the rate the Government appeared to be back-pedalling over the Convention, it would be back-pedalling over its own credibility.[53] Foreign Affairs officials prepared a paper setting out the arguments against a unilateral ban by New Zealand on mining in the Ross Dependency. This paper pointed out that the other countries with an active presence in the Dependency—the United States, the Federal Republic of Germany and Italy—did not recognise the New Zealand claim and would accordingly not recognise any action by New Zealand purporting to make the area a park. Effective controls on the use of any area in Antarctica could only be put in place on the basis of decisions taken collectively under the Antarctic Treaty. Legislative or other action by New Zealand applying to the Ross Dependency which challenged collective decision-making would be inconsistent with CRAMRA and would prevent New Zealand's ratification of it. On the other hand, New Zealand as a party to the Convention would have the power to veto exploration and development activity anywhere in Antarctica (on the grounds that environmental standards had not been satisfied) and thus keep the Dependency free from mining activity for so long as New Zealand wished. New Zealand could, moreover, adopt legislation of an interim nature to give effect to the existing moratorium until such time as CRAMRA entered into force; this would prohibit all forms of mining activity by New Zealanders anywhere in Antarctica and by anyone in the Ross Dependency.[54]

Cabinet took account of this submission in approving the White Paper, deciding that New Zealand would apply 'an automatic veto' against any proposal for mining in the Ross

Dependency, and that interim legislation should be introduced along the lines proposed by the Ministry.[55]

The Ministry now found itself hoist with its own advice. It felt obliged to warn Ministers against saying publicly that New Zealand would 'automatically veto' any proposal for mining in the Ross Dependency. This might imply that the Government was less concerned about mining operations elsewhere in Antarctica. It could convey the misleading impression that, under the Convention, countries claiming sovereignty over territory in Antarctica would have greater powers of control over the areas they claimed in respect of the lifting of the ban on exploration and development. Finally, a statement that New Zealand would exercise an automatic veto, whether in the Dependency or elsewhere, would be a powerful disincentive to adherence to the Convention by countries such as the United States, United Kingdom, Japan and the Soviet Union which, unlike New Zealand, viewed the possibility of access to Antarctic minerals as a merit of the Convention.[56]

This last, it might be thought, was a double-edged and dangerous argument to use to Ministers who were already having doubts, perhaps more extensive than officials appreciated at the time, about the political wisdom of strong support for the Convention. The Ministry's advice also presented some difficulty for Ministers in facing cross-questioning from the press on the inner meaning of the White Paper.

In a press conference to 'launch' the White Paper on 9 August, Palmer, who had replaced Lange as Prime Minister the previous day, made it 'absolutely clear that our policy in relation to mining is that we are against it. We've always been against it, but we do recognise that that requires . . . the agreement of all the Antarctic Treaty partners'. At the moment there was no such agreement, but there was a moratorium, 'and the CRAMRA negotiations are a very useful method of controlling it at the moment, and preventing it at the moment'. When asked whether New Zealand was now backing away from the Convention, Palmer replied in the negative: New Zealand's position was still one of support for the Convention 'as being the best practical way of vetoing mining in the Antarctic'. He had fallen into the trap against which officials had tried to warn him. Did that mean, he was asked, that if the Convention came into effect New Zealand would automatically veto all mining applications? He was getting into deep water, as his reply showed:

> You can't make that claim because if you start saying that they say you're not a *bona fide* treaty partner because you are in a situation where you ruled out what the Treaty provides for. So you can't bind yourself in that way because it's bad faith . . . But the fact is that what you can say is that you have complete veto power on mining because all the parties . . . have to agree before any can take place.[57]

The questioner had put his finger on the point. The Government had, in fact, decided to veto any mining in the Ross Dependency, irrespective of whether an application to mine there complied with the environmental requirements in the Convention or not. So it *was* bad faith.

(The relevant Article in the Convention, Article 41 paragraph 2, was in every draft from MR/17 onwards. It seems to have attracted curiously little attention during the negotiations. Did all the negotiators accept that consensus meant unanimity, and that therefore any member of the Commission could veto mining anywhere in Antarctica? It is strange those countries which wished to keep open the possibility of engaging in mining operations in Antarctica should have found this acceptable.)

The White Paper was now circulated to New Zealand's Antarctic Treaty partners. It was presented as a serious new initiative for an integrated and binding environmental regime comprising a range of conventions covering the nine issues listed in the White Paper. These were described in the White Paper as collectively forming an Antarctic park concept, but posts were instructed to stress that it differed from the Australian proposal for a single all-embracing Convention which, in New Zealand's view, would take an extraordinarily long time to negotiate if indeed it were negotiable at all. The New Zealand proposal that the range of issues listed in the White Paper be discussed at an SCM in 1990 fitted in well with the Chilean proposal for a broad discussion of environmental questions at the forthcoming ATCM. The guidance telegram claimed that none of this meant that the Government's position on the Minerals Convention had changed. Australia had turned its back on the Convention, at least for the time being; New Zealand had not. New Zealand regarded the Convention as an element of the integrated environmental regime that was already in place.

The telegram drew attention to the intention to introduce domestic legislation, stressing that this would be of an interim nature, designed to give effect to New Zealand's commitment to the moratorium until the Convention entered into force. The White Paper was not asserting that following the entry into force of the Convention New Zealand could purport through legislation to block mining activity in the Ross Dependency. New Zealand was well aware that prospecting which met the requirements of the Convention could proceed without further authorisation and that decisions to identify an area as potentially suitable for exploration and development were taken collectively through the institutions of the Convention.[58]

Although this was legally correct, it did not exactly square with the Government's policy on mining in the Dependency as stated in the Cabinet minute.[59] It is not altogether surprising that American officials greeted the Paper with some reserve. While acknowledging that the proposed legislation seemed to be consistent with the moratorium, Scully warned that the formal attitude of the United States would have to be that it did not accept that New Zealand had a right to legislate for nationals other than New Zealanders in the Ross Dependency.

Scully regarded New Zealand's environmental proposals as a useful initiative, but considered that they should be dealt with at an ATCM, and not an SCM. This, the Washington Embassy pointed out, was not just a question of nomenclature. Scully's point was that environmental questions should be dealt with directly under the aegis of the Antarctic Treaty and not—as living and mineral resources had been, and as Australia envisaged in its world park proposals—in conventions separate from the main Treaty. (Presumably he had in mind 'agreed measures' or simply

ATCM recommendations, although this was not spelt out.) Scully also felt that more emphasis should be placed on the 'very good' environmental provisions in CRAMRA.[60]

The British authorities were even less enamoured of the White Paper than the Americans. The High Commission in London reported that Heap—the Foreign Office official most directly concerned with Antarctic matters—was clearly troubled by his perception that New Zealand's underlying premise was closer to Australia's than to Britain's. The Australian approach, he suggested, was to try to 'preserve the continent in aspic'. This reflected a conservationist view which was basically opposed to the presence of man in Antarctica because of the 'alleged' fragility of the ecosystem. In his opinion, this view was based on ignorance of the vast scale and robustness of the Antarctic environment. Britain considered it a very dangerous misconception because it implied that all activity in Antarctica must be regulated to minimise its impact. The alternative (British) thesis was that the treaty system should be concerned to maximise Antarctica's potential contribution to the welfare of mankind, both now and in the future. This approach governed Britain's attitude to the Minerals Convention, starting from the proposition that if Antarctic minerals could be economically exploited they should be, subject to necessary rules concerning adequate protection of the environment. The Minerals Convention provided just that.

Heap maintained that within the provisions of the Convention it would not be possible, given the current state of technology, to identify an area for offshore oil development. In the absence of a gigantic oil spill, the major threat to the Antarctic environment would come from external phenomena such as global warming, and scientific research would need to be stepped up to monitor such effects. Margaret Thatcher had written to Hawke stressing the benefits of scientific research in Antarctica and asserting that the environmental impact of that research was virtually nil at present.

Although Heap also described the New Zealand White Paper as a useful initiative, he emphasised that there were two different schools of thought about Antarctica—the one wanting it to be left alone to avoid damage, and the other wanting to make maximum use of it to alleviate the problems of the rest of the world. He referred to the pressure that the forecast doubling of the world's population by 2030 would put on its resources.[61] By implication, New Zealand appeared to belong to the first school and Britain to the second. Indeed this conversation showed that there was a wide gap between the New Zealand Government's perception of the purpose of CRAMRA and that of the British Government. The gap had, no doubt, been there for quite a long time, but had been masked during the course of the negotiations.

It may be remarked that the British position as expounded by Heap (he emphasised that its formal position had yet to be embodied in ministerial instructions for the Paris ATCM), would tend to strengthen the case for considering Antarctica as part of the common heritage of mankind, rather than the claimant stand on national sovereignty. In later exchanges, New Zealand's officials acknowledged that there was a clear difference between Britain and New Zealand on the acceptability of mining in Antarctica, even though both countries supported the Convention. New Zealand's very deep reservations about mining, they asserted, were 'of long standing and informed our position in the negotiation'. New Zealand did not accept the idea that Antarctica could alleviate the resource problems of the rest of the world. British officials, on the other hand, believed that the Convention arose from the view that Antarctic minerals could not be left out of the world minerals equation; some Consultative Parties, including the United Kingdom, continued to believe that Antarctica should not be banned from contributing to world minerals demand.[62]

Australia and France, meanwhile, had reached an agreed position on the protection of the environment in Antarctica. Referring to their 'shared concerns' about CRAMRA, the prime ministers of the two countries declared that mining in Antarctica was not compatible with the fragile environment. Australia and France would therefore call at the Paris ATCM for a convention covering every aspect of the protection of the environment and dependent or associated ecosystems in Antarctica, and would propose an SCM in 1990 to draw up and adopt a convention along these lines.[63]

Given the protracted nature of the negotiations that had preceded the conclusion of previous agreements forming part of the Antarctic treaty system, this was an ambitious timescale. The French Prime Minister, when asked about his Government's attitude to CRAMRA, did not reject it outright but said that if the proposal for a comprehensive environmental convention succeeded, there would be no need for it. And he added:

> If we do not succeed, but that is not what I have in mind, we will have to have another look at the situation—which would be an unpleasant one—and we will have to talk again to Australia.[64]

Subsequently, however, an Australian official had told the New Zealand High Commission in Canberra that Rocard had held back publicly out of concern for the American and British positions. Mitterrand, he said, had told Hawke privately that France would not sign and Rocard's office had spoken to Australian officials in the same sense. The official also acknowledged that Australia was lobbying other countries, not only in favour of their own proposal, but against signature of CRAMRA.[65]

In New Zealand, at the end of August, the Department of Conservation organised consultations with non-governmental representatives, as envisaged in the White Paper.

It was evident that some bodies, such as ASOC, continued to suspect the Government's motives and to urge that it repudiate CRAMRA and join Australia in working for a no-mining regime embodied in a single convention.[66] There was especial suspicion of the attitude of Foreign Affairs officials and, it would seem, pressure for the replacement of Beeby as New Zealand's chief representative at Antarctic meetings. Russell Marshall wrote to the Prime Minister and to Woollaston on 28 August that the NGO community appeared to have the impression that Beeby was to be removed as leader of the New Zealand delegation. This notion, he said, had no substance, but if anyone else was considering such a move, he totally rejected it. In view of Beeby's personal mana and experience in the field of Antarctic diplomacy, New Zealand would be foolhardy not to take advantage of those qualities to advance New Zealand's objectives at the forthcoming ATCM. To replace Beeby at this time would be seen as an expression of no confidence in his stewardship and in New Zealand's previous painstaking efforts. While the domestic politics of the issue could arguably be best handled by the Ministers and Departments with environmental responsibilities, it did not follow that those people should take on the diplomatic responsibility as well. Beeby, Marshall added, had served successive governments with absolute loyalty and considerable skill. He expected loyalty and received it: loyalty should be a two-way street. Palmer agreed about Beeby. In a minute which showed that he had indeed had approaches on the matter, he said that he had 'told anyone who asks that I am resistant to such a proposal'.[67]

The New Zealand NGOs who would have liked to see Beeby removed from his leadership role were evidently not alone in this sentiment. During the May preparatory meeting for the ATCM it had been tentatively agreed that an informal meeting of heads of delegations would convene before the ATCM to discuss arrangements for the negotiation of the protocol on liability called for in Article 8 of the Minerals Convention. It had been intended that this meeting might be held in Madrid, but the Spanish authorities evidently got cold feet in view of the developing opposition to CRAMRA on the part of France;[68] it was decided therefore that the meeting should be convened by New Zealand and held in Paris in the United States Embassy. It was now also proposed that the meeting should consider 'other issues relating to the protection of the Antarctic Environment'.[69] At this point the Australian High Commissioner in Wellington (Rob Laurie) approached Beeby, 'obviously on instructions', to suggest that as New Zealand had a proposal to make on the additional item; Beeby should stand aside in favour of a more neutral Chairman. After thanking him for 'this delicate suggestion' (Beeby recorded), Beeby told Laurie that he believed he was capable—and that others knew this—of distinguishing between the role of a Chairman and that of an advocate for a New Zealand position.[70]

Despite the vigour with which Australia was pushing its no-mining policy, New Zealand officials were aware that support for it among Australian Ministers was not uniformly enthusiastic. A senior Australian official told New Zealand representatives of an informal meeting among Australian Ministers in which Gareth Evans had told Hawke that it was desirable to keep open the CRAMRA option. Hawke, however, did not consider it feasible to talk publicly of a fall-back position; that simply undermined your objective. When asked for his view, the Minister of Defence, Kim Beazley, had pointed out 'rather rudely' that he had not been present in Cabinet when the decision on the new policy had come up. He felt there were important strategic considerations which had not been fully taken into account, and he did not like the policy. After a blunt rejoinder from Hawke, Beazley had simply walked out of the room. The official believed that Evans recognised that Australia might need to come back to the Convention. The reason for the new Australian policy had obviously been the election result in Tasmania in May 1989, in which the Green party had acquired the balance of power.[71]

Following the consultations with non-governmental organisations at the end of August, a New Zealand working paper was produced, approved by Ministers, circulated to other Consultative Parties and—unprecedentedly—made public in New Zealand. The paper recorded cautiously that 'a measure of agreement' had been reached with the non-governmental organisations. (It seems that a final agreed-upon report never emerged from the consultations.) The paper consisted mainly of an elaboration of the measures proposed in the White Paper. Additional elements were proposals for the establishment of an Antarctic Treaty secretariat and a standing working group on the environment. Notably absent was a repetition of the assurance in the White Paper that New Zealand was not turning its back on CRAMRA, although continued support was implied in, for example, a proposal for the development of rules on liability for damage caused by activities other than mineral resource activities, for which 'specific arrangements had been made or were in contemplation'.[72] Nor was there any mention of CRAMRA in the Prime Minister's media release covering the working paper.[73] When asked at a press conference whether New Zealand would ratify the Convention at the Paris meeting, Palmer said that that depended on the outcome of the Paris meeting. If there was a consensus on a total prohibition of mining activity on Antarctica there would be no need for CRAMRA. If there was no agreement, CRAMRA would be needed.[74]

This was another significant step away from the Convention. Some other Consultative Party would have to take the responsibility for rejecting a total ban on mining and ensuring the continuing relevance of the Convention. The paper did not, of course, satisfy ASOC, because it did not explicitly support the Australian world park proposal, nor repudiate CRAMRA. The Opposition spokesman for the Environment echoed ASOC's criticism, saying that the measures outlined in the paper still supported the 'increasingly discredited' Convention and that until the Government supported a total ban on mining, its advocacy of other protective measures was inconsistent and incomplete.[75]

Understandably, the Fifteenth ATCM met in an atmosphere of some tension. There was some uncertainty about the composition of the New Zealand delegation. Beeby was to have been accompanied by the Director-General of Conservation, but at the last minute the Secretary for the Environment was substituted. Of the two representatives of non-governmental organisations included in the delegation, one (Alan Hemmings) publicly criticised the Government's policy as set out in the White Paper and took a pot shot at the Foreign Affairs officials most closely associated with the negotiation of CRAMRA:

> . . . a certain pettiness is evident, with considerable aggravation that the environmental 'high ground' has been stolen by the Aussies, and that a major international agreement championed by New Zealand may be in jeopardy. For a small but powerful group of officials in the Ministry of External Relations and Trade, defence of the Minerals Convention seems to be a matter of personal honour.[76]

This was not calculated to contribute to smooth working relations between the Government and NGO representatives on the delegation. After the meeting the Secretary to the Environment submitted his own 'personal' report, including a number of observations and recommendations that caused his Foreign Affairs fellow-delegates some unhappiness.[77]

The Paris ATCM was held concurrently with a Commonwealth Heads of Government Meeting in, of all places, Malaysia—whose Prime Minister, it will be recalled, was the leading proponent of treating Antarctica as part of the common heritage of mankind, and of placing it under United Nations supervision. Against the likelihood that Malaysia might raise the issue in the CHOGM, the Paris delegation reported progress on 19 October.

While good progress on a number of environmental issues had been made, the delegation said the success of the meeting hung in the balance because of a fundamental disagreement over the terms of reference for the proposed special meeting in 1990 and on the related question of a meeting on the liability protocol. A significant majority of countries—including the United States, the United Kingdom, the Soviet Union, Argentina and Chile—wanted to pursue a parallel approach to negotiations on comprehensive measures of environmental protection and to the follow-up of the Minerals Convention. Australia, on the other hand, was reluctant to agree to a recommendation calling for the liability negotiations to begin because it implied, acceptance of the CRAMRA process. There was considerable irritation with the Australians at the meeting: a number of countries, notably the Soviet Union, Argentina, Sweden, Norway and the German Democratic Republic, were annoyed because Australia had misrepresented their positions on the minerals issue in its publicity campaign against CRAMRA; and there was irritation at the proposition that a country was either pro-environment and anti-CRAMRA, or pro-CRAMRA and anti-environment. One consequence of this irritation was a hardening of opposition to the idea of an Antarctic Secretariat, in which Argentina was joined by Brazil, the German Democratic Republic and India.[78]

The delegation wanted New Zealand Ministers present at

the CHOGM meeting to speak to Hawke. Before the meeting began the Australian Prime Minister had written to Palmer urging cooperation between the two delegations but saying bluntly that Australia would not be able to support the commencement of negotiations on a liability protocol and would speak out against it.[79] Palmer had pointed out in reply that New Zealand had not proposed such discussions, as Hawke's letter had suggested, but that there had been a consensus at the preparatory meeting in Paris, in which Australia had participated; that there should be informal consultations in advance of the meeting on both the environmental issues and the question of the liability protocol.[80] The exchange, however, had made it clear that the hard Australian line was coming from Hawke himself and that any softening would require his agreement.

While there is no record of what may have transpired between the Prime Ministers at Kuala Lumpur, it seems that Hawke may have been persuaded to soften his stand. At the end of the ATCM, the New Zealand delegation reported to Ministers that it had been a success 'both for the Treaty system and for New Zealand'. Environmental issues had dominated the meeting. A clear majority had favoured an approach that would build on the existing achievements of the treaty system. The New Zealand paper had received widespread support, although 'a couple of the more conservative countries' had expressed reservations about its proposals for compulsory dispute settlement procedures and the establishment of institutions to promote environmental protection measures.

The delegation reported that Australia and France, despite the media campaign they had waged outside the meeting, had not received a great deal of support for their proposed comprehensive convention. Many countries expressed concern about the relationship between such a convention and existing treaty arrangements. The proposal seemed to ignore the environmental protection measures already adopted under the treaty system—including CRAMRA.

After a general debate on the environment, consultations had been held under Beeby's chairmanship to work out the terms of reference for an SCM on environmental protection in 1990. This received virtually unanimous support. A number of countries also insisted, in the face of Australian opposition, on a parallel recommendation for the convening of a meeting on liability. This was achieved through compromise language put forward by New Zealand.[81]

The major sticking point in the final hours of the meeting arose from France's insistence that the recommendation for the environment meeting should refer specifically to the French proposal that Antarctica be declared a nature reserve. This was strenuously resisted by a number of countries on the grounds that, as a result of the publicity campaigns conducted by France and Australia, this expression had become equated with an end to CRAMRA. French obduracy prevailed, however, and a preambular reference was included to the French and Australian proposals, as well as those of New Zealand, the United States, Chile and Sweden.

Contrary to media reports, the delegation noted, New Zealand played no part in opposing the convening of a meeting on environmental protection, and indeed strongly supported it, New Zealand's chairmanship of the consultations had made a major contribution towards resolving a potential impasse. If there was a downside to the meeting, it was the extent to which some countries, notably France and Australia, used the occasion to play domestic politics. There were, in fact, two negotiations going on in Paris. One was inside the room where the hard work was being done by a few delegations. The other was outside the room where France, in particular, and also Australia, were promoting their position on the Minerals Convention as being the only true environmental stance.[82]

Despite their divergent objectives, the Australians too professed to be happy with the outcome of the meeting, and grateful to Beeby for his efforts to bring about an agreed compromise which, as they put it, did not prejudice Australia's position on CRAMRA. (The relevant recommendation was for a meeting to 'explore and discuss all proposals relating to Article 8 (7) of the Convention'. The Australians believed that their radical approach 'had time on its side'. The intense public interest in Antarctica, they told the New Zealand High Commission in Canberra, was a phenomenon which some Consultative Parties might find uncomfortable, but which they would have to get used to.[83]

In a press statement, the Prime Minister rejected suggestions that New Zealand had not played a constructive role at the Paris meeting, and noted the acknowledgment by the French Chairman and others that through its chairmanship of the environmental consultations, the New Zealand delegation had been instrumental in resolving the difficulties. On what New Zealand's future policy would be, in particular in regard to ratification of CRAMRA, he was silent.[84] The New Zealand NGOs, meanwhile, continued their personal attacks on Beeby for allegedly joining with American and British representatives in 'an attempt to frustrate and defeat the Australian proposal' for a world park.[85]

As mentioned, a separate report on the meeting had been prepared by Roger Blakeley. His comments on CRAMRA showed a disposition to distance New Zealand from the Convention. It was 'quite wrong', he said, for the press to say that New Zealand had joined the United States and the United Kingdom in actively defending CRAMRA. There were six Consultative Parties, he noted, which were either not intending to sign the Convention or had reserved their position: Australia, France, Belgium, Italy, the Federal Republic of Germany and India. On the other hand, 'several' countries had expressed their commitment to CRAMRA. In fact, as he listed them, there were eleven: Argentina, Sweden, German Democratic Republic, the Soviet Union, the United States, South Africa, Poland, Norway, Japan, Finland, and the United Kingdom. Not to mention New Zealand. (And he should probably have mentioned Chile.) There was a need, he said, to review New Zealand's future strategy on CRAMRA in the light of the ATCM.[86] In a subsequent radio interview, he said that if the United States decided not to ratify, it might well influence others not to ratify, 'and then you may well see a shift of opinion coming in behind a no-mining regime, which our Government has said in the White Paper would be consistent with its policy objectives'. He noted that some countries which had spent six years negotiating the Minerals Convention now felt some form of obligation towards it. To move these nations was not going to be easy and would require 'some skilful negotiation and probably some major public, pressure within those various nations so it may take some time for that shift to happen'.[87] He, it seemed, was ready to give the process a healthy shove in what he regarded as the right direction. Although he recommended in his report that officials should meet to consider the next steps, his own views had been given to Ministers and the general public without any apparent prior consultation.

At the CHOGM, Malaysia proposed the inclusion in the communique of a paragraph recognising the increasing international interest in Antarctica and expressing support for every effort to ensure its 'permanent protection and conservation as a vital resource of the global environment'. New Zealand tried unsuccessfully to have all reference to Antarctica deleted. However, by demanding that the text be balanced by a specific commendation of the Antarctic treaty system, the delegation secured agreement to an anodyne formulation which 'noted existing conservation measures and shared the conviction that every effort should be made to protect and conserve that unique territory'.[88]

In November, the Prime Minister told Parliament that a complete ban on mining in Antarctica would be supported by New Zealand if all other treaty partners would agree.[89] The following month, at his request, the officials committee submitted its recommendations on future policy to the four Ministers concerned. Even before they had met, it was becoming clear that pressure from within the Government for the public abandonment of New Zealand's position as a leading supporter of CRAMRA was increasing. On 28 November, Palmer told a meeting with environmental officials that he wanted to change New Zealand policy to make a clear statement that New Zealand would not ratify the Convention until after the

1990 SCM.[90] In response to a note from David McDowell—now Chief Executive of the Prime Minister's Department—Beeby told him that the Foreign Minister was opposed to any public announcement if it were decided to defer ratification of the Convention. An announcement would not satisfy the NGOs, would weaken New Zealand's ability to promote other aspects of Antarctic environmental protection, and would increase the possibility of no-rules mining. McDowell had suggested that such an announcement would 'bring pressure on both sides of the table' at the 1990 SCM in Santiago. Beeby couldn't see it. There was, he argued, little prospect of resolving the impasse at Santiago and none whatsoever of resolving it by deciding to set aside the Minerals Convention. At the right time it would be necessary to look at imaginative solutions to break the log-jam. Strengthening the existing moratorium might be one way of achieving that but Beeby thought it most unlikely that there would be agreement to such a solution in the short term. In his opinion, any solution that might be eventually agreed upon would have to involve a continuing role for the Minerals Convention; but this would require a bigger change of heart on the part of Australia than domestic political considerations in that country would seem likely to permit before the Santiago meeting. Beeby suggested, therefore, that New Zealand should try to avoid an unproductive debate about CRAMRA at Santiago. Instead it should concentrate on developing and refining those elements of the New Zealand working paper which were not implemented at the Paris ATCM.[91]

The paper submitted to Ministers on 19 December acknowledged that the Government was faced with a problem. On the one hand, within the Antarctic treaty system, New Zealand was widely regarded as a leading advocate for the protection of the Antarctic environment, and its credibility and influence within the system were very high. On the other hand, the Government had received bad press domestically, and the false impression had been created that the Government was on the wrong side of the divide in Antarctic matters.

Since the Paris meeting, the paper noted, the Convention

had been signed by two more countries, making 19 in all before the signature deadline of 25 November.[92] Of the countries that had chosen not to sign, only Australia and France were 'truly significant'. There was, however, an impasse that was unlikely to be resolved for some time; in this situation officials were agreed that in preparation for the Santiago meeting the Government's position on comprehensive protection for the environment should be vigorously developed and that this was not the time to recommend a major change on New Zealand policy. A decision to press ahead with ratification of CRAMRA would not help to solve the impasse. On the other hand, an announcement that New Zealand was not going to ratify the Convention would not change the position of the principal supporters of the Convention and could deepen the impasse even further. Officials considered, therefore, that the question of ratification should be left in abeyance. Ministers might say publicly that ratification was not a priority either domestically or internationally, and for that reason there were no plans to add the preparation of legislation needed for ratification on to an already overcrowded legislative programme. Officials would prepare a new policy statement for the Prime Minister to issue early in 1990, and then develop a comprehensive working paper to be promoted at the SCM later in the year.[93]

At the end of January 1990 Palmer reshuffled his Cabinet, dropping those members who had signified their intention not to stand again in the general elections, which were due to be held later in the year. Among those relegated to the back benches was Russell Marshall, who throughout had been the strongest supporter in Government of a policy of sticking with the Convention that its own officials had been instructed to negotiate. At about the same time the Australian Prime Minister, who had a warmer relationship with the New Zealand Prime Minister than with Palmer's predecessor, paid a visit to New Zealand in connection with the Auckland Commonwealth Games.

It seems that either in preparation for his talks with Hawke, or during them, Palmer decided that New Zealand's policy on the Antarctic environment should be brought into broad alignment with Australia's. When he learnt of this, Marshall wrote Palmer an impassioned memorandum. He questioned whether the present policy was an electoral liability: Antarctica had not figured in a recent poll among the top five environmental concerns of New Zealand voters. It was in domestic environmental issues that gains needed to be made. The Hawke/Cousteau approach, Marshall said, was unlikely to commend sufficient support from governments to have international legal effect. The Australian position was not even fully supported by France. Mitterrand had refused to promise Hawke that France would never sign. France's problem was the popularity of Cousteau, who did not even understand how the Antarctic treaty system worked, and whose views on the French nuclear weapons testing programme at Mururoa cast doubt on his environmental judgment.

While a change in New Zealand's policy would no doubt be cheered to the echo by Greenpeace, Cath Wallace and Jacques Cousteau, Marshall said, the effect on the Government's and Palmer's international reputations would not be good. Palmer would be seen as posturing and diplomatically irresponsible. Australia's refusal to sign had shaken CRAMRA but not terminally. Abandonment by New Zealand would pull the plug on it. The reaction of the United States and the United Kingdom needed to be taken into account: it would certainly not help Palmer's efforts to improve the New Zealand/United States relationship. Marshall ended:

> Now that you know that Hawke is going to the polls next month, and that the ground may move again soon after that, why move now? Please don't make international fools of us now for very limited short-term domestic and trans-Tasman gain! PS: If you do change our stance, I hope that I am out of the country at the time.[94]

Backbench MPs have little clout, and lame ducks even less. Marshall's *cri de coeur* went unheeded. It was too late: Palmer had committed himself to Hawke, and a change of Government in Australia was clearly not in his Government's interests in a year when it too would have to go to the polls.

Early in February, New Zealand officials visited Washington

for bilateral consultations on environmental issues, including the protection of the environment in Antarctica. American officials, they were told, had reached the conclusion that it would be unwise to press Congress to ratify the Minerals Convention at that time. Influential congressmen such as Senator Gore were responsive to environmental groups which favoured setting aside the Convention, and might well come up with a congressional resolution that could cause the executive branch to investigate alternatives. American officials were therefore giving consideration at the working level to the possibility of a protocol to CRAMRA which would not only beef up the environmental protection through the liability provisions, but incorporate a long-term, legally binding extension of the moratorium. In addition, they contemplated the possibility of a second protocol, in this case to the Antarctic Treaty itself, which would incorporate as legally binding elements much of the Australian and French initiatives, and pick up the new ideas in the New Zealand working paper submitted at the Paris ATCM. A joint New Zealand/United States venture was a possibility.

The Americans had been encouraged in this line of thought by discussions with the Australian Minister for the Environment, Senator Richardson, who had raised the question of a possible compromise with their Embassy in Canberra. Richardson had apparently indicated 'in some detail' that Australian Ministers could live with an arrangement under which the liability protocol would be used to beef up the environmental protection, and Australia's economic interests 'would be given something, especially on anti-subsidies'.

New Zealand officials were told that the Americans were concerned their strategy should not result in the demise of CRAMRA; there was widespread acceptance both in the administration and in Congress that this could result in a destabilising stalemate which could quickly unravel the Antarctic Treaty itself. A permanent ban on mining was non-negotiable. But it was now felt that instead of proceeding to seek early Senate ratification of CRAMRA it would be better to engage in some lateral thinking to supplement, not replace it.[95]

In mid-February officials in Wellington reported this important development in American thinking to their Ministers, and at the same time produced the new policy statement envisaged in their December report in the form of a draft Cabinet paper and a suggested media release. Officials told Ministers that in their view the ideas being considered by the Americans offered promising new leads in the search for a break in the current impasse. The draft Cabinet paper was designed to facilitate further discussion of these ideas but because of the strict confidence for which the Americans had asked, it did not refer to them directly.[96]

On 19 February Ministers considered the draft and approved it for submission to Cabinet, subject to one significant amendment. Without mentioning the American suggestion for a protocol to the Antarctic Treaty, the paper suggested that there might be a creative solution to the present disagreement on the final form of the comprehensive protection regime. It recommended that Cabinet reaffirm the Government was, and always had been, opposed to mining in Antarctica, and that if there was a consensus among the Treaty partners for a permanent ban on mining, that would be in accord with New Zealand's policy goals. Cabinet should note that there were dangers in the current impasse. New Zealand should concentrate on helping to resolve the deadlock, and to this end should 'set aside' consideration of whether or not to ratify CRAMRA; explore ways of resolving the impasse with its Treaty partners; and work for the greatest possible protection of the Antarctic environment at the Chile SCM in October. Such protection could be achieved through innovative measures, as proposed in the White Paper and New Zealand's working paper at the Paris ATCM, 'which could be described as an Antarctic Park concept'.[97]

The paper as drafted by officials had recommended as one of the ways of resolving the impasse an extension of the existing moratorium for a substantial period, say, three decades. Ministers directed that New Zealand should aim for a *legally binding* moratorium—i.e., a moratorium not necessarily linked to the entry into force of CRAMRA.

The day before Ministers had issued this direction, Palmer had received from Greenpeace's General Counsel, Duncan Currie, a lengthy legal critique of CRAMRA which (according to Currie) Palmer himself had requested. Currie contended that to ratify the Convention in the belief that the ratifying state could veto every proposal to open up an area for mining, and thus ensure that no mineral activity should take place in Antarctica, would not constitute a 'good faith' ratification. There was an obligation on states to examine each proposal on its merits, and in particular its environmental consequences. The consensus required by Article 41 was a consensus that identification of an area for purposes of mining was consistent with the provisions of the Convention, not on whether or not mining should be permitted. Currie noted that Palmer had acknowledged the problem of bad faith.

Currie further argued that for New Zealand to legislate to prohibit all mining in the Ross Dependency would not be consistent with ratification of the Convention. The proposed interim legislation would have to be repealed when the Convention came into force, thus demonstrating clearly CRAMRA's true nature as a Convention allowing and facilitating mineral activities in Antarctica'.

Currie, finally, questioned the argument that there was no current obstacle to the commercial extraction of minerals in Antarctica. In his opinion, the fact that the 1977 Recommendation for a moratorium was made under Article IX of the Antarctic Treaty meant that it must be consistent with the Purposes and Principles of the Treaty, and thus gave weight to the contention that commercial exploitation was outside those purposes.[98] (This rather convoluted argument does not take into account the negotiations leading up to the adoption of the Antarctic Treaty, in which reference to mineral resources was deliberately excluded.)

Although Currie's paper may have raised (or intensified) legal doubts in Palmer's mind about CRAMRA, it is unlikely that it affected Cabinet's deliberations on the matter one way or the other. The revised Cabinet paper was approved on 26 February,[99] and New Zealand's decision to 'set aside' ratification of the Convention was announced publicly by none other than Hawke, even before Palmer could issue his press release. Palmer's decision, Hawke crowed, 'would give even greater impetus to Australia's efforts with France to create an Antarctic wilderness reserve'. Hawke was especially appreciative of this change of position by New Zealand

> because it is the country after whom the Convention, the proposed convention, is named, the Wellington Convention . . . If it's seen around the world now that New Zealand has come aboard with Australia and France that's going to have a very significant psychological impact . . . An initiative which in the beginning was regarded as Mission Impossible is now shaping up as one which will be accomplished.[100]

This was perhaps not exactly the way in which Palmer would have chosen to present New Zealand's new stand. A creative solution to the impasse was needed, he told the press. The debate about CRAMRA was 'wasting energies'. In the light of that, the Government had decided to set aside the ratification of CRAMRA by New Zealand. It was important for the Antarctic Treaty community to recognise that the time had come to move constructively in the direction of the Australian and New Zealand proposals on environmental protection measures. New Zealand had decided to explore a range of possible solutions to the current impasse, including a long-term, legally binding moratorium on mining activity in Antarctica. It might be necessary to have a look at a thirty year moratorium to replace the current 'informal agreement'.

When asked whether New Zealand was abandoning CRAMRA, Palmer hedged, saying that New Zealand had set aside the idea of ratifying it 'for the moment' and was looking for 'more creative solutions'. But, he added, what had happened over CRAMRA was that it was now beginning to threaten the Antarctic treaty system. He denied, rather unconvincingly, suggestions from reporters that New Zealand was following Australia in giving priority to domestic political considerations. New Zealand's concern, he said, was to preserve the Antarctic treaty system and if the impasse over mining continued there was a danger of increased pressure at the United Nations, from the Malaysians and others, to break the treaty system which was in New Zealand's best interests.[101]

The Government's announcement was debated in Parliament, as a matter of urgency, the following day. When pressed by the Leader of the Opposition to say whether the Government had 'completely abandoned' the Convention, Palmer declined to accept that description of the Government's position; but when asked whether 'putting aside' its support for the Convention meant that it could reinstate the Convention as the preferred option if it did not make progress in some other form, Palmer replied that no, it did not.

The debate that followed took Parliament into the realm of mythology. When Woollaston asked the Prime Minister to confirm that when the Government took office it was necessary to redefine the instructions to the New Zealand negotiators to 'put environmental protection at the head of the list, because it had been ignored in instructions given to them by the National Government', Palmer replied:

> That is my understanding. The philosophy that dominated the National Government of the day was 'think big'. It would have allowed 'think big' in Antarctica, and that would have been a disaster.[102]

That was not what he had said to Greenpeace in 1984.

Few of those senior politicians who had taken part in the decision-making on New Zealand's role in the negotiation of the Convention intervened in the debate. One who did, Warren Cooper, was at pains to distance himself from the process:

> The Ministry of Foreign Affairs . . . was pushing too hard for the minerals regime. It was not the politicians; it was the foreign affairs people who supported the idea. It was an international junket. There were people from all over the world meeting every six months and studiously working towards some end that we would never achieve.[103]

It was true that in 1983 Cooper had expressed reservations about the viability of a minerals regime within the Antarctic treaty system (in the privacy of an ANZUS Council meeting), but this was not what he had said to a correspondent in 1988. A range of myths were trotted out by Government speakers.

Walter Nash had advocated a world park in the 1950s. The Third Labour Government had 'formally proposed' a world park at the Eighth ATCM in Oslo in 1975. The National Government had 'backed off' that proposal. Its instructions to officials negotiating the convention had put environmental protection of Antarctica 'about last on the list'.[104]

Now that the Opposition had come out in favour of an outright ban on mining in Antarctica, there was no disposition on the part of any of its members to defend the record of the Muldoon Government on the environmental issue. That record was, in fact, a quite respectable one. The instructions issued by Cabinet in 1977 stipulated as the criterion of a minerals regime that it should protect the Antarctic environment to the maximum practicable.[105] In 1983, after discussion in Cabinet, the brief for the New Zealand negotiating team was strengthened to provide that no exploitation should take place until the judgment could be made that the impact on the environment would be limited and in conformity with rigorous standards spelt out in the regime.[106] What was totally absent in the debate was any disposition on either side to acknowledge that from 1975 to 1988 the New Zealand Government in office, whether National or Labour, had been a prominent advocate of the need for a minerals convention, and that in accordance with successive Cabinet directives its representatives had taken a leading role in the negotiations for such a convention. As one Opposition member (Doug Graham) put it: 'Frankly, I am interested only in 1990, and in what will happen in the next few years'.[107]

The shift in New Zealand's position, although it had come about incrementally over a period of months, appeared as a volte-face to some of the Consultative Parties, and was by no means kindly received by them. The Uruguayan charge seem to have made a special trip from Canberra to voice the concerns of his Government and those of other Latin American Consultative Parties. The Uruguayan Government was 'gravely disappointed' at the apparent U-turn in New Zealand's position. Uruguay believed that CRAMRA contained detailed and widely acceptable provisions for the protection of the environment, and therefore continued to support it. In Uruguay's assessment, France and Australia had been completely isolated at the Paris ATCM, and there was no subsequent evidence to suggest that they would achieve anything in their attempts to undermine the Convention. A number of other countries, especially in Latin America, shared Uruguay's view that New Zealand's decision to set aside the Convention had been misguided. Moreover, the content and manner of New Zealand's announcement had led Uruguay to question its bilateral relationship with New Zealand. Uruguay and a number of its neighbours had seen New Zealand as an important partner on a wide range of issues, for example as a fellow member of the Cairns Group in the Uruguay round of GATT negotiations. The inconsistency in New Zealand's Antarctic policy led to a question whether New Zealand could be trusted in those negotiations.[108]

New Zealand, Australia and France were, however, not the only Treaty countries in which environmentalist organisations were bringing increasing pressure to bear on government policy-makers to take a stronger line against the exploitation of mineral resources in Antarctica. In Chile, for example, a new Government succeeded the Pinochet regime, and New Zealand diplomats were informed that the new Ministers wanted environmental issues in Antarctica given the highest priority.[109] Although Chile had already taken an initiative in regard to the Antarctic environment, this was a radical shift from its traditional position on sovereignty, if the statement could be taken at face value.

While the United States still regarded a permanent ban on mining as non-negotiable, the discussion of these new ideas surely signalled the beginning of a shift, not dissimilar from what had taken place in New Zealand, away from unequivocal support of CRAMRA. With New Zealand's public decision to put off ratification indefinitely, it must have become clear to the other Consultative Parties that Australia and France were not—as the Latin Americans may have hoped—in an 'isolated position', and that a consensus based on support by the Consultative Parties for the Convention was not to be had. There was thus a real danger, as suggested by Palmer, that with the Treaty partners in disarray the initiative might be seized by the proponents of a United Nations regime. A new proposal was therefore needed—whether as a supplement to CRAMRA or an alternative to it—to enable the Consultative Parties to regain the initiative and build a new consensus. It was towards this objective that the more active of the Consultative Parties now bent their minds in preparation for the Santiago SCM, scheduled for November.

XIV

AN ENVIRONMENTAL PROTECTION PROTOCOL

The 'second protocol', adumbrated in February 1990 by American officials to deal with environmental protection in Antarctica differed in form from the Franco-Australian proposal in that it would be a protocol *to the Antarctic Treaty* and not a stand-alone Convention. It differed also from the New Zealand proposal in that it would embrace all environmental issues within a single instrument, rather than deal with them in a range of measures or agreements. In content, it differed from the Franco-Australian proposal in that it was clearly not intended to replace CRAMRA, but to stand alongside it. It thus constituted a third possible approach to the development of the comprehensive system of environmental protection called for in Recommendation 1 of the Fifteenth ATCM.

During a visit to Washington in April, Beeby was informed that following inter-agency discussions there was now an agreed American position based on retention of CRAMRA, with additional environmental protection measures in the form of a protocol to the Antarctic Treaty, and some kind of delay in the initiation of any minerals activity under CRAMRA in the form of a moratorium. The protocol would comprise a set of principles, a schedule of existing and future legally binding measures, a secretarial infrastructure and a compulsory dispute settlement procedure.

American officials envisaged a discussion of these ideas with New Zealand, British, Norwegian and possibly one or two Latin

American representatives in a small group in advance of a Nansen Institute meeting in Oslo in May, where they could then seek the blessing of a wider group. It would be best, they thought, to 'allow the Franco-Australian wave to break' before attempting to put forward other ideas.[1]

Also in April, France and Australia circulated a revision of their proposal to all Antarctic Treaty parties. Although it did not specify that their 'comprehensive regime' should take the form of a convention, it did so perhaps by implication, envisaging that Antarctica would be declared a 'nature reserve—land of science', and proposing new machinery to give effect to its provisions. In describing the components of a regime, the revised paper drew extensively on the New Zealand working paper submitted to the Fifteenth ATCM.[2]

By the end of April, when a seminar on Antarctica was held at the Australian National University, the Australians had become aware that a rival proposal was being discussed by American and British officials. Predictably they were not pleased. They assumed that while the concept of a protocol to the Antarctic Treaty might be regarded as more radical in form, it would be less radical in content than their own proposals. More important, perhaps, was the fact that domestically their initiative was firmly identified in the public mind as a proposal for a new convention.[3]

In May, a meeting was held in Wellington with environmentalist and scientific bodies and individuals concerned with Antarctica, in preparation for which both government and non-governmental participants were invited to submit their ideas in writing. Some participants, notably the representatives of the Auckland University Antarctic Policy Group (Hemmings), ASOC and Greenpeace, continued to be critical of the Government's failure to adopt the Franco-Australian proposals *in toto*, and in particular of its failure to give up explicitly on CRAMRA and adopt a pro-active stance against Antarctic mining.[4] These representatives came away with their suspicions reburnished and undimmed. Cath Wallace expressed concern that there were still some powerful groups opposing a no-mining conservation regime for Antarctica, and that some officials left open the retention of

CRAMRA. 'Environmentalists,' she said, 'have nominated the abandonment of the Minerals Convention as a key election goal.'[5]

Reporting to Ministers, the officials who had taken part in the consultations noted that while all the NGO organisations and individuals had agreed with the Government's position on environmental protection and opposition to mining in Antarctica, there had been differences on the question of CRAMRA. Some NGOs, such as ASOC, ECO and Greenpeace sought a commitment to the complete abandonment of CRAMRA, whereas others saw value in retaining the Convention while a more comprehensive environmental protection regime was negotiated. There was also disagreement about New Zealand's role in the negotiation of the liability protocol to CRAMRA. Some NGOs considered that there should be no further discussion of the liability issue, some favoured 'low-key' participation in the talks, while others favoured an active role, bearing in mind the possible applicability of the liability protocol to broader environmental protection measures.[6]

Officials followed up this report by preparing a lengthy Cabinet paper. This took into account also the discussions with some Treaty partners which had taken place concurrently with the Nansen Institute meeting. The NGO consultations had shown that there was strong support for a leading New Zealand role at Santiago in promoting a comprehensive environmental protection regime and in opposing mining in Antarctica. There was 'good news' from the talks in Oslo: some creative thinking had been going on 'similar to ideas under consideration by New Zealand officials', about how such a regime could be developed. It seemed that a New Zealand proposal would achieve maximum impact if presented as a draft outline treaty: this would 'pick up the desire expressed by a large number of the NGOs for the Government to promote a single over-arching instrument on environmental protection'. One promising possibility would be to put forward a protocol designed as a supplement to the Antarctic Treaty. This would be very close to the Franco-Australian proposal for a separate convention, but would solve the problem of the relationship between this instrument and the other components of the Antarctic treaty system. The protocol would not deal with the mining issue. It had been clear from the discussions at Oslo that countries who supported CRAMRA, including the United Kingdom, the United States, Argentina, Chile, Norway, the Soviet Union and Japan, were not prepared to agree to including a permanent unqualified ban on mining, which would contradict their position on CRAMRA. It would be necessary to treat the mining issue separately. The Australians and French seemed to have reached the same conclusion and had made the mining ban a less central element in their April draft. (The Franco-Australian paper envisaged the establishment of a list of activities which could not be kept within acceptable limits and should therefore be prohibited. Provision should be made for particular classes of activity to be added to or deleted from the list. Australia and France would see mining as an activity that should be prohibited—but the paper did not make it clear whether they would insist that it be included in the prohibited list *ab initio*.) It had been suggested during the NGO consultations that the use of mining be set aside in the same way that the Antarctic Treaty set aside the contentious issue of sovereignty. It would be essential, however, to emphasise at Santiago that the New Zealand Government was committed to a no-mining position.

The paper noted that the moratorium adopted at the same time as CRAMRA was weak. (The Final Act of the Convention had stipulated that the participants would 'urge their nationals and other States to refrain from Antarctic mineral resource activities as defined in the Convention pending its timely entry into force'.) Other parties recognised the danger that such a moratorium might lose its effect with the passage of time, and there was a willingness to consider the adoption of a more formal moratorium until the basic disagreement over mining was resolved. There was a difference of view, however, as to whether such a moratorium should or should not be linked to CRAMRA; a number of the major Treaty partners would accept a moratorium only if it were linked to the entry into force of the Convention, while on the other hand there was no sign that Australia and France would modify their position in support of a complete ban on mining.

The paper did not come down on one side or the other: officials, it said, wished to consider further the possibilities of developing an effective moratorium proposal that would move the treaty parties away from the current stalemate.

The paper recommended that Cabinet agree in principle that New Zealand's position at the Santiago meeting should include the presentation of a draft environmental protocol to the Antarctic Treaty; that it should make clear New Zealand's stand against mining; that officials should continue to explore the possibility of New Zealand's proposing a long-term, legally binding moratorium on mining; and that the delegation at Santiago should take 'an appropriately low-key approach' to the negotiations on the liability protocol to the Minerals Convention.[7]

When Cabinet considered these recommendations it made two significant amendments to them. It said that the proposal for a protocol to the Antarctic Treaty should be launched as a New Zealand initiative by the Prime Minister. The Cabinet paper had not adverted to the fact that the idea of dealing with the environmental issues in this way had originated with the United States, although the Minister of Foreign Affairs and Trade had been informed of American thinking in February.[8]

The second amendment said that New Zealand should promote a long-term, legally binding moratorium on mining *independent of CRAMRA*.[9] Officials from MERT were concerned by this decision and asked their Minister and the Prime Minister to reconsider it. They argued on the one hand that such a moratorium was unlikely to be acceptable to some of the treaty parties, and on the other that it would be environmentally weak, since there would be no rules to govern mining in place when the moratorium came to an end—however lengthy a period might be stipulated. The submission suggested that a preferable alternative might be a moratorium that would last indefinitely until such time as a high majority of ATCPs were agreed that the ban on prospecting should be lifted; but there was no need, at this stage, to decide on any particular form of moratorium.[10]

These arguments evidently did not convince. When nearly

three weeks later Palmer publicly announced New Zealand's new policy (Cabinet had rejected a draft press release attached to the Cabinet paper), he said specifically that the Government had decided to push for a moratorium which was independent of the Minerals Convention.

Palmer also refuted any suggestion that the Government had some kind of hidden agenda in regard to CRAMRA. This was simply not true. 'We have set it aside. *I see no need to come back to it.*[11] [Author's emphasis.] This passage in the press statement was evidently added at the last minute, presumably by the Prime Minister himself. He thus took yet another step away from the Convention—indeed he had now got almost as far from it as it was possible to go.

American officials appear to have taken New Zealand's new policy, and its reassertion of an intention to take a leading role, in stride. The new Assistant Secretary of State for Ocean and Environment Affairs, Buff Bohlen, told the New Zealand Embassy, 'only half in jest' that he was 'pretty comfortable' with New Zealand's approach and indeed the United States was now 'only following New Zealand's lead'. American officials acknowledged that there was no prospect of CRAMRA entering into force until some additional environmental measures had been put in place. De-linking the two questions, as New Zealand had suggested, and dealing with the environmental protocol first, was a means by which consensus could be achieved and the cooperative process restored. There would not be too much difficulty in extending the voluntary moratorium, provided the negotiation of the protocol could be pursued expeditiously.[12]

ASOC was not appeased. It wanted Palmer to publicly 'abandon' CRAMRA and

> to resist the proposals from our Ministry of External Relations and Trade, and from the pro-mining states such as USA, West Germany and Japan, for a form of agreement that could allow the Minerals Convention to be brought in at a later date as part of the environmental agreement, perhaps after a moratorium of a few decades.[13]

In mid-July, Beeby attended a seminar on the Law of the Sea under the auspices of the University of Kiel. It had been agreed beforehand that the officials who had been involved in the discussions at Oslo of an environmental protocol to the Antarctic Treaty might stay on for an extra couple of days in Kiel to explore the concept further. Those attending came from New Zealand, Norway, Chile, Argentina, India, the United States, the United Kingdom and the Soviet Union. (Ironically, the Federal Republic could not be represented, because of a change in the leadership of their Antarctic team.) This was a productive meeting which produced—no doubt on the basis of much preliminary work by some representatives—a full draft of the proposed protocol.

On his return Beeby reported developments to the other departments concerned. It had been agreed that a two-step procedure might be followed: first, the circulation to ATCPs of an outline paper, followed shortly afterwards by the draft protocol. It had been noted that if all the governments represented at Kiel were not in a position to put their names to the latter document, the problem could be solved by putting it forward in the name of one delegation only; and it was noted that New Zealand was already committed by the Prime Minister's statement of 6 July to present a draft protocol. (Thus the difficulty, if it was a difficulty, of putting forward the work of a committee as a New Zealand initiative, would be neatly avoided.)

The proposed structure—a protocol with annexes that would form part of the protocol but could be added to subsequently—was preferable, Beeby argued, to the Franco-Australian proposal for a comprehensive convention, which would inevitably take years to negotiate if it were decided that agreement must first be reached on all the elements to be included. The structure proposed in the Kiel draft acknowledged the undeniable fact that the enhancement of environmental protection for Antarctica must be a continuing process. It would also eliminate the doubts entertained by some ATCPs about the legally binding character of recommendations adopted under Article IX of the Antarctic Treaty.[14] It would avoid the need for new institutions that would erode the authority vested in ATCMs by Article IX of the Treaty.

On the other hand, if all those involved in the Kiel meeting could persuade their governments to commit themselves to the proposals, in particular Argentina, this would commit them to the proposed infrastructure in the Antarctic Treaty, including a secretariat (which Argentina had hitherto opposed).[15]

Notable absentees from the Kiel meeting were, of course, representatives of Australia and France. The proposals for a protocol could be construed as a move to gazump their initiative. Beeby had, however, expounded New Zealand thinking at a meeting of Australian and New Zealand Foreign Affairs lawyers immediately before setting off for Kiel. After describing the advantages that New Zealand saw in a protocol over a convention, Beeby had remarked that if ATCPs tried unfruitfully to resolve the mining issue in Santiago this could prevent important progress on other fronts including environmental protection. The Australians had said that their policy was in an evolutionary process, and that they had not yet committed themselves to circulating a text at Santiago. But it seemed that they were still strongly attached to the concept of a convention.

On the question of mining, the Australian officials said their position was clear. Australia wanted a ban: it was uneasy about a time-fixed moratorium and would prefer an open-ended one, although that would be difficult to distinguish from a ban. They acknowledged that Australia's principal aim at Santiago was to get its ideas for a comprehensive environmental protection regime adopted and realistically would not be going there to achieve a ban on mining.[16]

Be that as it may, the adoption of an outright ban on mining was the crucial difference between the proposals of Australia and France on the one hand and the protocol drafted at Kiel on the other: and this was the rock on which New Zealand's continued participation in the Kiel group—perhaps even in a leading role—was to founder.

On 3 August the Leader of the Opposition spoke about Antarctica to an environmental conference in Christchurch. Moratoriums, he said, were only temporary:

> I share the disappointment of thousands of New Zealanders that our present Prime Minister, who is also Minister for the Environment, has thus far refused to commit his Government to support the call to ban mining in Antarctica—with an election looming he will probably change his mind tomorrow. The sight of the election gallows I am sure will concentrate his mind.
>
> . . . It is not good enough for the Labour Government to simply 'set aside' the convention and blandly commit itself to seeking new initiatives. The initiatives . . . are already on the table.
>
> The next National Government will, in conjunction with Australia, actively promote the concept of a world wildlife park for Antarctica. I will expect my Minister of the Environment to take a leading role in persuading those treaty nations less enthusiastic about a total ban . . . that it is the only responsible option . . . [At Santiago] this country will advocate the implementation of a single convention for Antarctica, a key feature of which will be a total ban on mineral exploitation now and in the future.[17]

Thus the position of the Opposition was fully aligned with that of the Hawke Government (and of ASOC). Not surprisingly, in talks with Hawke in August Palmer acknowledged that electoral considerations were also in his mind. He wanted to make an electoral impact with New Zealand's proposal, he said, and that would determine the timing of its presentation.

It had been necessary, Palmer told Hawke, to show that New Zealand was divorced from CRAMRA.[18] It might be thought that this had been done with sufficient clarity in Palmer's statement of 18 June. It now seemed necessary, however—perhaps as a reaction to Bolger's speech—to promulgate the decree absolute. On 23 August Palmer told a TV interviewer that

> There is no difference between our policy and the Australian policy. We have said in relation to the mining convention that we aren't going to ratify; we've set it aside; that means we've abandoned it.
>
> . . . We have said in our Government Paper of last year that we are going to legislate against mining in Antarctica, in that part of it that we control, and we are. We are for permanent bans on mining in Antarctica.[19]

(What the White Paper had said on the latter point was that:

> Ultimately, changing world opinion may lead the Treaty nations to reach a consensus that Antarctica should be accorded permanent protection from extraction industries *in toto*. Such a consensus, if reached, would be in accord with New Zealand's policy goals.

The White Paper went on to make it clear that in the absence of such a consensus, the proposed New Zealand legislation would be of an interim nature pending the entry into force of CRAMRA.)[20]

Palmer's rewording of his Government's position was greeted with rejoicing by the environmental lobbyists. 'We are jubilant,' said Cath Wallace. 'It is a great day for the penguins.'[21] After having had consultations with the NGOs, officials sat down to prepare yet another Cabinet paper. After much argument a revised draft was produced, but the departments were unable to reach full agreement on their recommendations.

Cabinet was advised that the Kiel package had a number of strong attractions. It removed the fundamental problem thrown up by the Franco-Australian proposal for a separate convention: what was the relationship to be between that convention and the existing legal instruments of the Antarctic treaty system, including the Treaty itself. It would also allow the Treaty parties to move quickly to get the basic principles of environmental protection into place, without having to wait until all the detailed provisions had been negotiated. The package offered, in the opinion of officials, the prospect of real progress at the Santiago meeting. New Zealand had been given the opportunity, if it wished, to circulate the draft protocol prepared at Kiel, and thus of taking the leading role in presenting a proposal that had a good chance of success. On the other hand, the Kiel package was not ideal from the New Zealand point of view. The institutional arrangements were less fully elaborated than New Zealand would want, and the absence of the annexes would be characterised by the New Zealand NGOs and the Opposition as indicating support for a partial solution and a lack of commitment to the comprehensive regime which the Government had said it wanted. Officials therefore advised against New Zealand's taking any role in promoting the Kiel package but suggested it should devote its efforts to a more comprehensive approach. At the same time, it was important not to attack or otherwise undermine the Kiel proposals. That would alienate a number of the most influential Antarctic Treaty countries and New Zealand would almost certainly be excluded from any future discussions in this group, thus losing considerable influence within the Antarctic treaty system. The structure underlying the Kiel package did offer the best prospect of achieving environmental protection within a realistic timeframe. A New Zealand initiative could 'employ the structure to advance the elements' set out in the White Paper. A presentation at Santiago along these lines

> would not prejudice the possibility of a consensus on the Kiel approach while maintaining New Zealand's capability of playing an influential role and therefore help the promotion of a New Zealand protocol as a credible and innovative initiative.

Cabinet may well have been bemused by this attempt to paper over interdepartmental disagreement. It was clear, in any event, that policy-making was becoming more and more NGO-driven. In consultations with the NGOs, officials had been unable to convince them that the chances of resolving the mining issue at Santiago were negligible, and that leaving that issue to be dealt with in an annex to the protocol would be preferably to insisting on the inclusion of a ban on mining in the main body of the protocol, if that were to totally frustrate progress in the negotiation of a general environmental regime. NGOs were unconcerned at the suggestion that this could delay the achievement of any agreement, possibly for years, even assuming there was an initial agreement to start negotiations on a mining ban. There was no agreement between officials and NGOs on this point. In bringing the NGO view to the attention of Cabinet, officials suggested that it would be unproductive for New Zealand to stand aside from the position of most, if not all, of the Consultative Parties that the mining issue and the question of a comprehensive should be treated separately.

The Cabinet paper noted that there had been no consideration at Kiel of how the mining issue should be dealt with. The question whether a mining ban should be by way of a moratorium, as Cabinet had decided in June, or by a permanent ban, had been discussed with the NGOs. Officials had attempted to convince the NGOs that the purpose of the moratorium was to achieve a ban on mining and that there was really no difference between the NGOs' position and the Government's. The NGOs would not accept this assurance—perhaps not altogether surprisingly. They demanded that the New Zealand position for Santiago incorporate the negotiation of a permanent ban. They made it clear that if Ministers did not meet them on this point they would make it an issue in the forthcoming election campaign. Since the meeting with the NGOs, the paper noted, the Prime Minister had indicated that the Government favoured a permanent ban.

Officials therefore recommended that New Zealand should support as comprehensive a protocol as possible, which would incorporate a permanent ban on mining. The disagreement among officials related not to that point, but to the form the New Zealand draft protocol should take. The Ministry of the Environment favoured a single protocol that would contain in its body all the rules required to regulate all activities in Antarctica including a ban on mining. The other departments involved—Conservation, Prime Minister's, DSIR and MERT favoured 'a single protocol whose body contains the basic principles of environmental protection applying to all activities in Antarctica, provisions on dispute settlement, plus a series of annexes containing additional rules governing specific activities in Antarctica *including a ban on mining*'. [Author's emphasis.]

The Ministry of the Environment believed that its favoured option was 'the best way of staking out a maximum New Zealand position'. It would create incentives for the inclusion of important elements such as environmental impact assessment procedures to be negotiated and agreed as early as possible. Conversely, the other departments thought it much more likely that such an approach would cause the achievement of any agreement to be considerably delayed. It offered no solution to the problem, inherent also in the Franco-Australian proposal, that all issues, including the difficult ones like liability, would have to be negotiated before there could be any progress. Nor would it solve the problem of the legal status of past and future recommendations by ATCPs under Article IX of the Antarctic Treaty. The other departments considered that their favoured option also offered the opportunity to stake out a 'maximalist' New Zealand position. An agreement need not be delayed until all the difficult issues were resolved. There would be widespread agreement that important elements, including environmental impact procedures, should be negotiated and agreed at the earliest possible date prior to the adoption of the Protocol.[22]

It is a measure of the influence now wielded by Ministry of the Environment officials and the NGOs with Ministers, in particular the Prime Minister, that Cabinet decided to go for the option advocated by that Ministry. It is a reasonable assumption that Ministers were concerned at the likely reaction of the environmental NGOs to a proposal that the mining ban should be relegated to an annex which might or might not be adopted at the same time as the protocol, or which might not be agreed to at all, and which, if adopted subsequently, would be subject to a separate ratification procedure.

At any rate, Cabinet decided on 3 September 1990 that New Zealand's position for the Santiago meeting would be to favour a single protocol which would contain in its body all the rules to regulate all activities in Antarctica, including a ban on mining. Fortunately, perhaps, it also agreed that the New Zealand delegation should have flexibility on the means of advancing the elements of the New Zealand approach. It was decided that the Prime Minister would announce the policy in a speech on 8 September, and that a New Zealand draft protocol should be circulated to the ATCPs *and made public* a month before the Santiago meeting.[23]

The Prime Minister was thus well placed to flourish his environmentalist credentials in the election campaign: but fate intervened. On 4 September, after setting 27 October as the election date, he was dumped by the Labour Caucus from the leadership of his party. His place was taken by Mike Moore who, although he had been and continued to be Minister of Foreign Affairs and Trade, had not made the Antarctic negotiations one of his principal interests. The 8 September speech was given by Philip Woollaston.[24] Palmer decided not to remain in politics and so, although he retained his Environment portfolio outside Cabinet, he did not play a significant part in the election campaign. Neither, for that matter, did the Antarctic environment issue.

Cabinet's decision that New Zealand should aim for a permanent ban on mining as an integral element of an environment protocol effectively ruptured New Zealand's association with the rest of the Kiel group. The reaction of the other participants—in particular the British, Americans and Norwegians—can only be guessed at.

On 29 August legislation was introduced in Parliament to prohibit mining by anyone in the Ross Dependency and mining by New Zealanders anywhere in Antarctica. Briefing for New Zealand's overseas posts asserted that the draft legislation was consistent with New Zealand sovereignty in the Ross Dependency and was not contrary to Article IV of the Antarctic Treaty.[25] (In other words, the legislation did not purport to strengthen the New Zealand claim.) Nevertheless representations were received from the United States, the Soviet Union and Japan. The United States, recalling that it neither asserted nor recognised claims to territorial sovereignty in Antarctica, and did not therefore recognise New Zealand's claim to 'the New Zealand Antarctic territory', rejected New Zealand's right to regulate United States nationals for any purpose and could not accept legislation purporting to do so with regard to possible mineral resource activities in New Zealand's claimed territory. If such legislation were enacted the United States would be obliged to lodge a formal protest. (The United States' note did not refer to its own 'basis of claim', asserted on other occasions.)

The United States went on to rebuke New Zealand for a 'unilateral action' which, in its view, would neither strengthen the Antarctic system nor help to restore the consensus which was needed if Antarctic environmental issues, including the issue of possible minerals activities, were to be satisfactorily dealt with. The Soviet Union made the same point, suggesting that New Zealand's action could trigger similar steps by other claimant governments; this could have a negative impact on the forthcoming Antarctic conferences, and would encourage 'extreme approaches leading to the disruption of the Antarctic Treaty system'.

The Foreign Ministry responded to the representations of the three Governments that New Zealand sovereignty in the Ross Dependency long predated the Antarctic Treaty. The fact that New Zealand was legislating in respect of the Dependency was neither a new claim nor an enlargement of an existing claim. A large body of New Zealand law already applied to the Dependency.[26] The Australian Government received similar representations in regard to comparable legislation, and made a similar response.[27] The Australian legislation was actually passed in March 1991. The New Zealand legislation was not enacted until December 1994.

The Cabinet decision of 3 September obviously brought New Zealand's policy closer to Australia's, but differences about the modalities remained. New Zealand officials in Canberra were informed that Australia and France had decided to circulate a draft convention at Santiago. An attempt would be made to meet the objection that a convention would take decision-making powers away from the ATCM, and to put such decision-making 'more squarely within the Treaty framework'. Australian officials emphasised that there would be no weakening in their position on a mining ban, which would be written into the new instrument. Australia would push hard for prospecting to be banned along with mining, and expected the British to be especially difficult on this point. The Australian Government, their officials said, had been under fire for 'backsliding' on a number of domestic 'green' issues which were complicated by economic considerations. There were no such complications in respect of Antarctica, and the Government would wish to play the issue for all it was worth in terms of showing its environmentalist credentials. There was no softening of the brief from Hawke, who intended to make a further statement on Antarctica in the run-up to Santiago.[28]

New Zealand officials, in consultation with the NGOs, carried out Cabinet's directive to draft a 'comprehensive' protocol, one which included as much substance as possible in the body of the instrument, rather than in annexes. As presented to the SCM (which was held at Viña del Mar, a coastal resort some distance from Santiago), it ran to some 61 articles. It included chapters establishing institutions, prohibiting mining, protecting 'Antarctic values', establishing environmental impact procedures and monitoring programmes, providing for waste management and the prevention of marine pollution, providing for a code of practice to regulate tourism, setting out the procedure for dispute settlement, and ending with the usual machinery clauses. There was, in addition, a schedule on arbitration, and provision for eight annexes. The draft did not contain rules relating to liability for damage to the Antarctic environment, but it was the stated intention to prepare stringent rules after further consultation with New Zealand's Treaty partners.

The institutions provided for in the New Zealand draft included an Antarctic Environmental Protection Inspectorate, an Advisory Committee for Environmental Protection and a Secretariat. The Consultative Parties were required to oversee the implementation of the protocol at Consultative Meetings, taking into account the views of the Advisory Committee.

Mineral resource activities were to be prohibited on the continent of Antarctica and on all Antarctic islands, including all ice-shelves south of 60° south latitude, and in the seabed and subsoil of all adjacent off-shore areas up to the deep seabed. This language was taken from Article 5 of CRAMRA and was designed to avoid conflict with the provisions of the Law of the Sea Treaty.

The article dealing with entry into force provided that this should take place when an unspecified number of the Consultative Parties had ratified the protocol. It thus seemed designed to avoid the requirement of unanimity specified for the entry into force of the Antarctic Treaty itself and subsequent recommendations of ATCMs (including the Agreed Measures for the Protection of Fauna and Flora) and also the complicated formula in Article 62 of CRAMRA. It also seems likely that ratification by a substantial majority of Consultative Parties was what the drafters had in mind, in contrast to the eight ratifications required to bring the Convention on Marine Living Resources into force. Unlike CRAMRA and CCAMLR, the draft contained no provision for withdrawal.[29]

In submitting the draft protocol to Cabinet, the Associate Minister of Foreign Affairs and Trade noted that many suggestions from the NGOs had been included. However, ASOC had wanted to go further and embody 'a presumption against human activity' in Antarctica. This, the Cabinet paper pointed out, would be contrary to the Antarctic Treaty itself, which provided for complete freedom of scientific activity. The protocol would nevertheless considerably strengthen the standards of environmental protection, together with the means by which the acceptability of all human activity was to be judged.[30]

The draft protocol was submitted to Cabinet on 23 October and released to the media by the Prime Minister on 25 October.[31] The general elections took place on 27 October, resulting in a win for the National Party led by Jim Bolger with a large majority. The approval of the draft protocol was thus the last decision of the Fourth Labour Government on Antarctic matters. Because of his other duties following the change of Government, Beeby was unable to attend the SCM in Viña del Mar, and the New Zealand delegation was instead led by the head of MERT's Legal Division, Frank Wong. The new Ministers were briefed on New Zealand's position as represented by its draft protocol, and agreed to the continuance of the existing policy, including negotiating flexibility for the delegation on the structure of the protocol and annexes.[32]

The five members of the Kiel Group, following New Zealand's defection (Argentina, Norway, the United Kingdom, the United States and Uruguay), circulated to other ATCPs the outline of a draft protocol that had been agreed by that group. The United States, in endorsing that outline, emphasised its view that no unnecessary burdens should be placed by the protocol on the planning and conduct of scientific research in Antarctica. In formulating annexes to the protocol, priority attention should be given to marine pollution, waste disposal, environmental impact assessment, and an annex based on the agreed measures for the conservation of Antarctic fauna and flora. The United States saw no need for work on these annexes to be completed as a precondition for the conclusion of the protocol, or for a list of future annexes to be agreed in preparing the text of the protocol. The United States' position thus differed from New Zealand's in relegating to annexes four important elements included in the body of the New Zealand draft, and in not committing the United States to any position on the issue of Antarctic mining.[33]

At the SCM the United Kingdom and the United States each circulated a draft protocol on similar lines, and an indicative draft convention prepared by Australia and France was co-sponsored by Belgium and Italy.[34]

The gap that had opened up between the positions of New Zealand and the United States (which claimed the support of the United Kingdom, Norway, the Soviet Union and the Latin Americans, among others) was demonstrated when American comments on the New Zealand draft were elicited on the eve of the SCM. Scully, a long-time collaborator with New Zealand officials on Antarctic matters, said bluntly that the State Department was opposed to the inclusiveness of the New Zealand draft, especially the ban on mining. Apart from the fact that the United States did not favour a permanent ban, they believed that to focus on this issue would detract from the work needed to enhance environment protection measures—the *raison d'etre* for the meeting. It was unfortunate that the NGOs had raised false expectations that a minerals ban could and should be achieved at Viña del Mar. The United States could generally support those aspects of the New Zealand draft that followed the Kiel framework, but did not think it helpful to put everything in the one document: the device of employing annexes provided flexibility when amendments to parts of the protocol needed to be made.

The bottom line for the United States, according to Scully, was that it did not support either a permanent ban on mining or an indefinite moratorium. It would agree to 'a time-specific, events-specific moratorium that could be extended by consensus'. Environmental safeguards like those in CRAMRA would have to be in place before the moratorium was lifted.[35]

The differences represented by the various drafts were therefore wide, and the prospects 'for agreement at Viña del Mar did not look especially bright. After ten days of negotiations the New Zealand delegation reported an impasse in the working group dealing with the principles and structure of an environmental regime. Although the proposal for a draft convention requiring prior authorisation of activities had caused widespread apprehension and attracted very limited support, its proponents continued to insist that their draft should have equal status to any compromise proposals that might be made. In particular, they insisted that prior authorisation of activities should be enshrined as a principle, and that the description of Antarctica as a 'nature reserve, land of science' must be retained.

On the question of a mining ban, there was a different line-up. Australia and New Zealand maintained their insistence on a mining ban within the body of the instrument, while Japan argued equally strongly for regulation by CRAMRA alone. There was a trend (supported by the United States, the Soviet Union, Chile and Brazil) towards the concept of a moratorium, though its duration and provisions for its review remained open questions. While it was accepted that minerals would have to form part of any package, there was little prospect of agreement on this issue at Vina.

On the question of the structure of the protocol, New Zealand had come under pressure from France, Norway, the United States, the United Kingdom, the Soviet Union, Chile and Brazil, all of whom considered that apart from principles, institutions, dispute settlement, possibly the principle of environmental impact assessment and inspection and (if agreed) a minerals prohibition, everything else should go into annexes. For all of them it was important to separate the general principles and rules which would have continuing application from the detailed regulations that would require regular modification and updating for their effectiveness. If these detailed rules were included in the body of the instrument, the legal systems of a number of countries would require legislative ratification of every amendment, whereas amendments to annexes could be brought into effect by executive decision. In light of this situation, the delegation sought authority to accept structural changes to the draft protocol and to decide what went into the body and what went into the annexes, on the understanding that it would maintain the New Zealand position that the mining ban must remain in the body of the protocol. This authority was granted.[36]

A number of delegations—Australia, Brazil, Chile, France, New Zealand, Norway, the United Kingdom, the United States and the Soviet Union—met privately to try to hammer out a compromise. The Norwegian representative (Rolf Andersen) then put together a draft which attempted to merge the four proposals on the table. His paper, which drew considerably on the New Zealand draft, came to be accepted as the basis for future work. The question of the mining ban continued to be a point of contention. Andersen included an article prohibiting mining in square brackets in the body of the protocol. This was acceptable to Brazil, Chile, the United Kingdom, the United States and Soviet Union delegations as not prejudicing their view of how the minerals issues should be addressed. Australia and France, on the other hand, insisted that the brackets be removed. In further discussion, however, it became clear that a number of influential delegations who had reservations about the substance of the bracketed Article were prepared to consider a form of moratorium, and that Australia and France were prepared to go along with such an approach. An Article was drafted by the Chilean Chairman which would provide for a rolling 50-year ban; this could be reviewed at the request of a substantial majority of Consultative Parties, which would trigger a process for negotiating new rules on mining to be adopted by consensus. Except for Japan and New Zealand, the principals of the delegations consulted considered that it would be possible to seek the approval of governments to a text drafted on this basis. Australia and France had slightly different approaches. Australia did not want to specify the duration of the moratorium but agreed that it could be reviewable. France wanted a reviewable 50-year ban, but did not want any reference to how mining should be regulated if the ban were lifted. Japan could not agree to any moratorium.

It was New Zealand, however, which now adopted the purest 'environmental' stand. The New Zealand delegation said that while it would be prepared to convey the Chilean ideas to Wellington, it was not in a position to negotiate anything along these lines. The Andersen draft of a permanent ban met New Zealand's requirements, even if it had to remain for the time being in square brackets. The delegation could offer no assurance that the Government could accept anything less. The delegation told the Australian delegation that a reviewable prohibition was not a permanent ban, and that if a new draft Article along these lines were included, it would feel obliged to say so publicly. Given the public position of the Hawke Government, this was calculated to put the Australians on the spot.

In the ensuing impasse, the New Zealand delegation offered a compromise. The final report, they proposed, should indicate the widespread support for a limited ban, together with the fact that some delegations were committed to a permanent ban and others to CRAMRA. In return, the square brackets would be removed, with a few dots at the end of the Article to indicate the need for further work. This solution was adopted. The delegation reported that, although the draft protocol now contained an unlimited ban, support for a form of moratorium was undeniably growing.

The delegation reported that it had also been instrumental in maintaining a strong environmental approach to the other key issues, the procedures for environmental impact assessment and the role of the proposed advisory committee in relation to their application. The Australian position had been that there should be prior majority approval by the committee before an activity could proceed. The Australians first abandoned this position in favour of the New Zealand approach, that an activity should be suspended if there were a 'preponderant' view in the Committee that the activity was inconsistent with the principles set out in the protocol.[37] They then indicated that they were prepared to abandon the New Zealand proposal in favour of an alternative put forward by the United States and the United Kingdom which would simply require public notification some time before an activity could proceed. The issue was not settled at Viña del Mar, but was left in square brackets to be debated further in the next round.[38]

New Zealand also played a major role in the discussion of texts dealing with compliance and dispute settlement, but found itself rather alone in arguing for rules as tough as those in CRAMRA. New Zealand also received little or no support for the concept of an environmental inspectorate, although there was a reference to the possibility of collective inspection in the Andersen text. Argentina had dropped its objection to the principle of setting up a secretariat, but insisted that this should be decided 'by a regular ATCM, and not in the context of an instrument of environmental protection'. A proposal for a standing committee with decision-making powers, together with a technical and scientific committee, had been put forward by Australia, France, Italy and Belgium in the context of their draft Convention. This was strongly opposed by the Soviet Union, and the question of machinery remained open: the Andersen text provided for a 'Committee on Environmental Protection' which would formulate advice and make recommendations.[39]

(It may be noted here that the prohibition on mining in the Andersen text survived into the final version of the protocol, minus only the dots that supposedly indicated that further work on it was to be done. This work was not done, with the consequence that language in the draft article proposed by New Zealand, which corresponded with the relevant provision in CRAMRA and was designed to harmonise the protocol's area of jurisdiction with the provisions of the Law of the Sea Treaty concerning the deep seabed, does not now appear. There is thus an apparent conflict between the protocol and the Law of the

Sea Treaty in regard to mining in the deep seabed beyond the limits of national jurisdiction, but within the boundary of the Antarctic Treaty area.)

It will also be noted that at Viña del Mar New Zealand was the only Consultative Party to stand out against the concept of a moratorium or time-related ban. While a permanent ban was also the starting position of Australia and its co-sponsors of the draft convention, that instrument provided for its amendment at any time by unanimous decision of all the ATCPs and also for a review conference thirty years after its entry into force at the request of any Consultative Party. At that Conference a simple majority only of the Contracting Parties, including a majority of the Consultative Parties, would be sufficient to adopt any amendment.[40]

Although New Zealand thus had adopted the strongest environmental approach to the mining issue, this was not the impression that was conveyed back to New Zealand by the media and by (unofficial) NGO representatives. One press report, which came to New Zealand via Hobart, claimed that New Zealand was weighing in *against* the proposed mining ban. This was quickly denied and a corrected report appeared.[41] But Cath Wallace, who was in Viña del Mar under her own steam (which seemed to have built up to a strong head) was critical both of the bigger nations and of New Zealand, which she said was 'holding back from getting involved in the real scrapping'. The National Government had said that the New Zealand policy would be to move to support Australia and France: there was, she said, some surprise and indeed dismay that the Government had not come out and said so.[42] The Minister of External Relations and Trade (McKinnon) told the press that he was 'appalled and annoyed' at suggestions that the New Zealand delegation was fence-sitting and was not pushing the Government's stated commitment to a comprehensive ban on mining. Frank Wong and his team had been doing exactly what their brief required them to do in a thoroughly professional manner.[43] In a further statement at the conclusion of the meeting, the Minister noted that there was disagreement over the mining issue and the future of CRAMRA; but there was, he believed, a reasonable prospect of a full mining ban being agreed upon when the SCM resumed in Madrid in 1991.[44]

In preparation for that meeting, the Australians indicated their wish for close cooperation with New Zealand. At the end of January a representative from the New Zealand Embassy in Paris therefore attended a meeting of the cosponsors of the draft convention, together with seven 'like-minded' countries, to discuss possible amendments to the Andersen text, which the meeting accepted as the basis for further discussion. The meeting provided an opportunity for a 'careful' explanation of the Australian position on a mining ban. Australia wanted mining prohibited, full stop. The ban would be permanent in the normal legal sense. Australia did not propose that the instrument specifically say that mining would be prohibited forever. The proposal for review in the draft convention meant that any party to it could call for a review of any aspect, without implying any end to the ban. This was very different from banning for a finite period, or a moratorium which implied that mining could be undertaken after its expiry. France preferred the Andersen text, which did not imply that it could not reviewed. But face needed to be saved, and France was prepared to envisage a ban for a limited period, followed by a review, with the ban to stay unless all the parties agreed to change it. The French representative did not think it possible to reach agreement on a finite ban without guarantees about what would happen afterwards. He hinted that 'afterwards' could only mean continuation or non-continuation of the ban: CRAMRA, or CRAMRA's underlying principles, did not provide a valid fall-back.[45]

Shortly after this meeting the United States circulated a 'non-paper' to all ATCPs in their capitals. The paper suggested that 'the elements of a tolerable middle ground' had begun to emerge at Viña del Mar. These were:

(a) a legally binding moratorium in the range of 20 to 40 years;
(b) the moratorium to be lifted upon the expiration of that period, unless consensus were reached among the ATCPs to extend it; and
(c) the moratorium to cover prospecting, exploration and

> development, with safeguards to ensure that prospecting did not take place under the guise of scientific research and at the same time that legitimate scientific research was not inhibited.

The Americans, however, regarded the acceptability of such a moratorium as conditional on devising an agreed means of ensuring that the Minerals Convention, or an equivalent process for dealing with possible interest in minerals resource activities, was in place when the moratorium ended.[46]

There is no record of the New Zealand reaction to this demarche. Australia reacted 'strongly and negatively'.[47] It is a reasonable assumption that the New Zealand response, if any, was also negative.

In bilateral talks between Australian and New Zealand legal officials, the Australians indicated that their reaction to the American non-paper was to tighten up their own position. They were opposed to a moratorium, or to having CRAMRA 'click in' after 30 years. Nor did they like the word 'permanent', which in their view was without juridical meaning. They preferred the word 'prohibition' and favoured the Andersen text (minus the concluding dots) with the review provision that it contained (i.e., on the basis provided for in Article XII of the Antarctic Treaty). (The Australians appeared ready to contemplate a provision parallel to Article XII paragraph 2 of the Treaty, permitting the convening of a review conference 30 years after the protocol had entered into force; this may or may not have been what Andersen had had in mind.)

There was also discussion of the geographical scope of a mining prohibition. Beeby argued that it was important to avoid encroaching on United Nations Law of the Sea Convention authority over the deep seabed. There was also the problem of the continental shelf where it extended northwards beyond 60° south. In CRAMRA, he pointed out, there was a formula which included continental shelves but excluded the deep seabed. The discussion was inconclusive; it was suggested that the question might be dealt with in the Final Act—a suggestion that was seemingly not pursued.[48]

New Zealand officials nevertheless considered the point of

sufficient importance to include it in the Cabinet paper which was to constitute the brief for the New Zealand delegation when the SCM resumed the negotiations in Madrid in April. After interdepartmental discussion the proposed instruction in regard to mining was strengthened from requiring the delegation to seek 'as permanent a ban as possible' to 'New Zealand should work to ensure that the new regime includes a permanent ban on mining'. New Zealand's starting position would therefore be more hard-line than even that of Australia.

The Cabinet paper noted that the Andersen text did not give the Committee on Environmental Protection, which was to be set up under the new regime, any 'whistle-blowing' function. That regime would be strengthened by the inclusion within the Committee's role of the capacity to suspend activities that gave rise to environmental concerns. The paper stipulated that NGOs should be given observer rights on the Committee; there must be the strongest possible rules on compliance, response action, liability and dispute settlement; and if there was no agreement on establishing an Antarctic inspectorate, which was New Zealand's preferred option, the regime should retain the possibility of institutional inspection. The new regime must extend coverage to the burgeoning field of Antarctic tourism, and indeed all non-governmental activity on the continent; New Zealand should continue to take an active part in developing the protected areas network; the value of environmental monitoring as a means of ensuring compliance with the protocol should be promoted as an integral component of comprehensive environmental impact assessment. The paper noted that the establishment of an Antarctic Secretariat, which New Zealand favoured, would be considered not at the SCM but at the next ATCM, which was to meet in Bonn later in 1991.[49]

We shall see, as we go on, how far New Zealand was able to secure the incorporation of its wish-list in the protocol.

The Foreign Ministry was not happy with the toughening of the instruction on mining. On the eve of the discussion of the Cabinet paper in the Cabinet Environmental Committee, it advised its Minister that the Australian position was for a mining ban that might be reviewed after 30–50 years, subject to consensus on any change, and was coordinating this position with the co-sponsors of its proposals. It seemed that New Zealand could find itself in a minority of one and be accused of wrecking the possibility of consensus on an environmental protocol if it pushed too hard for a permanent mining ban. The Ministry therefore recommended, and the Minister agreed, that the Cabinet paper be amended to revert to the 'as permanent a prohibition as possible' formula.[50] The Cabinet Committee did not accept this language, but amended the instruction to read:

> There is a wide spectrum of views among the Treaty Parties on how best the minerals issue might be resolved. New Zealand's position is a permanent prohibition of mining. New Zealand officials should be in contact with other delegations to ascertain their position on this issue.

The delegation was to keep Ministers informed of major developments and seek further ministerial instruction.[51]

MERT officials had also indicated to their Minister that their patience with NGO attitudes had reached breaking point. The officials were finding it almost impossible to work with some representatives, especially Cath Wallace. She had, they said, publicly maligned two members of the delegation to the Viña del Mar meeting. The antagonistic approach of one of the two NGO members of the delegation made him more of a hindrance than a help. Since then officials had attempted to open up a constructive dialogue, but 'nothing less than the rigid acceptance and articulation of NGO views appears to be acceptable to [Wallace]'.

Officials had told the Minister that they regarded the Andersen text as very favourable to the New Zealand position. Although it differed structurally from the New Zealand proposals, in substance it included much of what New Zealand wanted, including a prohibition of mining. Wallace, on the other hand, characterised it as 'quick and dirty'. She disliked the fact that it was not identical to the New Zealand draft; she disliked the structure; she disliked the degree of priority given to science; and she believed major and extensive revisions would need to be made to it. Moreover, she was critical of the consultation process with the NGOs, of what the New Zealand delegation had been able to achieve at Viña del Mar, of the underutilisation of the NGO representatives at that meeting and of the level of seniority of the official delegates. She was therefore insistent that the NGOs be fully and formally involved in the formulation of the delegation's instructions for the Madrid meeting and on a more independent role for the NGO representatives there.

It really was not possible, officials told the Minister, to run an international negotiation, particularly one in which New Zealand's interests extended beyond environmental considerations to the Antarctic treaty system as a whole, if the NGOs felt—as they did—that they could dictate the New Zealand position and the process leading to its formulation. The Ministry therefore sought authority to *discuss* NGO proposals, in the consultations they were about to hold, but not to *negotiate* them; to tell NGOs that their views would be taken into account in briefing the delegation but that they should not expect to have a role in clearing the brief; that there would be one NGO representative at Madrid who would have to be acceptable to all the NGOs and to the Government; and that that representative would be subject to the direction of the delegation leader. The Minister agreed, subject to the admonition that the process of consultation should not be carried out in a hasty or perfunctory manner.[52] He duly wrote to Wallace and Barry Weeber (of Environment and Conservation Organisations of New Zealand [ECO]) asking for the nomination of a single NGO representative for the Madrid meeting, but warning that the current economic stringency made it extremely unlikely that the Government would be able, as it had at Viña del Mar, be able to offer any financial assistance.[53]

As the New Zealand Government firmed up its position, a message was received from the British Foreign Secretary (Hurd) seeking New Zealand's sympathetic consideration for a new British proposal about minerals. While Britain still believed strongly that CRAMRA provided the best solution to the problem, it now recognised that there was little prospect of its providing the urgently needed consensus. Nor, said Hurd, did he see any prospect of consensus in a ban of the kind proposed by New Zealand. The solution, in his opinion, lay in a moratorium providing the Consultative Parties with time and an incentive to decide how to deal with the problem in the future.

The British proposal, therefore, was to replace the terminal dots in the Andersen article prohibiting mining with the words 'in accordance with Annex X to this protocol'. Annex X would then provide for a moratorium of so many years, which would not extend automatically beyond that period. This would create an incentive for the parties to agree meanwhile on what should happen thereafter. A further article in the annex would require them to meet and agree on environmental safeguards as strong as those in CRAMRA, and on the procedures for deciding whether or not any mineral resource activities should be allowed to take place after the expiry of the moratorium.[54]

At least as far as New Zealand was concerned, the United Kingdom was still very much behind the play. McKinnon replied politely that a moratorium would not meet the New Zealand position, but that there seemed to be some positive elements in the British proposal that New Zealand would wish to consider further.[55]

The British proposals were published, but no public New Zealand comment was made. The Australians, however, issued press guidance to the effect that the proposals still contained some significant unacceptable elements. Australia believed that a fixed moratorium would create expectations of the inevitability of mining in Antarctica and run counter to international public opinion that it should not occur. The residual role envisaged for CRAMRA was unacceptable. Australia believed that 'an unqualified prohibition, amendable only by unanimous agreement in accordance with normal Antarctic Treaty procedures', as provided for in the Andersen draft protocol, offered a basis for a consensus.[56]

It appeared, however, that the Norwegians themselves did not regard a moratorium as being incompatible with the Andersen text. Andersen had intended the three terminal dots to signify that an addition to the sentence would serve to qualify the currently unqualified prohibition.[57] The Norwegian approach was thus apparently not too different from the British. The United States' approach to the question of mining also appeared broadly similar to that of the United Kingdom; it was working to elaborate a moratorium proposal.[58] The Germans indicated that they were in favour of an indefinite ban, which could nevertheless be lifted at some fairly distant date by a strong majority (say, three-quarters).[59] Not surprisingly, New Zealand posts were told that there was a wide spectrum of positions on mineral activities and that it remained the most divisive issue in the negotiations. Environmental impact assessment (EIA) had been another 'problematic' issue at Viña del Mar, and New Zealand would be working to firm up the role of the proposed environment committee's 'whistle-blowing' function in the EIA process.[60] This contrasted with firm opposition on the part of the Americans to giving the Committee any decision-making powers. The Australians were even more pessimistic than New Zealand officials about an early agreement, saying in press briefing that it would take several more rounds of meetings to persuade all the parties that a ban was necessary.[61]

The SCM resumed its meeting in Madrid from 22 to 30 April. An early development was an announcement by Japan that it now favoured a moratorium on mining until technology was advanced enough to safeguard the Antarctic environment.[62] The NGOs continued to pursue their technique of keeping the New Zealand delegation up to the mark by accusing it of backsliding. The delegation leader (Wong) was obliged to issue a statement rejecting allegations in the NGO bulletin that New Zealand was said to be considering moving from a permanent ban to a 60-year moratorium. The delegation, it was claimed, was nearly invisible, and its projection of the Government's stated policy was very weak.[63]

In fact the New Zealand delegation was arguing—in private—for a position stronger than other delegations were prepared to accept. It was reported to the Minister after two days of informal negotiation that a consensus was emerging on the following elements:

> (a) a prohibition on mining without time limit;
> (b) no review of any of the provisions in the protocol for 50 years;
> (c) after 50 years, any amendment to the protocol could be adopted by a majority of parties including a majority of the ATCPs;
> (d) in the case of minerals, however, the prohibition could not be lifted until a binding regime on minerals had entered into force. That regime would not enter into force until ratified by three-quarters of the ATCPs, including all the states that were ATCPs at the time of the adoption of the protocol.

New Zealand was arguing for a much longer 'holiday' than 50 years and that the prohibition should be liftable only by consensus. Australia and France, while they preferred a 60 year period, were prepared to go along with 50 years, and the lifting of the prohibition by something less than a consensus. It was understood that Hawke and Rocard had agreed to this approach. The delegation sought approval in principle to the four points, subject to approval by Ministers after the meeting. McKinnon agreed after consulting the Prime Minister.[64]

This was not, of course, anywhere near what New Zealand ASOC members had wanted. In meetings with officials before Madrid, they had proposed a review holiday of 999 years, subsequently modified to 200 years, with a decision to lift the ban requiring a consensus of all the parties.[65] At the end of the Conference, however, ASOC put out a press release in Madrid 'applauding' the compromise draft. Even Cath Wallace said that though it was not perfect, it went a long way towards protecting Antarctica from mining.[66] In talking to a radio interviewer, however, she was less enthusiastic, pointing to the difficulty of casting a veto against the wishes of a majority, and to the fact that if there were ever an agreement to lift the prohibition, 'something very like the Antarctic Minerals Convention' would be required to regulate mining.[67]

After the meeting the delegation reported on the difficulties that had been encountered in producing the compromise. While the meeting had been supposed to focus on the Andersen text, the situation had been complicated by the 'four' (Australia, Belgium, France and Italy) who had produced a rival draft. Although based on the Andersen text, it had proposed a decision-making role for the Environmental Protection Committee, a classification of the acceptability of activities, and a 'second guess' on the form of the eventual instrument—all propositions which had been comprehensively rejected at Viña del Mar. It was clear, moreover, that little progress would be made until there was settlement of the minerals issue.

In addition to the shift on the part of Japan, the Germans finally came off the fence and argued for a permanent ban—but signalled that they considered the objective to be unachievable and that they were therefore prepared to consider the conditions on which the ban might be lifted. The United States and the United Kingdom were also prepared to accept an unlimited prohibition, provided it was on 'the right conditions'. That set the scene for a negotiation on the duration of the review period and the conditions on which the ban could be lifted.

As at Viña del Mar, it was again Andersen of Norway who produced a text that offered 'a definitive solution of the minerals issue in the context of an overall regime as a package'. What he proposed was an indefinite prohibition with a 45-year review period requiring a double consensus at both the adoption and ratification stages to lift the ban. The 'four' were evidently prepared to compromise at a 50-year review period, dropping one of the consensus decisions. That left New Zealand alone to argue for a longer period and the retention of the double veto. The United States delegation, on the other hand, was not prepared to go beyond a 50 year 'holiday' and a single consensus. They had the support of the Soviet Union and the United Kingdom. The New Zealand delegation was confident that what was on offer was in effect a permanent ban, but in terms of its instructions it felt obliged to hold out for more. It received no support and agreed, therefore, to refer the package back for consideration. The package, it noted, had since been praised 'fulsomely' by the international NGOs and those from Australia and 'with more restraint' by the New Zealand NGOs.[68]

In a letter to the New Zealand members of ASOC, Cath Wallace said that 'privately we are very pleased about the progress made in Madrid; a draft protocol is to be put to governments which would ban minerals activity, very likely permanently'. However, she said, it was important that, to maintain negotiating power, New Zealand and the NGOs remain publicly somewhat reluctant to sign.[69]

The New Zealand delegation had also taken the lead in seeking to strengthen other parts of the Andersen text against stiff American resistance. The draft provided for NGO representation on the Environment Protection Committee and for the appointment of 'institutional' Antarctic inspectors. The New Zealand delegation had chaired the negotiations on environmental impact assessment and, with the Australians, played the major role in developing the agreed procedures. Because of the fixed time periods built into the procedures, the Committee for Environmental Protection would have effective oversight of the regime. (The Committee was not, however, given the power to suspend activities for which New Zealand had argued at earlier meetings and which was one of the desiderata in the March Cabinet paper.)

It was unclear, said the delegation's report, whether the package would ultimately be acceptable to the United States and the United Kingdom. The delegation was nevertheless optimistic. Arrangements had been made for a final meeting in Madrid from 17 to 23 June with a view to adopting the protocol. The date 23 June was the thirtieth anniversary of the entry into force of the Antarctic Treaty. Hopes to celebrate this serendipitous anniversary were, however, soon to be dashed.

At first, the news was encouraging. John Major, who had replaced Margaret Thatcher as British Prime Minister in November 1990, took the advice of the Environment Secretary (Michael Heseltine) against that of the trade and energy Ministers and 'warmly welcomed' the outcome of the Madrid meeting. The effect of the provisions of the draft protocol, he noted, was that there could never be mining in Antarctica unless all the current Consultative Parties agreed.[70] In making this statement, he contradicted a Foreign Office Minister who had told Parliament only a few days before that the British position recognised that mining 'may indeed be a possibility and that we should have a plan to cope with it'.[71]

When the New Zealand Minister of Conservation (Denis Marshall) visited Washington later in May, he was told by Bohlen and Scully that the issue was 'still very much under consideration' by the various government agencies. Scully said that concerns would relate not to any desire to preserve exploitation options but to the precedent that would be created by signing an agreement with such a long period of abstinence and an effective veto on review. This might affect the administration's position on the Arctic Wildlife Refuge, where it would be proposing 'limited and controlled' exploration. There might also be concern that prospecting would take place under the guise of science. The only way that could be allayed was to require prompt disclosure of data, and—according to Scully—there was no prospect of getting agreement to that within the time-frame of the next Madrid meeting. The Embassy detected a difference of emphasis between Bohlen and Scully. Bohlen said that 'Tucker and I have the champagne on ice'. Scully said privately that he detected a feeling at the upper levels in the State Department that Bohlen had got out in front of the policy and could have the rug pulled out from under him. The Embassy—no doubt reluctant to be the harbinger of bad news—thought that Scully's perception was unduly influenced by his long involvement with CRAMRA. 'Congressional pressure alone . . . would make Baker think twice' about rejecting the draft protocol. There was no longer a pro-mining constituency in Congress but on the other hand strong support for protecting the Antarctic environment.[72]

On 10 June, Scully gave another veiled warning that United States acceptance of the protocol should not be taken for granted, and indeed that some amendment could be expected to be sought to the decision-making rules in regard to review. The United States, he said, was reluctant to agree to a regime where it could have its interests blocked by, say, Ecuador. The decision would come from the Secretary of State (Baker) who would not be deterred from standing out from the protocol by the likelihood of the United States becoming internationally isolated on the issue. Baker's attentiveness to congressional opinion, he added, needed to be weighed against the administration's lack of sympathy with Senator Gore![73]

Two days later, the United States made a *demarche* to the Consultative Parties which, while it welcomed the Andersen text as offering the basis for restoration of the consensus, bluntly rejected the provision 'which would permit anyone of the current 26 ATCPs to prevent entry into force of an amendment lifting the prohibition on Antarctic mineral resource activities' and did not offer a means of resolving the impasse that would be created if a single party or a small minority were to block such an amendment. The United States proposed therefore to add provisions, analogous to those in the Antarctic treaty, to enable any party to withdraw if an amendment adopted by a simple majority had not entered into force within a reasonable period, not to exceed three years. This right of withdrawal would apply only to amendments affecting the article of the protocol dealing with mineral resources. With this addition, the United States could accept the Madrid package.[74]

New Zealand Ministers were informed that according to the United States delegation, they had little room for manoeuvre: neither the Secretary of State nor the White House could accept maverick countries blocking a negotiated deal. Some countries, such as Britain and the Soviet Union, were advocating 'understanding' of the American position. Others, such as France, seemed ready to consider the proposal. Australia was deeply unhappy. The New Zealand delegation was instructed to explore whether there was room for movement in the United States position and whether it was possible to meet its concerns while maintaining a veto or something like it for key Antarctic countries. (The adjective 'key' is significant; it seems that officials may have had in mind the sort of voting provisions found in CRAMRA that gave special weight to the votes of claimants and the two states asserting a basis of claim.)[75]

The NGO reaction was predictable. It was 'quite outrageous,' said Cath Wallace,

> for the [United] States to pretend, and I think no one is taken in, that they're proposing something small. What they're proposing is to dismantle the ban and to simply allow any country, and it's quite clear they consider they're the ones who are likely to do this, to just walk away from the Antarctic minerals ban any time they feel like it after the first 50 years . . . I'm personally pretty angry. I got a little letter from George Bush the very same half hour that I heard about what the United States had done on this and George Bush was telling me that it was great I'd been working for the environment . . . and wouldn't it be a good thing if everyone worked for the earth and all this stuff. [Then] I get this message . . . saying that the United States has completely tried to put the kybosh on this attempt that 25 other countries agreed to have permanent protection for the Antarctic environment and the permanent minerals ban.[76]

New Zealand Ministers were also disturbed. On 17 June they authorised the delegation to sign the protocol, should it be opened for signature at Madrid, on the basis of a paper prepared before the United States *demarche* had been received.[77] The New Zealand Embassy in Washington was instructed to join the Australians and others in urgent representations to the State Department. The response suggested, by implication, that the United States had room to compromise and that their proposal was designed to encourage some movement towards easing the difficulties they had with the veto provision.[78]

Two days before the session was due to end, the New Zealand delegation reported that it had reached a crunch point, at which a decision must be made about the American demand that the mining prohibition be subject to the possibility, after 50 years, that a country could withdraw from the protocol. New Zealand and Australia had fought hard to resist the American demand. With a number of other delegations they had almost achieved an outcome which would have left in place a 'disguised' veto on any proposal to lift the mining ban. The proposal, which was again put forward by Andersen, was to add a paragraph which read:

> No modification or amendment shall be adopted unless it contains an agreed means for safeguarding the interests of all States referred to in Article IV of the Antarctic Treaty and applying the principles embodied in that Article.

The disguised veto was, presumably, compressed in the word 'agreed'. It is unclear whether, as the delegation believed, the United States would in the end have bought this formula. In any event, they were not obliged to take the lead in rejecting it. To the dismay of the New Zealanders, a number of countries including France, Italy and Belgium, found the proposal too obscure to meet the need for something explainable to the public in simple terms. They then insisted on returning to the original American proposal which two days earlier they had labelled as unacceptable. In addition, Argentina opposed the proposal in the mistaken belief that it failed adequately to protect the interests of claimant states. At that point the New Zealand delegation moved from the floor an amendment to the original United States proposal to provide that any change to the mining ban could only be adopted by consensus. This too was rejected. New Zealand was thus faced with a choice between accepting the United States package or vetoing the whole protocol. If it rejected the protocol, it risked losing the environmental gains and could not be confident that there would be agreement on continuing the negotiations at a later date. A situation could arise where there were no new rules on environmental protection and no restriction at all on mining.[79] This was a stark choice. Australia and New Zealand were virtually alone: the remainder of the treaty parties were prepared to accept the United States' draft article.

In reality there was no choice. The Prime Minister and the Minister of External Relations and Trade agreed that McKinnon should consult his Australian counterpart, but indicate that New Zealand was not disposed to veto the protocol and, subject to the Australian view, should instruct the New Zealand delegation accordingly. Evans advised that the Australian Government's position was the same and that their delegation had been instructed to put up a vigorous fight but in the end to acquiesce in the adoption of the protocol.[80]

The message sent to the New Zealand delegation instructed it to express very strongly the Government's disappointment at the watering down of the moratorium [sic] on mining. It should clearly dissociate New Zealand from the position which the majority had adopted and continue to take whatever opportunities were available to improve the text. It should explore, in conjunction with the Australian delegation, the possibility of deferring adoption of the protocol for a 'cooling-off' period of two to three months. If, however, these efforts were unsuccessful New Zealand should not stand in the way of adoption of the protocol, while continuing to dissociate itself from the provisions about mining.[81]

The delegation reported no support for the cooling-off period. Attitudes in favour of adoption had hardened. Not only would France, Italy and Belgium agree to adopt the protocol but they were likely to sign it as well. Jacques Cousteau was said to have given it his blessing. The United States had threatened that if New Zealand proposed deferral, they would insist on the separation of the minerals issue from the protocol altogether. They would then engage in an endless debate about minerals so that it was never resolved. The delegation had therefore prepared a final statement which reflected its instructions. For a reason which will shortly become apparent, the statement was never delivered. It was noteworthy for its harsh criticism of the amendment article which, it said,

> gives rise to the possibility that after 55 years a country that is intent on undertaking minerals activities may attempt to do so in the very worst of circumstances—without any rules, environmental or otherwise, and in disregard of the interests of every other party. This can only alarm those who understand that the viability of the Antarctic Treaty system lies in the harmony of consensus. It must alarm those who sought to give the Antarctic environment permanent protection. Article 25 does not represent the position of the New Zealand Government.

The statement would have noted that the protocol also marked a real advance in areas such as environmental impact assessment, institutional inspection and dispute settlement. The delegation was particularly gratified that the dispute settlement provisions covered the Article dealing with compliance—in other words, a disagreement as to whether a Party had complied with the environmental requirements of the protocol could be challenged in either the International Court of Justice or the Arbitral Tribunal to be established under the terms of the protocol.[82]

The speech was not delivered because the protocol was not adopted at this session. The protocol was not adopted because the United States announced at the last minute that it needed more time to consider the amendment provision as it had emerged from the negotiations. That text, the New Zealand delegation pointed out in reporting this surprising development, differed significantly from the draft originally put forward by the United States itself only in that it stipulated a three-quarters majority of current ATCPs for the adoption of any amendment instead of a simple majority. (This was important as giving a collective veto to the seven claimants.) The United States claimed to be concerned that a single country or a small group could block an amendment supported by a majority of countries. (A single country could, however, veto the amendment only at the stage of entry into force, with the disagreeable consequence that any country could then withdraw from the protocol and engage in unrestricted mining.)

Following the American bombshell, virtually every delegation took the floor to say that they were prepared to accept the protocol as it stood and to express their disappointment at the tum of events. The United Kingdom indicated that if the United States had in mind to renegotiate the article, they should not ignore the possibility that others might wish to strengthen it.

In the circumstances, the New Zealand delegation did not indicate that New Zealand had been prepared to join in a consensus to adopt the protocol. Nor, in view of its instructions to seek a deferral, did it express disappointment that the action of the United States—which only a short time before had so strongly opposed deferral—had in the end been the cause of a delay. The delegation reported that the international NGOs considered that, defective as the final product was, it should be adopted lest the United States succeed in weakening it further. This feeling was widely shared among the delegations.[83]

The Minister of External Relations and Trade, taking a less philosophic view, issued an indignant press statement. The situation 'had gone from bad to worse'. New Zealand and Australia had fought a vigorous re-arguard action. The shift by a large number of Treaty countries had left them 'between a rock and a hard place'. When it came to the crunch, there was no serious support for a permanent ban. Nevertheless, some rules were better than no rules. It had seemed that a deal might be struck; but now it appeared that even the fallback position of a three-quarter majority voice to overturn the mining ban was still not enough.[84]

Considerable diplomatic pressure was applied to the United States to accept the protocol as it stood—Hawke wrote to President Bush and McKinnon called in the American Ambassador,[85] and no doubt there was domestic pressure on the administration that was even more effective. In any event, only a few days passed before Bush agreed to sign the protocol. In doing so he said that the protocol 'addresses our concerns and provides effective protection for Antarctica *without foreclosing the options for future generations*.[86] [Author's emphasis.] The New Zealand Government welcomed the decision and little more was heard of its misgivings about the amendment article. A three-quarters majority, said McKinnon, was 'a pretty good position'.[87]

Cath Wallace did not agree. The result was

> miles away from the really strong environmental protection we had in April. The United States hasn't really backed down, they've bullied countries like New Zealand that wanted a permanent ban into submission and it's a really irresponsible sort of agreement that we're looking at now.[88]

This was, however, rather a lone voice.

In September, Cabinet agreed that New Zealand should sign the protocol, subject to ratification.[89] The protocol was adopted, with some minor amendments, and opened for signature at the fourth session of the Eleventh SCM at Madrid, held on 3 and 4

October 1991.[90] The protocol entered into force on 14 January 1998 following its ratification by the 26 Consultative Parties who took part in the SCM, including New Zealand.

At the time of signature there were four annexes, on Environmental Impact Assessment, Conservation of Antarctic Fauna and Flora, Waste Disposal and Management and Prevention of Marine Pollution. These four annexes were adopted in 1991 together with the protocol and entered into force in 1998. A fifth annex, dealing with Area Protection and Management, was adopted at the Sixteenth ATCM in Bonn immediately following the October 1991 session of the Eleventh SCM where the protocol was opened for signature and entered into force on 24 May 2002.[91] There was provision for additional annexes, including in particular an annex containing rules and procedures relating to liability for damage arising from activities taking place in the Treaty area and covered by the protocol. The Final Act notes that the Arbitral Tribunal will not make determinations about damages until a binding legal regime has entered into force through such an annex. The final meeting of the SCM agreed that an inquiry procedure should be elaborated to facilitate resolution of disputes concerning the interpretation of Article 3 (Environmental Principles) with respect to activities undertaken in the Treaty Area.

Although the Final Act stressed the desirability of beginning work on the Liability annex at an early stage, there was a disposition at subsequent ATCMs to proceed rather slowly, lest difficulties over its content should slow up the entry of the protocol into force.[92] The Final Act also stated that liability for damage to the Antarctic environment should be 'included'. This was in contrast to most existing liability regimes, which dealt with liability for damage to property or loss of life, but many states felt the pristine Antarctic environment deserved a higher standard of protection even if they were not sure how to achieve this in practice.

The Sixteenth ATCM in Bonn later in 1991 reiterated the need for 'early consideration of a Liability annex', with the details left to the following ATCM to work out. However, the Antarctic and Southern Ocean Coalition (ASOC), an environmental NGO that followed the protocol's negotiation closely, submitted one of the first drafts of a Liability annex as an information paper to the Sixteenth ATCM.[93]

Substantive discussions on the Liability annex began in 1992 at the Seventeenth ATCM in Venice, which decided the liability regime should be developed through a group of legal experts, chaired by Professor Rüdiger Wolfrum of Germany. Wolfrum elaborated a first draft (known as the Chair's 'first offering'), circulated to parties in June 1993. The group met nine times between November 1993 and May 1998. Its work was based on draft 'offerings' prepared by the Chair, which became increasingly elaborate but achieved no breakthrough.[94]

The 1998 entry into force of the protocol spurred negotiations for a Liability annex, and the Twenty-first ATCM asked the group of legal experts to report to the Twenty-second ATCM in Tromsø on its progress. There were now two competing visions, as set out in that report: on the one hand the comprehensive Chair's 'eighth offering' and on the other a more limited proposal from the United States for a draft annex on Liability for Emergency Response Action.[95] The United States, supported by the United Kingdom, China, Russia, Japan, Norway and others, regarded the comprehensive regime as impracticable. Although some states supporting the comprehensive approach had significant Antarctic programmes—for example Australia, New Zealand and Italy—many did not maintain Antarctic bases and therefore faced little financial exposure from the broad-ranging regime they supported. The Twenty-second ATCM decided to wind up the group of legal experts, and that further negotiations of 'an annex or annexes on liability' would be undertaken in working group I of the ATCM.[96]

Don MacKay of New Zealand was appointed Chair of this working group at the Twenty-third ATCM in 1999 in Lima and sought to find common ground between the competing 'comprehensive' and 'limited' approaches. His approach was to take as a starting point the narrower proposed regime dealing with environmental emergencies, and to broaden out the coverage as far as consensus would allow, with any remaining gaps left to a future annex or annexes. This 'step by step' approach, as it became known, narrowed differences and meant both sides were prepared to work on the basis of one informal text produced by the Chair. It also sought to focus the negotiations on the practical situations liability needed to cover (such as small oil spills), to avoid dealing with issues in the legal abstract. The Chair produced several drafts, as the negotiations progressed and outstanding issues narrowed.[97]

The Liability annex (Annex VI) was adopted at the Twenty-eighth ATCM in Stockholm in 2005.[98] It requires those operating in Antarctica to take measures to prevent environmental emergencies, requires prompt and effective response action should an environmental emergency occur, and imposes financial liability for the costs of response action (such as containing an oil spill). It does not create liability for irreparable damage to the environment itself, which reflects adamant resistance from the United States and others during the negotiation of the Liability annex, who viewed this as impracticable. However, in a compromise, the ATCM decided when adopting the Liability annex to defer the issue of irreparable damage to future negotiations. Nor does the Liability annex cover fishing vessels, as this was opposed by several states, but this issue could also be addressed in a future annex.[99]

The ATCM also adopted Decision 1 (2005), which provided that within five years the ATCM would take a decision on the establishment of a time-frame for the resumption of negotiations 'to elaborate future rules and procedures as may be necessary' relating to liability for irreparable damage. The adoption of this decision was a key element of the final package for those countries that had originally pushed for a comprehensive regime.

Decision 1 (2005) recorded the parties' decision to evaluate annually the progress towards Annex VI entering into force and, not later than five years from the adoption of the annex, to consider the time-frame for the resumption of negotiations, in accordance with Article 16 of the protocol, to elaborate further rules and procedures as may be necessary relating to liability for environmental damage.

Five years after that Decision was taken, the parties agreed Decision 4 (2010) (which supersedes Decision 1 [2005]), deciding to continue to monitor progress towards Annex VI entering into force; extending the time-frame for considering the resumption of negotiations on further rules and procedures on liability to 2015, and requesting the Committee for Environmental Protection to consider environmental issues related to the practicality of repair or remediation of environmental damage in the circumstances of Antarctica, in order to assist the ATCM in adopting an informed decision in 2015 related to the resumption of the negotiations.

This Decision was in turn superseded by Decision 5 (2015) which deferred until 2020 the decision on the establishment of a time-frame for the resumption of negotiations on liability in accordance with Article 16 of the protocol, or sooner if parties so decide in light of progress made in approving Measure 1 (2005). More than ten years after its adoption, the Liability annex has been approved by only 12 of the 28 Consultative Parties needed for its entry into force.[100]

Some Consultative Parties have also promoted an annex on tourism, but there has been no agreement on this method of dealing with the issue. Five Consultative Parties put forward a proposal at the Seventeenth ATCM for comprehensive and binding regulations to govern tourism, in the form of an annex, but others, including New Zealand, the United Kingdom and the United States considered that the protocol, as it applies to all human activity in Antarctica, already provided the necessary regulatory mechanisms.[101]

The Final Act recorded agreement at the Fourth Session of the SCM that, pending entry into force of the protocol, current constraints on Antarctic mineral resource activity should continue. The meeting noted that the harvesting of ice was not considered as a mineral resources activity, and that if it should become possible in the future, it should not be covered by the mining ban but should be subject to the other provisions of the protocol. The meeting noted also that the rights and obligations of parties to CCAMLR and the Antarctic Seals and Whaling Conventions should not be affected by the protocol, nor would the Final Act prejudice the legal position of any part under Article IV of the Antarctic Treaty. The meeting urged Contracting Parties to the Antarctic Treaty to apply the annexes to the protocol to the extent possible pending entry of the protocol into force, and to do what they could to bring about entry into force as soon as possible.

The Final Act contains nothing to clarify the question of the area of application of the protocol, but allows states signing or ratifying the protocol to make declarations or statements, provided that these do not modify its legal effect in its application to that state. Chile, in signing the protocol, took the opportunity to declare that the mining prohibition was understood to apply to the whole territory to which it claimed sovereign rights in Antarctica, and to the continental shelf, even if it extended beyond 60° south. In the area south of that latitude, Chile reaffirmed the collective commitment (in the Final Act) to make appropriate efforts to ensure that no one carried out activities in the Treaty area which are contrary to the Treaty and the protocol.[102]

It was widely accepted during the negotiation of the protocol that a permanent Secretariat would be required if it was to operate effectively, bearing in mind in particular that the functions of the Committee on Environment Protection would include consideration of the Environmental Evaluations produced by parties in respect of all significant new activities on Antarctica. No progress was made on this issue during the negotiation of the protocol, or at the subsequent Sixteenth and Seventeenth ATCMs. It appeared that the principal obstacle to progress was the attitude of Argentina, which considered that the establishment of a Secretariat might constitute an infringement of its sovereignty. It seemed, however, that this objection might not be insuperable, if it were proposed that the Secretariat should be located in Argentina. There were doubts whether that would be acceptable to the United Kingdom or to Chile. New Zealand took the view that the Secretariat could be located in the country of the Secretary-General's nationality, moving as the appointment changed. The United States, as depositary to the

Antarctic Treaty and protocol, also offered to provide a home for the Secretariat.[103]

Argentina in fact offered in 1992 to host the Secretariat in Buenos Aires. However, it was not until 2001 that the United Kingdom indicated at the Twenty-fourth ATCM in St Petersburg that it was ready to join the consensus on this location. The report of that ATCM contains statements from the Argentine Defence Minister and the United Kingdom Foreign Secretary in response, from which it is apparent much behind the scenes negotiation had taken place. The statements indicate Argentina took various steps to address the United Kingdom's concerns, including appointing a civilian head of Argentina's CCAMLR obligations including control of illegal, unregulated and unreported fishing in the CCAMLR Convention Area, and ratifying Annex V of the Protocol on Environmental Protection to the Antarctic Treaty (on protected areas). The Antarctic Treaty Secretariat commenced operation on 1 September 2004 in Buenos Aires.[104]

XV

A BALANCE SHEET

The New Zealand delegation in Madrid reported that the mood, following the signature of the protocol, was one of euphoria. In the end the apprehensions that consensus among the Antarctic Consultative Parties on important questions was elusive, it said, had proved unfounded. Not only was there now agreement to prohibit minerals activities on the continent, but there was in place a comprehensive system for the protection of the Antarctic environment.[1]

The delegation emphasised the positive achievements of the negotiators, which were considerable. The protocol imposes an absolute ban on mining for at least 50 years from its entry into force on 14 January 1998.[2] The ban can be lifted at any time by unanimous agreement of all the Consultative Parties (by invoking the amendment procedure in Article 12 of the Antarctic Treaty); but the likelihood of such unanimous agreement is so remote that it can be dismissed. On the other hand, fifty years after the entry of the protocol into force, the prohibition of mining can be lifted by a vote of three-quarters of the 26 Consultative Parties which joined in the adoption of the protocol. While this permits a 'collective veto' by the seven claimant states, only one of them would have to break ranks for that 'veto' to disappear.

It may seem that to assemble 20 votes in favour of lifting the ban would be an insuperable obstacle. That may well turn out to be the case. But fifty years is a long time. In the seventies, the policy of the New Zealand Government was resource-driven. It had been demonstrated, in successive oil shocks, that the principal users of liquid fuel did not control the principal sources of supply. Had it been conclusively established at that time that there was an Alaska-scale oilfield in Antarctica, it is a reasonable assumption that extraordinary efforts would have been set in train to develop the technology required for its extraction. What will happen when, as it eventually must, the world's known reserves of oil and natural gas dwindle to a level where competing demands can no longer be met? Will the technology for the production of alternative fuels already be in place, or will there be a gap to be bridged? It does seem possible, as I suggested earlier, that the opportunity to review the operation of the protocol could arise just about the time that pressure to relax the prohibition on mining in Antarctica—no doubt under appropriate safeguards—reaches sufficient strength to change the policies of governments. In the nineties their policies were strongly influenced by environmental considerations, and because of this were more directly sensitive to public opinion. At present there is no desperate worldwide shortage of vital mineral resources, such as oil—rather the reverse, in fact. It cannot be assumed that this will still be the case in 2050, or that then or at some later date economic and strategic needs will not prevail over concerns for the environment and the conservation of nature in a distant and largely uninhabited continent.

At that point there could well be a conflict of interest between the southern hemisphere Consultative Parties located relatively close to Antarctica and the major industrialised countries in the northern hemisphere. If it came to the crunch, there is no question where the balance of power would lie. Four of the southern hemisphere Consultative Parties claim sovereignty over sectors of Antarctica, but their claims are recognised only—to the extent that their claims do not overlap—by other claimants. Their right to enforce legislation applying to their Antarctic territories against foreign nationals is likely to be challenged.

Are there, in fact, large mineral resources in Antarctica? This has to be established. If, as is generally accepted, Antarctica was at one time contiguous to Australia in a supercontinent known as Gondwanaland, there is no reason to suppose that Antarctica is less mineral-rich than Australia. There could well be huge quantities of oil in the continental shelves in the Ross and Weddell seas: or there could be none. Prospecting is forbidden by the protocol, but some could possibly be conducted in the guise of scientific research.

The protocol unquestionably provides a more comprehensive regime for the environmental protection of Antarctica than has existed up to the present. Understandably, however, the New Zealand delegation in its reporting tended not to draw attention to the extent to which, in a number of areas, the agreed provisions of the protocol fell short of what New Zealand had proposed in the draft it had submitted to the SCM at Viña del Mar and of the objectives set out in the Cabinet paper of March 1991.

In a candid assessment, following the Viña del Mar meeting, a member of the New Zealand delegation recorded that 'the wider membership of the Treaty was not prepared to accept an approach, which some saw as inherent in the Franco–Australian proposal, that was predicated on the concept that activities in Antarctica would be subject to approval by an international environmental institution'. The majority evidently considered such a proposition as 'inconsistent with the sovereignty of states and the guarantee of freedom of science contained in the Antarctic Treaty.[3] But it was not only France and Australia who wanted to impose some form of supra-national control over activities in Antarctica. The March 1991 Cabinet paper also noted that the Viña del Mar text did not give the Environmental Protection Committee a 'whistle-blowing' function and expressed the hope that it would be empowered to suspend activities that gave rise to environmental concerns.[4] But a New Zealand proposal that would have allowed an activity to be stopped, if it were the preponderant view in the Committee that the activity was harmful, did not survive. The Committee's role is entirely advisory, and a whistle can be blown only through the disputes procedure which, one suspects, an individual Consultative Party might well hesitate to invoke against another.

There is provision for inspection in the protocol, but it does not go much beyond the inspection provisions in the Antarctic Treaty itself, and falls a good deal short of New Zealand's original proposal for an Environmental Inspectorate with extensive duties and powers. The Minerals Convention contains, in Article 12, much more specific provisions for institutional as well as national inspection.

The protocol envisages attendance by NGOs at meetings of the Environmental Protection Committee as observers, but only by invitation and not by right. Whereas the 1991 Cabinet paper insisted that the new regime must extend coverage to 'the burgeoning field of tourist activities', there is no agreement among the ATCPs on the desirability or content of an annex on tourism, and New Zealand itself now leans to the view that tourists should simply be regarded as subject to the general provisions of the protocol applying to all human activity.[5] The rules and procedures for dealing with liability for damage are a contentious issue. The liability annex to the protocol was adopted in 2005, and creates liability for the costs of response action to an environmental emergency (such as containing an oil spill), but not for irreparable damage to the environment itself as no agreement could be reached on this. In compromise, the ATCM decided when adopting the Liability annex to defer the issue of irreparable damage to future negotiations.'

As already noted, the protocol forbids all mineral activities within the Antarctic Treaty area, i.e., south of 60° south. It thus covers areas of the deep seabed which under the Law of the Sea Convention are part of the common heritage of mankind and subject to the regime in Part II of that Convention. There is consequently an apparent conflict between the protocol and the LOS Convention (which has entered into force since the protocol was adopted) and parties to the LOS Convention who become party to the protocol would seem to be in breach of Article 311 (6) of the Convention.[6]

How much better a deal, therefore, did the protocol represent—from the environmentalists' point of view—than did CRAMRA? The Convention had a number of weaknesses, perhaps the most important of which was a widespread public perception, never effectively countered, that its purpose was to open up Antarctica for mining. Its very title—a Convention on the

Regulation of Antarctic Mining Activities—gave colour to that perception. Moreover, the Convention did allow prospecting—under strict rules—so that the discovery of, say, an enormous oilfield could have led to correspondingly enormous pressure for authorisation of the next stage, exploration. After the Convention had been negotiated—but not during the negotiations—New Zealand Ministers and officials made much of the veto which, in theory at least, any member of the CRAMRA Commission could cast against any proposal to open up any area in Antarctica for mineral exploration and development. Whether it would be politically expedient for a country such as New Zealand to make use of this power is another matter. The exercise of a blanket veto against any mineral activity in Antarctica—as environmentalist NGOs would no doubt expect—or of an 'automatic' veto against any mineral activity in the Ross Dependency, irrespective of whether the proposed activity was regarded by other members of the Commission as consistent with the Convention, could have undesirable consequences. Parties sponsoring a mining proposal could take New Zealand to disputes settlement on the grounds that the veto had been exercised in bad faith and in an arbitrary manner; or alternatively, they could simply exercise their right to withdraw from the Convention in accordance with Article 65 after giving two years' notice, and engage in a mining activity without the restraints imposed by the Convention.

On the other hand, the Convention gives the claimant states which are prepared to contemplate mining activity within their claimed territories extensive powers to control such activities. Thus New Zealand would have a major say, through the Regulatory Committee in question, in regard to the conduct of any mining operation in the Ross Dependency. Should the protocol be amended to permit mining at the end of the 50-year period, New Zealand would have no such special rights—unless CRAMRA were to be revived at that point. Article 25(5) (a) of the protocol requires that there should be a binding legal regime on Antarctic mineral resource activities in place before the prohibition is lifted. This could be CRAMRA, but equally it could be some other instrument which did not give claimants special rights and which did not necessarily contain the strict provisions for the protection of the environment that are a feature of CRAMRA. As its principal author has pointed out, the standards and procedures set out in the Minerals Convention are as tough as they are, precisely because they were negotiated well in advance of any serious commercial interest in mining.[7]

It would be easy to gaze in the rear-vision mirror and to claim that the six years spent in negotiating the Minerals Convention was a waste of time and scarce resources—not least on New Zealand's part. To do that would be to misread totally the diplomatic atmosphere in which the negotiations were conducted. In the mid-seventies some ATCPs were reluctant to contemplate any regulation of mineral exploitation in Antarctica. Then they were brought to accept a non-binding moratorium. In due course they came to recognise that binding rules were essential if there were not to be a free-for-all which could end in conflict and chaos. They also recognised that, from the point of view of the countries actively engaged in scientific work in Antarctica, a minerals regime forming part of the Antarctic Treaty system was much to be preferred to treating the continent as part of the common heritage of mankind, and attempting to negotiate a regime under United Nations auspices. As the negotiations proceeded, environmental considerations came to assume increasing priority. Public concern to preserve the Antarctic environment, stronger initially in southern ATCPs like New Zealand, assumed a global dimension.

It would have been possible for the Labour Government that took office in New Zealand in 1984 to switch the policy and come out for a prohibition of mining in Antarctica. That would have followed comfortably enough from its election manifesto, with its heavy emphasis on the need to preserve the fragile Antarctic environment. But the manifesto did not repudiate the proposed minerals regime which New Zealand had taken the lead in negotiating. Wisely, the new Ministers accepted officials' advice that a regulatory convention offered the best hope for the Antarctic environment. Had it sought a mining prohibition at that time New Zealand's would have been an ineffectual voice. The desire to keep the mining option open was general among the Consultative Parties until the end of the decade and CRAMRA continued to offer the best consensus for the protection of the Antarctic environment. The United States, under the Bush administration, remained determined until the very end to ensure that mining might still be possible one day. If that day ever comes, CRAMRA may still be needed.

ACRONYMS

ANZUS	Australia, New Zealand, United States Security Treaty
ASEAN	Association of South-east Asian Nations
ASOC	Antarctic and Southern Ocean Coalition
ATCM	Antarctic Treaty Consultative Meeting
CCAMLR	Convention on the Conservation of Antarctic Marine Living Resources
COFI	Committee on Fisheries
COMECON	The Council for Mutual Economic Assistance
CRAMRA	Convention on the Regulation of Antarctic Mineral Resource Activities (
DSIR	Department of Scientific and Industrial Research
ECO	Environmental and Conservation Organisation of Aotearoa New Zealand
EEC	European Economic Community
EEZ	Exclusive Economic Zone
EIA	Environmental impact assessment
FAO	Food and Agriculture Organization
ICJ	International Court of Justice
ISA	International Seabed Authority
IUCN	International Union for Conservation of Nature
IUU	Illegal, unreported, unregulated fishing
LOS	Law of the Sea
MERT	Ministry of External Relations and Trade
NAM	Non-aligned Movement
SCM	Special Consultative Meeting
SCAR	Scientific Committee on Antarctic Research
SCOR	Scientific Committee for Ocean Research

NOTES AND REFERENCES

VII: Conservation: The Protection of Fauna and Flora

1 See *A Wise Adventure I*, Chapter VI, page 252.

2 PM208/1/10 Part 1, letter of 8 July 1959 from Secretary of Internal Affairs to Secretary of External Affairs, minute by J K Cunningham.

3 Ibid. SCAR circular 35 of 9 February 1960 reported a resolution on the protection of wildlife adopted at an Antarctic Symposium held in Buenos Aires the previous year.

4 Ibid, RDRC meeting on 17 March 1960.

5 Ibid, report on 21 October 1960 by NZ Embassy of discussion with Washington Consultative group.

6 Ibid, memorandum of 8 December 1960 from Secretary of External Affairs to Charge, Washington reporting discussion with Dr Brian Roberts of the Foreign Office.

7 Ibid, SCAR circular 51 of 14 February 1961 and attachments.

8 PM208/5/9 Part 1, memorandum of 17 February 1961 from Secretary of External Affairs to Charge Washington. PM208/1/10 Part 1, memorandum of 27 March 1961 from Secretary to Charge.

9 PM208/10/1 Part 1, NZ brief dated July 1961 for first Consultative Meeting.

10 Recommendation I-VIII, 24 July I961.

11 Ibid, telegram 407 of 11 July 1961 from NZ High Commission, Canberra to Minister and reply in telegram 342 of 12 July.

12 Ibid, second Consultative Meeting document P3 of 17 July 1962.

13 Ibid, memorandum of 28 May 1962 from Secretary of External Affairs to NZHC London (drafted by Tony Small).

14 See *A Wise Adventure I*, Chapter VI, page 247, Article VIII of Treaty.

15 PM208/1/10 Part 1, memorandum of 28 June 1962 from NZHC London to Secretary of External Affairs.

16 The second Consultative Meeting, held in Buenos Aires, was somewhat unproductive and unsatisfactory from the viewpoint of the more activist delegations, in part because of inadequate preparatory work. New Zealand had a particular problem because it had no resident representation in Argentina. It proposed that future meetings should be held in a capital where all Consultative Parties were represented, in the Embassy of the next host country. South Africa made a proposal for the creation of the nucleus of a secretariat: New Zealand hoped that future meetings would be in Washington, but neither proposal succeeded. The British proposal on jurisdiction was withdrawn, and never raised again at later meetings. Much more extensive

preparatory work was undertaken in advance of the third Consultative Meeting held in Brussels in 1964.

17 PM208/1/10 Part 1, memorandum of 15 May 1963 from Secretary of External Affairs to NZ Mission, Brussels.

18 Ibid, note of 7 January 1964 from US Embassy, Wellington to Ministry of External Affairs.

19 Ibid, reply of 22 January 1964 (drafted by Chris Beeby).

20 PM208/5/9 Part 3, memorandum of 17 December 1963 from Acting High Commissioner, Canberra to Secretary of External Affairs, and enclosure.

21 Ibid, opinion of 23 December 1963 (Chris Beeby).

22 Ibid, memorandum of 21 April 1964 from NZHC London to Secretary of External Affairs, reproducing a Foreign Officer letter. Reference was made in the letter to the definitions of a treaty in McNair's Law of Treaties (1961) and in Sir Gerald Fitsmaurice's first report on the Law of Treaties to the International Law Commission (A/CN4/1O1).

23 Ibid, memorandum of 3 April 1964 from NZ Embassy, Washington to Secretary of External Affairs.

24 Ibid, memorandum of 7 May 1964 from Beeby to Quentin-Baxter.

25 PM208/1/10, Part 2, New Zealand brief for Third Consultative Meeting, 29 May 1964.

26 Ibid, report of New Zealand delegation, 3 July 1964, paragraph 49.

27 Ibid, Departmental paper of 17 March 1964, prepared as a brief for the New Zealand representative on the working group in Brussels.

28 Ibid, memorandum of 6 April 1964 from NZ Head of Mission, Brussels to Secretary of External Affairs.

29 Ibid, memorandum of 14 May 1964 from NZHC London to Secretary of External Affairs and enclosure.

30 Ibid, memorandum of 26 May 1964 from NZHC London to Secretary of External Affairs.

31 Ibid, telegram 1296 of 29 May 1964 from Minister to NZHC London.

32 Ibid, telegram 47 of 1 June 1964 from New Zealand Mission, Brussels to Minister, 'From Templeton'.

33 Ibid, report of the NZ Delegation, 3 July 1964, paragraph 50.

34 Ibid, part 3 memorandum of 10 August 1966 from NZHC London to Secretary of External Affairs, with letter of 9 August 1966 from David Anderson, Foreign Office.

35 Ibid, part 2, memorandum of 27 April 1964 from Beeby to Quentin-Baxter.

36 Ibid, report of the NZ delegation, paragraphs 23-38.

37 Ibid, Annex C (forwarded under memorandum of 6 April 1965 from NZHC London to Secretary of External Affairs) pages 1-3.

38 Ibid, pages 13-23.

39 Of the Consultative Parties which attended the 1964 meeting the last to accept the Agreed Measures was Japan. It did so on 1 November 1982 (208/51/1, note of that date from MFA, Tokyo to Embassies of the Consultative Parties).

40 Ibid, report of NZ delegation, paragraph 22.

41 'Brazil, China, Germany, Italy, India, Netherlands, Poland Republic of Korea, Spain and Uruguay. ATCM Decision 1 (2011) decided 'these measures are

no longer current and that the Parties do not need to take any further action with respect to them' and was adopted by ATCM XXXIV in Buenos Aires on 1 July 2011.'

42 PM 208/1/10, part 3, letter of 30 September 1965 from Department of External Affairs (Small) to ARC Wellington.

43 Ibid. Telegram 659 of 31 August 1966 from NZ Embassy Washington to Minister contains translation of Chilean note setting out proposed amendments.

44 Ibid, Report of NZ Delegation to the Fourth Consultative Meeting, Santiago, 3-18 November 1966.

45 Ibid, note for file by Alan Doyle, 27 February 1967.

46 Section 6A of the amended Act, repealed by Antarctica (Environmental Protection) Act 1994 section 57(1).'

47 Memorandum of 24 March 1970 from Secretary of Foreign Affairs to Law Draftsman (missing from PM 208/1/10, located in Law Drafting Office file).

48 PM 208/1/10 Parts 3 and 4, PM 208/1/10/1 Part 1. United Kingdom Antarctic Treaty Act, 27 July 1967 (C65).
The instructions to the New Zealand Law Draftsman (memorandum of 24 March 1970) proposed that the British Act be followed in the extension of its application to the high seas. When the Law Draftsman queried this proposal, it was decided that the legislation should 'encompass the making of regulations extending to the high seas on the understanding that, initially, they would not do so and would be expressed not to do so'. (Note by Beeby on memorandum of 11 June 1970 from Law Draftsman to Secretary of Foreign Affairs.)
It was also intended to follow the British legislation in taking power to make regulations to give effect to any recommendation agreed by the Consultative Parties to the Treaty: but this provision was rejected by the Cabinet Committee on legislation (PM 208/1/10/1 Part 1, note on copy of the Bill from Beeby to Templeton, undated, about July 1970).

49 SR 1971/278, revoked by Antarctica (Environmental Protection) Act 1994 section 57 (2).

50 Notified to depositary (United States) on 23 December 1971. Bush *op cit* Vol 1 page 168 (not on Foreign Affairs file).

51 Ibid, pages 97-98.

52 Decision 1 (1995).

VIII: Conservation: The Convention on Seals

1 PM 208/1/10 Part 3, memorandum of 29 March 1966 from NZHC London to Secretary of External Affairs and enclosure.

2 Ibid, telegram 809 of 2 September 1966 from Minister to NZ Embassy, Washington.

3 Ibid.

4 Ibid, Foreign Office draft of Agreed Measures, 23 August 1966.

5 Ibid, memorandum of 27 September 1966 from New Zealand Embassy, Washington to Secretary of External Affairs reporting on preparatory meeting

in Santiago, page 17.

6 PM 208/5/14 Part 1, memorandum of 5 December 1966 from NZ Embassy, Washington to Secretary of External Affairs, with report of New Zealand Delegation to Fourth Consultative Meeting, page 27.

7 Ibid, memorandum of 24 April 1969 from NZ Embassy, Paris to Secretary of External Affairs, with report of New Zealand Delegation to Fifth Consultative Meeting, pages 7-9. British draft convention in document ANT/26.

8 Report of the Sixth Antarctic Treaty Consultative Meeting, Tokyo, 19-31 October 1970, paragraph 10.

9 PM 208/1/10 Part 4, memorandum of 28 April 1970 from NZHC London to Secretary of Foreign Affairs.

10 Ibid, memorandum of 12 June 1970 from NZHC Canberra to Secretary of Foreign Affairs.

11 Ibid, memorandum of 2 July 1970 from NZ Embassy, Tokyo to Secretary of Foreign Affairs.

12 Ibid, telegrams 406 and 412 of 9 and 13 October 1970 from NZHC Ottawa to Wellington.

13 Ibid, letter of 15 June 1970 from RJ Glen to Minister of Marine and reply of 30 June 1970 from Minister of Foreign Affairs, referring to Glen's letter to the *Press*.

14 Ibid, New Zealand brief for Sixth Consultative Meeting, undated, October 1970.

15 Ibid, document APS/2/Rev 1 of 30 October 1970.

16 PM 208/1/10/2 Part 1, memorandum of 17 November 1971 from Secretary of Foreign Affairs to PM Holyoake wrote 'seen' on the submission—a favourite tactic for disposing of unwelcome proposals.

17 Ibid, file note of 14 December 1971 recording a call at the Ministry by a Japanese Embassy official.

18 208/51/1, memorandum of 6 May 1982 from NZ Embassy, Tokyo, to Secretary of Foreign Affairs and enclosure, extract from *Mainichi Shimbun,* 8 February 1982.

19 PM 208/1/10/2, aide-memoire of 13 January 1972 from US Embassy, Wellington.

20 Ibid, paper of 5 January 1972 by B B Roberts, FCO.

21 Ibid, memorandum of 25 January 1972 from Secretary of Foreign Affairs to High Commissioner, London, and enclosure.

22 Ibid, report of New Zealand delegation, forwarded on 11 April 1972 (covering memorandum from NZHC London on 208/51/1).

23 Poland acceded to the Convention on 15 August 1980, Italy on 2 April 1982, Germany (Federal Republic of) on 30 September 1987, Canada on 4 October 1990 and Brazil on 11 February 1991.'.

24 New Zealand withdrew from the Whaling Convention effective 30 June 1969, and re-adhered I5 June 1976.

25 Article 8.

26 Article 9.

27 Report of NZ Delegation (see Note 22), paragraphs 21 and 56.

28 Article 6.

29 208/51/1 statement of 12 June 1972.
30 Ibid, memorandum of 15 February 1978 from NZHC London to Secretary of Foreign Affairs.
31 208/1/10/1, Statement of 5 June 1975.
32 208/51/1, letter of 14 November 1977 from Minister of Foreign Affairs to G S Martin, Project Jonah.
33 NZ Statutes 1978 Vol 2, P855.
34 106/22/16, memorandum of 14 August 1978 from Secretary of Foreign Affairs to NZ Embassy, Washington (not found on Wellington file, copy retrieved from NZHC London).
35 Ninth Meeting of Consultative Parties to the Antarctic Treaty, Recommendations 1 and 2, 7 October 1977.
36 208/55/21 Part 3, telegram 727 of 18 November 1986 from Wellington to NZ Embassy, Moscow (Embassy's memorandum of 4 November 1986, not on file).
37 Ibid, file note by Hamish Cooper, Economic Division, 17 November 1986.
38 Ibid, telegram 1090 from NZ Embassy, Moscow to Wellington.
39 Ibid, telegram 524 of 8 June 198Tfrom NZ Embassy, Moscow to Wellington.
40 Ibid, memorandum of 25 June 1987 from Secretary of Foreign Affairs to Minister.
41 Ibid, statement to press by Minister (Lange) on 3 August 1987.
42 Ibid, *Tass*, 5 August 1987.
43 See note 40.
44 701/16/4/2 Part 1, note of 31 July 1987 from Foreign Secretary to NZHC London. Australian ratification deposited 1 July 1987, Convention entered into force for Australia 31 July.
45 Ibid, Part 2. Press release from FCO, 30 August 1988. Brazil, Canada and Sweden were also invited to participate as observers.
46 Ibid, telegram 1926 of 21 September 1988 from NZ Embassy, Paris to Wellington containing report from New Zealand representative at the Conference (Frank Wong).
47 Ibid, fax 289 of the same date containing his opening statement.

IX: Conservation: Marine Living Resources

1 Recommendation VIII-1O, 20 June 1975.
2 PM208/1/10/1, part 1. Baleen whale diet—see minutes of meeting between F Popper (FAO), and NZ officials, 2 February 1977, page 5. Crabeater seal diet—see SCAR Bulletin, SCAR/SCOR meeting on living resources of the Southern Ocean, 23-24 August 1976, page 240.
3 PM208/1/10/1 Part 1. Paper of 26 January 1976 by R B Thomson, Antarctic Division, DSIR. PM208/2/1 Part 1, telegram 521 of 15 June 1970 from NZ Embassy, Tokyo to Wellington, remarks by Thomson reported in *Japan Times*.
4 PM208/1/10/1 Part 1, file note of 29 March 1976 by T J Groser.
5 PM208/44/1 Part 2, ANT6 of 26 May 1975.
6 Ibid, ANT6 of 26 May 1975.

7 Ibid, telegram 3729 of 16 June 1975 from NZHC London to Wellington, 'From delegation in Oslo.' Recommendation VIII-10.
8 See *A Wise Adventure I*, Chapter VI, page 229
9 PM208/1/10/1 Part 1, telegram 1058 of 18 November 1975 from Wellington to New Zealand Embassy, Rome. FAO document C75/19 paragraph 22.
10 Ibid, telegram 1767 of 17 December 1975 from Wellington to NZ Embassy, Paris.
11 Ibid, memorandum of 11 May 1976 from Secretary of Foreign Affairs to DSIR, Trade and Industry, Agriculture and Fisheries, and Fishing Industry Board.
12 Ibid, report of SCAR/SCOR meeting at Woods Hole, 23-24 August 1976 (see note 2).
13 PM208/45/1, report (dated 13 June 1977) of New Zealand delegation to preparatory meeting held 14-18 March 1977.
14 PM208/1/10/1 Part 2, telegram 297 of 1 April 1977 from Wellington to NZ Embassy, Rome.
15 Ibid, Cabinet paper CP(77)179 of 10 March 1977, from Minister of Foreign Affairs and Cabinet Minute CM77/8/27 of 14 March 1977 (on 208/46/1 Part 1).
16 Ibid, telegram 2540 of 12 April 1977 from NZHC London to Wellington, telegram 1127 of 15 April 1977 from NZ Embassy Washington to Wellington, and telegram 2089 of 15 April 1977 from Wellington to NZHC London.
17 Ibid, telegram 250 of 28 April 1977 from NZ Embassy, Rome to Wellington.
18 Ibid, telegram 1404 of 20 July 1977 from NZHC Canberra to Wellington.
19 Ibid, text under cover of undated memorandum (mid-October 1977) from NZHC London to Wellington.
20 208/2/1 Part 3, telegram 1821 of 15 September 1977 from NZHC Canberra to Wellington.
21 208/46/1 Part 2, telegram 6144 of 22 September 1977 from NZHC London to Wellington.
22 Report of the Ninth ATCM, London, 19 September-7 October 1977, paragraph 10.
23 Convention on the Conservation of Antarctic Marine Living Resources, Article IX(2).
24 208/46/1, Part 2, NZ delegation report in telegram saving 3 of 10 October 1977 from NZHC London to Wellington. (See also memorandum from Paris, 21 November 1977, and enclosure on 208/5/14 part 3).
25 ATCM Recommendation IX-I paragraph 5. See also Chapter X, page 74.
26 208/1/10/1 Part 3. Telegram 7 of 16 January 1978 from Wellington to NZ Embassy, Santiago.
27 Ibid, Report of FRG Expedition in 1975/76 under memorandum of 28 November 1977 from NZ Embassy, Bonn to Secretary of Foreign Affairs.
28 Ibid, telegram 26 of 27 January 1978 from NZ Embassy, Santiago to Wellington.
29 Ibid, memoranda of 15 and 16 February 1978 from DSIR and Fisheries Division, MAF, to Secretary of Foreign Affairs.
30 ANT/SCM/17 of 8 March 1978 and ANT/SCM/17/REV2 of 15 March

1978. REV 1 not found.

31 Ibid, Article IV, para 2.

32 Ibid, telegrams 611 and 614 of 16 March 1978 from NZHC Canberra to Wellington contain the delegation report and the interim report of the Canberra session.

33 Ninth Consultative Meeting, Recommendation IX-2(iii) paragraph 3(e).

34 See *A Wise Adventure I*, Chapter V, p. 192. The Antarctic convergence had originally been proposed by the Soviet Union as the northern boundary of the Antarctic Treaty area.

35 208/1/10/1 part 4, memorandum of 4 April 1978 from NZ Ambassador, Paris to Secretary of Foreign Affairs.

36 Ibid, telegram 2149 of 10 July 1978 from Wellington to NZ Embassy, Washington.

37 Research suggests that the assertion of prior jurisdiction was over-simplified and perhaps overstated.

See the account of New Zealand's efforts to licence whaling in Chapter II. In 1926 the Norwegian government, on the basis of a report from its Consul-General in New Zealand, challenged a reported New Zealand claim to exercise jurisdiction in the Ross Sea beyond the three-mile limit. The British authorities immediately denied that there was any truth in the assertion, and the New Zealand government confirmed that 'New Zealand has in no way claimed the Ross Sea as territorial waters other than that portion of it within the three mile limit.' They also admitted to the British government that they could not prevent unlicensed ships from operating in the Ross Sea so long as they stayed outside territorial limits, and moreover that it was impossible to police the territory to ensure that they did not in fact encroach into territorial waters. (See G48A/3(i), despatch of 2 February 1926 from SSDA to GG, GH No 509/26, and memorandum of 19 May 1926 from PM to GG).

The question came up again in 1929 after the revised Ross Sea Whaling Regulations had been promulgated and New Zealand ministers again acknowledged that they applied only to operations within the three mile limit (See *A Wise Adventure I*, Chapter II, pages 50–51, notes 101 and 102). As to the question of their continuing validity, note Small's opinion in 1955, Chapter II page , notes 59 and 109.

38 *Foreign Affairs Review*. Vol 28 Nos 3 and 4, page 29, address to NZ Antarctic Society, 26 April 1978.

39 208/1/10/1 part 4, memorandum of 31 July 1978 from NZ Delegation to Secretary of Foreign Affairs.

40 Ibid, part 3, telegram 611 of 16 March 1978 from NZHC Canberra to Wellington.

41 Ibid, part 4. Annex 1 to Delegation report (see note 39).

42 Letter of 1 August 1978 from Norrish (NZ Ambassador, Washington) to Keating (not on file). Oelofsen was a South African representative.

43 See note 39.

44 208/1/10/1 Part 4, file note 7 July 1978. Delegation comprised M Norrish (Washington), D Holborow (Santiago) and D MacKay (New York Mission).

45 WP/32 of 28 July 1978.

46 See note 36.

47 208/1/10/1, Part 5, memorandum of 28 September 1978 from NZ Embassy, Washington to Secretary of Foreign Affairs.

48 Ibid, annex F.

49 See Note 36.

50 208/1/10/1 Part 5, annex A contains French amendment to Article I of the Convention, which establishes the boundaries of the Convention area.

51 Ibid, telegrams 3511 and 3535 of 25 and 26 September 1978 from NZ Embassy, Washington to Wellington.

52 Ibid, telegrams 1668 and 1764 of 28 September and 12 October 1978 from Wellington to NZ Embassy, Paris, and reply in Embassy's 1741 of 16 October.

53 Ibid, telegrams 1741 of 16 October 1978 from NZ Embassy, Paris, 2400 of 20 October from NZHC Canberra, and 2302 of 23 October from NZHC London.

54 Ibid, telegram 6876 (misnumbered 8676) of 20 October 1978 from Wellington to NZHC London.

55 Ibid, memorandum of 3 October 1978 from Secretary of Foreign Affairs to his Minister, circulated to other Ministers.

56 Ibid, file note of 31 October 1978 by Colin Keating.

57 Ibid, part 6. Telegram 2106 of 19 March 1979 from NZHC London to Wellington contains reports of New Zealand representative (Keating) at informal discussion held in Australian Embassy, Berne, 12- 16 March 1979. All the Antarctic Consultative Parties and the EEC were represented. The Chairman's statement on the islands issue is also on file (14 March, footnote of 16 March).

58 Ibid, 'Points relating to the EEC proposed by Australia as a basis of consensus in relation to the EEC issue,' not dated.

59 'Ibid, telegram 671 of 22 March 1979 from NZHC Canberra and reply in telegram 974 of 28 March.

60 Ibid, memorandum of 29 March 1979 from Secretary of Foreign Affairs to his Minister, and letter of 6 April 1979 Keating/Plimmer (Deputy HC Canberra).

61 Ibid, part 7. Telegram 2490 of 9 July 1979 from NZ Embassy, Washington to Wellington contains report of NZ representative to talks held in Washington from 25 June.

62 Ibid, note of 18 July 1989 from US Secretary of State to Embassies of Antarctic Consultative Parties, enclosing revised texts of several articles, with suggested statement on Kerguelen and Crozet and French alterative draft.

63 Ibid, 'Note by the Chairman of the Information Consultations on Antarctic Marine Living Resources conveyed to the Representative of Australia,' 4 October 1979.

64 Ibid, telegram 3767 of 8 October 1979 from NZ Embassy, Washington to Wellington.

65 See Note 63. The final paragraph of the statement reads:

> The understandings set forth in paragraphs 1-4 above, regarding the application of the Convention to waters adjacent to the islands of Kerguelen and Crozet, also apply to waters adjacent to the islands within

the Convention area over which the existence of state sovereignty is recognised by all Contracting Parties.

66 Final Act of the Conference on the Conservation of Antarctic Marine Living Resources signed at Canberra on 20 May 1980.
Paragraph 5 of the Chairman's statement, as quoted in note 65 above, remained unchanged.

67 208/51/2 Part 1 circular letter of 21 April 1980 from ASOC to Prime Minister (and presumably to other Antarctic Treaty Governments).

68 Ibid, telegram 3413 of 25 April 1980 from NZHC, London to Wellington.

69 Ibid, memorandum of 29 April 1980 from Secretary of Foreign Affairs to Minister.

70 Ibid, telegram 1358 of 9 May 1980 from NZHC Canberra to Wellington.

71 Ibid, telegram 1472 of 19 May 1980 from NZHC Canberra to Wellington.

72 Ibid, opening statement by New Zealand representative (W R Mansfield), 7 May 1980.

73 Ibid, see note 71.

74 New Zealand ratified the Convention on 8 March 1982.

75 Convention on the Regulation of Antarctic Mineral Resource Activities, Article 2(1).

76 The Antarctic Convergence is defined in Article 1(4) for the purposes of the Convention by lines of latitude and longitude. From 150° E to 50° W the boundary of the Convention area is the same as that of the Antarctic area. Thus the New Zealand subantarctic islands, Auckland and Campbell, are excluded, as are the Falkland Islands and the southern tip of South America. Elsewhere, however, the boundary runs at higher latitudes (up to 45° in one sector) and thus includes a number of sub Antarctic islands not in the Antarctic area, including Kerguelen and Crozet

77 Bush, op cit, Vol 1, page 403.

78 For historical catch data see CCAMLR Statistical Bulletin 1990 volume 2 (1980-1989). Current krill catch limits are set by CCAMLR Conservation Measures 51-01 (2014), 51-02 (2014), 51-03 (2014) and 51-07 (2014).

79 Ibid, part 4. Telegram 676 of 26 September 1984 from NZ Consulate-General, Noumea contained NZ delegation report.
(The Commission's request to all parties to refrain from a directed fishery of *notothenja rossii* did *not* constitute a formal conservation measure).

80 Ibid, Part 10, Report of New Zealand representative at Sixth Commission meeting 2-6 November 1987 (Mike Donoghue, DOC).

80a For historical catch data see CCAMLR Statistical Bulletin 1990 volume 2 (1980-1989). Current icefish catch limits are set by CCAMLR Conservation Measures 42-01 (2014) and 42-02 (2014).

80b For historical catch data see CCAMLR Statistical Bulletin 1990 volume 1 (1970-1979), 1990 volume 2 (1980-1989) and 2000 volume 12 (1990–1999). Current toothfish catch limits are set by CCAMLR Conservation Measures 41-02 (2014), 41-02 (2014), 41-03 (2014), 41-04 (2014), 41-05 (2014), 41-06 (2014), 41-07 (2014), 41-08 (2014), 41-09 (2014), 41-10 (2014) and 41-11 (2014).

80c 'The toothfish catch documentation scheme was established by CM 170/

XVIII (1999) and the latest version is CM 10-05 (2014). The non-contracting party vessel IUU list was established by CM 118/XVI (1998) and the latest version is CM 10-07 (2009). The contracting party vessel IUU list was established by CM 10-06 (2002) and the latest version is CM 10-06 (2008).

81 The CCAMLR System of Inspection was established in 1989. New Zealand provides reports of its CCAMLR inspections to the Commission and to the flag state of the inspected vessel. See the CCAMLR website www.ccamlr.org for further information.

82 Ibid, part 11. Reports of New Zealand activities for 1986/87 (CCAMLR-VI/MA/15 of 26 October 1987) and Fax of 10 October 1988 from Ministry of Foreign Affairs to Executive Secretary, CCAMLR.

83 NZ Statutes 1981, No 53. Antarctic Marine Living Resources Act, passed 20 October 1981, came into effect 1 January 1982.

84 701/16/4/1 Part 2, Report of 14 September 1981 by Ministry of Foreign Affairs to the Foreign Affairs Committee of Parliament

X: Mineral Resources: The Need for a Regime

1 PM154/2/6 part 1, memorandum of 12 July 1945 from Secretary, DSIR, to Secretary of External Affairs.

2 Ibid, memorandum of 17 December 1945 from Minister of External Affairs to NZHC, London.

3 *Evening Post*, 9 January 1947, 13 April 1948, 1 June 1951.

4 PM208/211, part I, Statement by Minister of 16 May 1951.

5 Ibid, memorandum of 17 October 1956 from Director, Geological Survey (R W Willett) to Secretary, DSIR.

6 Ibid, letter of 5 January 1960 from White to Jermyn.

7 Ibid, memorandum of 12 June 1961 from Secretary of External Affairs to NZHC Canberra. Memorandum referred to Report of Senate Committee on Foreign Relations, 23 June 1960.

8 Ibid, letter of 7 August 1969 from David Gillman, Venture Associates Pty, Sydney and replies from the Prime Minister (Holyoake) on 2 September 1969 and 20 March 1970.

9 Ibid, memorandum of 15 October 1969 from NZHC Canberra to Secretary of External Affairs.

10 Ibid, memorandum of 30 September 1969 from Secretary of External Affairs to New Zealand diplomatic posts in Antarctic Consultative Party capitals.

11 Ibid, see note 9.

12 Ibid, memorandum of 17 October 1969 from New Zealand Embassy Washington, to Secretary of External Affairs.

13 Ibid, memorandum of 23 October 1969 from NZHC London to Secretary of External Affairs.

14 Ibid, memorandum of 28 November 1969 from Secretary of External Affairs to diplomatic posts.

15 Ibid, note of 19 December 1969 from New Zealand Embassy Tokyo to Embassies of Consultative Parties.

16 Ibid, brief paper on Mineral Exploration and Exploitation, October 1970.

17 Ibid, letter of 14 October 1970 from White to Wade.

18 Ibid, letter of 27 October 1970 from Wade to White, with text of New Zealand statement. New Zealand Delegation Report dated 21 December 1971 (sic).

19 Ibid, ECOSOC document E/C.7/5 of 25 January 1971.

20 Ibid, telegrams 52, 55 and 75 of 12 and 17 February and 3 March 1971 from New Zealand Mission, New York, to Wellington.

21 Ibid, memorandum of 28 Apri11972 from NZHC London to Secretary of Foreign Affairs.

22 Ibid, ANT/17, 18 October 1972, draft recommendation by United Kingdom (included a proposal for agreed measures and an interim moratorium). ANT 17/Rev 1 (proposed inclusion in agenda of next Consultative Meeting and interim moratorium).

23 Ibid, ANT/2, 27 September 1972.

24 Ibid, ANT/44, 2 November 1972.

25 Ibid, ANT/37, 31 October 1972.

26 Ibid, Recommendation VII-6, 10 November 1972.

27 Ibid, memorandum of 16 January 1973 from Secretary of Foreign Affairs to PM.

28 PM208/2/3 part I, file note of 6 March 1973 by Peren of advice from Thomson, Antarctic Division, DSIR.

29 PM208/2/3/1 part 1, memorandum of 24 February 1974 from NZHC London to Secretary of Foreign Affairs (Note: This file is actually Part 2 of PM208/2/3. To add to the confusion, there is another file 208/2/3 containing papers on a later conference on Antarctic Minerals.)

30 PM208/2/3 part 1. Contains report of New Zealand representative (Kear), July 1973.

31 PM208/43/1 part 1. Memorandum: of 29 October 1973 from Director-General, Department of Lands & Survey to Secretary of Foreign Affairs.

32 Ibid, memorandum of 12 November 1973 from Secretary of Foreign Affairs in reply.

33 Ibid, telegram 304 of 15 April 1975 from Wellington to New Zealand Mission, Geneva. 'We have had excited calls from Japanese—and British representatives . . . 'UNEP proposals were contained in document UNEP/GC/31, 'which we cannot locate'.

34 Ibid, telegram of 21 April 1975 from Wellington to Uniterra, Nairobi, conveying message from Rowling to Strong.

35 Ibid, telegram of 25 April 1975 from Strong to Rowling.

36 PM208/44/1, part 1, memorandum of 4 October 1974 from Secretary of Foreign Affairs to NZHC London.

37 Ibid, telegram 62 of 27 February 1975 from New Zealand Embassy, The Hague, to Wellington.

38 Ibid, part 2, telegram 2936 of 14 May 1975 from NZHC London to Wellington.

39 My emphasis.

40 PM208/44/11 part 1, memorandum of 29 May 1975 from Secretary of Foreign Affairs to Prime Minister, approved by PM and approval conveyed

to New Zealand delegate (Craw) 3 June 1975.

41 Ibid, press statement of 9 June 1975.

42 Interview with Charles Craw, 3 August 1990. No record survives of the New Zealand statement, which may have been made off the cuff. It would not be correct to say that New Zealand made a formal proposal, on which other delegations were required to take a position.

43 Telegram 3882 of 23 June 1975 from NZHC London to Wellington.

44 Eighth Antarctic Treaty Consultative Meeting, Recommendation VIII-14.

45 Ibid, Final Report, paragraph 15.

46 See note 43.

47 PM208/2/1 part 2. Memorandum of 2 July 1976 from Secretary of Foreign Affairs to Minister.

48 Ibid, memorandum of 29 June 1976 from Secretary of Foreign Affairs to Minister, and Minister's J minute.

49 PM208/45/1, memorandum of 6 April 1976 from NZHC London, and enclosure.

50 Ibid, telegrams 267 and 268 of 4 May 1976 from Permanent Mission, New York to Wellington.

51 Ibid, telegram 266 of 6 May 1976 from Wellington to Permanent Mission, New York.

52 Ibid, telegrams 275 of 6 May 1976 from Permanent Mission New York and 2860 of 14 May 1976 from NZHC London to Wellington.
PM208/2/1 part 2, telegram 1508 of 21 May 1976 from NZ Embassy Washington to Wellington.

53 PM208/2/1 part 2, telegram 820 of 25 June 1976 from Wellington to NZ Embassy, Paris.

54 Ibid, telegram 848 of 1 July 1976 from Wellington to NZ Embassy, Paris.

55 Ibid, telegram 717 of 7 July 1976 from NZ Embassy Paris to Wellington
PM208/45/1, Report of New Zealand Delegation, 5 August 1976, paragraph 16.

56 PM208/46/2, document RPS-10. (Attached to final report of the Special Preparatory Meeting.)

57 Ibid, document RPS-7.

58 Ibid, document RPS-6.

59 Ibid, document RPS-14.

60 Chapter VI, note 28.

61 PM208/45/1, report of New Zealand Delegation, paragraphs 25–35.

This would no doubt be an interesting point to argue if the matter ever came to international adjudication. It should be noted that the 'common heritage' Area as finally defined in the LOS Convention is 'the seabed and ocean floor and subsoil thereof beyond the limits of national jurisdiction' (not the *deep* seabed), that the seabed is not assigned any geophysical or geographical limits in that Convention, and that the expression 'sea-bed' is in fact used in the definition of the continental shelf.

62 Ibid, paragraphs 53-59.

63 PM208/46/2, Final Report of the Special Preparatory Meeting, Annex 3 (Report of the Working Group on the Legal and Political aspects of Mineral

Exploration and Exploitation in Antarctica.)

64 PM208/2/1, part 2, telegram 1 of 14 July 1976 from NZ Embassy Paris to NZ Embassy Moscow.

65 Ibid, *Evening Post*, 30 August 1976.

66 Ibid, memorandum of 28 October 1976 from Secretary of Foreign Affairs to Acting Minister, and CM76/44/19 of 11 November 1976, Secretary of the Cabinet to Minister.

67 Ibid, memorandum of 4 November 1976 from Secretary of Foreign Affairs to DSIR, Treasury, Commissioner for the Environment, Energy Resources and Agriculture and Fisheries, with draft Cabinet paper .

68 PM208/1/10/1, memorandum of 24 November 1976 from Commissioner for the Environment to Secretary of Foreign Affairs.

69 208/46/1, part 1, memorandum of 1 December 1976 from Assistant Director-General, DSIR to Secretary of Foreign Affairs.

70 Ibid, Treasury report No 4653 to Minister of Finance, March 1976.

71 Ibid, letter of 9 May 1977 from Keating to McArthur (Ambassador, Paris).

72 Ibid, memorandum of 14 March 1977 from Secretary of Foreign Affairs to Minister.

73 Ibid, memorandum of 10 March 1977 from Minister of Foreign Affairs for Cabinet (CP(77)179), and memorandum CM77/8/27 of 14 March 1977 from Secretary to the Cabinet to Minister.

74 208/2/1 part 3, draft Cabinet paper dated 27 August 1979.

75 208/46/1 part 1, memorandum of 20 June 1977 from NZHC London to Secretary of Foreign Affairs.

76 208/2/1 part 3, telegram 1721 of 13 July 1977 from Wellington to NZHC Canberra.

77 Ibid, telegram 4446 of 28 July 1977 from Wellington to NZHC London.

78 Ibid, letter of 15 August 1977 from Talboys to Peacock.

79 Ibid, memorandum of 27 September 1977 from NZHC Canberra to Secretary of Foreign Affairs and reply of 3 October 1977.

80 Ibid, letter of 15 September 1977 from Peacock to Talboys.

81 Ibid, memorandum of 12 September 1977 from Secretary of Foreign Affairs to the Commissioner of Energy Resources and Secretary to the Treasury.

82 208/46/1, part 2, telegram 5651 of 22 September 1977 from Wellington to NZHC London.

83 Ibid, telegram 6144 of 22 September 1977 from NZHC London to Wellington.

84 Ibid, telegram 5842 of 29 September 1977 from Wellington NZHC London.

85 Ibid, telegram 6463 of 5 October 1977 from NZHC London to Wellington.

86 ATCM Recommendation IX- 1paragraph 8 reads:

> They urge their nationals and other states to refrain from all exploration and exploitation of Antarctic mineral resources while making progress towards the timely adoption of an agreed regime concerning Antarctic mineral resource activities. They will thus endeavour to ensure that, pending the adoption of agreed solutions pertaining to exploration and exploitation of mineral resources, no activity shall be conducted to explore or exploit such resources. They will keep these matters under continuing examination.

87 208/46/1 part 2, Saving telegram 3 of 10 October 1977 from NZHC London to Wellington.
88 208/2/1 part 3, note of departmental) meeting held on 29 November 1977.
89 Ibid, CEC paper of 11 May 1978. The Departments involved in its preparation were Agriculture and Fisheries, Defence, Energy, Foreign Affairs, Prime Minister's, Scientific and Industrial Research, Trade and Industry, Transport and Treasury.
90 Ibid, hand written minute.
91 Ibid, memorandum of 17 August 1978 from Secretary of Foreign Affairs to Minister.
92 Ibid, memorandum 21 June 1979 from Secretary of Foreign Affairs to Minister, approved 27 June.
93 Ibid, document ANT(79) PM LP2, 2 July 1979. Informal paper on Mineral Exploration and Exploitation submitted by New Zealand.
94 Ibid, telegram 2490 of 9 July 1979 from NZ Embassy, Washington to Wellington.
95 208/47/1, CM79/33/6 of 3 September 1979.
96 Ibid, press statement of 12 September 1979.
97 Ibid, telegram 3680 of 12 September 1979 from Wellington to NZ Embassy Washington (draft of speech).
98 Ibid, telegram 3767 of 8 October 1979 from NZ Embassy Washington to Wellington. The reference to 'an ingenious form of words' is obscure. There was in fact no reference to the moratorium in either the relevant recommendation of the Tenth Consultative Meeting (Recommendation X-I) or in the report of the Working Group on this question (ANT/X/47 of 4 October 1979). The failure to recall Recommendation IX-I (see note 86) was a notable omission. At the Eleventh Consultative Meeting, however, it was recommended that governments 'take account' of the 1977 moratorium in elaborating the minerals regime. This recommendation was presumably intended to extend the validity of the moratorium until such time as a regime was in place, but did not affect its non-binding character.
99 208/2/1 part 4, file note of 5 February 1980 by Keating.
100 Ibid, telegram 2930 of 25 July 1980 from Wellington to NZ Embassy Washington and telegram 3526 of 5 September 1980 from Embassy to Wellington. .
101 208/51/2 part 1, telegram 805 of 27 August 1980 from NZ Mission Geneva to Wellington, 'for Norrish from Templeton'.
102 personal letter of 15 October 1980 from Keating to Mansfield.
103 208/2/1 part 4, telegram 4890 of 12 December 1980 from NZ Embassy, Washington to Wellington.
104 701/16/5, memorandum of 17 March 1981 from Secretary of Foreign Affairs to Minister.
105 Ibid, memorandum of 28 May 1981 from Secretary of Foreign Affairs to Minister, covering draft Cabinet paper.
106 Ibid, Treasury report T62/11 of 17 June 1981.
107 208/2/1 part 4, memorandum of 11 June 1981 from Secretary of Foreign Affairs to Minister.

108 701/16/5/1, memorandum 12 January 1982 from Secretary of Foreign Affairs to Minister.

109 Eleventh Antarctic Consultative Meeting, Recommendation XI-I, 7 July 1981.

110 70/16/5, telegram 2947 of 10 July 1981 from NZ Embassy Washington to Wellington containing NZ delegation report on the Eleventh Consultative Meeting.

111 As reported in March, see note 104.

112 See note 109, paragraph 6 of the Recommendation.

113 Ibid, paragraph 7(iv).

114 See note 110. Telegram 2947, paragraph 15.

115 The 1982 Convention, unlike the 1958 Convention, defines the Continental shelf as extending at least 200 nautical miles from the coast, whether or not it in fact does so as a natural feature. The Final Act of the Fourth Special Antarctic Consultative meeting records that:

> The Meeting also agreed that the geographic extent of the continental shelf as referred to in Article 5(3) of the Convention would be determined by reference to all the criteria and the rules embodied in paragraphs 1 to 7 of Article 76 of the United Nations Convention on the Law of the Sea.

XI: Mineral Resources: Negotiating a Convention

1 Argentina invaded the Falklands on 2 April 1982, only two months before the first session of the Fourth Consultative Meeting on Mineral Resources was due to convene in Wellington. New Zealand responded by *jnter alia*, breaking off diplomatic relations with Argentina, expelling its Ambassador and closing its Embassy. As the interests of Argentina were not taken over by any other diplomatic mission, there remained no means of direct diplomatic communication between the two countries. It was initially by no means certain that Argentina would attend the June meeting; after the overthrow of the Allende government in Chile, the Soviet Union had broken off diplomatic relations and thereafter made it known that it would not attend any Antarctic meetings in Chile or host any meetings in Moscow. (It may be noted. that of the eleven sessions of the Fourth Minerals meeting, none were in fact held in Chile, the Soviet Union, Argentina or the United Kingdom.) It is, of course, a frequent occurrence for states to participate in multilateral meetings alongside states with which they have no diplomatic relations—less frequent, perhaps, alongside states with which they are engaged in active hostilities. It is a credit to all concerned, and to the durability of the Antarctic Treaty, that its demilitarisation provisions were respected during the Falklands war, and that the Antarctic meetings schedule was not disrupted. The New Zealand authorities indeed came close to postponing the June meeting until September, but were strongly dissuaded from doing so by the United States, with support from other Consultative Parties, and by the fact that in the end both Britain and Argentina decided to attend. (701/16/5/1 Part 2, telegram of 3002 of 7 May 1982 to NZHC London and to other posts, telegram 2041 of 10 May 1982 from New Zealand Embassy Washington to Wellington.)

2 Eleventh Consultative Meeting, Recommendation XI-I, paragraph 2.

3 AMR/SCM/25. This document was not dated but was circulated to the participants on 13 December 1982 (701/16/5/1 Part 4, memorandum of 15 December 1982 to posts).

4 Perhaps inevitably, the draft Convention did in fact become more detailed as session succeeded session. Its scope was limited, however, to non-renewable resources ('all non-living natural non-renewable resources, including fossil fuels, metallic and non-metallic minerals') and thus excluded renewable resources such as ice, which in 1982 was the subject, of an Argentinian paper, AMR/SCM/8. Renewable resources would have had to be dealt with in a separate negotiation if that had been thought necessary. The question of liability also required further elaboration which would have involved the negotiation of a further protocol. (Article 8 of the Convention and Final Act.)

5 Recommendation XI-I, paragraph 5(d).

6 LOS Convention 1982, Article 82.

7 701/16/5/1 part 2, memorandum of 24 May 1982 from Minister of Foreign Affairs to Cabinet.

8 Ibid, part 4, memorandum of 2 July 1982 from Secretary of Foreign Affairs to Minister.

9 principally Keating (stationed in Washington), Bill Mansfield (Head of the Legal Division, MFA) and Beeby (Assistant Secretary, MFA).

10 701/165/2 part 1, telegram 4651 of 10 December 1982 from Wellington to NZ Embassy Washington, 'For Keating from Beeby'.

11 Ibid, memorandum of 31 January 1983 from Secretary of Foreign Affairs to Minister.

12 ANT(83)MR/17, Personal Report by the chairman on the Meeting on Antarctic Mineral Resources held in Wellington 17-28 January 1983. This was described as an 'informal' meeting, but this meant only that the full range of interpretation and translation services were not provided.

13 701/16/5/2 part 1, telegrams 64 and 65 of 3 February 1983 from Wellington to NZ Mission New York, repeated to other posts.

14 Beeby to author, 15 February 1990. The other NZ draftsmen were Keating and Mansfield. Keating contributed many innovative ideas, including this one.

15 The various drafts of MR/17 are discussed on pages 131, 133–35, 144–45, 149, 151, 153–55, 157, 160–62, 174, 179, 183, 185, 187–88, 191, 193–96, 198–203, 216, 218, 245

16 701/16/5/4, telegram 5503 of 30 June 1983 from NZHC London to Wellington reported discussion with British officials of German attitudes. The British thought the Germans were also worried about Beeby taking a major role because they did not like Beeby's paper, being 'wedded to the idea of co-administration', and thought that his chairmanship of a legal/political group would give impetus to his proposals.

17 701/16/5 part 3, letter of 11 May 1983 from Beeby to Keating and reply of 9 June.

18 Article 20 of the draft Convention in MRlI7 provided that the regulatory committee should consist of (a) the state sponsoring an application to mine,

(b) the claimant state (or states) to whose territory the application related, (c) the US and USSR, (d) up to two parties to the Convention designated by the sponsoring states, provided that (a) plus (c) plus (d) added up to no more than four and (e) up to three parties designated by the claimant state, provided that (b) plus (e) added up to no more than four. This formula provided a balance if the sponsoring state was a non-claimant, but Scully correctly pointed out that the balance would be upset if the sponsoring state was the claimant state for the territory in question or another claimant state.

19 701/16/2 part 1, telegram 494 of 5 August 1982 from New Zealand Mission, New York to Wellington.

20 The suspicion was partially confirmed more than a year later when a copy of Mrs Gandhi's letter to Mahathir was made available to a New Zealand representative. Mrs Gandhi, telling Mahathir of India's scientific expedition, declared that India had 'kept away' from the Antarctica Treaty because its position was that 'a few countries should not have the right to expropriate natural and other resources in territories outside their own, as some countries have done in Antarctica'. India was now looking at the Treaty again within the framework of the recently concluded Treaty of the Law of the Sea, but 'would not do anything and to the best of our ability we shall not allow others to take any steps, which could be considered detrimental to the interests of developing countries'. (701/16/2 part 7, telegram 619 of 22 September 1983 from NZHC Kuala Lumpur to Wellington.)

21 701/16/2 part 1, telegram 557 of 20 August 1982 from Wellington to NZ Mission, New York, repeated to Kuala Lumpur and other posts.

22 UNGA, 37th session, tenth Plenary Meeting, 29 September 1982 (Verbatim Record, page 132).

23 701/16/2 part 2, telegram 496 of 23 September 1982 from NZHC, Kuala Lumpur to Wellington.

24 Ibid, telegram 2 of 5 January 1983 from Wellington to NZ Mission, New York 'For Harland from Templeton'. The NZ Permanent Representative, Bryce Harland, was dispatched to New Delhi to patrol the corridors and report developments at the NAM meeting. A note was also sent to the Indian High Commission in Wellington in acknowledgement of advice about the Indian Antarctic expedition, agreeing to provide assistance if practicable, and indicating that cooperation between New Zealand and India in Antarctica would be greatly facilitated if India became party to the Treaty. (Note from Indian HC of 9 December 1982 and reply of 5 January 1983, parts 2 and 3 of file.)

25 Ibid, telegram 734 of 9 October 1982 from NZ Mission, New York to Wellington.

26 Ibid, memorandum of 12 October 1982 from Secretary of Foreign Affairs to Minister, telegram 1885 of 15 October 1982 from NZHC Suva to Wellington, and telegram 780 from Wellington to NZ Mission New York.

27 Ibid, memorandum of 4 November 1982 from NZHC Kuala Lumpur to Wellington.

28 Ibid, telegram 1132 of 26 October 1982 from NZHC Ottawa to Wellington, 'For Templeton from Beath'.

29 Ibid, part 4, file note of call on Minister of Foreign Affairs on 31 March 1983 by Abdul Kadir, Malaysian Parliamentary Secretary of Foreign Affairs. Cooper told Kadir that those who thought Antarctic minerals would shortly lead to an economic bonanza had 'stars in their eyes'. Significantly, Cooper left the defence of New Zealand's claim to sovereignty in the Ross Dependency to Beeby.

30 Ibid, part 3, memorandum of 25 March 1983 from NZ Mission, New York and attachment.

31 Ibid. The Malaysian paper is filed under date 11 March 1983. The 'Enterprise' to which it refers is the agency to be created to conduct international mining operations in the seabed under the provisions of the LOS Convention (Article 170).

32 Ibid, part 4. The paper' 'Discussion of Antarctica in the United Nations: Informal Note (Revised)' -' is dated 13 April 1983.

33 Ibid, telegrams 320 of 18 May 1983 from NZ Mission New York, 2144 and 2224 of 25 and 31 May 1983 from NZ Embassy, Washington to Wellington.

34 Ibid, telegram 1419 of 27 April 1983 from Wellington to NZ Mission New York, repeated to Washington and other posts.

35 Ibid, telegram 2229 of 31 May 1983, 'for Beeby and Mansfield from Keating'. The telegram went on to express concern about the need to protect the position of the claimants in the negotiation of the regime:

> . . . The already slim elements of the claimant position in MRII7 must remain if we are to demonstrate to the outside world that we have any real interest left. On no account can we permit the modification of Article XX along lines that would· submerge or conceal the fact that the reason why a particular claimant is a member of the Regulatory Committee and has a veto is simply because the activity in question is being carried out in territory over which It) he(sic) maintains a claim to sovereignty.

36 Ibid, part 5, telegram 750 of 1 July 1983 from NZ Embassy, Bangkok to Wellington.

37 Ibid, telegram 769 of 5 July 1983 from NZ Embassy, Jakarta, reported Indonesian views along these lines.

38 701/16/5 part 3, telegram 4958 of 14 June 1983 from NZHC London to Wellington. Memorandum of 15 June from Beeby to Hensley, Permanent Head, PM's Department.

39 Ibid, telegram 3996 of 15 June 1983 from Wellington to NZHC London and other posts.

40 Ibid, ECO Vol XXIII, No.1, 11-22 July 1983. ('ECO is an occasional newspaper published by Friends of the Earth and others at international meetings of environmental importance.')

41 Ibid, part 4. The paper (CS (83)564) was taken by Cabinet on 11 July 1983 and referred to an *ad hoc* Committee with power to act. The Committee met on 13 July and again on 20 July, when it adopted additional instructions for the delegation (AH (83) M10).

42 Ibid, telegram 770 of 15 July 1983 from Wellington to NZ Embassy Bonn, and personal message for Beeby from Templeton, unnumbered.

43 Ibid, telegram 721 of 16 July 1983 from NZ Embassy, Bonn to Wellington.

44 Ibid, AH (83)M10 (see note 41).
45 Ibid, telegram 3041 of 19 July 1983 from NZ Embassy, Washington to Wellington.
46 Ibid, telegram 756 of 22 July 1983 from NZ Embassy, Bonn to Wellington and memorandum of 19 August 1983 from NZHC London to Wellington.
47 Ibid, see note 42.
48 Ibid, press statement issued 8 August 1983.
49 Ibid, see report from NZHC London, paragraph 10 (note 46).
50 701/16/2, part 6, memorandum of 9 August 1983 from NZHC Canberra to Wellington and enclosure. The Australian PM (Hawke) wrote to Mahathir on 27 July asking him to defer inscription of the item until they could 'jointly address' the issues which the Malaysian initiative had raised. Hawke made it clear in this letter that the change of government in Australia had not altered Australian policy on Antarctica, which continued to be based on the Antarctic Treaty system and participation in the negotiation of a minerals regime. Mahathir's reply indicated that Malaysia was determined to go ahead with its item at the 38th session, but that it would be limited in scope to a request to the Secretary General to undertake a study and make a report (telegram 593 of 23 August 1983 from NZ Mission, New York, to Wellington).
51 Ibid, part 7, telegram 695 and fax 694 of 19 September 1983 from NZ Mission, New York to Wellington forwarded Malaysian draft resolution.
52 Ibid, document A/38/439 of 21 September 1983.
53 Ibid, telegram 705 of 21 September 1983 from NZ Mission, New York to Wellington.
54 Ibid, memorandum of 7 September 1983 from Secretary of Foreign Affairs to Minister.
55 Assembly Resolution 38177 of 15 December 1983.
56 701/16/2, part 8, telegram 11793 of 29 December 1983 from NZHC London to Wellington. 70111615 part 5, telegram 371 of 28 January 1984, paragraph 10.
57 701/16/2, part 5, E (83)120 of 16 October 1983.
58 Ibid, E(93)M39 Part II, 18 October 1983.
59 Ibid, telegram 4272 of 12 November 1983 from Wellington to NZHC Canberra, transmitting a letter of 11 November from Cooper to Hayden.
60 Ibid, letter of 18 November 1983 from Hayden to Cooper.
61 Ibid, file note of 12 December 1983 by Beeby.
62 Ibid. Much to the exasperation of the Secretary of Foreign Affairs, in whose absence the Minister had approved their attendance. This must be positively the last time, he said, that the Assistant Secretary and Head of the Legal Division should be away together on Antarctica matters (Minute of 5 December 1983 on submission to Minister of 22 November). It wasn't.
63 Ibid, telegram 11756 from NZHC London to Wellington; file copy undated, probably 24 December 1983.
64 Ibid, memorandum of 11 January 1984 from Harry Keys, for Commissioner for the Environment, to Beeby.
65 Ibid, letter of 10 January 1984 from Secretary of Foreign Affairs to Yamashita, Japanese Embassy.

66 Ibid, telegram 371 of 28 January 1984 from NZ Embassy, Washington to Wellington.

67 Informal Personal Report of the Chairman of the Working Group on Antarctic Mineral Resources (Bonn, July 1983: Washington, January 1984). This contained parallel texts of MR/17 and MR/17 Revision, the latter dated 29 March 1984. Some corrections were subsequently circulated. r

68 See note 18 for the original text of this article in MR/17. The revision appears to have been largely based on an informal suggestion from the United States representative (Scully), sent to Beeby shortly before the revised text was issued. (701/16/5 part 6, telegram1055 of 12 March 1984 from NZ Embassy, Washington to Wellington.)

69 Beeby to author, IS February 1990.

70 Ibid.

71 701/16/5 part 1, CEC paper dated 2 May 1984.

72 Ibid, E(84)MI5 Pt 5, 8 May 1984.

73 Ibid, telegram 1507 of 8 May 1984 from NZHC Canberra to Wellington.

74 Ibid, ECO Vol XXVIl Nos 1-3, 22-31 May 1984.

75 Ibid, telegram 1103 of 1 June 1984 from NZ Embassy, Tokyo to Wellington.

76 Ibid, telegram 1111 of 1 June 1984 from NZ Embassy, Tokyo to Wellington.

XII: Mineral Resources: Reaching Agreement

1 See *A Wise Adventure I*, Chapter VI, note 30.

2 701/16/7 part 3, (about) July 1984.

3 Ibid, letter of 7 August 1984 from PM to R Wilson, Greenpeace International.

4 Ibid, letter of 17 August 1984 from PM to Miss V Young, Coordinator, Focus on Antarctica.

5 Ibid, part 4, letter of 1 October 1984 from Acting Minister to Richard Northey.

6 Ibid, memorandum of 16 October 1984 from Minister to Minister of Tourism (Moore had raised the issue orally).

7 Ibid, memorandum of 25 October 1984 from Minister of Overseas Trade and Marketing (Moore's principal portfolio) to Prime Minister.

8 Ibid, memorandum of 12 November 1984 from Minister of Tourism to Minister.

9 Ibid, memorandum of 21 November 1984 from Secretary of Foreign Affairs to Minister.

10 Ibid, letter to PM or Minister from Convenor, NZ Organising Committee ASOC of 6 November, 22 November, 3 December and 12 December 1984 and 11 January 1985. In her letter of 6 November Wallace said:

> ASOC was very disappointed in your response to our recent criticism of the negotiations by the Antarctic Treaty Consultative Parties of the Antarctic Minerals Regime.
>
> You said in your press statement of 23 October that:
>
> 'It has been suggested . . . that these negotiations could lead to conflict from environmental damage. This is a totally irresponsible comment from people who ought to know better.'

> You later said: 'I just cannot take this criticism of the negotiations seriously. It seems to me that the worst thing that we could possibly do at the moment is to walk away from a constructive and responsible negotiating process. These people seem to be saying that if there is a gap in the present law do nothing and Antarctica will remain a wilderness.'
>
> In your discussion of the issue on *Morning Report* on Wednesday 24th, you called me mischievous'.
>
> Calling us 'irresponsible' of 'mischievous' does us an injustice. We hope that you will consider our views much more carefully than that. We appreciate that you have probably only heard them second-hand from the Press and from the officials of the Ministry of Foreign Affairs. We are not irresponsible. Nor are we mischievous. We have been closely involved in monitoring and analysing the minerals regime since the first meeting in Wellington in June 1982. We liaise with the ASOC alliance of about 120 groups in 22 countries which are concerned about Antarctica and have considered the issues carefully.

11 Ibid, memorandum of 19 February 1985 from Secretary of Foreign Affairs to Minister. One 'correspondent' wrote to the Secretary:

> Thank you for your letter of 21 November 1984 acknowledging a postcard about Antarctica. I am sure I sent no post card on Antarctica. Liquor in supermarkets—yes, or in favour of fluoridation, or abolition of corporal punishment, or homosexual law reform. You seem to have done your best to protect the Antarctic environment. (17 December 1984)

12 Ibid, letter of 20 February 1985 to Cath Wallace.

13 Ibid, memorandum of 19 February 1985, see note 85.

14 701/16/5 part 9, notes of Canberra discussions dated 23 November 1984. (The meeting was held from 17-21 September.)

15 Resolution A/Res/39/152 adopted 17 December 1984 UN Study in document A/39/584.

16 701/16/5 part 9, ER(84)15 of 7 December 1984 approved by Cabinet 12 December. (See memorandum to posts of 9 January 1985.)

17 Ibid, part 10, memorandum of 22 March 1985 from Secretary of Foreign Affairs to Minister. (Copy of Rio package non-paper is on Part 12, out of date order.)

18 memorandum Beeby to author, 23 March 1990.

19 Ibid.

20 Ibid, and point 3(c) of the Rio package.

21 Ibid.

22 Ibid, and point 6 of the Rio package.

23 701/16/5 part 10, telegram 1828 of 28 March 1985 from NZ Embassy, Washington to Wellington.

24 Ibid, part 11, telegram 2738 of 4 April 1985 from NZHC London to Wellington.

25 Ibid, telegram 404 of 29 April 1985 from NZ Embassy, Brussels to Wellington.

26 Ibid, letter of 28 June 1985 from British Acting High Commissioner to Beeby and enclosure.

27 Ibid, part 12, letter of 7 August 1985 from Fennessy, Australian High Commission, to Keating.
28 Ibid, telegram 2908 of 8 August 1985 from NZHC Canberra to Wellington.
29 Ibid, file note of 15 August 1985.
30 Ibid, New Zealand record of claimants' meeting dated 3 September 1985. (Meeting held 26-29 August.)
31 Ibid, part 11, letter of 10 July 1985 from Ian Nicholson, DFA Canberra, to Keating.
32 Ibid, part 12, telegram 6033 of 1 August 1985 from NZHC London to Wellington.
33 Ibid, letter of 13 August 1985 from Keating to Nicholson.
34 Ibid, transcript of Prime Minister's press conference, 5 September 1985.
35 Ibid, part 13, letter of 10 February 1985 from James Barnes, The Antarctic Project, Washington DC, to Minister for the Environment and reply of 17 May 1985.
36 Ibid, part 12, telegram 1101(m) of 11 October 1985 from Wellington to Washington and other posts.
37 *New Zealand Herald*, 6 March 1986.
38 701/16/5, part 14, memorandum of 2 April 1986 from Beeby to Keating, with attached summary account of the discussions.
39 Beeby says that 'the Soviet Union was excluded because Rybakov was being so bloody-minded that his presence . . . would have done more harm than good. The FRG was excluded for the same reason' (Beeby to author, 23 March 1990).
40 701/16/5 part 14, memorandum of 2 May 1986 from Secretary of Foreign Affairs to Minister, c covering delegation report.
41 Ibid, letter of 16 May 1986 from Director-General, DSIR (A J Ellis) to Secretary of Foreign Affairs.
42 Ibid, part 15, reply of 6 August 1986 and file note of 15 August 1986 by Hilary Willberg.
43 Ibid, part 14, letter of 28 July 1986 from Beeby to Commissioner for the Environment (Ken Piddington).
44 Ibid, part 15, memorandum of 7 October 1986 from Secretary of Foreign Affairs to Minister, telegram of 8 October 1986 to Graham and reply of 10 October 1986. The Ministers were Marshall (Conservation), Goff (Environment) and Woollaston (parliamentary Undersecretary to both).
45 *Eye Witness*, 30 September 1986.
46 NZPD, Vol 475, P4988, 16 October 1986.
47 701/16/5 part 15, letter of 22 October 1986 from Wallace to Minister, and reply of 28 October.
48 Ibid, part 14, telegram 819 of 7 July 1986 from NZ Embassy, Bonn to Wellington.
49 Ibid, parts 14 and 15, telegrams 3798 of 10 July and 4748 of 26 August 1986 from NZ Embassy Washington. In the end only two Americans attended.
50 Ibid, telegram 7060 of 18 August 1986 from NZHC London to Wellington.
51 Ibid, MR/17 Rev 2, 19 September 1986.
52 Ibid, telegram 293 of 23 September 1986 from Wellington to NZ Embassy,

Santiago, contained a watching brier' for the New Zealand representative at the claimants' meeting.

53 Ibid, see note 127.

54 Ibid, Chairman's personal summary of conclusions, Santiago Claimants' Meeting 24-29 September 1986, forwarded by New Zealand representative (Alistair Hercus) 2 October 1986. The Chairman was Nicholson of Australia.

55 Ibid, memorandum of 16 October 1986 from Secretary of Foreign Affairs to Minister.

56 Ibid, memorandum of 23 October 1986 from Secretary to Minister and enclosure.

57 Ibid, part 16, telegram 3637 of 13 November 1986 from NZ Embassy Tokyo to Wellington.

58 Ibid, memorandum of 30 January 1987 from Secretary for the Environment to Secretary of Foreign Affairs and enclosure.

59 Ibid, part 17, telegram 774 of 10 March 1987 contains agenda for the claimants meeting.

At the 1986 Tokyo meeting Australia and the United Kingdom had circulated a draft article (34 bis) which read:

> Having regard to the position under the Antarctic Treaty of States asserting rights of or claims to territorial sovereignty in Antarctica, and their special position under this Convention, including their responsibilities in relation to management schemes, any state which in relation to an area is a state referred to in Article 29(2) (a) shall be entitled to receive [a special share, to be defined] of net revenues or payments in kind arising from mineral resource activities in that area.

60 Ibid, file note by Beeby, 12 March 1987.

61 Ibid, memorandum of 6 March 1987 from NZHC Canberra and enclosure.

62 Ibid, telegram 332 Mis of 6 March 1987 to Washington and other posts.

63 MR/17 Rev 3, 2 April 1987 (not on file).

64 701/16/5, part 18, statement issued by Chairman of negotiations at 10th session of Special Consultative Meeting on Antarctic Resources in Montevideo, 20 May 1987.

65 Ibid, note by Beeby and summary of his statement to the final meeting at Montevideo, 15 June 1987.

66 Ibid, memorandum from Beeby to MFA, 27 May '1987.

67 Ibid, see note 141.

68 Document URU98 of 15 May 1987.

69 701/16/5 part 19, memorandum of 9 September 1987 from MFA to Deputy PM.

70 See note 141.

71 701/1615 part 20, letter of 7 December 1987 from Colin Keating to Alistair Graham. See also documents of the November 1987 meeting held in Auckland, A/13 Revs 1-6.

72 See note 141.

73 701/16/5 part 18, ASOC papers under cover of 11 June 1987.

74 Ibid, letter of 19 June 1987 from PM to Helen Clark.

75 701/16/7 part 8, letters of 23 and 26 June 1987 from Clark to PM.

76 Ibid, letter of 17 June 1987 from Wallace to PM.
77 Ibid, letter of 8 July 1987 from PM to Wallace.
78 Ibid, part 19, MR/17 Rev 4 of 26 November 1987.
79 Article 5 in both MR/17 Rev 4 and final text.
80 Article lO in MR/17 Rev 4.
81 Chapter VII of MR/17 Rev 4.
82 Document A32 Rev 3 of 19 November 1987.
83 Document A43 of 17 November 1987 and NZ notes of meeting of 18 November.
84 Australian papers of 11 and 12 November 1987 (special claimants share and anti-subsidies) and NZ notes of meeting of 12 November (item 8, economic issues).
85 Article 44 of MR/17 Rev 4, Article 46 in final text. Documents A51 and A60, NZ Notes of meeting of 20 November 1987.
86 UNGA resolutions 40/156C of 16 December 1985 and 41/88C of 4 December 1986.
87 UNGA resolutions 42/46A and B of 30 November 1987.
88 701/16/9 part 9, telegram1834 of 1 December 1987 from New York Mission to Wellington.
89 Ibid, part 8, telegram 3064 of 2 September 1987 from Wellington to NZHC Canberra, 1162 of 29 September 1987 to New York, and 3029 of 2 October 1987 from Canberra to Wellington.
90 Ibid, telegram 1375 of 27 October 1987 from Wellington to New York.
91 701/16/5 part 20, MR/17 Rev 5, 3 February 1988.
92 Ibid, part 21, delegation report of 25 February 1988 on the eleventh session of the minerals negotiations, 18-20 January in Wellington.
93 Article 47 of MR/17 Rev 5. The version (Article 49) eventually embodied in the Convention made no provision for arbitration but merely for 'reconsideration' by the Regulatory Committee.
94 701/16/5, part 21, telegram 264 of 4 March 1988 from NZ Embassy, Bonn, to Wellington (from 1 Beeby).
95 Ibid, letter of 19 April 1988' from Australian High Commissioner to Minister, April 1988 and enclosure.
96 Ibid, part 22, telegram 1307 of 26 April 1988 contains Marshali's reply to Hayden.
97 Ibid, memorandum of 26 April 1988 from Beeby to Minister of Foreign Affairs, copied to other Ministers. For the 1984 Cabinet paper, see page 213 and note 92.
98 Ibid, part 21, fax of 18 October 1988 from MFA to MFA Oslo (from Beeby to Rolf Andersen). Also paper by Beeby supplied to author.
99 The final text of paragraph 2 of Article 5 appeared in Chairman's paper CH54/Rev 2 of 29 May 1988 (see folder of Chairman's papers in MFAT archives). I found no record of the discussion which led to the acceptance of this formulation. Earlier discussion on 17 and 18 May did not produce agreement (Caughley's notes) but document 074/Rev 1 produced at the latter meeting came very close to the final text.
100 Argentinian proposal in document 118 of 29 May, Chairman's revision in

129/Rev 2 of 31 May, discussed in Chairman's consultations of that date where the American amendment was accepted with some reluctance on the part of the Soviet Union and Brazil (Caughley's notes).

101 Beeby to author, 27 December 1991.

102 Ibid, also Caughley's notes.

103 Ibid.

104 Ibid. See also 701/16/5 part 22, telegram 499 of 1 June 1988 from Wellington to NZ High Commission, New Delhi, and reply in telegram 438, same date.

105 701/16/5 part 22, notes prepared for Beeby's statement in plenary, 2 June 1988: 'I should like to recall that when the issue of liability was under discussion I stated my understanding that Article 8(10) precludes [sic: does not preclude] a defence based on sovereign immunity'.

106 Beeby to author, undated note.

107 Final Report of the Fourth Special ATCM on Mineral Resources, page 8, statement by Jean-Pierre Puissochet.

108 701/16/5 part 22, press statement of 2 June 1988.

109 Christchurch, 4 June 1988.

110 701/16/5 part 22, letter of 3 June 1988.

111 Ibid, fax 82 of 8 June 1988 from New York Mission to Wellington. The Assembly resolution referred to in the statement was No. 42/46 of 30 November 1987.

XIII: Mineral Resources: A Convention Under Fire

1 701/16/5 part 23, letter of 22 August 1988 from Warren Cooper to Carol Stewart, Antarctic Campaign Coordinator, Greenpeace.

2 Ibid, telegram 1995 of 29 August 1988 from NZHC Canberra to Wellington.

3 Ibid, referred to in Canberra's 1995. Statement itself not on file

4 Ibid, circular telegram of October 1988 from wellington to most diplomatic posts.

5 Ibid, parts 23 and 24 telegram 5802 of 26 October 1988 from Wellington to NZHC London, and reply in telegram 5552 of that date. Telegram 1115 of 27 October 1988 from NZ Embassy Rome. Telegram 1451 of 4 November 1988 from NZ Embassy Brussels.

6 Ibid, part 24, telegram 2282 of 9 November 1988 from NZ Embassy Paris to Wellington.

7 Ibid, telegram 5978 of 7 November 1988 from Wellington to NZHC London, telegram 5744 of 8 November from NZHC London to Wellington (record of Palmer/Hawe conversation) and telegram 5817 of 14 November from NZHC London to Wellington.

8 *Sydney Morning Herald*, 21 November 1988.

9 Article 8, paragraph 7 of the Minerals Convention.

10 Eigam, 25 November 1988.

11 701/16/5 part 24, telegram 2394 of 28 November 1988 from NZ Embassy Paris to Wellington.

12 Ibid, telegram misc. 46 of 26 November 1988 from Wellington to all posts.

13 Ibid, letter of 3 December 1988 from Northey to Marshall.

14 Ibid, minute by Gerard van Bohemen on Marshall's reply to Northey, 20 December 1988.
15 Ibid, letter of 20 December 1988 from Palmer to E Hem and others.
16 Ibid, *Calypso Log* August 1988.
17 Ibid, letter of 12 January 1989 from Beeby to Cousteau (follow-up to their meeting).
18 Ibid, file note by Beeby, 18 January 1989.
19 Eigam, 16 January 1989 reporting interview of 13 January.
20 701/16/5 part 25, telegram 356 of 1 March 1989 from NZ Embassy Paris, to Wellington.
21 Ibid, telegram 693 of 7 April 1989 from Wellington to New York Mission.
22 Ibid, telegram 658 of 21 April 1989 from NZ Embassy Paris to Wellington.
23 *Le Monde*, 24 April 1989.
24 Document PREP/WP/1, 2 May 1989.
25 Document PREP/WP/14, 11 May 1989.
26 701/16/3/6 part 1, telegram 756 of 16 May 1989 from NZ Embassy Paris to Wellington.
27 CPD Senate, pages 1650-6.
28 *Sydney Morning Herald*, editorial 25 November 1988, news items and commentary, 4 and 6 May 1989, *The Australian*, 5 May 1989.
29 Melbourne 2 May 1989.
30 701/16/5 part 26, telegrams 1344 and 1346 of 22 May 1989 from Wellington to NZHC Canberra.
31 Ibid. The first draft of this message was dated 18 May.
32 Ibid, statement of 22 May 1989, faxed by NZHC Canberra.
33 Ibid, part 27, letter of 15 June 1989 from Hawke to Lange.
34 Ibid, part 26, telegram 1310 of 26 May 1989 from NZ Embassy Washington to Wellington.
35 Ibid, part 27, telegram 1840 of 1 June 1989 and memorandum of 6 June 1989 from NZHC London to Wellington.
36 Ibid, part 26, telegram 835 of 24 May 1989 from Wellington to NZ Embassy Paris, and telegram 819 of 25 May from the Embassy confirming delivery of the message.
37 NZPD Vol 498, page 10919, 30 May 1989.
38 701/16/5 part 27, press release of 1 June 1989.
39 Ibid, letter of 12 June 1989 from Marshall to Evans.
40 *Dominion*, 15 June 1989.
41 701/16/5 part 27, memorandum of 16 June 1989 from Minister of the Environment to Ministers of 1 Foreign Affairs, Conservation, and Science and Technology.
42 Ibid, part 28, memorandum of 27 June 1989 from SERT to D-G Conservation, Secretary for the Environment, and Manager, Antarctic Division, DSIR (Logan).
43 Ibid, memorandum of 28 June 1989 from Secretary for the Environment to SERT.
44 Ibid, memorandum of 11 July 1989 from Beeby, McDowell, Blakeley and Logan to Ministers of Foreign Affairs, Conservation, Environment, and

Science and Technology, enclosing draft Cabinet paper for signature by Minister of Foreign Affairs.

45 Ibid, Cabinet Policy Committee minute, POL(89)M23/4 of 19 July 1989 and Cabinet minute CAB(89)M25/16 of 24 July 1989.

46 Ibid, proposals handed by Hawke to Lange at Tarawa, 10 July 1989.

47 NZPD Vol 499, page 11281, 18 July 1989.

48 701/16/5 part 29, memorandum of 25 July 1989 from SERT to Ministers of Foreign Affairs and External Relations and Trade, and Associate Minister, enclosing draft white paper under signature of the four officials (see note 44).

49 Ibid, fax of 28 July 1989 from van Bohemen (MERT) to McDowell (Conservation) covering draft of , White Paper showing amendments by Woollaston, Tizard (Minister of Science) and the PM's' office.

50 701/16/3/6 part 2,letter of 28 August 1989 from R G Norman, Chairman of RDRC, to Beeby.

51 See previous chapter, note 79.

52 *White Paper on Antarctic Environment* laid on the table of the House of Representatives, 8 August 1989 (Government Printer).

53 701/16/5 part 29, letter of 31 July 1989 from Minister of Foreign Affairs (Russell Marshall) to Beeby.

54 Ibid, paper submitted by SERT on 31 July 1989 to Minister of External Relations and Trade (Mike Moore) at his request. (Apparently both Marshall and Moore had asked for papers.) This paper was circulated to Cabinet by the MERT Ministers.

55 Ibid, Cabinet Policy Committee minute POL(89)M25/1 of 2 August 1989. (The Committee had been empowered by Cabinet to act.)

56 701/16/3/6 part 1, memorandum of 4 August 1989 from SERT to Minister of Foreign Affairs for reference to other Ministers.

57 701/16/5 part 29, transcript of PM's press conference, 9 August 1989.

58 701/16/3/6 part 1, circular telegram of 10 August 1989 to posts.

59 See note 55.

60 701/16/3/6 part 2, telegram 2189 of 21 August 1989 from NZ Embassy Washington to Wellington.

61 701/16/5 part 29, telegram 2869 on 1 August 1989 from NZHC London to Wellington.

62 701/16/3/6 part 3, telegram 3027 of 5 September 1989 from Wellington to NZHC London, and reply in telegram 2946 of 7 September 1989.

63 ibid part 2, fax 720 of 18 August 1989 from NZHC Canberra to Wellington.

64 Ibid, fax 721 of 18 August 1989 from NZHC Canberra to Wellington and posts.

65 Ibid, telegram 2223 of 30 August 1989 from NZHC Canberra to Wellington and posts.

66 Ibid, Analysis of the White Paper, Cath Wallace (ASOC) August 1989.

67 701/16/5 part 29, memorandum of 28 August 1989 from Minister of Foreign Affairs to PM and Minister of Conservation, with marginal comments by PM.

68 Ibid, telegram 1789 of 22 August 1989 from Wellington to NZ Mission New York containing message from Beeby to MulIoz-Seca, and replies from

Mission in telegrams 1414 and 1425 of 28 and 29 August 1989.
Also letter of 4 September 1989 to Beeby from Mulloz-Seca, Sub-Director-General of Air, Land and Sea Cooperation, Spanish Ministry of External Relations. On file 701/16/3/6 part 3.

69 701/16/3/6 part 3, telegram 1422 of 8 September 1989 from Wellington to Paris and other posts.

70 Ibid, telegram 2729 of 14 September 1989 from Wellington to NZHC Canberra.

71 701/16/5 part 29, file note of 4 September 1989 by NZ Deputy High Commissioner, Canberra. The Tasmanian election result on 13 May was Liberals 17, ALP 13, Greens 5 (*Keesings* 1989, page 36658).

72 701/16/3/6 part 3, fax 128 of 21 September 1989 from Wellington to NZ Embassy Paris and other posts. Document XV ATCM/WP/4.

73 Ibid, press statement of 26 September 1989.

74 Ibid, transcript of PM's press conference, 26 September 1989.

75 *Dominion*, 27 September 1989

76 Ibid, 3 October 1989.

77 701/16/3/6 part 4, telegram 2 of 19 October 1989 from NZ Embassy Paris to CHOGM delegation and posts.

78 Should refer to appropriate source for irritation and hardening of positions against establishment of Antarctic secretariat following Australia's characterisation of states as either pro-CRAMRA and anti-environment or pro-environment and anti-CRAMA.

79 Ibid, part 3, letter of 29 September 1989 from Hawke to Palmer.

80 Ibid, part 4, telegram 340 of 2 October 1989 from New York Mission to NZHC Canberra contains Palmer's reply to Hawke.

81 Final Report of the 15th ATCM, Recommendations XV-1 and XV-2, pages 43-47.

82 701/16/316 part 4, telegram 5 of 21 October 1989 from NZ Embassy Paris to CHOGM delegation and posts.

83 Ibid, telegram 2875 of 31 October 1989 from NZHC Canberra to Wellington.

84 Ibid, press statement of 25 October 1989.

85 Ibid, transcript of Radio NZ news, 23 October 1989 (Cath Wallace). Dominion, 22 October 1989 (Colin Benson).

86 Ibid, report on XVth ATCM by Secretary of the Environment, forwarded to Beeby by Blakeley, and by PM to Foreign Minister on 26 October 1989.

87 Ibid, transcript of interview of Blakeley by Maggie Barry, Radio NZ, 26 October 1989 .

88 Ibid, part 5, telegram 10 of 22 October 1989 from CHOGM delegation to Wellington.

89 NZPD Vol 53 page 13719, 23 November 1989.

90 701/16/3/7 part 1, notes of weekly meeting of Minister of Environment with officials, 28 November 1989 .

91 701/16/5 part 30, letter of 12 December 1989 from Beeby to McDowell (McDowell's letter of 8 December not on file).

92 Argentina, Brazil, Chile, China, Czechoslovakia, Denmark, Finland, GDR,

Japan, Republic of Korea, New Zealand, Norway, Poland, South Africa, Sweden, USSR, UK, USA, Uruguay.

93 701/16/3/6 part 5, memorandum of 19 December 1989 to Acting Minister of Foreign Affairs and Ministers for the Environment, Research Science and Technology, and Conservation, signed by Beeby on behalf of officials from MERT, PM's Dept, Environment, Conservation and DSIR Antarctic Division.

94 701/16/5 part 30, memorandum of 15 February 1989 from Marshall to PM.

95 701/16/3/7 part 1, telegram 3712 of 8 February 1990 from NZ Embassy Washington to Wellington, reporting on NZIUS environment consultations.

96 701/16/5, secret file, memorandum of 16 February 1990 from officials (as in note 93) to their Ministers, covering draft paper for Cabinet Policy Committee.

97 Ibid, part 30, memorandum of 20 February 1990 from Blakeley to Beeby, McDowell, Edmonds (Conservation) and Logan, enclosing 'final version of Cabinet paper, amended as directed by Ministers of 19 February'.

98 Ibid, fax of 18 February 1990 from General Counsel, Greenpeace to PM.

99 Ibid, CAB(90)M5/12 of 26 February 1990.

100 Ibid, press release by Australian PM and interview transcript, 26 February 1990.

101 801/16/3/7 part 1, telegram 4458 of 26 February 1990 from Wellington to Canberra and other posts contains press statement by Palmer and press conference transcript, 26 February. The fact that Hawke's statement came out first was alluded to by Opposition MPs (NZPD Vol 505, pages 157 and 162, 27 February 1990).

102 NZPD Vol 505, pages 147-148.

103 Ibid, page 169.

104 Ibid, speech by Woollaston, page 164. For Nash's attitude, see *A Wise Adventure I*, Chapter V, pages 10 and 12 of typescript. New Zealand would work for a regime which 'would provide for free access for scientific and economic purposes' (my emphasis). For discussion of the 1975 'proposal' see Chapter X.

105 See Chapter X, page 24 of typescript.

106 See Chapter XI.

107 NZPD Vol 505, page 165.

108 701/16/5 part 30, memorandum of 30 March 1990 from Acting Secretary of External Relations and Trade to Acting Minister of External Relations and Trade, for passing to PM and Minister of Conservation.

109 701/16/317 part 1, telegram 749 of 10 March 1990 from NZ Embassy Santiago to Wellington.

XIV: An Environmental Protection Protocol

1 701/16/3/7 part 2, draft telegram prepared in NZ Embassy Washington during Beeby's visit in April 1990, together with US position paper of 26 March 1990 (the telegram was *not* despatched).

2 Ibid, *aide-memoire* delivered jointly by Australian High Commission and

French Embassy on 19 April 1990.

3 Ibid, telegram 4467 of 26 April 1990 from NZHC Canberra to Wellington.

4 Ibid, three ASOC papers of 22 April 1990, together with 'A Critique of the Government's Antarctic Environmental Policy'.

5 Ibid, ECO/ASOC press statement, 4 May 1990 (out of date order).

6 Ibid, part 3, memorandum of 22 May 1990 to the PM (and Minister for the Environment), the Associate Minister of Foreign Affairs and Trade (Fran Wilde), and the Ministers of Conservation and Science, signed by officials of the four Departments.

7 Ibid, part 4, memorandum to Cabinet from the above Ministers (sent up for signature on 7 June 1990).

8 701/16/3/6 part 5, memorandum of IS February 1990 from SERT (Beeby) to Minister (Moore).

9 701/16/3/7 part 4, CAB(90)M19/12 of 18 June 1990.

10 Ibid, memorandum of 25 June 1990 from SERT to Minister, with enclosure, for reference to PM.

11 Ibid, 6 July 1990. There are two versions of the press statement on file, one marked 'the uncorrected version',

12 Ibid, telegram 5345 of 25 July 1990 from NZ Embassy, Washington, to Wellington.

13 Ibid, ASOC media release of 29 July 1990.

14 See Chapter VIT, pages *et seq* of typescript, for discussion of the legal status of ATCM recommendations.

15 701/16/2/1 part 1, memorandum of 24 July 1990 from SERT (Beeby) to Chief Executives of Conservation, Environment and PM's Department and the Antarctic Manager, DSIR.

16 Ibid, extract of NZ record of Australia-New Zealand legal talks, held 10-12 July 1990.

17 701/16/3/7 part 5, notes of Bolger's address to 'Environment and Conservation Organisations of New Zealand Inc.'

18 Ibid, extract from NZ record of Palmer/Hawke talks, undated.

19 Ibid, transcript of TVNZ interview.

20 See previous chapter.

21 701/16/3/7 part 5, ASOC press statement, 24 August 1990.

22 CAB (90) 646 of (about) 29 August 1990 (copy of complete final text supplied from DOC Antarctica file).

23 701/16/3/7 part 5, CAB (90) M30122 of 3 September 1990.

24 Ibid, text of speech on file.

25 Ibid, telegram 1073 of 15.September 1990 to all posts.

26 701/16/5 part 31, informal notes delivered to MERT on 17 and 25 September 1990 by US and Soviet Union Embassies. Formal note of 23 January 1991 from Japanese Embassy. Telegram 6297 of 27 September 1990 from Wellington to NZ Embassy Washington (also to Moscow and Canberra).

27 701/16/317 part 5, telegram 5910 of 17 September 1990 from Canberra to Wellington.

28 Ibid, file note of 21 September 1990 by First Secretary, Canberra (Mark Sinclair).

29 Document XI ATSCM/2 of 18 November 1990.

30 701/16/3/7 part 5, draft Cabinet paper circulated to Ministers of the Environment, Conservation and Science, and the Associate Minister of Foreign Affairs and Trade on 18 October 1990, under cover of a memorandum signed by Simon Murdoch (PMs), Blakely (Environment), Mansfield (Conservation), Beeby (MERT) and Logan (DSIR). For submission to Cabinet by Fran Wilde (Associate Minister, MERT)

31 Ibid, RNZ *Morning Report* and *New Zealand Herald*, 26 October 1990, press statement by Prime Minister of 25 October covering release of draft protocol. Cabinet minute not on file.

32 Ibid, part 6, submission to PM and Ministers of External Relations and Trade, Environment, Conservation and Science of 8 November 1990. This submission was presumably approved. '701/16/2/1 part 1, *aide-memoire* from US Embassy, updated (?) September 1990. Five-power outline not on file.

34 Documents Xl ATSCM/3, /4 and /1 of 18 November 1990.

35 701/16/2/1 part 3, telegram 6280 of 13 November 1990 from NZ Embassy, Washington, to Wellington.

36 701/16/3/7 part 6, telegram 1149 of 29 November 1990 from NZ Embassy, Santiago, to Wellington and fax of 3 December in reply.

37 Document XI ATSCM, Article 33.

38 Draft of Annex I to the Protocol, Environmental Impact Assessment Procedures, Article 4 (no document number). Neither the Australian nor the New Zealand proposals for preventing or stopping undesirable activities survived into the final text of Annex I.

39 701/16/317 part 6, telegrams 1158 and 1163 of 4 and 8 December 1990 from NZ Embassy Santiago to Wellington containing the NZ Delegation's interim and final reports on the outcome of the SCM.

40 Document XI ATSCM 1.

41 701116/317 parts 6 and 7, *Dominion*, 5 and 6 December 1990.

42 Ibid, part 6, RNZ Good Morning NZ transcript of 30 November 1990. See also memorandum from Beeby to Ansell (SERT) of 23 November. Wallace later complained to McKinnon that she had been misreported (letter of 11 December on part 7).

43 Ibid, press statement by Minister 4 December 1990.

44 Ibid, press statement of 9 December 1990. Christchurch Press, 10 December.

45 Ibid, part 7, telegram 3732 of 30 January 1991 from NZ Embassy Paris to Wellington.

46 Ibid, 4 February 1991.

47 Ibid, telegram 7073 of 8 February 1991 from NZHC Canberra to Wellington.

48 Ibid, NZ record of MERT/DFAT legal talks, 21 February 1991.

49 Ibid, ENV (91)8 of 25 March 1991.

50 Ibid, memorandum of 26 March 1991 from Acting Secretary, MERT, to Minister. (Approval on copy on DOC file.)

51 Ibid, ENV(91)M4/2 of 26 March 1991.

52 Ibid, memorandum of 4 March 1991 from Acting Secretary to Minister, with his annotations.

53 Ibid, letter of 27 March 1991 from Minister to Cath Wallace and Barry

Weeber (ECONZ). (A grant of $2,000 was subsequently made available.)
54 Ibid, part 8, message of 26 March 1991 from Foreign Secretary to Minister, with British proposals.
55 Ibid, letter of 8 April 1991 from Minister to Foreign Secretary.
56 Ibid, telegram 7587 of 8 April 1991 from NZHC, Canberra to Wellington.
57 Ibid, telegram 665 of 3 April 1991 from NZ Embassy, The Hague, to Wellington (the Ambassador was dually accredited to Oslo).
58 Ibid, telegram 7305 of 10 April 1991 from NZ Embassy Washington to Wellington.
59 Ibid, telegram 2421 of 3 April 1991 from NZ Embassy, wellington.
60 Ibid, telegram 5116 of 2 April 1991 from Wellington to NZ Mission New York and other posts.
61 Ibid, telegram 7613 of 9 April 1991 from NZHC, Canberra to Wellington, with extract from Melbourne of that date.
62 Ibid, Reuters report, 23 April 1991.
63 Waikato Times, 27 April 1991.
64 701/16/3/7 part 8, submission of 29 April 1991 from Acting SERT to Minister.
65 Ibid, letter of 20 April 1991 from Cath Wallace to Minister.
66 Ibid, ASOC media release in Madrid, 30 April 1991.
67 Ibid, *RNZ Morning Report*, 30 April 1991.
68 Ibid, fax of 1 May 1991 from New Zealand delegation to Wellington.
69 Letter of 1 May 1991 from Wallace, Convenor ASOCNZ in Madrid (DOC file).
70 UK Hansard, 10 May 1991, answer to written question *Independent*, 14 May 1991.
71 UK Hansard, 26 April 1991, speech by Parliamentary Under-Secretary for FCO Affairs (Mark Lennox-Boyd).
72 701/16/3/7 part 8, telegram 7649 of 23 May 1991 from NZ Embassy Washington to Wellington.
73 Ibid, part 9, telegram 7737 of 10 June 1991 from NZ Embassy Washington to Wellington.
74 Ibid, fax of 12 June 1991 from van Bohemen (in Madrid) to Wong (in Wellington).
75 Ibid, memorandum of 14 June 1991 from SERT to Minister.
76 Ibid, RNZ Morning Report transcript, 17 June 1991.
77 Ibid, CAB (91) M23/14.
78 Ibid, telegram 8474 of 17 June 1991 from Wellington to NZ Embassy Washington, replies in telegrams 7792 and 7806 of 17 and 19 June.
79 Ibid, fax of 20 June 1991 from NZ delegation to Wellington
80 Ibid, part 10, fax of 21 June 1991 from Keating (Deputy Secretary, MERT) to McDowell, Mansfield, Blakeley and McFarlane (DSIR). Out of date order.
81 Ibid part 9, fax of 21 June 1991 from Minister to Wong.
82 Ibid, fax of 22 June 1991 from NZ delegation to MERT.
83 Ibid, fax of 24 June 1991 from NZ delegation to MERT
84 Ibid, press statement of 23 June 1991. (This was apparently issued before the delegation report had been received.)

85 Ibid, telegram 7859 of 27 June 1991 from NZ Embassy, Washington to Wellington. Press statement of 28 June 1991 by Minister recording the representations he had made to the US Ambassador (Della Newman) .
86 Ibid, Reuters report of 3 July 1991, statement by President
87 Ibid, RNZ Midday Report, 4 July 1991.
88 Ibid, RNZ Morning Report, 5 July 1991.
89 Ibid, part 10, CAB (9I)M38/33 of 16 September 1991.
90 Document XI ATSCM2/3/2 of 3 October 1991, with some minor amendments.
91 Document XVI ATCM WP54, 17 October 1991, Annex to Recommendation VI-I0.
92 701/16/3/8 part 2, report by Mike Prebble (MFE) on 16th ATCM, 1 November 1991. Also memorandum from Prebble to MERT, DOC and MFE, 17 July 1992 (DOC file).
93 Document XVI ATCM IP55 'Annex on Liability and Compensation for Antarctic Activities' submitted by ASOC.
94 Document XVIII ATCM WP2 'Liability Annex to the Protocol on Environmental Protection to the Antarctic Treaty' submitted by Germany.
95 Document XXII ATCM WP1 'Liability – Report of the Group of Legal Experts' submitted by Norway.
96 Decision 3 (1998) ATCM XXII, Tromsø.
97 Documents XXIII ATCM WP41 'Personal Report of the Chairman of the Liability Discussion in WG1'; ATCM XXV, WP 14 'Chairman's Draft'; ATCM XXVI, WP33 'Chairman's draft of Annex VI to the Protocol on Environmental Protection to the Antarctic Treaty 'Liability arising from environmental emergencies"; ATCM XXVII, IP110 'Revised Chairman's draft of Annex VI to the Protocol on Environmental Protection to the Antarctic Treaty. 'Liability arising from environmental emergencies"; ATCM XXVIII, WP47 'Revised Chairman's Draft of Annex VI to the Protocol on Environmental Protection to the Antarctic Treaty – 'Liability for Environmental Emergencies'.
98 Measure 1 (2005) ATCM XXVIII, Stockholm.
99 For further accounts of the negotiation of the Liability annex and analysis of the agreed text, see for example: Michael Johnson 'Liability for Environmental Damage in Antarctica: The Adoption of Annex VI to the Antarctic Environmental Protocol' 19 Geo. Int'l Envtl. L. Rev. 33; Elana Geddis 'Protecting the Antarctic Environment: Liability for Environmental Emergencies in Antarctica' Resource Management Journal Issue 3, Vol XIII, November 2005 at page 28.
100 Copies of all ATCM decisions and measures are available at www.ats.aq
101 701/16/3/8 part 2, telegram 2957 of 18 October 1991 from NZ Embassy, Bonn, to Wellington containing NZ delegation report on 16th ATCM. Memorandum from Prebble (note 92) and memorandum of 23 November 1992 from Paul Dingwell, Consultant to IUCN, to D-G, IUCN reporting on 17th ATCM.
102 Document of the 4th session of the Eleventh SCM, 3-4 October 1991, unnumbered and undated.

103 See note 93.

104 ATCM XXIV report, paragraphs 20–24 and appendices 2 and 3. Decision 1 (2001) decided that 'the Antarctic Treaty Secretariat shall be established in Buenos Aires following the development of necessary modalities and agreements, which the Parties shall urgently pursue' and Measure 1 (2003) set out the mandate of the Secretariat and attached the Headquarters Agreement. Other practical matters such as the allocation of contributions between Parties and staff and financial matters were also agreed at ATCM XXVI in Madrid in 2003, allowing the Secretariat to commence operation the following year.

XV: A Balance Sheet

1 701/16/3/7 part 10, telegram 2910 of 7 October 1991 from NZ Embassy Bonn to Wellington.

2 Article 25 of the Protocol. Fifty years from entry into force until a review conference could be convened. If an amendment were adopted by the Conference by a three-quarters majority, three years would be allowed for ratification. If any ATCP 'vetoed' the amendment by failing to ratify within the three year period, a further two years must elapse before withdrawal of a party to the Protocol could take effect and prospecting for minerals could begin: 55 years in all.

3 701/16/318 part 1, report by Gerard van Bohemen, 18 March 1991.

4 Chapter 13, note 49.

5 701/16/3/8 part 2, telegram 2957 of 18 October 1991 from NZ Embassy Bonn to Wellington. Report by Paul Dingwall on 17th ATCM, 23 November 1992 (DOC file).

6 701/16/317 parts 8 and 9. Telegrams 8352 of 31 May 1991 from Wellington to NZ Embassy Washington, and reply in telegram 7737 of 10 June 1991.

The New Zealand lawyers originally favoured the definition of the area in which mining would be prohibited by a formula similar to that in the Minerals Convention, Article 5, which was designed to avoid conflict with the Law of the Sea Convention. After the April 1991 session of the SCM, however, they changed their minds and indicated to some other A TCPs in advance of the June meeting that, 'after full reflection', their preferred approach was to define the area covered by the Protocol as coinciding with the Antarctic Treaty area, i.e., the area below 60° south. If other delegations had difficulties with this in respect, either of the deep seabed south of 60° south or of continental shelves generated by islands or extending northwards from Antarctica beyond 60° south, they would accept the CRAMRA formula as their next preference. There had been no discussion of this issue at the April meeting of the SCM, and presumably the preferred New Zealand approach was shared by most, if not all, delegations at the June meeting. The considerations that caused the New Zealand lawyers to change their minds are not known.

7 701/16/5 part 30, letter of 14 June 1990 from Beeby to McDowell.

INDEX

Adélie Land, airstrip in, 166, 228
Agreed Measures on Fauna and Flora
    drafting of, 17–27, 241
    and Environment Protection
        Protocol, 286
    implementation of, 26–29
    as legally binding, 30
    substantive articles, 24–26, 28, 49
    unanimity rule, 29–30
Andersen, Rolf, 207, 288–90, 292–95, 297–98, 300–1, 303–4
Antarctic Act 1960 (NZ), 13, 16
Antarctic and Southern Ocean Coalition (ASOC), 66, 144–45, 166, 181, 185, 197–98, 249, 252, 270–71, 274, 277, 285, 299, 301, 310
Antarctic Marine Living Resources (AMLR) Convention, *see* marine living resources, conservation of
Antarctic Research Programme, New Zealand, 100, 113, 166, 168
Antarctic toothfish, 72
Antarctic Treaty 1959
    Consultative Meetings, *see* Antarctic Treaty Consultative Meetings (ATCMs)
    Consultative Parties to, *see* *individual countries*
    Contracting Parties to, *see* *individual countries*
    and environmental protection, *see* Environment Protection Protocol
    and fauna and flora, *see* fauna and flora, conservation of
    jurisdiction under, *see* jurisdiction in Antarctica
    and marine living resources, *see* marine living resources, conservation of
    and mineral resources, *see under* mineral resources regime, need for; Minerals Convention (CRAMRA), negotiation of
    and seal conservation, *see* seals, conservation of
Antarctic Treaty Consultative Meetings (ATCMs)
    First Meeting (1961), 13–14, 76
    Second Meeting (1962), 14, 16
    Third Meeting (1964), 16, 20, 31
    Fourth Meeting (1966), 27, 31–32
    Fifth Meeting (1968), 27, 45
    Sixth Meeting (1970), 32, 77
    Seventh Meeting (1972), 79
    Eighth Meeting (1975), 44–45, 83, 87, 266
    Ninth Meeting (1977), 47, 50, 52, 58, 67, 102, 106–7
    Tenth Meeting (1979), 63, 65, 108, 110, 113, 116
    Eleventh Meeting (1981), 112, 115, 118–19, 127–28
    Twelfth Meeting (1983), 142
    Fourteenth Meeting (1987), 202
    Fifteenth Meeting (1989), 229, 231–32, 252, 269–70
    Sixteenth Meeting (1991), 309–10, 313
    Seventeenth Meeting (1992), 310,

312–13
Twenty-first Meeting (1997), 310
Twenty-second Meeting (1998), 310
Twenty-third Meeting (1999), 310
Twenty-fourth Meeting (2001), 314
Twenty-eighth Meeting (2005), 311
Antarctica [Environmental Protection] Act 1994, 27
Antarctica Act 1960, 27
Antarctica Act 1961, 16
Antarctica Amendment Act 1970, 27
Arbitral Tribunal, 127, 157, 191, 200, 205, 219, 307, 309
Arctic, 133, 140, 144, 302
Arctic Wildlife Refuge, 302
Argentina
in environmental regime negotiations, 253, 272, 275, 285, 290, 305, 313–14
and the Falkland Islands, 126, 141
fauna and flora, approach to, 20, 25
internationalisation concerns, 89, 141
jurisdiction in Antarctica, 15, 22–24, 56, 313
marine living resources, approach to, 45, 49–50, 63
in mineral resources regime negotiations, 77, 79–81, 89, 95, 97, 99, 106, 113, 115, 118, 125, 130, 133–34, 141, 156, 170, 178, 182, 195, 202, 208, 217, 221–22, 233
seal conservation, approach to, 35
Secretariat in, 11, 313–14
Association of South-east Asian Nations (ASEAN), 143–44
Atlantic Ocean sector, 71–72
Auckland, 198, 203–5
Auckland Islands, 36
Auckland University Antarctic Policy Group, 270
Australia
in environmental regime negotiations, 238–39, 242, 245, 248–49, 251–56, 259–61, 263–64, 267, 269–70, 272, 276–77, 283–84, 286–93, 297–301, 303–6, 308, 310, 317
fauna and flora, approach to, 18, 24–25, 28
marine living resources, approach to, 45, 48–50, 59, 62–63, 103–4
in mineral resources regime negotiations, 75, 77, 96–98, 103–8, 113, 126, 128, 130, 149, 153, 159–60, 162, 167, 175–76, 178–80, 185–86, 188–90, 194, 201–2, 206–11, 214, 217, 219–20, 222
Minerals Convention, objections to signing, 224–26, 228–36, 238, 246, 251, 256, 259–60, 267
seal conservation, approach to, 33, 42
Australia, New Zealand, United States Security Treaty (ANZUS), 102–4, 148, 265
Australian National University, 270

Baker, James, 303
Barnes, James, 177
Beardmore Glacier, 169
Beazley, Kim, 251
Beeby, Chris, 116, 127–29, 131–32, 134–36, 146, 149–51, 153, 155, 157, 161, 169, 171–72, 174, 178, 180–83, 188–92, 197–98, 200, 203–4, 208–9, 217, 222–24, 228, 237, 249–50, 252, 254–56, 258, 269, 275–76, 285, 293
Belgium, 198, 256, 286, 290, 300, 305–6
Berne document, 64
birds, protection of, 12, 70
Blakeley, Roger, 237, 256
Bohlen, Buff, 274, 302
Bolger, Jim, 235, 239, 277, 285
Bonn, 144, 146, 149, 151, 153–54, 208, 294, 309
Brazil, 36, 137, 151, 155, 170, 178,

182, 214, 217, 220, 226, 253, 287–88
see also Rio de Janeiro ('Rio package')
Brennan, Keith, 50, 91
Britain
in environmental regime negotiations, 247–48, 253, 256, 260, 270, 272, 275, 283, 285–88, 290, 298, 300–301, 303, 307, 310, 312–14
and the Falkland Islands, 126
fauna and flora, approach to, 13–14, 16, 19, 22–23, 25–26
jurisdiction in Antarctica, 21–23
marine living resources, approach to, 47–48, 58–59, 61, 66, 70
in mineral resources regime negotiations, 77, 79–80, 87, 92, 98, 106, 108, 113, 119, 125, 130, 151, 154, 159–60, 170, 173–76, 178, 180, 182, 184, 187–89, 194, 208, 215, 217, 219, 247–48, 296–97
Minerals Convention, signing of, 225–26, 228, 232, 234–35, 256
seal conservation, approach to, 32, 34–36, 38–39
British Discovery Committee, 74
Brussels, 16, 21–22, 26, 28, 173
Buenos Aires, 11, 14, 52–58, 115, 314
Bush, George, 304, 308, 321

Cairns Group, 267
Campbell Islands, 36
Canada, 33, 36, 140, 144
Canberra, 11, 13, 18, 51–52, 54–56, 103–4, 142, 175, 188, 232, 256, 266, 283
Canterbury University, 34
Caracas, 44, 84
Cenozoic, 98
CH/60 (document), 218
Chile
in environmental regime negotiations, 245–46, 253, 255, 267, 272, 275, 287–89, 313
fauna and flora, approach to, 12, 20, 24, 26
internationalisation concerns, 26, 89, 115
jurisdiction in Antarctica, 15, 22–24, 26–27, 56, 92
marine living resources, approach to, 45, 49–51
in mineral resources regime negotiations, 77, 79–81, 89, 91–92, 95, 97, 106, 113–15, 117, 125, 130, 133–34, 156, 170, 178, 182, 195, 208, 217, 222
Minerals Convention, signing of, 226, 233
seal conservation, approach to, 35, 37
China, 137, 190, 214, 220, 310
Christchurch, 33, 165, 169, 215, 276
claimant/non-claimant state issues, *see under* mineral resources regime, need for; Minerals Convention (CRAMRA), negotiation of
Clark, Helen, 181, 197
coastal state jurisdiction, 52–53, 55, 59, 62, 106, 120–21, 128
Commission on the Conservation of Antarctic Marine Living Resources (CCAMLR), 50–51, 57–59, 61–63, 67–70
Committee on Natural Resources of the Economic and Social Council, 79
common heritage, Antarctica as, 46–47, 84–85, 96, 98–99, 117, 122, 126–27, 134, 136, 141–43, 148–49, 152, 234, 248, 253, 318, 320
Commonwealth Heads of Government Meeting (CHOGM), 253–54, 257
conservation
of fauna and flora, *see* fauna and flora, conservation of
of marine living resources, *see* marine living resources, conservation of

of mineral resources, *see under* mineral resources regime, need for; Minerals Convention (CRAMRA), negotiation of
of seals, *see* seals, conservation of
of whales, *see* whales, conservation of
Conservation, Department of, *see* Department of Conservation (DOC)
Consultative Parties to Antarctic Treaty, *see individual countries*
continental shelf, mineral exploitation in, 80, 84–85, 97–99, 107, 110, 113, 118, 121–22, 125–26, 128, 130, 199, 284, 293, 313, 317
Contracting Parties to Antarctic Treaty, *see individual countries*
Convergence, Antarctic, 52, 66, 68
Cooper, Warren, 119, 144, 148, 224, 265
Council for Mutual Economic Assistance (COMECON), 60, 63
Cousteau, Jacques, 226–28, 260, 306
crabeater seals, 24, 31, 38, 44
Crozet archipelago, 56, 59, 64–65
Currie, Duncan, 263

Dam, Kenneth, 149
Department of Conservation (DOC), 227, 236–37, 249, 280
developing countries
marine living resources, interest in, 70
mineral resources, interest in, 84, 93, 97–98, 100, 122, 127, 135–44, 147–48, 155, 157–59, 182, 184, 187, 214–15, 220
Doidge, Frederick, 75

Eastern Europe, 60
Economic Committee, Cabinet, 101, 109–10, 153, 158
economic interests, 32, 50, 56, 58–59, 61–62, 75–80, 84–86, 96–98, 104–5, 115, 123, 127, 135–44, 147–48, 155, 157–59, 167–68, 175, 210–15, 261, 316
Ecuador, 302
election (1981), 119
election (1984), 158, 163–64, 167
Emerson, Craig, 230
Energy Resources, Ministry of, 104, 106–9, 185
Environment, Commission for, 154, 180, 185, 187
Environment, Ministry of the, 236–37, 280–81
Environment and Conservation Organisations of New Zealand (ECO), 161, 271, 296
Environment Protection Convention, Antarctic, 238
Environment Protection Protocol
annexes, 309–14
within Antarctic Treaty framework, 269, 271–73, 275–76, 278–79, 283, 313
area of application, 293, 313
Committee functions, 284, 289–90, 294, 298, 300–301, 312–13, 317
decision-making powers, 283, 290, 300, 302–5, 307–8, 315
dispute settlement provisions, 269, 284, 287, 290, 294, 306–7, 309, 317
draft instruments and proposals, 269–81, 283–308
entry into force, 284–85, 299, 301, 308–10, 313, 315
impact assessment provisions, 280–81, 284, 286–87, 289, 294, 298, 306, 309
inspection procedures, 284, 287, 290, 294, 301, 306, 317–18
liability protocol, 284, 294, 309–12, 318
mining under, 272, 276–82, 284, 286–306, 308, 315–16, 318
moratorium, 272–74, 287–89, 291–93, 297–98, 306
NGO consultation, 270–71, 278–81, 284–86, 291, 294–96,

298, 300–301, 304, 307–8, 318
scientific research and, 270, 285, 290
secretariat, 269, 276, 284, 290, 294, 313–14
Environmental Impact Assessment group, 187
Environmental Protection Agency, Antarctic, 177
Environmental Protection, Committee for, 301, 312–13, 317
environmentalism
Environment Protection Protocol, *see* Environment Protection Protocol
environmental protection regime negotiations, 238–39, 242, 245–49, 253–314 *passim*, 317–21
liability protocol, 191, 195, 199, 203, 209–10, 216, 219, 225, 230–32, 234, 250–55, 261, 271, 273, 284, 309–12, 318
and marine living resources, 44, 66–67, 69–70
in mineral resources regime negotiations, 73, 83, 88, 90–92, 97–100, 105–6, 109, 111, 113–14, 116–17, 121, 123, 127, 131, 140, 145–48, 150–51, 154–55, 158–61, 163–64, 166, 177–78, 180–81, 185–87, 192–95, 197–200, 203, 207, 209–10, 212–13, 215, 221–22, 225, 250, 253–59, 318–19
Minerals Convention, objections to signing, 224, 226–34, 236–37, 250–51, 256–68
mining ban, 88–89, 145, 161, 164, 180, 228, 230–31, 233, 235, 237–40, 243–45, 248, 252, 257, 261–62, 266–67, 272, 280–82, 284, 286–92, 294–305, 308, 315–16, 318
NGOs, *see* non-governmental organisations (NGOs)
Equatorial Guinea, 73
European Economic Community (EEC), 42, 56, 60, 62–63, 66–68
Evans, Gareth, 230, 236, 251, 305
Exclusive Economic Zone Act 1977, 40
exclusive economic zones (EEZs), 39–40, 43, 50, 53, 56, 61–63, 66–67, 73, 84, 100–101, 120
External Affairs, New Zealand Department of, 12–13, 18, 26, 75
External Relations and Trade, Ministry of (MERT), 237, 239–40, 252, 280, 285, 291, 295, 305, 308
see also Foreign Affairs, Ministry of, and Foreign Affairs and Trade, Ministry of

Falkland Islands, 36, 126, 141
Falla, Robert (R A), 12
fauna and flora, conservation of
Agreed Measures, advantages/disadvantages of, 29–30
Agreed Measures, drafting of, 17–27, 241
Agreed Measures, implementation of, 26–29, 69
Agreed Measures, substantive articles of, 24–26, 28, 49
jurisdiction issues affecting, 13–16, 20–24, 26–28
see also marine living resources, conservation of; seals, conservation of
Fauna Protection Advisory Council, 12
Final Act of the Conference on the Conservation of Antarctic Marine Living Resources, 66–68
Finance, Ministry of, 101
finfish, 70–72
Finland, 226, 256
Fisheries Resources and Exploration Division, 37, 47
fishing
catch allocation, 49–50, 58, 61, 63, 67, 70–73
commercial interests in, 33, 45–49, 51–52, 54–56, 58, 60,

69–72, 98
environmental concerns over, 66–67, 69–70, 73
illegal, unreported and unregulated (IUU), 72–73, 314
Fishing, Committee on (COFI), 47–48
Food and Agriculture Organisation (FAO), 37, 46–48
Foreign Affairs and Trade, Ministry of, 273, 282, 294–95
see also External Relations and Trade, Ministry of (MERT), and Foreign Affairs, Ministry of
Foreign Affairs, Ministry of, 46–47, 51, 81–83, 90, 93–94, 100–106, 110, 115–16, 118–19, 122, 130–31, 140, 151, 153, 163, 165, 180–81, 227, 236–37, 243, 252–53, 265
see also External Relations and Trade, Ministry of (MERT), and Foreign Affairs and Trade, Ministry of
Forest and Bird Protection Society, 12
France
airstrip in Adélie Land, 166, 228
in environmental regime negotiations, 248–49, 254–56, 264, 267, 269–70, 272, 276, 283, 286–90, 292, 299–300, 303, 305–6, 317
fauna and flora, approach to, 25, 122
marine living resources, approach to, 52, 56, 59–60, 62–66
in mineral resources regime negotiations, 80, 108, 125, 173, 178–79, 182, 187, 190, 207–8, 217, 221–22, 233
Minerals Convention, objections to signing, 226–30, 235, 249–50, 256, 259–60, 267
nuclear testing, 81, 260
Fraser, Peter, 74, 240
Friends of the Earth, 35

Gandhi, Indira, 137, 139
Geneva, 84
Geological Survey, Director of, 81
German Democratic Republic, 187, 205, 253, 256
Germany, 36, 298, 300
Germany, Federal Republic of
in environmental regime negotiations, 274–75
marine living resources, approach to, 42, 51
in mineral resources regime negotiations, 133–34, 137, 149, 151, 154, 157, 167, 170, 182, 184, 191, 195, 200–201, 204–5, 208, 233
Minerals Convention, objections to signing, 256
Ghazali, Tan Sri, 144
Glomar Challenger, 80
Gondwanaland, 125, 316
Gore, Al, 261, 303
Graham, Alistair, 180–81
Graham, Doug, 266
Great Britain, *see* Britain
Greenpeace, 144, 164, 207, 222, 224, 242, 260, 263, 265, 270–71
Group of 77, 93, 127, 136
see also developing countries

harvesting of marine living resources, 49–50, 59, 66–67, 69–70
Hawke, Robert, 230, 232, 235, 247, 249, 251, 254, 259–60, 263–64, 277, 284, 289, 299, 308
Hayden, Bill, 144, 149, 153, 208, 210
Heap, John, 194, 247–48
Heard Island, 71–72
Hemmings, Alan, 252, 270
Heseltine, Michael, 301
Hobart, 68, 153, 178–80, 182–83, 291
Holyoake, Keith, 39
Howard, John, 230
Hurd, Douglas, 296–97
hydrocarbons, 80, 118, 125

icefish, 71–72
India, 136–37, 139, 151, 170, 182, 198, 214, 220, 253, 275
Indian Ocean sector, 71–72
insects, protection of, 12
Institute of International Affairs, New Zealand, 145
International Council of Scientific Unions, 13
International Court of Justice (ICJ), 18, 81, 191, 307
International Geophysical Year (1957), 75, 241
International Seabed Authority (ISA), 99, 111
International Union for the Conservation of Nature (IUCN), 67, 82
internationalisation of Antarctica, 22, 25–26, 47, 78, 89, 96, 115, 136, 139, 141–42
Italy, 36, 137, 182, 256, 286, 290, 300, 305–6, 310

Japan
  in environmental regime negotiations, 272, 274, 282, 287–89, 298, 300, 310
  marine living resources, approach to, 33–34, 53, 55–56, 61, 72
  in mineral resources regime negotiations, 88, 97, 108, 133, 151, 154, 157, 182, 187, 190–91, 195, 200, 205, 217, 244, 256
jurisdiction in Antarctica
  coastal state jurisdiction, 44, 52–53, 55, 59, 62, 106, 120–21, 128
  and fauna and flora, 14–16, 20–24, 26–28
  and marine living resources, 39–40, 44, 46, 51–59, 62
  and mineral resources, 84, 86, 99, 103, 106, 120, 125, 128–29, 131, 138, 144, 167, 175–76, 183–84, 188–90, 210, 220–21, 248
  in Ross Dependency, 13, 86, 246, 282–83

Kear, David, 81
Keating, Colin, 93, 97, 115, 117, 135, 150, 175
Keating, Paul, 225–26, 230
Kerguelen archipelago, 52, 56, 59, 64–65
Keys, Harry, 187
Kiel ('Kiel package'), 275–76, 278–80, 282, 285–86
Kirk, Norman, 80, 82
Knox, Professor G A, 34
krill, 34, 44–47, 51, 66, 71
Kuala Lumpur, 139, 254
Kunlun (vessel), 73

Labour Party, 85, 90–91, 122, 163–64, 167, 212, 239–41, 266, 277, 281, 285, 320
Lalonde, Brice, 228, 235
Lands, Director-General of, 82
Lange, David, 163, 165–67, 192, 197–98, 230–32, 235, 240, 244
Latin America, 79, 87, 89, 95–96, 119–21, 131, 135, 195, 266–67, 269–70, 286
  see also Argentina; Chile; Uruguay
Laurie, Rob, 250
Lauterpacht, Eli, 48
Law of the Sea, 44, 46, 49, 54, 60, 84–85, 87, 93, 106, 109, 111, 114–15, 117–18, 120–21, 126, 128, 134, 136, 142–43, 157, 162, 178, 199, 216, 275, 284, 290–91, 293, 318
liability protocol for environmental damage, 178, 191, 195, 199, 203, 209–10, 216, 219, 225, 230–32, 234, 250–55, 261, 271, 273, 284, 294, 309–12, 318
Lima, 310
Logan, Hugh, 237
London, 33–34, 47, 51, 61, 95, 102

MacKay, Don, 310
Madrid ('Madrid package'), 250, 292, 294, 296, 298–99, 301–4, 308, 315
Mahathir Mohamad, 137–40
Major, John, 301

Malaysia, 137–44, 151–52, 154, 171, 223, 225, 241, 253, 257, 264
Mansfield, Bill, 115
Marine Living Resources Act 1981 (NZ), Antarctic, 73
Marine Living Resources, Commission on the Conservation of Antarctic (CCAMLR), 50–51
marine living resources, conservation of
 AMLR Convention, contemporary application of, 72–73
 AMLR Convention, drafting of, 47–68, 241
 AMLR Convention, implementation of, 68
 AMLR Convention, need for, 44–47
 AMLR Convention, substantive articles of, 68–71
 within Antarctic Treaty framework, 68, 241
 environmental concerns, 44, 66–67, 69–70, 73
 Final Act of the Conference on, 66–68
 jurisdiction issues affecting, 46, 51–55, 58–59, 62
 scientific research on, 45–47, 57, 69
 sovereignty issues affecting, 49–60, 62–66
 voting procedure, 56, 59–60, 63, 66
 see also fauna and flora, conservation of; seals, conservation of; whales, conservation of
marine mammals, 31, 39–40, 42, 70
Marine Mammals Protection Act 1978, 40
Marine Mammals Protection Bill, 39
Marsden, Ernest, 74
Marshall, Denis, 302
Marshall, Russell, 177, 194, 211, 236, 249–50, 259–60
Maruia Society, 223
McDonald Island, 71–72
McDowell, David, 237, 258
McKinnon, Don, 291, 297, 299, 305, 308
Meetings, Antarctic Treaty Consultative, *see* Antarctic Treaty Consultative Meetings (ATCMs)
Middle East, 122
mineral resources regime, need for
 within Antarctic Treaty framework, 68, 77–80, 83, 85, 92, 95, 99, 101, 103, 105, 108–9, 111–12, 117, 121, 241
 claimant/non-claimant state issues, 84–85, 87, 89, 96–97, 101–4, 106–21
 'common heritage' issue, 84–85, 96, 98–99, 117, 122
 developing countries' interests, 93, 97–98, 100, 122
 dispute settlement, 111
 draft instruments, 93, 97–98, 105, 108, 111–15
 environmental concerns, 83–84, 88, 90–92, 94–95, 97–100, 105–6, 109, 111, 113–14, 116–17, 121, 123, 225, 250
 within environmental protection regime, *see under* environmentalism
 'exploitation' issues, 77, 79–83, 85–86, 88–93, 97–99, 101, 104–6, 108–9, 111–12, 121–22
 'exploration' issues, 77, 79–86, 88–93, 98, 102, 104–5, 108–9, 116, 121
 headquarters, 118
 jurisdiction and sovereignty issues, 84–85, 87, 92, 96, 99, 103–4, 106, 109, 111–13, 120
 Law of the Sea application, 84–85, 87, 93, 109, 111, 114–15, 120–21
 moratorium, 29, 80, 85, 89–91, 94–95, 99–100, 104–5, 107–8, 112, 114, 122

Nansen Foundation Conference, 80–82
'prospecting' issues, 77–78, 116
scientific research and, 74–75, 79–81, 100–102, 106, 109, 113, 116, 121
sharing of revenue, 84, 89–90, 97–98, 112–13, 117
within United Nations framework, 79, 82, 86, 90, 92–93, 97, 109
Minerals Convention (CRAMRA), negotiation of
Advisory Committee functions, 127, 154, 156, 186, 193–94
within Antarctic Treaty framework, 129–30, 136–37, 141–42, 146, 152, 154, 163–64, 179, 196–97, 209, 214, 254, 264–65, 320
area of application, 128, 190, 199, 202–3, 216
'basis of claim' issues, 132–33, 157, 217
claimant/non-claimant state issues, 124–26, 129–36, 138–39, 143–44, 149–50, 154, 156, 167, 172–76, 179–80, 182–84, 188–90, 192, 201, 204–6, 210–11, 214, 216–18, 226, 319
Commission functions, 127, 131, 133, 135–36, 154, 156, 159–60, 172, 178, 183, 186, 189, 195–96, 200, 204–5, 213–14, 217, 220
'common heritage' issue, 126–27, 134, 136, 143, 148–49, 152, 234, 248, 253, 318, 320
costs, 159–60
decision-making powers, 127, 131–33, 135–36, 148, 150–51, 154, 159–60, 169, 171–74, 177, 180, 183–84, 186–87, 190, 193–94, 200–201, 213, 217–20, 245, 263, 319
developing countries' interests, 127, 135–44, 147–48, 154–55, 157–59, 182, 184, 187, 214–15, 220
dispute settlement, 154, 158, 161, 178, 187, 191, 195–96, 200, 204–5
draft Convention, 131, 133–35, 144–46, 149, 153–62, 171–72, 174, 178–80, 183–221 *passim*, 245
entry into force, date of, 190–91, 196–97, 216–17
environmental concerns, 127, 131, 140, 145–48, 150–51, 154–55, 158–61, 163–64, 166, 177, 180–81, 185–87, 192–95, 197–200, 203, 207, 209–10, 212–13, 215, 221–22, 224–25, 247–48, 250, 253–68, 270–71, 318–20
'exploitation'/'development' issues, 145–46, 149, 155–56, 158–61, 166–68, 171, 175–77, 181, 186–87, 207, 218–19, 221–22, 319–20
'exploration' issues, 145–46, 154–56, 158–60, 166, 176, 183, 186–87, 207, 212–13, 218, 221–22, 319
Final Act, 216–17, 219–21
headquarters, 151, 153, 165, 168, 197, 215
inspection procedures, 186, 200, 203–4, 212–13, 318
jurisdiction and sovereignty issues, 120, 125, 128–29, 131, 138, 144, 167, 175–76, 183–84, 188–90, 210, 220–21, 248
Law of the Sea application, 126, 128, 134, 142–43, 157, 162, 178, 216
moratorium, 146–47, 158, 161, 181, 202, 223, 231–32, 236, 246, 262, 264, 269, 272–74, 320
NGO representation, 160, 164, 168, 185, 192, 207, 213, 249–51, 253
'prospecting' issues, 154–56, 158–60, 162, 178–79, 195, 207, 212, 319
regulatory bodies, 127, 129, 131–

33, 135–36, 153–54, 156, 159, 170, 172, 174, 177, 180, 183–84, 186–87, 189, 191–96, 200–201, 204–6, 212–14, 217–18, 220
'Rio package', 169–75, 177, 180, 184
scientific research and, 127, 129, 137–39, 144–45, 158, 160, 163–66, 168, 213, 247
sharing of revenue, 125–26, 128, 143, 157, 159, 175–76, 185, 188–90, 201, 206–7, 210, 214–15, 217, 219–20, 224–26
signing issues, *see under* Minerals Convention (CRAMRA), signing of
subsidisation of activities, 201, 206–7, 210–11, 217, 219, 224–25, 261
within United Nations framework, 136–37, 141–43, 146–49, 152–54, 201–2, 225, 253, 264, 268, 320
Minerals Convention (CRAMRA), signing of
Australian objections, 224–26, 229–36, 238, 251, 256, 259–60, 267
environmental objections, 224, 226–34, 236, 250–51, 256–68
French objections, 226–30, 235, 250, 256, 259–60, 267
New Zealand approach to, 224–27, 229–32, 235–36, 238–40, 243–44, 246, 251, 256–59, 262, 264–67, 277
New Zealand policy review following, 236–52, 256–68, 278–79
mining ban, 88–89, 145, 161, 164, 180, 228, 230–31, 233, 235, 237–40, 243–45, 248, 252, 257, 261–62, 266–67, 272, 276–82, 284, 286–92, 294–305, 308, 315–16, 318
Mission to the United Nations, New Zealand, 137
Mission to the United Nations, United States, 142–43
Mitterrand, François, 228, 249, 260
Montevideo, 180, 191–93, 196, 198
Moore, Mike, 165–67, 282
moratorium on mineral exploitation, 146–47, 158, 161, 181, 202, 223, 231–32, 236, 246, 262, 264, 269, 272–74, 276, 280, 287–89, 291–93, 297–98, 306, 320
MR/17 (draft Minerals Convention), 131, 133–35, 144–45, 149, 151, 153–55, 157, 160–62, 174, 179, 183, 185, 187–88, 191, 193–96, 198–203, 216, 218, 245
Muldoon, Robert, 101, 181, 266
Mururoa, 260

Nairobi, 235
Nansen Foundation Conference, 80–82
Nansen Institute, 270
Nash, Walter, 54, 91, 121, 136, 228, 239–41, 266
National Parks, World Conference on, 82, 89
National Party, 122, 198, 239, 241, 265–66, 277, 285, 291
Negroponte, John, 65
Nehru, Pandit Jawaharlal, 136
New Delhi, 141, 220
New International Economic Order, 136–37
New York, 93, 95, 142, 171, 202, 223
New Zealand
in environmental regime negotiations, 238–39, 242, 245–49, 253–314 *passim*, 317–21
fauna and flora, approach to, 12–18, 20, 22–29, 241
High Commission (Canberra), 18, 104, 249, 256
High Commission (Kuala Lumpur), 139
High Commission (London), 21, 34, 74, 87, 95, 247
High Commission (New Delhi), 220

jurisdiction and sovereignty
in Antarctica, 13–16, 20–24, 27–28, 39–40, 43, 51, 53–57, 78, 84, 86, 101, 109, 129, 138, 243, 282–83
marine living resources, approach to, 45–56, 59, 61–62, 66–67, 103–4, 122, 241
in mineral resources regime negotiations, 77–80, 84–86, 88, 90–123 *passim*, 129–31, 133–40, 142–44, 146–48, 153–55, 157–223 *passim*, 318–21
Minerals Convention, approach to signing, 224–27, 229–32, 235–36, 238–40, 243–44, 246, 251, 256–59, 262, 264–65, 277
Minerals Convention, policy review of, 236–52, 256–68, 278–79
seal conservation, approach to, 31–35, 39–43
Non-aligned Movement, 136–37, 139, 141, 143, 145
Non-Consultative Parties to Antarctic Treaty, 161, 169, 171, 177, 184, 190–92, 196
non-governmental organisations (NGOs)
in environmental regime negotiations, 249–51, 253, 256, 258, 270–71, 278–81, 284–86, 291, 294–96, 298, 300–301, 304, 307–8, 318
in mineral resources regime negotiations, 160, 164, 168, 185, 192, 207, 213, 249–51, 253, 258
Norrish, Merwyn, 55
Northey, Richard, 164–65, 227
Norway
in environmental regime negotiations, 253, 269, 272, 275, 285–88, 297–98, 300, 310
marine living resources, approach to, 45, 59
in mineral resources regime negotiations, 92, 108, 157, 170, 182, 189, 217
Minerals Convention, signing of, 226, 256
sealing interests, 24, 32–33, 35–36, 43
Noumea, 235
nuclear testing, 81, 242, 260

Oelofsen text, 55
O'Flynn, Francis Duncan, 176, 181
oil exploration and exploitation, 84, 87, 92, 97–98, 100, 104, 107, 122–23, 140, 146, 181, 315–17
Order in Council, 14
Oslo, 87, 91–93, 100, 241, 266, 270–72, 275
Oxman, Bernard, 87

Palmer, Geoffrey, 164, 194, 235–36, 239–40, 244, 250, 252, 254, 257, 259–60, 262–65, 268, 274, 277–78, 282
Paris, 32, 52, 60, 93–95, 97, 100, 102–3, 105, 108, 117, 177, 225–26, 233, 239, 248, 250, 252–56, 258, 261–62, 292
Patagonian toothfish, 72
Peacock, Andrew, 103–5
pelagic sealing, *see* seals, conservation of
petroleum exploration and exploitation, 77, 81, 84, 98, 109–10, 113, 122, 125, 140, 166
Piddington, Ken, 180–81
Pinochet, Augusto, 267
Pinto, Chris, 93
Poland, 36, 53, 55–56, 72, 139, 256
pollution, 12, 111, 178, 242, 284, 286, 309

Quai d'Orsay, 226, 228
quotas, 34, 39, 58, 61

Reagan, Ronald, 134, 143
Richardson, Graham, 261
Rio de Janeiro ('Rio package'), 167, 169–75, 177, 180, 184
Rocard, Michel, 228–29, 235, 249, 299

Ross Dependency
administration of, 13, 110
as exclusive economic zone (EEZ), 39–40, 43, 61, 73, 100–101
jurisdiction over, 13–16, 27–28, 39–40, 43, 54, 78, 86, 101, 129, 138, 167, 206, 243, 246, 282–83
mineral resources in, 75–76, 86, 100–102, 106–7, 109–10, 113, 129–30, 140, 159, 164, 166, 168, 206, 214, 227, 243–46, 263, 282–83, 319
Order in Council 1923, 14
Research Committee (RDRC), 13, 242
Ross Sea, 53, 72, 80, 92, 98, 102, 104, 110, 113, 122, 130, 140, 166, 317
Rowling, Wallace (Bill), 39, 83–84, 240–41
Russia, 310
Rutherford, Ernest, 74
Rybakov, Yuri, 169–70

Salmon, Guy, 223
Santiago, 24, 51, 183, 185, 258–59, 268, 271–73, 276, 278–81, 283–84
Science, Ministry of, 100, 236
Scientific and Industrial Research, Department of (DSIR), 74, 78, 81, 122, 180, 185, 237, 280
Scientific Committee for Ocean Research (SCOR), 47, 57
scientific research
and Environment Protection Protocol, 270, 285, 290
on marine living resources, 45–47, 57, 69
on mineral resources, 74–75, 79–81, 100–102, 106, 109, 113, 116, 121, 127, 129, 137–39, 144–45, 158, 160, 163–66, 168, 247
on seals, 34–35, 40–41
Scott Polar Research Institute, 75
Scully, Tucker, 116–17, 135, 169–70, 232–34, 246–47, 286–87, 302
Sea, Law of the, 44, 46, 49, 54, 60, 84–85, 87, 93, 106, 109, 111, 114–15, 117–18, 120–21, 126, 128, 134, 136, 142–43, 157, 162, 178, 199, 216, 275, 284, 290–91, 293, 318
Sea Mammal Motivational Institute, 35
seabed, mineral exploitation in, 78, 84–85, 93, 98–99, 113, 115, 120–21, 126, 134, 136, 143, 199, 203, 284, 291, 293, 318
seals, conservation of
commercial sealing interests and, 24, 30–31, 33, 38, 40–43, 49, 71
Convention, drafting of, 32–38
Convention, ratification of, 39–43
and Environment Protection Protocol, 312
outside Antarctic Treaty framework, 32, 68
policing of, 37, 43
public interest in, 33, 35, 40–41
scientific research and, 34–35, 40–41
see also fauna and flora, conservation of; marine living resources, conservation of
seas, high, 28–29, 31–32, 61, 199
Second World War, 74
Secretariat, Antarctic, 11, 252–53, 269, 276, 284, 290, 294, 313–14
Secretariat, United Nations, 79
Senate Foreign Relations Committee (USA), 76
Sierra Club, 35
Songhua (vessel), 72
South Africa, 35, 56, 59, 198, 201, 226, 256
South Georgia, 36, 71–72
South Pacific Fisheries Organisation, 60
South Pacific Forum, 238
South Victoria Land, 75
sovereignty
on 'basis of claim', 120, 132–33, 157, 217, 282, 303
coastal state sovereignty, 52, 55
economic development and,

75–76, 96, 103–4, 108–9, 111, 120, 167, 248, 316
and fauna and flora, 16, 21, 23, 25, 27, 30
and marine living resources, 44, 49–57, 59–60, 62–66
mineral resources and, 125, 128–29, 131, 138, 175–76, 183, 188–90, 206, 210, 220–21, 282–83
Soviet Union
and East–West tensions, 150–51, 161–62, 170
in environmental regime negotiations, 253, 272, 275, 286–88, 290, 300, 303
fauna and flora, approach to, 25
jurisdiction in Antarctica, 52–53, 55, 282–83
marine living resources, approach to, 52–53, 55–56, 61, 63, 71–72, 98
in mineral resources regime negotiations, 81, 88–89, 97–98, 100, 114, 117–18, 120, 125, 127, 130–35, 139, 143, 149–51, 154, 156–57, 161–62, 170, 172–74, 178–79, 182–84, 205, 207, 215, 217
Minerals Convention, signing of, 226, 256
seal conservation, approach to, 36–37, 40–41
see also Russia
Spain, 250
Special Committee on Antarctic Research (SCAR), 13–14, 31–32, 36–37, 45–47, 67, 81
Special Conservation Area, Antarctica as, 25, 49
Special Consultative Meetings (SCMs), 121, 126, 144, 148, 158, 174, 177–78, 184–85, 187, 190, 192, 198, 202, 213, 216, 232, 238, 245–46, 255, 258, 262, 268, 284–86, 292, 294, 298, 308–9, 312, 317
Sri Lanka, 48, 93
St Petersburg, 314
Stockholm, 44, 311
Strong, Maurice, 83–84
Suva, 140
Sweden, 226, 253, 255

Taiwan, 70
Talboys, Brian, 39, 53–54, 93, 103–5, 119
Tarawa, 238
Tasmania, 68, 153, 251
Territorial Sea and Exclusive Economic Zone Act 1977 (NZ), 52
Thatcher, Margaret, 247, 301
Third World, 88, 96, 100, 105, 115, 134, 147
see also developing countries
Tokyo, 32–33, 77, 155, 158, 161, 167, 170, 180–81, 185–86, 188–89, 193, 219
toothfish, 72–73
tourism, 29, 165, 242, 284, 294, 312, 318
Treasury, 101–2, 104, 106–7, 119

United Kingdom, *see* Britain
United Nations
Charter, 18–20, 30
Conference on the Human Environment 1972, 44
Development Programme, 46
Environment Programme (UNEP), 44, 83–84, 93, 137, 235
General Assembly, 48, 93, 115, 118, 126, 137, 141–42, 151, 167, 201–2, 214
and mineral resources regime, 79, 82, 86, 90, 92–93, 97, 109, 136–37, 141–43, 146–49, 152–54, 201–2, 225, 264, 268, 320
Secretariat, 79, 153
United States (USA)
and East–West tensions, 126, 150–51, 161–62, 170
in environmental regime

negotiations, 246–47, 255, 260–62, 267, 269–70, 272, 274–75, 285–88, 290, 292–93, 298, 300–308, 310–14, 321
fauna and flora, approach to, 13, 16–19, 25
jurisdiction in Antarctica, 15, 20–21, 28, 87, 99, 282
marine living resources, approach to, 45, 48, 55–56, 59, 61, 63, 66
in mineral resources regime negotiations, 76–77, 79–80, 88–92, 96–99, 103, 107–8, 110, 114, 116–17, 125, 130, 133–36, 149–51, 154, 156–57, 159, 161–62, 167, 170, 172–74, 178–79, 182–84, 187, 194–95, 204–5, 207–8, 214–15, 217–21, 246–47, 253
Minerals Convention, signing of, 226, 232, 256, 261
Mission to the United Nations, 142–43
ratification of Antarctic Treaty, 17, 30
seal conservation, approach to, 32, 34–38

Upton, Simon, 198
Uruguay, 188, 190, 220, 226, 266–67, 285

Venice, 310
Viña del Mar, 284–87, 290–92, 295–96, 298, 300, 317

Wade, Hunter, 78
Wallace, Catherine, 145, 166–67, 181, 185, 197–98, 222–23, 260, 270, 278, 291, 295–96, 299, 301, 304, 308
Washington, 57–58, 60–61, 63, 80, 92, 95, 103, 110, 114–17, 143, 151, 153–54, 172, 246, 260, 302, 304
Weddell Sea, 317
Weddell seals, 38, 41
Weeber, Barry, 296
Wellington, 24, 40, 79, 81, 126, 140, 148, 170, 180, 188, 191, 202, 206–7, 209, 211, 216, 225–27, 262, 264, 270, 289
Wellington, HMNZS, 72
whales, conservation of, 38–39, 44, 49, 53, 70, 312
Whaling Convention 1946, 36, 38, 70–71
Whangaroa meetings, 178, 182–83, 188, 190–91
White, Lloyd, 78
White Paper (on mineral resources policy), 238–49, 251–52, 257, 262, 278–79
wilderness park, Antarctic, 231, 233, 238–39, 264
Willett, R W, 81
Wilson, Roger, 144
Wolfrum, Rüdiger, 191, 310
Wong, Frank, 285, 291, 298
Woolcott, Richard, 232–33
Woollaston, Philip, 235, 240, 243, 249, 265, 282
world park, Antarctica as, 25, 29, 82–83, 89–92, 94–95, 100, 122, 149, 223, 228, 230, 236–37, 239, 241, 243, 252, 256, 266, 277

Yongding (vessel), 72

Zegers, Fernando, 95, 114–15, 117, 170